Moving Pictures and Classic Images

Moving Pictures and Classic Images

Memories of Forty Years in the Vintage Film Hobby

SAMUEL K. RUBIN
FOREWORD BY LEONARD MALTIN

McFarland & Company, Inc., Publishers
Jefferson, North Carolina, and London

Library of Congress Cataloguing-in-Publication Data

Rubin, Samuel K., 1918–
Moving pictures and classic images : memories of forty years in the vintage film hobby / Samuel K. Rubin ; foreword by Leonard Maltin.
p.   cm.
Includes index.

ISBN 0-7864-1757-9 (softcover : 50# alkaline paper)

1. Motion pictures—United States. 2. Motion pictures—United States—Societies, etc. 3. Motion pictures—Collectors and collecting—United States. I. Title.
PN1993.5.U6R83   2004   791.43'0973—dc22   2004004450

British Library cataloguing data are available

©2004 Samuel K. Rubin. All rights reserved

No part of this book may be reproduced or transmitted in any form or by any means, electronic or mechanical, including photocopying or recording, or by any information storage and retrieval system, without permission in writing from the publisher.

Front cover: (background) ©2004 Corbis Images; (inset) Sam K. Rubin

Manufactured in the United States of America

McFarland & Company, Inc., Publishers
Box 611, Jefferson, North Carolina 28640
www.mcfarlandpub.com

Table of Contents

Foreword by Leonard Maltin   1
Preface   3

1. The Beginnings!   5
2. I Get Letters   23
3. End of an Era   32
4. The Prelude   36
5. Editerribles   39
6. The Film Fan Organizations and Conventions   87
7. Film Collectors and Collecting   136
8. Dealers and Distributors   160
9. People!   180
10. The Stars   191
11. Flashbacks   202
12. Wondering and Wandering   230
13. The Westerns   244
14. Jungle Stuff   256

Index   267

Foreword

by Leonard Maltin

Sam Rubin was the first person to publish one of my articles. I was 13 years old, and didn't dare to tell him that when I submitted my manuscript. After he accepted the piece, I confessed the truth, and was happy to discover that he didn't care. He liked what I wrote, and that's all that mattered. When we met in person, a short time later, we became good friends.

Sam started his magazine *The 8mm Collector* as a means of getting in touch with other people around the country—indeed, around the world—who shared his love of silent films. He wasn't a professional writer or a trained editor, but he provided a welcome vehicle for people like me who wanted to express themselves.

Being an old-movie buff or collector in those days was a lonely proposition. There weren't video stores on every street corner or cable television stations running classic films around the clock. There was no Internet to offer chat rooms and bulletin boards.

Sam was a furniture dealer in Indiana, Pennsylvania, who collected silent films in the 8mm home movie format. His quest in those days was to find a perfect print of his all-time favorite film, the 1925 classic *The Lost World*. He patched together the best copy he could by buying every print he was able to find and extracting the best-looking sections of each one. But there weren't many (if any) like-minded souls in Indiana.

That's what inspired Sam to reach out to his fellow fans, and they responded. *The 8MM Collector* eventually became *The Classic Film Collector*, and finally *Classic Images* ... but its purpose never changed. The magazine continues to celebrate what we call the Golden Age of Hollywood some 40 years after its founding.

I'm sure Sam never dreamed that his hobby would one day become a full-time occupation, but after the magazine was purchased by a professional publisher, he actually made that leap. I'm just as certain that he never thought there would be a time when virtually every household would have at least one videocassette or DVD player, and classic films would be widely available in beautiful, restored editions.

Still, we movie buffs remain a minority group. Young people today aren't exposed to the great films and great stars of the past, as I was, growing up in the first television generation. Old movies were inescapable back then, filling every

Leonard Maltin, renowned screen and television authority, with Lillian Gish, beloved silent movie star, at one of the film lovers' conventions.

local TV channel into the wee hours of the morning. A kid could discover Laurel and Hardy or Bogart or W.C. Fields and become intrigued. Revival theaters in major cities made it possible to see those wonderful movies on a big screen.

Nowadays, we live in an age of specialization. Video killed off most of the revival theaters, and old movies appear only on the exclusive old-movie channels. Kids can tune in a radio station that plays only their kind of music, and a TV network that's designed for their particular demographic. No one in broadcasting sees any reason to broaden their audience's cultural horizons.

It's left to the true believers like Sam Rubin and those who have followed in his footsteps to celebrate the great films of the past and help to keep them alive, toward a time when young people finally discover their worth. That's why I am glad Sam has gathered his columns together here, to share his lifelong enthusiasm. I only hope it's contagious.

By the way, even though I've moved on to DVDs like so many other people, I've never gotten rid of my original 8mm collection. In fact, I wound up buying Sam's fabled 8mm print of *The Lost World*. I wouldn't trade it for anything.

Preface

If you enjoy classic motion pictures, pick this book up gently, and with great care. It won't bite you, but it may cause you to depart from your established lifestyle and turn you into a classic film fan. This is about the silent and early sound screen and the people who love and collect film, videos and everything about that field of entertainment.

Long ago, someone invented the world "memorabilia," which encompasses all the memorable items generated from the memory of the early screen: books and magazines of the era, biographies of the stars, posters, photographs, autographs and about anything else emanating from that era.

This book is about the publication *Classic Images* and the film fan movement. *Classic Images* was born in 1962 as a six-page, rather crude affair entitled *8mm Collector*. It was aimed at collectors of 8mm versions of the early classic movies. It rapidly expanded to include 16mm and was retitled *Classic Film Collector*.

It continued to grow and with the advent of video, it was once more enlarged and retitled *Classic Images*. Its scope included all sizes of film, all types of movie memorabilia, tales of old Hollywood and every facet related to the early film. Still being published, it is tabloid-size, completely in print, and at times has had more than 100 pages. It is affectionately called the "Film Fan's Bible."

Inside this book I have related experiences I have had while editor of that fine journal. What may confuse you is that I have written the names of three different women as my wives. Yes, I was married three times and each of them had shared these happenings with me. I have been so lucky in three happy marriages!

Nathalia (Sissy) was my first wife and mother of our two children, JoAnne and Jay. Sissy developed leukemia and died.

Several years later I married Lois, who developed breast cancer and died.

Then, several years later I married Audrey. We've been together for ten years and a happy marriage it is!

Like Sissy and Lois, Audrey is attractive, intelligent, sociable and loving. We have a happy, contented home based on love!

Though the marriages were riddled with tragedy, lengthy hospital confinements and long terms of bereavement, I still consider myself fortunate to have had these partners in marriage.

As I said before: I'm lucky!

I had a lot of fun doing this book; I sure hope you like it. You will realize that some of the short articles are repeats of material that previously appeared in my Classic Clips department of *Classic Images*.

For clarification, so as you won't think I have lost my marbles, I would like to explain that, in writing and assembling the material to be included in this book, I have reproduced articles originally written for *8mm Collector, Classic Film Collector*, and *Classic Images*.

In order to maintain the flavor of the contents, I have made no attempt to update the time element of the various articles. I may seem to be writing of past activities as if they had just happened. And, I might mention individuals who have passed away since the items first appeared.

It was a long job leafing through back issues in order to select which columns I wanted to grace the pages of this book. It is possible there may be some duplication of facts or events which I overlooked, or deliberately left in, to illustrate an item in the column. Please accept my apologies. I burned a considerable amount of midnight oil!

—S.K.R., March 2004

1
The Beginnings!

A brontosaur in a prehistoric jungle sneered during a showing of the 1925 *The Lost World* in a theater in a Pennsylvania town about 30 miles from Pittsburgh.

There was a closeup of the monster's head, leaving no doubt he was sneering! His upper lip was covered in a disdainful gesture, indicating, in a subtle way, his power over all the other denizens of that ancient wilderness (other giant reptiles, human cave dwellers, miscellaneous assorted beasts).

This groundbreaking movie featured a variety of such creatures, masterfully animated by the wizard of that art, Willis O'Brien.

That particular moment of that particular film planted the seed which was to become *Classic Images*, the publication which was to eventually become the bible for film fans, classic movie addicts and movie collectors.

Mesmerized, I was sitting in my favorite fourth row seat, in the theater we called "The Ranch House," when that sneer occurred. It is entirely possible that I did not blink my eyes during that entire feature. I returned, three or four times, to see that thriller again. At each viewing I waited, in anticipation, to see that fascinating reptilian gesture once more.

Years passed! I ran the entire gauntlet from public school through college and a four-year hitch in the Army during World War II. My wife, Sissy, gave birth to JoAnne and Jay.

Now, we fast forward to 1961. I was leafing through an issue of *Popular Photography* when a tiny ad caught my attention. It was offering the 1925 *The Lost World* for sale in 8mm. This had to be the long-remembered film of my youth. I wondered if the dinosaur was still sneering.

The check for *The Lost World* went out in the next mail.

The 8mm feature arrived! It was an abbreviated five-reel version of *The Lost World*! At that time I was unaware that the original was released in ten reels. And, at that time, I wouldn't have cared!

Eagerly, I opened the package and immediately threaded the film into the projector, which had been sitting there since the day I ordered the movie. Yes, it was my old friend, *The Lost World*. But what terrible quality! The entire feature was difficult to watch. I packed it up with a note and returned it for replacement.

After another feverish wait, a replacement print arrived. It was as bad as the first! Now I was perturbed! An angry letter accompanied the return package mailed to the dealer. A third print arrived! This time the pictorial quality was acceptable—

The author with Bessie Love, heroine of the groundbreaking 1925 film *The Lost World*, inspiration for the birth of *8mm Collector*.

but the images were reversed! Our characters greeted each other with left-handed shakes. Because this print was not difficult to view, I decided to keep it and not be concerned about how they shook hands. However, to this day, I still wonder how the image could be reversed and the titles remain legible.

That unhappy transaction deeply disturbed me; I wanted to do something about it. I have always loved journalism. I had studied it in school and became active with a publication in practically every organization to which I belonged. I had been on the staff of the high school newspaper and became co-editor of *Froth*, the Penn State humor magazine. I started newspapers in the Boy Scouts, in men's clubs and even the Army when Uncle Sam drafted me.

So, "Why don't I start a publication for such movie addicts as myself?" It could be a vehicle for collectors: They could express their opinions about the quality of the classic movies obtained from the various dealers; and they could also evaluate the quality of service each dealer provided. It would enable film buffs to avoid problems such as I encountered.

The publication could also provide them with an advertising medium in which they could buy and sell their films, equipment and movie memorabilia (magazines, photographs, posters, press sheets, etc.).

Such a publication could enable collectors to get in touch with each other and could provide a market for dealer and film fan advertising. It could also generate interest in the hobby with stories about the classic movies and their stars, and generally cover the entire movie industry from the viewpoint of the collector.

"Sam, what a great idea!"

I contacted a printer and initiated the *8mm Collector* in 1962. It later evolved into *Classic Film Collector* in order to include the 16mm and other film sizes in its coverage. And, still later, it became *Classic Images* with the advent of video and could, therefore, encompass the entire field of movie interest for film fans and collectors.

I believe this could have been the start of the active film fan, movie collector movement in 1962. I am unaware of any such publication prior to that date.

The film buffs ate it up! Instant circulation! I received unexpected out-of-proportion response; so many contacts! The ensuing workload dumped a ton of pressure on that thing between my ears, causing me to lose the first of many of my hairs.

Despite the flood of interest and apparent workload that descended on me ... I loved it! Apparently the film buffs had been hungry for something like this: their own publication about their own corner of the collecting hobby!

Now, in their minds, they felt they were true movie fans. They could now continue to enlarge their collection of movie memorabilia (the films, the magazines, the photos and everything else about their favorite stars and films) by advertising them in this new medium, enabling them to contact other film buffs.

Some have attributed the introduction of the *8mm Collector* to the birth of the "Film Fan Movement." Anyways, I got so puffed up about it that I determined to go ahead and continue publication. I requested articles and movie-related material from these film buffs ... and, oh yes, to buy or sell advertising of movie collectibles.

In deference to my full-time furniture occupation, I planned the next issue to appear in approximately three months. And I started accepting advertising! At the beginning I was using cash from my pocket and from the minute flow of cash coming in from donations and scattered subscriptions. And I was accepting movie collectibles in payment for ads. (How do you think I was able to accumulate such a sizable collection?)

I was now able to really begin publishing! I established subscription and advertising rates and talked people (they were all eager) into sending articles and news about their movie-related activities.

I asked them to forward tidbits of information about their organizations and incidents about their favorite Hollywood people and their special interests.

The seeds I scattered with that first issue were fertilized by these fervent film fans and collectors, and they multiplied many times. I began to get letters and phone calls in increasing numbers.

An antique saying: "I looked, aghast, at the quantity of enthusiastic responses." Previously, I would not have minded this uproar which put me in a precarious position. I was one of the owners of a furniture store which kept me quite busy; what with six days of long store hours, many night appointments with potential customers, long weekends and frequent buying trips to the furniture markets to purchase additional inventory.

And, I had a family: my wife, Sissy, and a Russian selection of kids (one of "itch"): son, Jay, and daughter, JoAnne. They all had lives of their own and they wanted Dad to share them. So, Dad dug deep for a huge bottle of midnight oil and started taking care of the infant *8mm Collector* at night.

You ask: When did I sleep? Who slept?

At first I did my own typing of the rustic-looking (to me) publication. After all these years I still can't type efficiently, so the mechanics of publishing took me awhile.

The first issue was reproduced by the offset printing method. The final result: this first issue looked like it was mimeographed, and the print looked a little less than sharp! I was unhappy with the appearance of our debut, but was unable to help myself with so little time and limited finances.

The initial issue was printed on June 7, 1962. Featured was an article on slides by Kalton C. Lahue, historian and 8mm collector.

The second issue was mailed September 24th that year. It was quite an accomplishment in three months; there was so much to do! Sissy began giving me that look and the kids and I were beginning to annoy each other. I swear I dreamt this: The kids jumped into bed with me and each one grabbed an ankle and started gnawing on it!

However, I did get things resolved by the time the next issue went to press. I was able to blend my two pleasures: the classic movie activities plus my wife and two kids. We had a lot of fun taking rides, going to the movies, attending dances, sharing the kids sporting events and their other activities. And, I continued with the publication, of course. During all of this, I forgot what sleep was!

I continued to offer the readers the kind of stuff they wanted to read: quality previews of the home movie reproductions of film classics, articles on mood music, reporting on the activities of the distributors, projection hints and the many facets of their collecting hobby—the buying, selling and swapping of classic films.

Now, talented writers and artists began sending material to me. Much of it was so professional in content that it broke my heart. I had to return some ... no room!

By the time we printed No. 3 on December 31, 1962, I decided that the copy could be set up in print like any quality outstanding publication. I contacted a local printer to do the preliminaries. I did the layout and ran into trouble. Too much material for the available space; I couldn't get it all in! So, in order to include it all in the issue, I set it up into a larger space and had the entire page reduced to fit.

Now I was able to get everything I wanted to run in that smaller space. However, now the type was so tiny that many had trouble reading it. Then the complaints started rolling in. Even Stan Laurel, when he saw the issue, had plenty to say about the small type.

I know better now! I am a bit older and wouldn't be able to read the blamed thing without a magnifier.

However, at that time I was happy I was able to get so much of that massive amount of submitted material into the issue.

Interest, however, had not diminished. More and more subscriptions arrived with the subsequent increase in cash, enabling me to add more pages. Never mind the additional work; I was giving them more for their money!

INDIANA, PENNA.   NO. 1   JUNE 7, 1962

THE 8MM COLLECTOR———WHY?

I have no idealistic motives. I have no romantic dreams about the Collector. I hope to get sufficient response to publish further issues with more "meat" than this.

A publication of this type can be a one man job only from the standpoint of the mechanical work; especially when the one man is located in the wilds of Western Pennsylvania, away from all the film markets and distributors.

But, why publish the Collector at all?

If you are a collector of 8mm classic movies, how many times have you sent for a much-sought-for title, and paid the going price. When the film comes to you it is out of focus, or it is too contrasty, or it is too light, or too dark, or the titles more than fill the screen, or the pictures jump.

I do not know the mechanics of reducing the large size movies to 8mm. No doubt it is an exacting art, and difficult to do. But, why should we suffer if some joker makes a lousy dupe of a film, and cannot make a good print? He foists it on us at the regular price and we take the licking instead of "Mr. Botcher."

This publication is designed to aid 8mm serious collectors avoid these pitfalls by printing the experiences we have had with the various film sources, so that collectors may benefit from these experiences, pleasant or unpleasant.

Also— we all have movies we would like to buy, sell or exchange. The Collector can act as your trading post.

When new items are placed on the market, when new titles are released, when old titles are again put into circulation— this information can be spread by the Collector, only if all of you out there cooperate. If you know of something new or unusual, drop me a line and I will spread the good word.

Are these enough reasons for printing the Collector?

slide bonanza

by Kalten C. Lahue

(Mr. Lahue, historian and collector of the silent cinema classics is in the final stages of preparation of a manuscript on the silent serial with the tentative title: THE SERIAL QUEENS— A History of the Silent Serial. We wish to thank Mr. Lahue for the excellent article which follows.)

The collection of silent cinema classics has given me a great deal of entertainment, satisfaction and amusement over the past few years. My interest was first aroused when I realized that some of the reels of old film clips could very well be worked into my history classes. The reels of clips led me to wonder if perhaps some of the old comedies might not prove to be valuable for the same purpose. My investigations brought me into contact with the films of Ben Turpin and I was hooked for life. At first, I began to collect everything which I felt to be of value but over the years I've slanted my collection towards short length comedies.

During the early days of collecting, I worked part-time for an exhibitor whose family went back to the very early days of the motion picture. We talked a great deal about movies and the "good old days" and I was soon to find that his house was a veritable treasure house of cinema material. Everything that ever found its way into the house remained to this day. The cellar was a delightful discovery because I came into contact for the first time with genuine specimens of the old nickelodeon slide, 3 1/4 x 4 1/4 size. As many collectors are aware, Kent Eastin of Blackhawk Films had brought several sets of the "Coming Attraction" slides onto the marketplace in the familiar 2 x 2 size. Unfortunately they never caught on with collectors and when I got in touch with Kent, he felt unable to make use of them.

(turn to page 5)

Front page of *8mm Collector*, June 7, 1962.

The *8mm Collector* had expanded to ten pages for the April 1963 issue. I will try to name some of the people who contributed articles to this new venture. If I skipped your name, I apologize.

I have already mentioned Kalton C. Lahue as author of the first literary piece. Charles Tarbox, who headed "Classic Film Exchange," a film distributorship, wrote of the early Hollywood era in which he had lived.

Then we had Anthony Phillips, who drew and designed amazing replicas of old movie advertising. He also illustrated articles and designed larger-size illustrations which could be used as posters.

Oscar Estes was also a talented man. He was a prolific writer and artist and created beautiful illustrations for his articles.

Others from the early days of the *8mm Collector* were David Prestone, who specialized in prehistoric animals, and Bill Lest, who brought his artistic talents to our pages.

When I began publishing the *8mm Collector*, I mailed the first issue free of charge to addresses given to me by others. I requested money from the readers to cover future costs in getting this newcomer off the ground. I asked for anything from $1 and up!

To my surprise and gratification, enthusiastic readers submitted larger amounts than expected. Some sent a dollar, some five dollars, one, $10. In gratitude I entered their names in a fictitious group, Benevolent Society of Aching 8mm Collectors.

I had corresponded with Tom Seller. He and I decided to inaugurate a national film group. He came to my home in Indiana, Pennsylvania. Together we made plans for the proposed Society for Cinephiles. All those who, when funds were solicited, had contributed more than requested were given membership to the new society.

The first national meeting was to be held in Indiana, Pennsylvania, during the next Labor Day weekend. The Society for Cinephiles would then be established; officers would be elected. The site of the next convention would be decided, and many classic movies would be screened.

I was to be the host!

Our committee-of-two appointed Tom to act as first president until an election could be held at the first Cinecon. (I take credit for inventing the word Cinecon.) Tom did a monumental amount of groundwork to augment the publicity given the Cinephiles in the pages of the *8mm Collector*.

The Society for Cinephiles was officially established January 1, 1965. The first Cinecon was held at the Holiday Inn, Indiana, Pennsylvania, Labor Day weekend, 1965. Officers elected at the event were: W.C. Beeler, Jr., president; Robert Young, treasurer; and Tom Seller, Secretary. He later resigned in favor of Herman McGregor, Jr.

Irving K. Meginnis was the speaker at the first Cinecon banquet. Many silent films were shown. A cocktail party was held at our home in Indiana, and after the official viewings at the hotel were completed, the Cinephiles who did not immediately leave for home returned to my house and we projected more silent films. There were no sound films shown at the first Cinecon. Exhausted and happy, the Rubins retired early the next evening … very early.

Clark Wilkinson and John Schellkopf offered to sponsor the next Cinecon at Baraboo, Wisconsin.

My absolute favorite by Cal Dobbins. (It's framed over my desk).

Cartoon by Cal Dobbins of the author sweating over the latest issue of *Classic Film Collector*.

Here are some of my unofficial memories of that first gathering of the Cinephiles: The tremendous cooperation of Sissy, Jay and JoAnne was a key factor in putting the thing over. Sissy outdid herself in welcoming the Cinephiles to our home and assisting in the preparations at the Holiday Inn. Jay and JoAnne, in addition to many other assists, operated a shuttle service between Indiana and the Pittsburgh airport, 65 miles away, transporting members who would have never found Indiana, Pennsylvania … even if Jimmy Stewart *was* born there.

Site of the first Cinecon, Labor Day, 1965: the Holiday Inn, Indiana, Pennsylvania.

One of the finest persons I have ever met, Delos "Dutch" Campbell, who once played for Fred Waring, accompanied our films. Dutch, without any preparation, sat at the keyboard and played for the silents like he was born to the chore. Without music in front of him, with the lights out, he followed every bit of action and emotion which appeared on the screen with appropriate mood accompaniment. He was an expert pianist. He loved accompanying the silents, and even refused payment for the work.

I'll never forget Nick Kovalchick. Nick was a local scrap dealer, quite wealthy, who loved the silent films, and everything nostalgic. He purchased a narrow gauge railroad as a hobby because he liked old trains. Notice I did not say *model* railroad. This was an operating two-mile-track tourist attraction. (It had street cars, too.)

I am mentioning the above because Nick offered to set me up in a theater on the boardwalk in Atlantic City to screen nothing but silent films. I turned him down; I had a furniture store to operate.

The Holiday Inn went all out for us. There was not a single problem with the motel throughout the entire convention. They even added a few touches for us: a welcome sign for the Cinephiles on the marquee, and a special brick ice cream dessert with an ice cream motion picture camera in the center of each piece.

For the film program we saw such items as *The Big Parade, The Spanish Dancer, Square Deal Sanderson, The Road to Yesterday* and many others, including shorts.

Media cooperation was excellent. The local newspaper, the *Indiana Evening Gazette*, along with the *Johnstown Tribune-Democrat* and the *Pittsburgh Press*, reported the Cinecon, as did the Johnstown TV station, WJAC-TV. The Press put the story on its statewide wire service.

Time magazine sent a photographer to cover the event. He took many pictures and later called to substantiate the information. We looked forward to a substantial *Time* spread, but unfortunately the story was short-stopped at an editor's desk and never appeared. Some editors!

Now I am going to live dangerously and try to list, to the best of my memory, those who attended: the four Rubins; George Zoldac; Nick Kovalchick; Dutch Campbell; Robert and Tina Young; Robert and Betty Cooper, Irwin, Harriet and Ward Abelson (I don't remember if daughter Stacy was there); Joseph Zymanski; W.C. Beeler, Jr., and his wife; Robert Saxton; Mike Polacek; Bud LeMaster, Herman S. McGreggor, Jr., with son Mike; Tom Seller; Carl Dossin; Arthur Ude; James Canfield; Harold Kinkade; I.K. Meginnis; and Sam Gill. I may have missed some names, and I know I have missed some members of families of those who attended. For that I apologize! I don't remember as well as I used to (an understatement).

It was one of the thrills of my life to have all these enthusiastic collectors, people with interests identical to mine, making the long trip to Indiana, Pennsylvania, to meet, talk about, to enjoy and to thrill at these old films. In that 1965 meeting I made good friends who remain my friends to this day. I must thank *them* for making the first Cinecon one of my most memorable.

At that time I also coined a word which has returned to haunt me many times: Cinecosis. Here's how it was introduced in *8mm Collector*: "One of the members of the Cinephiles shifted to his seat to relieve his weary tailbone. He rubbed his bleary eyes and muttered an absurdity ... like 'Let's watch some more movies.' This was after hours of unblinking staring at the silent stars perform. Acute Cinecosis had set in ... incurable, contagious, and completely self-destroying."

I never did recover.

I so appreciate the efforts of the many people who submitted the vast amount of material which appeared in the pages of our publication for years. The writers and artists contributed a flood of articles and artwork through the period which I chose to call the Rubin Era of *Classic Images*.

What readers may not have realized was that none of the contributors were paid. These were real Cinephiles, originating their written or pictorial work for the love of the classic screen. Some of them continued donating their talents to *Classic Images* for long periods of time. We were a publication for and by film lovers!

I intended to honor these great people by naming them in this book and perhaps run a biography of each. I found that to be practically impossible with the space allotted me. Some of the issues in that Rubin era ran to over 100 pages.

What to do?

The decision: to run a list of names of some of the contributors and the type of material to appear in our pages for a couple of years, and then honor all of them by running their names in this book.

I didn't realize that even doing this would take plenty of time and space. I had to check all the names for spelling and I had to be careful not to miss any of these generous authors and artists.

So! A proclamation: I have gone through all the back issues in order to get all the names possible on the donor list. It was difficult! I may have missed some; I may have misspelled some. If your efforts appeared in *Classic Images* and I have failed to list your name, or if it is misspelled, you have my apologies!

It took a considerable period of time to wade through all those bound volumes of back issues; and, as you might guess, I had to stop frequently to read some of that stuff from past ages. I did get sleepy!

If I did not do right by you, I am truly sorry! Blame it on the arms of Morpheus! Back in that prehistoric age, a reader wrote that I take great pride in castigating myself. And now, *you* know why I called my goofs "Rubinerrs"!

Now, more and more quality material was submitted. Stuntman John Hagner's talent was introduced! Issue No. 9 brought innovations, plus more professional big-league articles and artwork.

The author in the early days of *Classic Images*.

Many of our 8mm collectors, to my surprise, also collected the larger 16mm size. We therefore introduced a new column to our pages "16mm Collector," written by Earle Ainworth.

Renowned author and TV personality Leonard Maltin began to show his talent with his "Research Unlimited" column. Sam Gill initiated "The Funnymen," Marty Kearns took over "The Book Nook" and Jack Hardy joined our cast with his "Comedy Classics."

In the winter of 1964, the *8mm Collector*'s banner headline read, "Society for Cinephiles to be activated Jan. 1st!" This was the first meeting date announcement for the new organization. The Cinecon was to be held in Indiana, Pennsylvania, over the Labor Day weekend.

Publication continued. Kalton C. Lahue introduced his promising "Continued Next

Week," with much to say about the serials. "Eye on the Distributors" also began at this time and proved to be an extremely popular feature.

Issue No. 12, Summer 1965, brought innovations to the pages of the *8mm Collector* with a variety of new features to tickle the palate of any classic film buff.

Lamar McCarty offered a compilation of 8mm features and where they could be purchased. Arthur Weld wrote about teaching history with 8mm. Alan Dodd, from England, introduced the innovative *International Collector* and Robert Young explained how to apply musical background for the silent productions. Artists for the Collector's pages contributed much to the appearance. Mike Avril began his cartoon series and other artwork was provided by Al Kilgore and Don Leet. Charles Crum began his illustrated reviews of the classics.

Clark Wilkinson offered Baraboo, Wisconsin, as the site of the next Cinecon, again to be held over the Labor Day weekend.

Ron Green contributed excellent artwork for Issue No. 13, Fall-Winter 1963. Bill McWilliams drew a top-grade sketch of Douglas Fairbanks, Sr.

By No. 14, Spring 1966, the size of the *8mm Collector* had grown to 40 pages. Art was contributed by my daughter JoAnne. Steve Kaplan took charge of Distributorscope.

An outstanding series of pictorial parodies by Wally Bradley debuted in this issue. They depicted how Hollywood stars would look if they had played a famous character. The first example: Stan Laurel portraying Robin Hood.

News arrived from I.K. Meginnis that the *8mm Collector* was presented to the Smithsonian Institute. John Hagner introduced his talent in this issue. Producer Sam Peeples wrote "Out Brief Candle," a biography of Rudolph Valentino.

Walter Dean introduced a

Wally Bradley drew a series of sketches entitled "IF." This one, of Stan Laurel, was among the most popular.

massive project which was to be run serially in our pages: "7,500 Feature Titles from 1919 to 1929," each to have credits and other information. It would take "many a month" before it would be completed.

Information on regional conventions began to appear in our pages as members of the Cinephiles planned their own gatherings to watch more rare movies and buy, sell and swap film and movie memorabilia.

A new masthead greeted our readers of No. 15, Summer 1966. The name of our publication had been changed to *Classic Film Collector*. At this time a new regional convention was announced for Richmond, Indiana.

Most contributors to the *Classic Film Collector* continued to offer their talents. Some would appear with a lone item and then not contribute anything for months. Other submitted their specialty items every month. Continuing his "IF" cartoons, Wally Bradley sketched Lon Chaney if he were to portray the Frankenstein monster.

Tom Fulbright, an avid Hollywood admirer, began a series of biographies of silent stars, most of whom he knew personally. Later he would introduce the Rosemary Award which he presented annually to a star of his selection.

Articles on Tarzan appeared in the *Collector* for many months. Most were written by Vernell Coriell, president of the Burroughs Bibliophiles. (Edgar Rice Burroughs was author of the Tarzan novels and many others.) Vernell wrote of "Tarzan in 8mm."

In this issue, a pictorial feature was introduced; it became a continuous series offering reviews of classic silent features. The photographs were supplied by Herman Weinberg.

A new look greeted readers of the *Classic Film Collector* in the Winter-Spring 1966, issue No. 17. This was the first to be partially typeset and printed. It had also grown to 52 pages.

In this issue, Bill Lest began his pictorial series "Sweethearts of the Silent Screen." Wally Bradley also drew a silent stars series.

At this point, things started to pick up. The number of pages in Issue No. 19 (Fall-Winter 1967) was increased to 64. Chris Collier began his "Chris from Across" column. John Schellkopf and John Harwood joined the roster of contributors.

All of No. 20, Spring 1968, was now typeset with enlarged letters, making for easier reading. Edgar Shew and Enrique J. Bouchhard joined the ranks of literary contributors. Joe Gish wrote of Rex Bell, and Raymond Lee penned *The Magic That Was Hollywood*.

Silent Movie Theater's John Hampton and Joe Gish were among the new people. The next issue introduced H.E. Bell into our ranks; Issue No. 22, Nancy Kurtz; then Bill McWilliams in No. 23 and R.R. Maskell in No. 24. Ernest Corneau, Lyle W. Nash, Gene Fernett and Lorang Berg added to the features in No. 24. Cal Dobbins, Maurice Trace, Lamar McCarty and Allan Hoffman came aboard in No. 25. Many quality people joined the ranks from No. 23 to No. 26. Manny Lest was one. *The Classic Film Collector* had reached 72 pages with, again, larger type for easy reading.

New were Kemp Niver, Ray Atherton and Anthony Slide.

The regular contributors continued to submit material. Mike Kornick came aboard. More writers and artists were attracted to the publication in this period of time.

1. The Beginnings! 17

A cinematic trio (from left): dedicated Cinephile Mike Kornick, the author and revered film pioneer Roy E. Aitken discuss the classic cinema at an early (1966) Cinecon.

Between Issues No. 26 and 29, new original works poured in. Manny Lest submitted lovely artwork and Sam Peeples supplied us with the shooting script of the original *The Lost World*, which we ran serially. The script filled in the gaps left by the shorter five-reel version available to collectors.

Denis Gifford, Ray Atherton, Dave Devensky, Chaw Mank and Bill Julison enhanced No. 26. G.D. Taverney and Bob Harman were in No. 27.

Alan Brock and Mary Meginnis were in No. 28. Dani's Doughnuts was the new addition for No. 29. Newcomer H.E. Bell graced No. 30.

Issues No. 31 (Summer 1979) through 39 (Summer 1973) brought newcomers Michael Pitts, Bill Nelson, Tom Brennen, Lt. Col. Escar G. Estes, Bud LeMaster, Sam Gill, Charles E. Carley, David Shepard, Kirk Crivello, Gerald Hamm, Frankie Larkins, Eldon K. Everett and my son, Jay Rubin, all of them lovers of the cinema.

More new names cropped up for the next ten issues: No. 40 (Fall 1973) to 50 (Spring 1976): David Butler, James Ennis, Bob Polunsky, Joe Franklin, David Meier, Carlos de Paulo Couta, Robert Semler, Ed Finney, Scott Eyman, Richard Lucy, F.C. McKnight, Paul Von Someron and Walter Scholz, all film buffs.

New people started between Issues No. 51 (Summer 1976) to No. 59 (Summer 1978): Marilyn Henry, Neville James, Arthur Lennig, John H. Whiting, Bown

Adams, Richard Lucy, Dan Aben, Audrey Totter, Kevin Brownlow, Buck Rainey, Edward Watz, Allen Green, H.E. Bell, John O'Leary and Ted Okuda.

Now we graduated from the quarterly status and began publishing bi-monthly. Our circulation grew and more names of movie addicts appeared on our pages. From No. 61 (Winter 1978) we welcomed to our midst these enthusiastic film followers: Mario DeMarco, Leonard Kohl, Saul Meth, Audrey Kupferberg, Michel Linders, Al Henry, Herb Gordon, Allen Greenfield, Chuck Anderson, Joe Collura, Seymour Stern, Stuart Oderman, Gunnar Lundquist, Jim Welsh and Gerhard Sundt.

From No. 67, Peter Squarini, Neville James, John McCarty, Jeff Cohen, George Katchmer, Michael Bliss, Chris Laube and Frank Poovey were added.

Then, from No. 76 (July 1981): Ted Newsom, Lewis G. Krohn, John Wright, Grady Franklin, Bo Bergland, James Bowden, Ray Loppnow and my wife Lois Rubin were also added.

At this point *Classic Images* graduated to a monthly publication.

New contributors were Art "Doc" Miller, Peter Gutman, Cal Dobbins, Bill Oates, Thelma Norton and Ray Nielsen.

Also new: A full-page quality art of a movie star was added to our front page! For easier research, an index of the contents was also included with the drawing!

David L. Smith, Dr. F.C. McKnight, Fred Robertson, Chris Laube and Daniel W. Horton were added in the July 1982 issue.

The January 1983 edition of *Classic Images* included avid film buffs Ed Chehan, Douglas Whitten, William D. Lucas, Tom Murray, Douglas C. Moore, Ashley O'Hara, Phil Golden, Mathias D. Freese, Wayne Schutz, Cliff Howe, Rick Decroix, Arthur Brokop, Ivor Lohman, Ted Ewing, Artura de Rosa Palhota, John Roberts and P.C. Caryannis.

Newcomers to Issue No. 102 and No. 103 were Tony Crnkovich, Mathias B. Freese, James V. Manago, Leon Calaquin, William J. Burgess, James Beuseline, Joe Empsucho, Alan B. Spater, Nick Nicholls, Christopher Krakora, Patrick McCarver, Bill Oates, Ed Crehan, Joe Carithers, Tim Eldred, Steve Risk, Patrick McCarver and Anthony Barron.

Issue No. 109 (June 1984) brought another group of newcomers to our pages: John Croydon, Daniel W. Horton, Ed Wyatt, Brian Taves, Peter DeLuca, Luther Hathcock, L.E. Ward, Thomas Banks, Lake Regal, R.E. Braff, Mike Martin, Conrad Love, Joyce A. Rogers, Tany Berman, Fritz Gutinger, Pierce Lyden, David Linderman, Scott Johnson, John J. Croft and Richard Gordon.

No. 120. Again we introduced new names and contributors: Stacey Narris, Edmund Whitman, Douglas J. Whitten, Arthur Pierce, George Zoldac and Bud Norris.

Issue No. 122 brought Isabel Withers, Norman Stewart, Michael Pitts, Blackie Seymour, Harv Bishop, Norman Rosenzeig, Alex Gordon, Albert Manski, Norman Paul, John Cocchi and Bruce Long to our pages.

Issue No. 126 added Charles P. Meddleton, Ted Reinhart, Leon Smith, Jack Nicholls, Linda Kowall, Michael Starr, Ralph Roberts and George E. Schatz.

John Aldrich joined the list in Issue No. 132; Jonathan Frid and Steve Randisi in No. 134.

Newcomers in No. 135 were A.V. Snyder, Herbert Smith, Peta Levi, Frank Thompson, Joseph C. Szyanski and Rich Wannen.

Dave Smith and Grady Franklin.

Peter Deluca, Paul Deane, Roy Kinnard, George Seltzer and William R. McDowell graced the pages of No. 138.

With No. 139 came Billy H. Doyle, Larry Byrd, Barbara Pruett, Dave Linden, Dr. Richard Seiverling, Peter Delvee, Theresa Bender and Bill Hagan.

Gil Carface, Bob Pontes and Jim Limbacher helped us celebrate our twentieth-fifth anniversary. That issue (144) was our largest, 132 pages. Also helping were Dennis W. Crow, Alex Bartosh, Ray Rizgonyl and Gunnar Lundquist.

In subsequent issues were Frank Thompson, Michael Katchmer, John Croydon, Erwin Dumbrille and Jordan R. Young. This issue *brought* tears to my eyes. An ad from Budget Video read GOOD LUCK SAM! WE LOVE YOU. I appreciated it then and I appreciate it *more* now. That was in October 1987. Thanks, you guys from Budget! This, at the end of the Sam Rubin Era, the twilight of our publishing career, was the last issue in which we greeted newcomers to our movie lovin' hobby: Mary Anne Landers, Jerry Rutledge, George Geltzer, Jay Rozgonyi, Sandra Quibb and Michael Moore.

Back in 1989, the Society of Cinephiles celebrated its twentieth-fifth anniversary in Cleveland. Chris Hall researched quite a bit of information for a program book and he assembled a superlative booklet which every Cinephile received.

It was chock full of fascinating material and history about the Cinephiles. It apparently took much research for the 40-page pamphlet and it was a beautiful and comprehensive piece of work. I am unaware if any of the members assisted him in the assembling of the pamphlet other than submitting short pieces for which they received by lines.

I enjoyed it tremendously. So much so that I stole some of it for this book. I lifted a narrative of the first Cinecon held in Indiana, Pennsylvania, which I wrote originally, and am duplicating here. I had already printed it in an issue of *Classic Film Collector*.

And, what I appreciated more, because I know it took considerable research to consolidate the material: a list of all past Cinecons, including date, location, and name of the sponsor. Also, an alphabetized list of the guests of honor at the past Cinecons, all 99 of them.

I know it wasn't easy, and right here and now I am thanking Chris Hall for doing the work of assembling those facts and saving me the effort.

June Havoc, who was honored with a Cinephile Award in 1974.

Cinecon Sites

    1965—**Indiana PA**—Samuel K. Rubin
    1966—**Baraboo WI**—Clark Wilkinson
    1967—**Chicago IL**—Irwin Abelson
    1968—**Hollywood CA**—Ed Finney and L. Dobbins
    1969—**Rochester NY**—Harrison Fist
    1970—**Dearborn MI**—Dennis Atkinson and Jim Limbacher
    1971—**Milwaukee WI**—Lou Fazzari
    1972—**Washington DC**—Howard & Elaine Kolodny
    1973—**Toronto Ont.**—Malvern Jacobs
    1974—**New Haven CT**—Bill Bissonnette
    1975—**Hollywood CA**—Marty Kearns
    1976—**New York NY**—Herb Graff
    1977—**Minneapolis MN**—Ron and Chris Hall
    1978—**Syracuse NY**—Ed Hulse
    1980—**Hollywood CA**—Marty Kearns
    1981—**Kansas City MO**—Doug Moore
    1982—**Davenport IA**—Samuel Rubin
    1983—**Chicago IL**—Robert Miller
    1984—**San Francisco CA**—Jon Mirsalis

1985—**New York NY**—Ed Hulse
1986—**Minneapolis MN**—Ron and Chris Hall
1987—**Orlando FL**—John Pipkorn
1988—**Saginaw MI**—Dennis Atkinson and Jim Limbacher
1989—**Cleveland OH**—Morris Everett, Jr.

*Cinephile Guests**

Roy E. Aitken—1966★
Bob Allen—1979★
Richard Arien—1975
Gertrude Astor—1975
Beverly Bayne—1972★
Madge Bellamy—1975
Ralph Bellamy—1980
Spencer Gordon Bennet—1975
Priscilla Bonner—1984★
Joe Bonomo—1976★
Eileen Bowser—1976, 1986★
Mary Brian—1975, 1984★
Betty Bronson—1968
Barbara Burgess—1968
David Butler—1975
Louise Campbell—1979★
Leo G. Carroll—1968
Gaylord Carter—1968
Lita Grey Chaplin—1968
Bernice Clair—1984★
Bob Clampett—1980
Gerald Clark—1974★
Jackie Coogan—1975
Richard Currier—1980
Viola Dana—1980
Rosemary DeCamp—1980
Ruth Donnelly—1976
Allan Dwan—1975
Kent Eastin—1969★
Madge Evans—1976★
William K. Everson—1972★
George Folsey—1980
Joe Franklin—1974★
Tom Fulbright—1973★
Lee Garmes—1977★
Anita Garvin—1980

Lillian Gish—1986★
Kathryn Grayson—1980
Ruth Hall—1977★
John Hampton—1968★
Hugh Harman—1980
T. Marvin Hatley—1980
June Havoc—1974★
Johnny Hines—1968
Victoria Horne (Oakie)—1975
Sam Jaffe—1980
Sybil Jason—1975
Chuck Jones—1975
Zena Keefe—1972★
Walter Kerr—1974★
Paul Killiam—1983★
Sidney Kingsley—1976
Arthur Kleiner—1977★
John Kuiper/Eastman—1978★
Audrey Kupferberg/AFI—1979★
Cullen Landis—1971
Rosina Lawrence—1978★, 1981
Robert E. Lee—1978★
"Babe" London—1968
Myrna Loy—1976★
Ben Lyon—1975
John McCabe—1988
Leonard Maltin—1973★
Patsy Ruth Miller—1973★
Jon Mirsalis—1983★
Colleen Moore—1967★
Pauline Moore—1981★
Ernie Morrison—1980
Ken Murray—1977★
Clarence Nash—1980
Grim Natwick—1980
Gene Nelson—1980

*Indicates that the guest received a Cinephile award (followed by the year).

Marion Nixon—1975
George O'Brien—1979*
Nell O'Day—1984*
Stuart Oderman—1971*
Kit Parker—1984*
Eleanor Powell—1975, 1980
Eddie Quillan—1985
Esther Ralston—1973, 1984*
Samson Raphaelson—1979*
Mrs. Wallace Reid—1975
Erik Rhodes—1979*
Hal Roach—1980
Samuel K. Rubin—1967, 1982, 1988*

Roy Seawrite—1980
Wini Shaw—1976
David Shepard—1970*
Anthony Slide—1986*
Gale Sondergaard—1980
John Springer—1976
Gloria Stuart—1980
Lyle Talbot—1975
June Travis—1983*
Jon Tuska—1971
Robert Vaughn—1981*
Lois Wilson—1972*
Jane Withers—1975

2

I Get Letters

Over the years the U.S. Postal Service has delivered 5,253½ letters to me as the editor of *Classic Images*. The half-letter was all that remained after the original was damaged in the delivering process. It was sliced diagonally from corner to corner.

To be truthful, I really don't know how many letters I did receive over the years. But, if they were all weighed, I would need a couple of trucks to carry the load.

However, I kept many of them and am having some reprinted here for our mutual pleasure. Most of these are from celebrities; most are complimentary, some are not. I'm exposing you to letters from movie people and *Classic Images* readers. The missives from people of the film industry tell me how they like the publication and "keep up the good work" sort of thing.

I especially like this one from Neil Hamilton.

August 6, 1964

Your letter has no date, neither does it have a signature, but it does have a request—namely—that I do something for nothing.

The answer is—*no!*

You may *n-o-t* reprint anything that Mr. Griggs may send you, nor for that matter, whatever anyone else sends you. Either how I met Mr. Griffith, or anything about the time I spent with him, but you may, should it be your desire, publish this letter in your magazine. Why not let your readers know that their editor is as stingy as he quite obviously is?

Your letter says, and I quote ... "I would certainly appreciate hearing from you on this."

You have heard.

Neil Hamilton

Undated

I do thank you for printing the story about me by Mr. Goldsworthy. However; Mr. Goldsworthy is a fine statistan but not much as a human interest writer. The ancient history referred to (my first marriage) was settled satisfactorily some fifty years ago, and has not been thought of since then. The list of films contained several in which I did not appear and omitted some—namely those with Mabel Normand—of which I was proud. I suggest to him that he come out here and we could talk over the whole thing, but he did not and so the most interesting part of my life—the ten years before I retired—were passed over with little or no comment. These years were spent in making films and teaching others how to make them in Iran, Iraq, Afghanistan, Pnom Penh, Istanbul and Manila. A great experience and a great way to close out a career which never took me away from what I knew best how to do.

Cullen Landis

Here are three letters from film pioneer R.E. Aitken, written in 1964 and 1966.

Undated

I am so glad to hear from you that you have a subscription list of over 350 old time enthusiastic silent movie day fanciers. Those were great days and I am always glad to visit with anyone who likes to hear about them. I have an old friend here at Waukesha who married a first cousin of mine. I started him and another cousin of his and hers wife, into the operation of a Nickelodeon in Wausau, Wis., in 1906. This is going back a bit in the silent days.

He lives a few blocks from me so it is often that we get together and have many a laugh over the crazy things that we had to do to get money into the till to pay for the film which generally came C.O.D.

They were both young. Neither had any amount of cash with which to start the show. I knew how to operate a machine, having had considerable experience in Chicago the year before with our own Nickelodeons. My brother and I had one on State Street and four others scattered about town. Operators were scarce then. No one knows much of anything about this new business. So I had to learn to operate and hire and teach new material.

The hot weather of the approaching summer closed us down. I then started to sell films for the film exchange in Chicago from whom I rented our film. We even opened a film exchange of our own in Milwaukee. So in starting my cousins up in the business I sold them a machine screen and film. I had just come from opening another Nickelodeon in La Crosse, Wis., for a gentleman who thought he would like to get into the business.

The experience in getting him started in no time at all (three or four days) was a strain, not only on me but this party and his family too. This would take too long to tell of because I want to go on and briefly speak of my cousins. I got them going and taught them how to operate and patch film. They told me later that when banana oil ran out they used spit to hold the film together. When business was bad they would go behind the theatre in the alley and shoot off a 22-caliber pistol, using blank cartridges.

They owned a one-reel western picture print, which they bought from someone and put this on. The shooting generally aroused some interest above normal, which helped the box-office. As our film exchange in Milwaukee was just getting started, our service was none too good. But they tell me that as soon as I left them and went to St. Louis to start another film exchange, they tried to find better film service. They did but instead of returning the film to the film exchange immediately after using, they rented it to a theatre in another nearby town. A horse and buggy served to carry it if train schedule was not just right.

Coming back to my book, which you speak of. The galley sheets have been received here and corrected. The publisher has received them and hopes to have an early fall release. When I have more data, I will let you know.

Many of your subscription clients must have had to do with early theatres and are therefore familiar with the operating booths of the early days. I was considerably amused one time in Miami when *The Birth of a Nation* was showing in a theatre there. I started quite a number of nickelodeons for people getting started in this new business when I started to travel for this Chicago Film Exchange around 1906 and 1907. So one afternoon just before show time I was standing in the lobby of this Miami theatre when a man asked me if I was Mr. Aitken. I said yes. Well he said I am the operator in this theatre and I wanted to meet you.

He said, right after your picture *The Birth of a Nation* was released (1915) and was being road showed I had a fairly good-sized theatre in Arizona. He said he did the operating. So when your road show crew came to put on the show they came right in and took over. He and you carried an advance man, an operator, a machine, which was not motor driven, a manager, an orchestra, plus advertising, etc. This man said he had one machine in his booth, which he turned by hand. He said they came right up in his booth and sawed another hole in the wall and set up the other machine too. He said for a fellow who had been cranking away ever since he started the theatre and to be able to sit down and cross his legs and watch the show with nothing to do but change reels he felt that he was on easy street for sure.

I expect that he and I would have visited much longer but one of the theatre owners reminded him that he was wanted in the booth as the matinee was about to start. He said further that to operate now with the wonderful projection equipment went beyond our imagination. This was in 1952.

My book will tell of the number of road shows we put on the road within a very short period after *Birth* was released in New York in March 1915. We had from 15 to 20 going before 1918 came around.

I hope that some of the boys who purchased the 8mm film will find the book a help to shed more interest in owning a print of this famous old film.

I wish you continued success.

R.E. Aitken

July 7, 1964

I liked the article on D.W. Griffith that Johnny Griggs wrote about—how he feels about Griffith's ability as a silent movie director and his ability in directing pictures with sound. There is a great difference. Some of these directors of today would probably not get to first base in trying to direct the silents. D.W. Griffith could make you want to hear the end of a story he would start to relate. He had a way of holding our interest.

I recall the many times I would listen to a story he had just read which he wanted to produce for us. We were always pressing him for better material from his directors (you know while he was in charge of our Fine Arts studio in Hollywood he had as many as eight or nine directors under him and was supervising each production) so probably the story was written by a more noted author and the price would be higher and he was selling us on the idea. But he made you listen. He no doubt was producing it as he was telling it.

I enjoyed the Billy Anderson material too. When we did get his films to sell through our film exchanges, they were always tops. Away back in the early days the Westerns were always in demand. And I guess they always will be. Even in England and throughout all my foreign office in the early days, Westerns went well and were the first in numbers over all films. Our American Film Company, which we called the "Flying A" brand, were mostly Westerns. We had Warren Kerrigan at that time and he became very popular as a Western star. He rode well and looked well.

And along with him we had Tom Ince making Westerns with Bill Hart as the star. So my foreign business was built up by selling Western films. They helped build the great interest in the movie business.

Well I could go on but much of the beginning will appear in my book, which I think will come forth this autumn. However, as it deals mostly with the creating *The Birth of a Nation*, I did not find too much space for so many other experiences that dealt with our getting into the production end of the business.

I am enclosing my check for $5 to apply on subscriptions. All best wishes for your continued success with the *Collector*.

Sincerely,

R.E. Aitken

August 18, 1966

I received my summer copy of the *Classic Film Collector*. I think it is a big improvement and I wish you much success in this venture.

I wish to thank you for the write-up about my book and the splendid publicity you added to it. I feel that you should sell quite a number of copies. You are a good showman and I should liked to have you around to help sell our programs when we were in the theatre business. Am sure we would have done more business.

Your manner is selling and getting up advertisement makes me think of a man that started a nickelodeon in St Louis soon after we opened our St. Louis Film Exchange in 1907. His name was Frank Newman and as the years passed he became one of the best theatre operators in the business. He was so particular about his show and the film he was to project that if there was any doubt about his getting the film I had promised him for his next change, he would almost shed tears. It almost broke me up too, in case I had to disappoint him. It made the office rather a gloomy place for a while.

After a successful operation in St. Louis, he decided to open a theatre in Joplin, Missouri. After a short time and his theatre was doing well, he got my brother and I to open a branch film exchange there too. He was a smart operator. It was really too far off the beaten path for an exchange, but Frank, I am sure, felt that this would give him a closer contact to *First Run Film* which most of the theatres wanted in those days. In his location in St. Louis, he paid us $50 for second run. That meant the downtown theatre paid around $75. And believe me, Frank saw to it that I, who was the boss of making up programs, gave it to him.

After a few months in Joplin he came to me and said, "I have a location in St. Joseph, Missouri, that I feel will make a profitable theatre venture." The building just needed fixing up and a good front added and we were in business. So he said I want you and your brother and Mr. John Freuler, of Milwaukee, Wisconsin, who was our partner there, to each put up enough to get me started there. We will split the profit four ways. He said I am sure that I can return your investment in a very short time. We all did as he suggested and within a few months we all had our money returned and dividends kept on coming with same results. We then backed him in a Kansas City venture for many years to come. He was a good operator.

Sincerely,
R.E. Aitken

October 5, 1963

Personally I think the Silent films were more effective for L&H, but the sound was of great value in enhancing the effects—dialog eliminated a lot of action & sight gags—I always feel that "action" speaks louder than words.

Sight gags had to be planned, they required timing and mechanics. Occasionally spontaneity would arise in the shooting of the scenes.

The pies were generally whipped cream, but in *Battle of the Century* film, we used 4,000 pies and they were actually real pies (filling et al.) and were supplied by the Los Angeles Pie Company. A fresh wagon load was delivered to the studio set each day of shooting that sequence.

The later to be famous were—Jean Harlow, Paulette Goddard, Lupe Velez, Fay Wray—George Stevens was our cameraman on many of our films, Leo McCarey, directed and supervised several.

We had friendly and pleasant relationships with all that worked in our films—many happy memories.

Before teaming with Mr. Hardy, I appeared in a Hal Roach "All Star" comedy series. In this particular film, I was cast as a "Crying Butler" (always whimpering—no matter what he was doing). It was a very effective mannerism, so I adopted this when I teamed with Mr. Hardy. (Frankly, I never liked doing it, but it became a part of L&H and I was stuck with it.)

My first movie was a two-reel silent titled *Nuts in May*, made at the "Bernstein Studio," Boyle Heights, California, in 1917.

My first official Team film with Mr. Hardy was *Putting Pants on Phillip*.

My only opinion on the L&H "home movie" situation—I regret we have no financial interest in them.

Trust this will be adequate for your purpose, Sam—you no doubt know there is a book published by Doubleday Co. Inc. written by John McCabe, titled *Mr. Laurel & Mr. Hardy* which covers the career of L&H, listing of films, dates, photos, etc. Maybe this would prove useful to you (information-wise).

Wish you good luck and success with your project.

Stan Laurel

Am enclosing a check for $60 for Poster Ad and would like to add it is very nice.

Yakima Canutt

June 10, 1967

Thank you very much for your good letter and for the three extra copies of *Film Collector* (they have not yet arrived however).

I'm so sorry I appear to have mislead you re—Beverly Bayne.

Of course I didn't know how these stories came to you, I just thought you had a staff, to members of which you would assign people you might be interested in.

As you mention that Mr. Fulbright "has others in mind." Maybe he would like to write a story on her.

I'm sure she would be more than happy. I understand she is thinking of making a return to the amusement world.

Another thank you and all good thoughts for you.

Olga Petrova

June 15, 1967

I'm sorry indeed about the enclosed. Since writing that letter to you the copies of *Classic Film Collector* have arrived and I thank you very much.

Since you have been—*are*—so generous as to say I may call on you again, wonder if I might have three copies of Mr. Fulbright's *first* issue of *our* story?

The second installment seems to have brought me inquiries.

With renewed apologies for my stupidity and my thanks.

(Madame) Olga Petrova

October 6, 1967

A friend of mine told me during the New York Film Festival, where I played for the Abel Gance films, that there was a short article about me in the last issue of your magazine, *Classic Film Collector*.

Would it be possible to get a copy of your magazine?

Thank you very much.

Arthur Kleiner

April 15, 1970

I think it's about time that I stop reading the *Classic Film Collector* over other people's shoulders. Thus, please cash, before somebody else beats you to my bank account, the enclosed $5. cheque for one year's subscription. I know it's only $4. But I think you were going to print some material that I sent you and would like an extra copy. If more, I'll send the diff.

It happens that on the *Studio Magazine*, April issue, is another story about my experience at Keystone, etc. Moreover, on the same Magazine are other quite interesting matter that seems to be the sort of stuff you want. I am sending you a copy of *Hollywood Studio Magazine* on a separate cover.

Whatever material I've sent you, if it's no longer of use to you, would you be so kind as to mail it back? Will refund postage. No hurry, take your time.

Best wishes,
Eddie LeVeque
Two finger typing. Both thumbs.

June 24, 1970

Are you one of my fans who would like to see me make the kind of pictures I made in the 40's and 50's? If a million and a half of you will lend me one dollar a piece, I can make ten pictures, starring myself and a young clean-cut actor, that will make the Saturday afternoon matinees fit again for yourselves and your children to see. Send the dollar to me with your name, address and Social Security number.

Advertisement from Don "Red" Barry.

January 1971

It is almost worth living to be eighty to find out that one has so many friends.

I am sincerely moved and deeply grateful for so many remembrances which reached me on my birthday. The problem is that there are too many—too many cables, telegrams, letters and cards—to allow for individual replies.

If I sat down today and started to acknowledge each 80th birthday message, by the time I finished I'd be 81.

So I am hoping you will forgive me and accept this acknowledgement in the spirit in which it is intended.

The cold print is really a disguise for a warm and grateful heart.

Thank you for remembering!

Fritz Lang

February 11, 1971

I hope I have the right address as it is not very clear on issue number 29 of *Classic Film Collector*. It could be either a one or a four. The printing is rather smeary, however it should be close enough for the postman to locate you.

It is about time that I subscribed to your very fine paper. The enclosed $5.25 is to cover the cost of one issue of number 29. I am interested in getting a copy of page 53 on which Mr. Glenn Shirley has compiled my directorial efforts from 1925. It will not be necessary to send the whole paper as I have another copy.... Just the sheet in an envelope.

Since I have survived the recent earthquake here I'll be interested to receive the *Classic Film Collector* in the future. The only complaint I have about the quake is that the chimney fell down on my car and damaged it to the extent of $1,100 dollars. Fortunately, I was covered by insurance.

Larry Edmunds book store on Hollywood Blvd. is all sold out of issue number 39 of the *Classic Film Collector*. Are there any other dealers out here who carry it? If there are, would appreciate knowing it.

Spencer G. Bennet

August 19, 1971

Your latest is a wonderful issue, and I am very happy to be part of it.
We thought you did an excellent job on layout and reproduction, and want to send our sincere thanks.

Bob Clampett

August 7, 1973

Thank you so very much for your complimentary copy of *Classic Film Collector*. I certainly enjoyed it—and am delighted to learn I came in "third"—in the Rosemary Awards.
May the *Classic Film Collector* have continued and greater success.

Constance Binney

September 10, 1973

I am informed that you published an article, or obituary, on the death of Pauline Bush, a silent star of the 1910-15 period. The issue of the magazine was three or four years ago.
It is extremely important to me that I find the date and place of her death so I may apply for a copy of the death certificate in order to settle some matters of my estate.
I have applied to the departments of Vital Statistics here in California, but they require a pin point of time and place of death before complying.
Can you please help me? If so, please send me a copy of the article and bill me at my address below. Congratulations on a great magazine.

Allan Dwan

January 14, 1966

I don't think it would be an exaggeration to say that yours is one of the most enjoyable and stimulating publications in the film field. I was very happy when someone turned over to me a copy of your 11th issue, although I've seen several other issues in the past. However, someone told me that you had folded over a year ago. The 11th issue, although I hope not your most recent, tells happy news.
Enclosed, by the way, is a check for all back issues, plus any you've had to date (except for #11), and for the next year.
It would be impossible not to say something regarding many of the interesting pieces you've run related to fantasy-horror type films. We would like to know what the possibility would be in granting us reprint rights on any which might interest us or on others you might like to suggest.

With best wishes,
Castle of Frankenstein
Calvin T. Beck, ed-in-chief

October 20, 1976

Just received from one of my friends a copy of the last number of your magazine and would like to express to you my warm appreciation of Bob Harman's rendition of my humble self among "The Queens."
It may amuse you to learn that I have several pals who tease me with that title. If possible could you have your public relation department send me some copies, in the hope that you agree that they should receive each a copy.

It would give me great pleasure if you were to accept the enclosed photograph for your collection.

With my sincere thanks.

Jetta Goudal

October 16, 1979

Glad you received the pictures. You mention writing an article. However several years ago, probably 1971–72, in *Classic Film Collector*, you ran a very good story. It was two full pages and I couldn't, at this time, add anything to that story.

If you want to write something to go with the pictures, I'm sure you can excerpt enough from that article.

It's always nice hearing from you.

Priscilla Dean

November 18, 1982

How nice of you to send me the letter about Robert Stack and the old films.

What actually happened was I had all my old films and sent them to the Museum of Modern Art. When Warner Bros. sold their back-log of films they took all their films from the museum, including mine. With the exception of a few films they have lost all of mine.

Meantime, Robert Stack bought my house and found an old film buried beneath a manure pile in the garden. We have never been able to discover how this happened. The film was an old movie, with my grandmother and me, and I have it. I wish it were true that Bob Stack had my films.

I do appreciate your trying to help me track down my films. It was nice hearing from you.

Colleen Moore Hargrave

April 29, 1983

Thank you for sending me the April issue of *Classic Images* containing Mike Pitto's story on me; he really researches. I didn't remember being in that many pictures.

I'm enclosing a check for three copies of the April issues, and three copies of the May issue. May is a good month for me, I'm going to be 76 on May 5th, that's because I was born in 1907 in St. Joseph, Missouri. But I grew up in Omaha and Lincoln, Nebraska.

I'm aware we might have been neighbors, across the Missouri.

Stay happy and healthy.

Benny Baker

May 24, 1983

I received a letter from Joe Callura and a copy of the article "Quite a Character John Qualen" in your *Classic Images* Issue #95.

I'd like to have 3 copies of the article, so I am enclosing my check for $5 for Xerox copies.

John Qualen

July 16, 1987

In your *Classic Images* Publication #145, there appears an article by Alex Bartosh on the Variety Arts Center of Los Angeles. I am very upset that Mr. Bartosh writes that *I donated* all of the Laurel & Hardy Memorabilia to that room. I did *not*. It is *on loan* and Mr. Bartosh knows that full well. The W.C. Fields Memorabilia is *on loan* and has not been *donated*....

I am getting mail each day now to the effect why did I do this ... how could I give up my collection which I have always stated I never would! Yes it is very upsetting to say the least!

The main problem is once something gets printed wrong it seems to be picked up all over the country by others and it multiplies and gets out of hand. If there is anything you can do to correct this mis-information I truly would be so grateful.

In another previous article in another publication, I was distressed by this and informed Mr. Bartosh by phone immediately. Now that its happened again I hope you might be able to correct this for me, as he is not attempting to correct it, himself!

We enjoy your Publication very much....

Lois Laurel Hawes

July 6, 1991

I am hoping that *Classic Film Collector* continues in publication, as I very much enjoyed the copies I saw some years ago.

In what was, I believe, an early Spring issue of 1977 you ran an article that was in fact a long interview with the former child star, Baby Peggy, with a drawing of her on the front page. Because I was the same Baby Peggy, the young author of that piece sent me a copy. However, in the course of a move across the State, that copy was lost. I am hoping it will be possible to obtain a copy or perhaps a Xerox of the original?

Under my present name I am also the author of two well-known books on early Hollywood, *The Hollywood Posse* and *Hollywood's Children: An Inside Account of the Child Star Era*. As I am now engaged in writing my autobiography, the above article would be of great value to my research.

Thank you very much for you kindness. If you have any questions please call me collect at the phone number listed below.

Diana Serra Cary (Baby Peggy)

January 13, 1988

Congratulations! You have found the release into the "world of travel" you have been waiting for so long.

We'll miss you, but wish you happy trails, where ever they may take you.

Please convey our congratulations and best wishes to Michael Bliss. He sounds like a winner and I'm sure he is, since he has been chosen in your long search for a replacement.

With Mr. Bliss' acceptance, I shall continue writing the column. We said we wouldn't, but *did*, do another book! It should be out April or May.

Mario DeMarco has again consented to edit for me. I think it will be what the fans have asked for, namely the badmen I rode with. I hope they like it.

As for me, I think it's a good finish to the other three volumes.

Once again, dear editor Sam, many thanks for all the courtesies and help you have given me. Our best always from our house to your house.

Now may all your wishes come true—that are good for you.

God Bless,
Pierce Lyden

3

End of an Era

In 1988, when I was 70 years old, I was unaware that my career as editor of the publication I had founded was about to come to a close. The end of the "Sam Rubin Era"!

The publisher of *The Muscatine Journal*, parent company of *Classic Images*, came up to me and said, "Sam, it's about time you retired!"

I wouldn't have been more shocked if she had taken a baseball bat (the old wooden kind) and broke it on my skull.

So, that was to be it! It was a long time since I started it in 1962.

She started to interview and hired Michael Bliss, a member of the Society for Cinephiles, who had been contributing to the publication with his continuing column "Technical Tips." I thought Mike was a good choice.

Everything looked under control until Mike gave us the news that he had a doctor's exam and was diagnosed as having a serious health problem. No Michael for *Classic Images*.

It was about a year after that fateful conversation with the publisher that I was informed that she had hired Sue Laimans as editor to replace me. With her came a friend, Jeannette Kopps, who was to be associate editor.

Here's what Sue had to say in her first issue as editor:

Classic Images, No. 157, July 1988:
In Laimans' Terms... by Sue Laimans

"Well, here I am ... the new editor of *Classic Images*. I can't tell you how many times I've pinched myself. I have loved old films since I was nine years old. Not only did the films intrigue me, but I was also fascinated by the lives of the stars.

My interest in old movies was encouraged by my Aunt Portia. Portia, who was born in 1901, loved the old films. She shared her memories with me of Hollywood gossip and of being a young girl playing piano for the silents in the little London Mills Theatre. I can still see Portia, lounging on her bedroom fainting couch, reading movie magazines and reminiscing about John Gilbert.

By the time I hit college, I found myself staying up til the wee hours just to see Greta Garbo in *Flesh and the Devil*. I was hooked.

So, when I first heard of Sam's intention to retire over a year ago, I became concerned. Like you, I too am a *CI* subscriber and my biggest fear (and perhaps yours) was that they would replace Sam with someone who would change *CI* to something else. I didn't know what kind of change, but maybe a current film newspaper or comics or (God forbid) nothing but video tape releases on the likes of *Golf Made Easy* and *Frankenstein General Hospital*.

I waited, uneasily renewed my subscription, and then came up with the surefire way to keep *Classic Images* classic—I applied for the job.

Since I'm currently employed full time with the corporation that owns the *Muscatine Journal*, which owns *CI*, assuming another full-time job was impossible. I knew I couldn't do it on my own. Who did I know that would put as much time, care and love into *CI* as it deserves? Jeannette Kopps.

Jeannette and I go back many years (let's just say 20 plus) to the days when we took journalism together. She had gone into social work out of college (I into the business world), and she later entered into advertising. She has been a sales rep (a good one, I might add) with another Lee Enterprises newspaper before she moved out of town.

Getting back on track, I called her before I formally applied with the opening statement, "I've got this terrific off-the-wall idea." We decided to present the idea of Jeanette doing the advertising, production, and general management of *CI* full-time, and I would do the editorial side only. We were determined to get the job, and finally we did!

We know that no one can ever replace the likes of Sam Rubin, and even trying has taken two people to do so. In working with him in the last few weeks, we are amazed at his unending knowledge and energy.

With a little luck we hope to provide you with the CI you have come to know and love for 26 years.

★ ★ ★

The two girls ran *Classic Images* for three years, doing a commendable job. Then, because of the amount of work entailed in putting this publication together and conflicts with other positions, they decided to call it a day.

Bob King had been hired several years prior to this. He was in advertising and circulation. However, he was a real film buff. He was well qualified, so Bob was made editor of *Classic Images* and Sue and Jeanette left.

Here's what he had to say in an issue after he was appointed to the position I didn't want to vacate:

"How I Started" by Bob King

I was always an avid movie goer! Back in '25, when I was much younger, one movie impressed me above all others. I saw it no less than four times.

Immediately following World War II, I was reading one of the Photography mags and noticed an ad listing some 8mm movies for sale. Among the titles I saw was The Lost World *starring Wallace Beery, Lewis Stone, Bessie Love and Lloyd Hughes. I couldn't believe my eyes, but there it was.*

I wasted no time in ordering it. After an agonizing six-week wait, it arrived. I trembled as I inserted the first reel in the projector. Sure enough, it was my well-remembered Lost World.

The above words were written by my predecessor, Samuel K. Rubin, in the first issue of *Classic Images* way back in 1962. At that time, Sam called his new publication

Sent to Sam upon his retirement by Tony Crnkovich, an artist who contributed so much beautiful artwork to the pages of *Classic Images*.

8mm Collector. With his characteristic dry humor, he explained that it was to be "published spasmodically." Subscriptions were free, and ad rates were $1 per page. The whole issue was cranked out on Sam's trusty typewriter. It wasn't much to look at, but it was the start of bigger things to come.

And now, 29 years and many spasms later, *Classic Images* is still going strong. For this we have Sam to thank. He's the man who made it happen.

But, of course, he couldn't have done it without a lot of help. Sue, Jeannette and many others have worked hard to keep *CI* healthy. And our many contributors have done an incredible job. Their combined knowledge of films is awesome. Each month they give us our chance to relive the magic of the movies.

Which brings us to you, the reader. Few publications can boast of such a dedicated following. Many of you have connections to the film industry; some of you have developed over the years an encyclopedic knowledge of films; others of you simply have a great love for films and film people. Together, you are keeping the movies alive.

Like you, I have a fascination with the movies. It all started one fine day in 1956 when I walked unsuspectingly into the old Varsity theatre in Iowa City. Before I could even make it to my seat I was stopped in my tracks, frozen in terror. On the giant screen above my head, looming out of the darkness, I saw Aliens and Earthmen killing each other in a fantastic running battle. I was shocked, appalled ... and fascinated. I was only six years old. The film was *Earth vs. the Flying Saucers,* and it is the beginning of my movie memories.

At first I was hooked on fantasy and science fiction, but over the years my tastes changed. I developed a love for all sorts of movies—Hollywood, foreign, good, bad, you name it. And somewhere along the line I developed a special fascination with the Hollywood films of the thirties and forties. They were my *Lost World*— the world as it was before I was born. Only the movies could take me there.

Movies and memories. Let's keep them alive. That's what *Classic Images* is all about.

★ ★ ★

Bob has done an admirable job with *Classic Images*. He has made many changes and has supervised the growth of the publication since the moment he took over the reins. It's now been 12 years; during that time he initiated a quarterly sister magazine, *Films of the Golden Age*, in 1995.

At a time when many hobby publications have ceased publishing, *Classic Images* and *Films of the Golden Age* continued to prosper. All indications are that this growth will continue.

If you are interested in contacting *Classic Images* for information or subscription, write to 201 E. Third St., Muscatine, IA 52761.

4

The Prelude

In 2001, I inserted the following hypnotic article in my *Classic Images* monthly column. I was absolutely flabbergasted by the response and proceeded with the project.

I knew it would be a lot of work and time. Braveheart that I am, I proceeded with this blankety blank book because so many people appeared interested in it. However, I did not know how much work and how much time it would take.

Frequently I would shake my mane (no time to see a barber) and give deep consideration to dropping the whole thing. On those occasions I would ponder on the problem and remember those fighting words that our ancestors used in a dire situation: "Remember the Maine." Then, I would rebuke myself and return to the trenches and resume digging up all these trivialities from the cemetery of ancient words which were printed in the past.

I would shout, "Onward!" and start hitting the keys of this monster of technology called a word processor and return to processing my words. Hope you enjoy them!

Here is the original article:

Classic Clips Book?

I pulled out my thinking cap and tried to organize my thoughts, so I could give myself quality time to make up my mind about an idea presented to me by Alice Levin, author of the Eleanor Powell biography.

She suggested that I do a book about the formation of the best publication in the world, *Classic Images*, and the subsequent birth of the Society for Cinephiles. And, I did give it serious thought. Don't forget that the *8mm Collector* evolved into the *16mm Collector*, and then it evolved into *Classic Images*. This took place over a period of 41 years. We're talking about hundreds of thousands of words which have appeared since that 1962 birth date.

She was talking about a lot of work! I stated that I would be happy to do it if there was enough interest. What you are reading now is the answer. I received a deluge of letters, some of which are reproduced here. Everybody wanted me to get to work on it.

So, I did! Even I did not realize how much sweat this would cause. But, dauntless Sam stiffened my upper lip and plunged in.

I have one thing to say to you. I sure hope you like it.

And here are some of the responses from the readers of *Classic Images*:

I think your work idea is terrific! I hope you will do it. I am a young lady who loves the classic movies—especially silent movies with Buster Keaton. A book sounds great!

Martha Jett

August 11, 2001

I don't want you to ruin your eyes—and you should get out of the hot sun—but I will be delighted to reread your vintage prose. Since Alice Levin started this, let her become your agent and find a publisher.

Jim Goodrich

I've only been reading *Classic Images* and *FGA* for a few months, but I've loved old movies since I was a little girl. I greatly enjoy your column; it's my favorite regular feature of the publication.

I like the way you describe the plots. Your summaries give me a very clear idea on whether I'd want to see the movie—and I've already bought a few videos you've reviewed.

Your reviews often make me feel like I've already seen the movie—which is good, because I couldn't possibly afford to buy them all! I also appreciate your comments on background music. An annoying score can ruin a silent movie.

Here's one vote in favor of your doing a book!

Kerry Lynch

Here is my opinion on the proposed book of articles which would ... or will capture the spirit of us classic movie enthusiasts.

Braveheart that you are I don't recommend that you take on a ton of work. It is not only the hours of backtracking through the old issues but the inevitable publishing deadline which always results in tension and anxiety.

I suggest that you submit a selected article from an old issue on an irregular basis to *Classic Images* to print as part of your Classic Clinic with a subtitle such as "Looking Back." A long article could be cut.

Lou McMahon

Sorry Lou, I couldn't resist this project. You were right; it was a lot of work!—Sam

I wanted to respond to your recent suggestion, carried in the August and September Issues of *Classic Images*, regarding a potential book comprised of selected articles from that same journal.

Personally, nothing would give me greater pleasure than to invest in such a volume. In the thirty plus years I've subscribed to the magazine, it is the one periodical which has afforded me the greatest pleasure. Without meaning to take anything away from its current editor, your years at the helm made it memorable, at least for me. There was magic to it back in the seventies, and either it has changed for the worse, or the passing years have afflicted my judgment.

In any event, register my vote as an enthusiastic "Yes!" I'd be honored to buy the book. Whatever the price, I'm sure its potential enjoyment would far outweigh the cost.

Frank Commins

Yes, please proceed with the *Classic Clips* concept! Your name on any written work—reviews, letters, etc., should be a bestseller! That's my vote.

Cal Francis

It is always with great pleasure that I read your very interesting columns "Sam Rubin's Classic Clinic."

Yes, it would be a great idea to publish your past articles in form of a book.

"Young" people like me (52 years), which have only recently joined *Classic Images*, have missed a lot of your articles; and I think that the other people will find interesting to read them again.

So Sam, please do it!

Thank you for sharing with us your fantastic knowledge, and be sure that we are looking forward to read your future columns.

Patrick Kuster

I don't guess that you remember me one of your first subscribers on the old *8MM Collector—yes, I will be very much interested* in a book of some of the great articles that you have written in the last 40 years. You really did movie fans a great favor by starting the *8MM Collector* which through the years developed into *Classic Images*. I have enjoyed your columns very much, keep up the good work.

I was born in 1920, I remember the silent days of film and the following days of the Golden Age. My likes in film are widespread from the B's to the A films.

I also enjoy the B Westerns of the 1930 and '40s—so many European films that were so good—the films from France in the 1930s.

I say again, yes I would be interested in a book on your articles.

Nick Fiorentino

P.S.: Sam, would you believe every time I pass a furniture store you come to my mind.

5
Editerribles

There comes a time in the life of every editor when he has something to say other than reporting events or occurrences. He wants to give his opinion on a happening, a complaint or a compliment he receives; or a speech; or ... *any*thing! He might even want to tell a joke, or make a personal announcement, or talk about candidates for offices, or about whatever he darn pleases.

He wants to editorialize. And when he does speak his piece, it's called an editorial, of course.

To me, an editorial would be out of place in an informal type of publication such as the *Classic Images* of the Sam Rubin Era.

Delivering our message in a casual, tongue-in-cheek sort of way, not nearly as serious as most editorials, just as easily gets our message across. We can broadcast our opinions, judgments, bellyaches and pains in the neck in any manner we wish. We can publicize movies, meetings, elections, or anything we want to: formally, informally, humorous or serious in our Editerrible!

I have selected *Editerrible* from the early days of the Sam Rubin Era of *Classic Images*. I hope you have as much fun reading them as I had re-reading them. Most are rather serious, some are humorous (I hope), and all offer samples of your editor's thinking.

8mm Collector, *No. 11*
Spring 1965

I am a hare-brained, ostrich-minded, short-sighted, ignorant nincompoop.

I have been collecting classic movies for years. I have been watching and thrilling at them. I have been thoroughly enjoying them. I was under the impression that I was watching the ultimate in fine movies when I projected one of the quality 8mm reproductions.

Until recently I made no attempt to add musical accompaniment to the films. And that is where I take the fur-lined, polka-dotted spittoon.

I have seen *The Lost World* no less than 15 times, and each time I have thoroughly enjoyed it. I recently became more deeply enchanted with *The Lost World*. I projected the classic with a musical background.

Since then I have projected other of my "old friends," musically, and it was like watching completely new presentations. The music added to my enjoyment tremendously.

You can be sure that there will be no more silent "silent" classics shown in my home. I have purchased a tape recorder and will have a musical presentation with each showing.

Much music is available for the collector. John Griggs, for example, will sell tapes for some of his presentations. He is, at present, advertising the tape of the soundtrack of the William S. Hart starrer *Tumbleweeds*. I believe that there will be a market for these tapes, and that the distributors should all make them available.

Years ago, when the silents were made and distributed to the theaters, music came with the print. Music for pianist, organist or orchestra. Much of the music was written for the particular movie it accompanied.

If you are showing your "silents" without music, you are "robbing" your viewers. These movies were made for music.

I have been showing movies without music. I have been extremely moronic about it.

But I am learning, and I am changing. What about you?

Classic Film Collector, *No. 16*
Fall 1966

"I feel that the *Classic Film Collector* is actually performing a *dis*service to serious-minded dealers as there is no distinction made between product which is legally available and with that which is not legally available."—R.F. Watson, Managing Director, Watsofilms, LTD.

The above statement is the climax of a letter sent to us by Mr. Watson.

The subject matter has been repeated, and again, in the pages of the *Collector*. And, once more I must state "my side" of the case.

As in the case of Watsofilms, they were releasing illegal prints. They discovered this fact, and removed them from sale. I began my publishing career by advertising and publicizing everything that was submitted. Now, if much of the same were sent in, I would hesitate about publicizing or printing it. I would be careful of the movies I "pushed!"

Now, we come to the critical point. How am I to determine whether a print is being released legally or not? I have stated in previous issues that I now require assurance from all distributors that their prints are legal. Further than that I will not go. I am not about to investigate every new movie that appears on the scene. I do not have the time, nor the inclination to do such. If a distributor issues an illegal print, and tells me that it is legal ... *he* is taking the risk. I sincerely believe that I have done my bit by asking him to check.

Now, let's discuss a situation in which the distributor assures me that his print is legal, and Mr. Kop E. Right writes to me and informs me he owns the rights to this particular movie. Just because Mr. Right claims ownership (and it has happened) does not *prove* ownership. Because he has made this statement to me does not mean that I should stop advertising that print, because he *says* he owns the rights. If Mr. Right does own the rights to this print, he should take legal action against the distributor and halt this illegal production.

According to Mr. Watson, such action is being taken. However, I have heard these rumblings for several years, and cannot understand the delay.

If Mr. Right owns the prints, the illegal production of these prints *can* be stopped. When such action is taken and when the distributor informs me that he no longer is able to produce and sell this print; then I will halt all publicity. And I sure hope that the actual print owner does not remove it from the market altogether, because then we may start talking about *him*.

Let's take a case. I know that there is a controversy concerning *The Black Pirate*. Because some person says that he owns the right to this movie, I cannot stop writing about the availability of this movie which, coincidentally, all three major distributors have, at one time or another, released. Two are still selling prints. When these distributors tell me that they can no longer reproduce *The Black Pirate*, I will stop advertising it.

I do *not* wish to advertise any illegal prints, and there are many of them, I know. But, I think that I would be doing the dealers a disservice if I *stopped* pushing a movie every time someone claims ownership. Let *him* prove it!

Classic Film Collector, *No. 18*
Summer 1967

The other day a fellow asked me, "Would you knowingly buy a desirable silent classic illegal dupe?"

Before I became involved with the *Collector* I would have unhesitatingly answered, "Yes!" In fact, I even tried the duping bit myself once, and got out from under that in a hurry.

Now, I "slyly" evaded answering the gentleman, and proceeded to retire to my cogitating corner to think the matter out.

I have given the matter considerable meditation.

If a person would ask me: "Would you knowingly buy a dupe of an art masterpiece?" Unhesitantly: "No!" Who wants a copy? Then he may ask, "Why do you not hesitate on making these negative decisions as you hesitated on the film dupe decision? Why the fine line of distinction?

The answer may be touchy, but I believe that I am echoing the sentiments of the collectors.

The silent movies are made for the enjoyment of the people. For this pleasure, we members of the movie-going populace reached into our respective pockets. Many of us missed these silent classics altogether. Many of us can remember only a portion of the silent era. Some of us lived through the entire period. We would like to see these movies to enjoy them again, or to see them for the first time. We wish to gain or regain the magic of this miraculous entertainment.

Now that miniature film sizes have, economically speaking in cost and space conservation, brought the possibility of ownership of these films within the reach of most of us, we want to see, enjoy and possess these prized films.

The copyright owner is able to give us these bits of nostalgic Americana, and we are willing to buy time. But, if he is sitting on his butt, and his rights, and permitting these movies to deteriorate without making any type of effort towards conservation; if he is disinterested in permitting people to enjoy these films (the reasons they were made), then he deserves a slight thump on aforesaid butt. He does not have the *moral* right to deprive the people of this enjoyment.

And the U.S. government feels the same about this. Else, why have a limitation on copyright time? Why let copyrights elapse at all?

Mechanically, these movies can be copied. And we can prize a copy much as an art collector will prize an original painting, watch or piece of jewelry. The individual watch or jewelry was made for one person's enjoyment. The movie was made for the enjoyment of many.

If the copyright owner is willing to make copies of his films, we are willing to buy them. If he won't duplicate his desirable item, he can't blame a duper for duping his dupes. If the copyright owner does not wish to go to the bother of duplicating his films (work, expense and time consumption), let him turn it over to someone who is willing to undergo this labor. Then he can reap profits from his valuable property by doing nothing.

The studio copyright owners could put a halt to illegal duping immediately, merely by making these classic films available for sale. Working with original negatives, and their fine labs, they could produce material, far superior in quality, to the dupes made from lesser quality material and less elaborate equipment.

It reminds me so much of the liquor situation during Prohibition. If a person wanted liquor, he was able to get it! The bootleg industry came to a virtual end with repeal.

I have corresponded with many collectors and distributors. I have yet, to my knowledge, personally met a distributor who does *not* own a print still under copyright, not being offered for sale to the public. He may not own this print with the intention of reproducing it and selling it for a profit. But, he does possess the print! And, how many of these prints were purchased from the original copyright owner, or his authorized agent? How much investigation was made concerning the source of the print when it was purchased?

All of the distributors cringe, and rightly so, when an illegal dupe is unintentionally mentioned in these pages. It cannot make for a healthy industry to have the market flooded by dupes. But, how many of the distributors fear the situation because they are solicitous of the illegal dupes they themselves possess?

I *will* go on record now and say ... if you are thinking of illegally duping a copyrighted movie, *don't*! If you are thinking of mentioning it in the *Collector*, forget it! *If* you want to go into film distributorship—fine, we can use you. The more distributors, the more collectors we will gather to our field. But, be sure you check the legality of the print you plan to reproduce.

Now, to get back to the original statement ... I don't think I'd care to run the risk of duping a copyrighted print myself. I can't recommend that anyone should. But, if someone should come up to me and say, "How would you like to buy a print of *Wings*?"

Answer: "How much do you want for it?"

Classic Film Collector, *No. 19*
Fall-Winter 1967

For many months I have been receiving letters from collectors deploring the fact that most of the ratings we give films (both Bud LeMaster and myself) are not critical enough.

It seems that we hesitate to give a film a bad name. Many reasons are offered. Perhaps, these people say, we are too friendly with the distributors and do not wish to antagonize them. Perhaps we do not screen them properly. Perhaps we are hesitant about passing our true feelings and judgment on these films. Perhaps we do not have the courage to say, "This is the way we see this film. It stinks."

Other reasons have been given, but the above seems to cover the territory fairly well.

Because determination of the quality of a film is definitely a personal judgment thing, and because each collector has different standards, each of us may come up with a different rating. Being that I can see, and understand, this problem, I can therefore sympathize with the people who have been tossing outraged remarks at us, who presume to judge the quality of the films. In most cases, if you notice, little is done with storyline because most of the films are known. We mostly attempt to state the quality of the particular print available.

Therefore, in order to pacify the people who disagree with the quality ratings given in the *Collector*, I announced last issue a rating plan whereby all collectors can participate, and submit their own ratings. We also planned to print their names and addresses so that other collectors can compare notes with them. This, then, was to stop the complaints.

Since last issue ... exactly two rating lists were submitted. One of these was by Bob Gray, who graciously agreed to tabulate and set up the department.

He had little work to do.

We will attempt to start the rating column. We will try it again next issue. If you want a rating column, with rating by the readers, submit yours. Because if the response for the next issue is not better than it was for this, we will discontinue our efforts and go ahead reporting them as we see them as we have in the past, as honestly and straightforwardly as we can. If you don't see eye to eye with us, you have had your chance to do something about it.

Classic Film Collector, *No. 20*
Spring 1968

Growing Pains

As the *Collector* continues to expand, the pulsating agony of torturous growing pains irritate us as we creep into the adolescent stage.

Ouch #1

The *Collector* is yet, unfortunately, basically a one-man operation insofar as mechanical make-up is concerned. The *Collector* is yet, more unfortunately, a hobby publication with work accomplished during available spare time. I would like the *Collector* to be my primary effort and interest. But, still more unfortunately, there is the small matter of livelihood.

Consequently when a siege of illness hits me, as had happened during (and a considerable time following) the issuance of #19, the *Collector* must take a back seat.

It all commenced months ago when I was attacked (one by one) by a series of aggravating ailments. I developed a case of the shingles, the flu, headaches, common (?) cold, ringing in my ears and other similar nonsense. Then a pain developed behind my (right-facing) eye, and my one eyelid drooped and I had trouble coordinating my vision.

The family physician recommended consulting an eye specialist, which I did. He could find nothing. He referred me to a neurologist. After his examination, the two doctors consulted! This consultation resulted in my commitment to a hospital. Then I went through an entire course in probing, penetration, photography and numerous and various tests including a spinal tap. The test verdicts were all negative.

The medical people then diagnosed a "viral" condition. A virus had possibly invaded my body, and the resultant conflict with my system caused all my problems.

They recommended a rest (which I took) feeling that the problem would correct itself. I had a week at home, two weeks in Florida and another week at home and most of the pain disappeared. However, as of this writing (Leap Year Day) the eyelid still droops, painful on occasions, and I still have trouble coordinating my vision.

I continue to wait for "Correction Day."

Ouch #2

I am continually attempting improved methods of *Collector* reproduction to diminish time consumption. The mechanical reproduction (before, and now) has been accomplished by the offset method. The material is pasted on a sheet, photographed and transferred from the negative to a metal plate. I do *not* get to see a proof after the paste-ups are placed in the hands of the printer. This is a roundabout method of apologizing for the putrid, sorrowful reproduction of many of the photos in the last issue. All photos are screened! The photos that appeared too dark in #19 did so because of using too fine a screen; the dots, of which the picture is comprised, came too close together after reduction. The photos this issue will be improved (it says here). We are not doing nearly as much reduction in an effort to counteract the countless complaints concerning the tiny type, which appears to have become the collector's trademark.

Also, for the same "lack-of-time" reasons, it is difficult and impractical for me to check, prior to publication, on such matters as the veracity of the advertising copy, as to the quality of the merchandise, ownership claims, copyright clearance, etc.

Therefore, I must make a policy statement ... right here, right now. Any merchandise offered for sale, or any claims made in the *Collector,* are not the property

The author at work at home in his basement office, Indiana, Pennsylvania, 1968.

of the *Collector*, and do not reflect the views of the *Collector* (me). These people have a right to offer any legitimate merchandise, or make any kind of claim, as long as they can deliver the merchandise and substantiate the claim. If the readers are mislead by false offers, or claims, I *do* want to know about them. On such complaint, I will contact the advertiser and hear his side of the story. As I have said in the past, unfortunately a few of our readers are not the fine, friendly, cooperative type which comprises the majority; consequently, it behooves me to hear both sides of the story before refusing any advertising.

Ouch #3

Also, because of our growth, the number of advertisers (regular and classified) has grown. Most of these, fortunately, are clean-cut, above board, upstanding people operating in a business-like manner. A scattered few are dirty, underhanded, slippery slobs. It is impossible for me to police the ads in the manner I would like to. If you have a complaint about one of the advertisers, let me know, and I will contact the party, and if the complaint is well-founded I will refuse his advertising. There is little more I can do in the limited time available to me. If this were a full-time, money-earning, lucrative project, I would pursue the villain to the very "The End."

Ouch #4

This is a real "hurtin'" ouch. The postal department "did it" to me again the first of the year by raising its rates. That, coupled with our perennial malady, increased size of the *Collector* (additional mailing weight) plus the more expensive new printing set-up, have blasted a devastating cavity in the financial "kitty." I will try to maintain prices, but a second "blow" of this nature will cause publishing the *Collector* to be tantamount to jumping off the Empire State Building using a handkerchief for a parachute.

> **policy statement**
> This is my policy on advertising: I reserve the right to refuse any and all advertising which I deem in bad taste, or which I feel is detrimental to the collecting field, or for any other reasons that may come to my peculiar Lilliputian brain. Amen.

Classic Film Collector, *No. 25*
Fall 1969

"I Saw Sparrows or Why Not Let the Collectors Have These Movies?"

If you are one of the early stars (or the progeny of such) and if you have your (or anyone else's) film to which you have the copyrights ... *why not make them available to the collectors?* Why not let the guys (or gals) who really revere your memory, more than anyone else in this land, buy your movies?

Who else in the country (other than the AFIs and the Museums) wants to perpetuate your (or your parents') memories?

How else are the films going to be shown to the general public in the manner they were intended, as the artistic entities they were? Elsewhere they will be burlesqued, satirized and displayed on TV and in the movies with a tongue-in-cheek approach and brutally ridiculed.

I saw *Sparrows* at the Eastman House at the Cinecon and I cried. I could watch it again and again. I trembled with Mary Pickford as she, with the children, made their perilous journey across the alligator-ridden swamp. I would take *pride* in owning and showing a print of *Sparrows* to others.

You, as the owner, may say: "I don't like anyone profiteering from these movies."

Then I will say, as rebuttal: Sure, a few of the collectors might attempt to make money on these films. *So what!* We're talking about *pennies*. The films will not be shown to huge theater audiences. They will not be nationally displayed and advertised. They will be shown (and proudly) to small groups. And, what's wrong if a few people do charge admission to moviegoers who *want to see your movies?* How else is your memory going to be perpetuated?

Some of you are allowing these films to be shown at the AFI and museums such as the Museum of Modern Art. *Great* ... for the people living in the cities.

How about we farmers who do *not* live in the cities? (Like the guy who is right now writing these lines in the middle of the night in the bathroom because he cannot sleep for thinking about it?)

Let's talk about *Sparrows* again. Here is a movie which is completely unavailable to us. Let us pretend that Mr. Joe Sneakmprint comes stealthily up to a collector and says: "You wantum spurious, illegal, unlawful print of *Sparrows*?" The collector jumps with joy and says, "You sneakum me a print!" After an interminable wait, ersatz print arrives (it is often a collector's nightmare in quality). Then you surreptitiously whisper to your friends, "Hey, come on over to my house, we're 'Sparrowing' tonight." Then, a very few get to see what is probably a very poor print, unworthy of the producers of the movie.

Wouldn't it be better (Mr. Copyright owner) if a collector could go to a legitimate dealer and say, "I want to buy a print of *Sparrows*?" You, Mr. C-owner, make your profit, the collector is happy with this "over-the-counter" print, and he can proclaim to the world…

"Tomorrow night," he exclaims, "at my house (or the Civic Center of the Sewing Circle, or the Boy Scout Meeting), I will show you the world-renowned Mary Pickford in *Sparrows*!"

And then he shows them a good-quality *Sparrows* in the dignified manner it should be shown to as many people as possible who are truly interested in the film as an art form, or as entertainment value rather than as a curiosity.

These profitable prints (profitable to you, Mr. C-owner) can be marketed through legitimate sources such as Blackhawk Films, the AFI, or some other reliable outlet.

Don't forget these customers would be the people who love these films and want to see them over and over again.

If you ask, "Who would like to have a print of *Sparrows* to show?," I would! And there are many more like me. Frankly, it aggravates the living daylights out of me that the people in the cities near the film centers can see such classics as *Sparrows*, *Peter Pan*, *Wings*, etc. They can attend the museums and the film festivals, such as the recent AFI showings in New York, and I must sit on my rural rear seeing only prints I am able to personally obtain or wait until the next Cinecon.

Last night I projected *Son of the Sheik* to a woman's group (and their husbands). They loved it … and I loved it … for the 14th time.

Classic Film Collector
Spring 1970

I have been the recipient of recent articles in which the readers have taken to task certain individuals, some of them *Collector* advertisers or writers. I have been forced to return the articles.

These articles blasted the subjects for lies, misrepresentation of facts, fraud and the entire gamut of unwholesome, unhealthy, nefarious activities. Instructions to me in one of the articles were that I was to print it exactly as written, making no changes. I returned it to the writer. I fear that he thinks I am a scoundrel who condones everything the "rascal" he wrote about has allegedly done; that I am afraid to print it for fear of turning an advertiser or contributor away from the *Collector* doors.

In a measure he could be right. When it comes to name-calling, accusations of *any* kind in the *Collector*, I am blithering, weak-kneed coward. I, and I alone, am responsible for the material in the *Collector*, not the authors! This is a hobby publication, *my* hobby. I am not averse to criticizing, disagreeing with, scolding an advertiser or writer in the *Collector*. But I will not accept anything for publication which might possibly have repercussions to *me* because what someone else has written will not hold "legal water." This *is* a hobby, and litigation in a matter such as this would not be overly popular with me.

Most of the material submitted does see print. I realize that these writers have spent much time in planning and research, and they receive no payment. Therefore, I feel a moral obligation to run practically everything that is submitted. However, much of it, unfortunately, does require editing. I remove as much extraneous material as possible, and I absolutely remove everything that could possibly have legal consequences.

Our collectors get rather angry about many things (and their anger often times has foundation) and they say (and write) some rather direct accusations which, in many cases, they would have difficulty in proving. I wonder if they would make these statements if they knew that the accused was going to take issue with the remarks and enter a libel suit. The allegations may possibly be true, but their statements cannot be protected with proof, documentary or otherwise. Then what? I, as editor-publisher, must never forget this.

If a writer or advertiser of the *Collector*, or any publication, makes a claim which you believe to be incorrect, feel free to write about it. Disagree with him, correct him, but don't call him a liar. If an advertiser has not delivered what he has advertised, let me know, but don't call him a crook. I will contact him. It may take me some time to get to it, for reasons we have previously emphasized, but I *will* get to it. Incidentally, always keep in mind that in the field of old films you are *not* going to get perfection every time because of the many factors we have endlessly discussed.

For the record: I cannot accept material for publication with the restriction "Don't change a word!" I reserve the right to edit anything that is sent to me. If you do not recognize this right ... please don't bother!

Classic Film Collector
Fall 1970

I have been charged with irresponsibility and, y'know, in this particular case I feel kind of semi-responsibility ... in fact, I feel downright sad and woebegone about it. It is seldom that I have to do any back-tracking in the *Collector*, because most of the people we might mention in an unkind manner deserve our mild rebukes which should, in most cases, be stronger. I find myself bending over backwards in order not to deliberately hurt someone. Their misdemeanors must be deliberate and malevolent in my mind, before I commence any I investigation or publicity.

I have digressed a bit before I get into the crux of the current matter in order to establish my "benevolent," "good-will towards all men" and "don't chastise anyone unless he really deserves it" attitude.

Now! An article was run last issue by Donald Mackenzie contradicting statements made in Arthur Miller's book *One Reel a Week*. When the article arrived, I read it with glee because, I felt, here were two outstanding movie citizens, who were instrumental in bringing some of our classics to the screen, disagreeing with each other; and here was a chance to get an interesting argumentative series in the *Collector*. Mr. Miller had been receiving the *Collector*, and he would, I felt, answer the charges. Here, I felt, were two of our senior film people with loads of wonderful memories of the past, and if I could get them in to a good old-fashioned "writing hassle," many gems of history, anecdotes and famous names would appear in the *Collector*.

I was wrong! The reason I was wrong is that just a few days after the last issue was mailed, I received the news that Arthur Miller had passed away. This was a shocker to me, because then it would appear that I was resorting to a type of yellow journalistic tactic which is quite prevalent in the publishing field today, that of jumping on a celebrity after he has passed away from the scene and tear him apart when he is not around to defend himself. I will never knowingly stoop to this sort of thing without definite proof; and the "crime" will have to be rather serious.

I was immediately called out on this by a prominent member of the collecting industry, who understandingly jumped all over me. I sent him a similar message to this which I am submitting here, but I don't think it was accepted; and I think that I have unwittingly lost a friend. I suggested that I reprint this letter, but he refused to permit this, in no uncertain terms. I am sorry about that, because he is a fine person and has done much for the collecting industry.

Now I have placed myself in front of a mirror for a self-appraisal and ask: "Would I have run the article had I known Mr. Miller had passed away?" And the answer has a difficult time coming forth. I argue with myself "Would I have toned the article down more than I had?" (The article was much stronger than appeared in the issue.) "Would I have returned the article with thanks and apology?" In attempting an honest diagnosis, perhaps I would have run the article in an altered form. (I am implying no incorrections, no misleading statements to Mr. Mackenzie's article. I think he was sincere. I think Mr. Miller would have sincerely answered the article, and given me, and you readers, that series of debates I was looking for.) Perhaps I would run it as a gentle, more disagreeing thing rather than the accusatory form it appeared. Perhaps I would have returned it "in toto" and forgot about it. I don't know. I can't pretend to know what I would do in such a situation until such a situation occurs.

This does not still my sense of irresponsibility. To the angry man who wrote to me (and anyone else who feels the same as he), I am sorry! Mr. Miller was a fine man. I met him, and respected him, in Hollywood. And I feel the same about Mr. Mackenzie. And if his heartfelt apology does not satisfy the dissenters, does not assure them that I meant no harm to the reputation of one of our respected ones, that I am sorry about that also.

Right now, I cease beating my head against the wall.

Classic Film Collector, *No. 35*
Summer 1972

I'm living in a dream world!

When I go to the movies, I like to walk out of the theater with a satisfied feeling. I like to see the good guy win and I like to see the villain get clobbered. I look for the happy ending; and even if I get the sad ending I like to see a "justified, satisfying, sad ending."

In so many of the contemporary movies the good guy is evil and the bad guy is worse, and neither receive their "just desserts." Evil triumphs and the hero strives futilely towards his goal, never attaining it. This is life! This is the way it is! I know it, but it's not necessary to go to a theater to watch it.

I go to the movies to "escape," not to watch brutal realism. I go to the movies to be *entertained*. I want to watch a picture and know it's going to end the way I would like it to end. I do not wish to fidget through some psychological upheaval and not know whether the poor people involved are going to "make it" or not. I don't mind the sweat of a horror film; I know the monster is due for a violent end, possibly to be resurrected in another picture. But, if this happens, I know he will "get it" again in the next picture, and again, in the next.

I realize that I am wrong; I know that what I expect does not depict life as it is; but I want to see it as I think it should be. I want to be entertained, and I am not entertained by much of the action which appears on the modern screen. Also, I am a sentimentalist, and it is extremely difficult to get sentimental at very many movies today, too. I love the fairy tales and could sit through a *Snow White* or a *Peter Pan* for showing after showing. *Robin Hood* puts me on, and so does *Zorro*. I'm nuts about *Tarzan*.

Therefore, when I am in the mood for a movie (and when I have time), instead of ambling to a theater to which the heroine wanders aimlessly into the night to have her baby at the denouement, after our hero has been brutally murdered, I will go down to my basement and watch my hero galloping off into the sunset with the heroine on his sturdy, faithful steed who has been instrumental in helping him get out of his difficulties.

I'm living in a dream world.

Classic Film Collector, *No. 45*
Winter 1974

The Signs Are Good

Has a leak been sprung in the dike? Have the bastions of the major studios been weakened? Will the trickle of major studio films for legitimate purchase in authorized versions for collectors become a stream? These questions are yet to be answered ... but the signs are good!

Many feature films have been available in authorized 8mm versions in England for several years. Many public domain titles are available in 8mm in this country now. And we have seen in past months Paramount releasing some rare titles through Ken, Columbia offering a mountain of blockbusters, Disney selling attractive titles for home use, and now we see MGM releasing titles through Cinema Concepts.

True, most of these releases are condensed versions, two reels at the most. However, I believe you will agree that it is a start. The MGM titles from Cinema Concepts are horror titles ... but, they *are* full-length.

As an observer, it appears to me that the major studios are finally realizing that the collector market can no longer be ignored. They perhaps feel that there *may* be money in this "pennyante" collecting game, perhaps they feel that they may be a potential financial bonanza in all those "freaks" out there who collect classic films, and who are wiling to put out good bread for them. (And their tribe is continually on the increase.)

Perhaps someone has advised them that these guys are going to get the films one way or another. Perhaps they now feel that it is better to release authorized, good-quality versions of their prints to the collectors, and reap the profits themselves, rather to let some no-goodnik duper make money on their sacred, untouchable titles.

And then, perhaps they are taking a good look at the big one, the best one ... Blackhawk Films ... and observing how that company is operating and what can be done when quality films are processed legally, efficiently and profitably. Then, they may also have noticed the tremendous wave of nostalgia sweeping the country; the hundreds of requests from libraries for films, and the ever-increasing interest of colleges and universities in the classics. Perhaps one of their officials reads the *Classic Film Collector* and is finding out what the collectors are really like. Perhaps they feel that the best way to beat the "film pirates" is to sell the same prints themselves in better quality; and frankly, in my opinion, that should do the trick. Who would want to buy a dupe when you can get a print from the original material?

And, most important, perhaps they have discovered, as did the professional sport teams about television, that ownership of these substandard size films will not prevent the collector and his viewing friends from going to the theaters to see the films, but instead may *increase* their desire to see the film in theater size just as the sport enthusiast would go out of his way to see his hero in the flesh after watching him on television. And, perhaps also, they may have discovered that a true-blue collector likes to watch a good film over and over again, and if one of his titles is shown on television, even though he has a copy, he will want to watch the TV showing in order to (1) enjoy it again, (2) see if his print is complete, or to see what has been cut from the TV version and (3) to check quality of his print against the TV print.

Perhaps enough collectors have infiltrated the ranks of the studios and distributors to make them realize all the above. I know a few collectors who *are* with the studios, or *are* in distribution.

All the above are "perhapses." But, I think the signs are favorable enough to warrant the first *Editerrible* in many a month. Collectors of abbreviated versions have a multitude of titles from which to choose. And, you collectors of features ...

I think your day is near! I think the studios and the print owners are "getting with it"!

Glory be!

Classic Film Collector, *No. 46*
Spring 1975

What About These Visits?

The collecting industry is in a nervous state at the present time. You get the feeling that you are sitting on an inflamed, festering boil and it's ready to erupt and cover you with all of its yellowish stuffing.

Witness the articles reprinted from other publications on the subject. They elaborate on the crackdown on the "film pirates" and, naturally, the emphasis is to publicize the better-known names ... like Roddy McDowall, who had an extensive film collection. I imagine that other well-known names, as well as many lesser-known names will also feel the bit of the investigation. Rumors of the secret investigation had reached us months before publicity finally broke.

What about the investigation? It is apparent that people have been stealing and duplicating many recent films and then re-selling them. This is wrongdoing! I have so stated many times in the *Collector*. Conversely I have also stated that I have no sympathy for the copyright owners who have withheld older movies, permitting them to disappear from the face of the earth; and I have a complete empathy with the people who are duplicating those films. Despite the recent activity in the collecting field, there are those copyright owners who are still apathetic, and many of our treasured classics are disappearing. I have also stated my position about not having the opportunity to view those films which are shown in the cities such as New York and Washington, being that I live in the country. And, I ask why shouldn't they be made available for the collector? They're not being shown on TV, or in the theaters. Apparently, to some extent, this is being rectified as more and more of the classics are being made available to the collectors in authorized versions.

However, I have thoroughly covered this territory in the past. Let's get on to freshly tilled soil.

Apparently many collectors are hearing knocks on the door ... and the fateful words, "I'm from the FBI." I have talked to several of the people who have heard that haunting tap ... and apparently the investigation is covering every phase of the field. However, the investigators appear to be searching for information on Ray Atherton, Roy Wagner, Gaine Films and others ... and most of the questions were directed that way. Questions such as "Have you bought from Wagner?," "Have you bought from Ray Atherton?," "What, where, when and how?," etc. And apparently they have been looking for corroborative material in their cases against these people. One collector informed me that the investigator was apparently not interested in any of the old classics ... or in 8mm. He was looking for recent material. Some of the collectors have been asked to go to Los Angeles to testify.

Be that as it may, I have heard many conflicting and confusing stories as to what the collectors have been asked, and what the investigators are looking for. I could not get a clear picture, so in order to try to get the matter cleared up, we contacted district FBI people, who knew nothing about it.

We called Assistant U.S. Attorney Chet Brown of the U.S. Attorney's Office in Los Angeles, who is in charge of the investigation. The information which Mr. Brown conveyed to us is quite bleak indeed, and it is difficult to determine whether Mr. Brown was using scare tactics, or if he really intends to pursue this to the end and result in contacting all collectors (as he would have to). If that is so, it might be a good thing for the economy because he will have to hire many, many more investigators to cover the thousands of collectors, this will produce more jobs and give our economy a tremendous boost.

Regardless, in essence, Mr. Brown stated that an intensive investigation is being carried on by the FBI in conjunction with the U.S. Attorney's Office. They are investigating film print piracy of motion pictures and TV programs on the basis of violation of the federal criminal law.

They are going after dupers, buyers, sellers, traders of all copyright material. Some of the possible charges: criminal copyright infringement, conspiracy, aiding and abetting, violation of interstate transportation.

According to Mr. Brown, this investigation has international proportions and they are even looking to South America for one source. Certain international laws are being violated as well. He said that he could not answer such questions as to what brought the investigation about, who they were focusing on and whether confiscated films would be returned, because the grand jury in Los Angeles is presently (Feb. 21) sitting in on these matters and he could not comment.

In regard to the question as to whether they were looking for certain types of copyrighted material, Brown said that anything under copyright is subject to this investigation. He said that this is an extensive investigation and they hope to bring many indictments. He also said that if and when indictments are brought in the pending case, this will not end the investigation. Brown said that anybody who has sent copyrighted films across state lines would be guilty of interstate transportation of illegal merchandise, which is a criminal offense.

He also said that the *Classic Film Collector* has run some ads with copyrighted material. He was to call back on this ... but he did not.

For further information, I questioned an attorney on the matter to get his opinion on what to do if that fateful knock comes to your door. There is only one response to this ... answer the door. I can only advise you to tell the truth. If you have material in your possession you are not sure of, and you do get a visitor, then tell him that you would like to make an appointment with him later through your attorney. Then ... see your attorney. Don't have any discussion with your visitor. You tell him that you feel you should have legal advice. If they present a search warrant, say that you would like to have your attorney look at it. If they insist on searching, you can do nothing. Let them look, but volunteer no information. Repeat: discuss nothing.

The above, of course, is if you feel that you have questionable material.

Frankly, from my own experience, I know that the average collector doesn't know a copyrighted movie from a corned beef sandwich. If someone has offered the collector a movie he would like to have, he does not go out and check the copyright before he buys it.

I am unable to check copyright on every film advertised in the *Collector*. However, a good rule of thumb to follow is: If a film is advertised openly in such publications as the *Collector* by a legitimate, well-known distributor ... then you are fairly safe. Distributors do not advertise openly any films they have not researched for copyright.

Now, in a saddened and bedraggled conclusion, I must forlornly state: Isn't it a pity what a few unscrupulous people, anxious to make a buck stealing these recent films, have done to our collecting field? It has put us all (including the ministers, the attorneys, the doctors, the teachers, the furniture people, etc.) under a cloud. Those who have bought some good old classic movies for their own personal entertainment are under suspicion and are placed in the same category as the bootlegger, the crook, the "film pirate" who is interested in only profiteering from the sale of these stolen films.

Ain't it a shame!

Classic Film Collector, *No. 49*
Winter 1975

Read this ... it's important to me and the future of the *Collector*; and you can help!

I am in a confused, befuddled quandary and must make a decision.

As you know, I am in the furniture business. The *Collector* is a hobby. It manages to always liquidate my spare (?) time down to an absolute nothing! I am constantly buried, hurried and worried!

During the day (Monday through Saturday) I have been kept occupied by the aforesaid furniture business. At nights (and Sundays and holidays) I have been like the proverbial beaver with the *Collector*.

Now ... I have decided that I would like to get out of the furniture business! That's where you can come in, because I don't know exactly what I want to do, or in what direction I wish to go. But, whatever it is, I want to do it *now*!

I have many friends and readers out there who know my qualifications and capabilities. However, some of you (fortunately) know nothing about me so here I am! I'm a graduate (BA) from Penn State. I know advertising; I know the publication game. I am familiar with most of the printing methods. I know business and merchandising and basic bookkeeping. And I have a deep-seated need to honor my word and my obligations. I am also a good listener.

Now that you have met me with the above questionable qualities in mind, do you have any ideas, suggestions, opportunities or offers for me? I would like to hear from you.

Although my initial tentative thinking is in terms of the publishing field, the advertising game, the film business, or in the area of promotion, I am not negating the thought of entering other fields. Primarily, however, I hope that someone can come through with a feasible plan to put the *Collector* on a regular, professional, paying basis.

For the first time in my life I am in a position where I am able (and willing) to (clichés) pull up the roots, weigh anchor and follow the wind ... in order to get into something I enjoy. My tendency is to lean towards the warm country to settle (south or west) but this is not a requisite. Any part of the country will do.

Any suggestions ... or ideas ... or offers out there? I am willing to travel anywhere to discuss any interesting propositions.

That all may result in what so many of you have been asking for ... more frequent publication of the *Collector* with a bona fide, educated, qualified proof-reader, to get rid of all those typographical errors which gnaw at the roots of my interior.

Classic Film Collector, *No. 58*
Spring 1978

"How About You?" or "The Great Film-Tape Controversy"

The innovation of video cassette tapes for home use at a realistic price level has the field wide open for controversy. The shootin' verbal war is about to begin.

When these tapes were first introduced, I said, with the approval of other "true-blue, dyed-in-the-wool, long-time collectors," that this sounds great—*but*—this is dehydrating our hobby. This is taking the meat and the enjoyment from our projection pleasures.

It's good that your movie will now come in a small cassette, virtually eliminating the massive storage problem. But, what pleasure is there in showing your prized possessions on the small video screen? How can you compare it with a beautiful projected picture? The pro–video taper says "Yes, it is a smaller picture, but you can also purchase a video tape projector which will give you the larger picture."

"But," I said, "you lose definition, sharpness and color when you do that."

And the pro–video taper says, "Yes, and isn't that also true with 8mm when you project the long throw for that larger picture?"

I said, "I think video tape is eliminating all the thrill of putting on a show. How about all these people who have set up miniature theaters in their homes?"

They say, "Baloney. You still get the thrill of showing your prized possessions, even if it is on the video screen."

Then they start shooting their cannonballs. "Look at the material you can legally buy on the open market on video tape which you cannot buy on film. Look at that list from 20th Century–Fox! And virtually all of the distributors are converting their titles to tape—it's so easy. And it eliminates practically all the lab problems. If there is an error, the tape can be erased and re-recorded. The only current problem is a potential delay because of a possible shortage in raw tape stock because of unprecedented demand. They also say that you can also record your movies directly from TV, thus making your own blockbusters. And if you get tired of a film, erase it and record another. Can you do that with film?"

I answer in a blustering voice, "Not too practical."

Then I said, "You can't accidentally erase film like you can tape." Tape man says, "Yes, but you can tear sprocket holes."

Then tape man comes through with his home run swing: "Take a print like *Hello Dolly* for $69.65. If you could buy it on film, what would it cost ... $400?"

I squeaked, "Something like that."

Then I said, "There are less service problems with a movie projector. The tape equipment is more sophisticated, containing so many more potential service situations ... and, you have two different pieces of electronic equipment dependent on each other. If either your TV set or the recorder malfunctions, you cannot show your tapes."

At the recent National Film Society Convention in Washington, D.C., I saw pre-recorded TV movies demonstrated. The quality surprised and saddened me. Because I thought, "This is good quality. Here is a good TV picture. We are going to lose many collectors because of this."

I feel, now, that we will retain many of the collectors because they feel as I do. Also the initial high equipment cost for video tape is a deterrent. I think also we will *gain* collectors from the ranks of those who buy videotape recorders—those who will really get bitten by the classic film collecting bug and wish to step up to that bigger, better picture offered by film.

So, here it is!

The tape man, though the initial equipment cost is greater, prefers the economy of cassette tapes, the ease of storage and the greater select on of titles which are forbidden to the film distributors. And he doesn't mind showing his movies on the miniature TV screen. "And what difference does it make," he asks, "if you collect tape or film? Aren't we collecting because of our love and enjoyment of the classic movies? Aren't we brothers under the skin? Aren't we striving for the same goals?"

I say: "I prefer the thrill of setting up a theater-type atmosphere: darkening the room and throwing a sharp, brilliant better picture on a large screen." Strangely enough, despite the many times that I have mumbled and cursed while threading a projector, and hoped that synchronization, lamp, take-up, etc., operate properly, I would miss that often tedious procedure. The oldtimer in me also states that nothing in this world will equal the smell when you first open that package upon the arrival of a brand-new, long awaited, highly desired film. Ambrosia!

What do you think?

I would appreciate hearing your pros and cons on this. If there is sufficient response, I'll set up a separate section for the controversy in the next issue.

This sounds like the beginning of the Standard 8, Super 8 controversy, and you know who won that one ... the film and equipment manufacturers!

Classic Film Collector, *No. 59*
Summer 1978

When you write a news story, you are to be objective. You report the facts and keep your personal opinions to yourself. You may want to slip a few comments into your article (and I often do), but you abstain. You are to be completely detached from your story and report on it, not editorialize.

But not so in an editorial! You can let it all out! You say what you think in the manner you want. So, you will pardon me if I do some "editerribleising" and express my thoughts abut the merger of those two greats: *Classic Film Collector* and Blackhawk Films. (Notice who was mentioned first!)

Attempting to use the proper restraint and decorum I will express my views in a single word ... *wow*!

I am a sleeper! Normally when I hit that pillow, I'm a goner. I don't hear a thing until the blasted alarm awakens me. Now I can sympathize with insomniacs. Recently my sleeping nights have become sleepless nights ... I am *that* excited!

Bleary-eyed, I write this. Here, apparently, is the fulfillment of my dreams!

The furniture store has been sold; I am now officially out of the furniture business! The new owners are neophytes and know nothing about the business. I have agreed to remain in the store until late October to help them get started and to help smooth the rough spots. It will be a long summer!

The Blackhawk people have purchased the *Collector*. I am to be editor-publisher. Here is the good part: I am to have control of the *Collector*! Whether there will or will not be changes in the *Collector* will be my decision to make. There will be alterations in the *Collector*! I have been dreaming (for years) of improvements and innovations. There is so much I want to do. These will come gradually as I feel my way.

The Blackhawk people have made only two requests and these have already been deeply imbedded in *Collector* policy from the start. No advertising of unlicensed copyrighted movies, and no promotion and advertising of pornographic movies. I have, in the past, refused contributions and advertising in both of these categories.

The first thing that Ted Ewing, president of Blackhawk, said to me was: "It's your paper, Sam. Run it the best you can. Run it as you have in the past. Play no favorites. If you review a Blackhawk film and it's a poor print, say so!"

Think of it! I will be able to spend my full time on the *Collector*! No more squeezing in *Collector* hours between meals and after regular daily toil, ruining my spare time, my vacations, my social life. The people of Indiana, Pennsylvania, no longer recognize me. I'm the night owl who doesn't go out.

But, that's all changing. Now I can spend time on all facets of the *Collector* to which I have been unable to do justice in the past. Such items as: Collectors' Court, distributor news, proper viewing and reviewing of films, coverage of the tape field, news on private collectors, their organizations, their conventions, etc. The *Collector* will be the *Variety* and the *Billboard* of the collecting industry. It will be *your* trade journal!

We hope to make the *Collector* into a major national publication. I will attempt to retain the format and the flavor.

Would you like to know what pleases me to the point of exhilaration? The fact that I will now be able to properly proofread the *Collector*. I have not been able to do this in the past. I admit that I am illiterate, but not as illiterate as the proof-readers made me. So many of the glaring errors in past collectors were not mine. And I imagine there should be some "lulus" in this column. The same proofreaders will be checking this. (I'll learn to keep my big mouth shut!)

All subscription commitments will be honored! You will receive as many copies of the *Collector* as your subscription calls for. We, no doubt, will publish more often than quarterly. So if you have three more issues to go on your subscription, you will receive three more issues, perhaps a bit sooner than you would originally have received them.

For the present, the free 25-word classified ad for subscribers will be retained! This could change! For the next issue, all advertising rates will remain the same. This *will* change! As we offer advertisers greater coverage and circulation, we will gently request (probably with a sledgehammer) that they pay the tariff on increased services, distribution and potential.

If this vehicle doesn't become a major influence in the movie collecting field, It won't be because I didn't manipulate every corner of my miniature brain for growth ideas. I want to strengthen our features to make them more attractive to all people. I hope to make every possible contact with people who know about circulation and distribution to add their thoughts to my own ideas of how to grow.

The ideas swirling around in my head are in combat! Each is striving for dominance because it wants to appear in the *Collector*.

I welcome suggestions. If you have thoughts of what should appear (or disappear) in the *Collector*, let me know. I would like to hear your ideas on additions or subtractions ... if you want additions or subtractions.

As I said ... *it's going to be a long summer.*

Classic Film Collector, *No. 60*
Fall 1978

Movie Memorabilia

I am in a peculiarly vulnerable position when it comes to movie memorabilia. You and I both know that the marketing of these old items is not helping to control added inflation. The exorbitant prices some of the items bring are sometimes a collector's nightmare.

We know the reason. It's the old story of supply and demand. As the supply diminishes and the demand increases ... the prices gently (?) begin to soar. Then, some enterprising journalist hears about it and he writes an article describing the beautiful old, venerable movie collectibles, and the massive amounts of cash they bring ... and then mentions that a leading publication in the field is the *Classic Film Collector*.

That is fine ... and I do enjoy and appreciate the publicity.

However I begin to receive letters: "Dear Mr. Rubin, I found an old movie poster behind the wallpaper in my bathroom. It's a poster of the actor George Gittelworth starring in *Rasputin's Roving Eyes*. I had to tear it a little, in taking it down, and some of the words are missing. How much is it worth?"

Or ... "Dear Mr. Rubin: I have an old scrapbook filed with movie star pictures" or "I have these posters which appeared in front of a theater" or "I found some old movie magazines," etc., etc., etc. "How much are they worth?"

These are examples of the many missives I receive. Because of all the massive publicity, everybody thinks that all movie material is worth a fortune.

How can I explain to these people that only some of the posters or magazines or lobby cards bring these high prices? How can I tell them the fable (they'll think) of the supply-and-demand story. How can I tell them that if a particular person is collecting material on a particular star, or genre, or particular type of magazine, of a particular movie ... he'll pay almost any sum to get a needed item, if he can afford it? But every piece of movie material is *not* worth high prices unless someone desires that particular item. In fact he'll pay *nothing* for it, because he does not want it!

Most of the reports I receive concerning film memorabilia are not in the blockbuster class, and there will be little or no demand for this material. I don't think the people inquiring will believe me ... because they read those articles proclaiming the value of old movie material. It is difficult to explain that old movie material is like any other antique. Someone must desire it before you can sell it.

Then I have another peculiar situation. Because of the *Collector* I am always looking for old material, especially those with illustrations, and especially the old trade journals like *Motion Picture News, Moving Picture World, Exhibitor's Trade Journal*, etc. However, I am looking for this material in order to build up any reference library so that when John Johns sends me an article I can find illustrations, and other references, for that particular article. I do not need anything on any particular movie or star. I can use material on any and all movies and stars. But, I can't use them as a collector, and I can't pay the collector prices for this material. So, when people write to me about material ... how can I tell them how much it is worth; especially without seeing it to evaluate it. And you wouldn't believe some of the erroneous descriptions I get when I myself am interested in *all* the material, but cannot pay the kind of prices they are expecting to hear on an evaluation when they ask, "How much is it worth?"

Now, I am talking to you, not the people who find the posters in the hayloft. If you have some material for sale (pictures, magazines, posters, etc.) from the old days, please don't write and ask, "How much is it worth?," or "Make me an offer." *Put a Price on It!* If it's too much I'll say, "No." If the price is right I'll buy it.

If you ask me, "Can you use it?," the answer is, "Yes! All of it. But I can't pay a lot of money for it. I can always use *Collector* reference material!"

Classic Images, *No. 61*
Winter 1978

We got growing pains!

As we stated in the story on the first page, the little ol' wormy *Classic Film Collector* has begun to wiggle a bit, preparatory to emerging from its cocoon.

Some of the many changes I have contemplated have been instituted in this issue. There are more to come. But, keep in mind the basic contents of the *Classic Film Collector* (from now on to be called *Classic Film/Video Images*) will remain the same. We will have the same type of material, expounded in the same ignorant manner in which we have always sprayed you. I will have more time now to invent more ignominious words and expressions.

You can read all about the good news and bad news of our changes in the story on the front page.

We will still continue to cover all phases of the classic screen ... including silents, early sound, animation, Westerns, fantasies, etc., etc. And we will continue coverage on all sizes and types of movies. We'll call it home entertainment now. We will pass on to you all the news that comes this way on Standard 8mm, Super 8mm, 16mm, 35mm and oddball sizes such as 9.5mm, etc. We will disseminate information on sound tape, videotape and sound and video discs, and anything else that may develop to enable us to watch (or listen to) the classic films at home, in this fluctuating field. The biographies, the obituaries, the reviews, the stories about stars, the history ... will all continue.

Things are still breaking for me, and to use an old cliché: I have to pinch myself. This can't be Old Man Furniture himself, Sam Rubin, doin' the thing he wants to do.

And how about the big news: Blackhawk's parent company, Lee Enterprises, Inc., has taken over ownership of the *Classic Images* through their division *The Muscatine Journal*? This has me dancing the journalistic jig. These people are *publishers*! These are people with the know-how to push the *Classic Images* to the top (if we can get anyone to read it once they have a copy in their hands). Facilities are available for me to do things I hadn't expected to do. I am absolutely enchanted with the idea.

As you can see by this issue, we are (as announced in the past) increasing the news coverage of the various distributors. We hope to bring you more and more information about what these people are doing to bring these desirable classics to your home.

Keep your eye on *Classic Film/Video Images*. We'll bring you all the news that nobody else will want to print because they don't care about the classics as much as we do.

As that famous Jazz Singer once said, "You ain't seen nothin' yet!" Keep watching! This is just the first episode.

Classic Images
May 1979

Not since Carter invented the Little Liver Pill has there been such an ado about a new product as the prevailing excitement over the video discs.

One brand is being test-marketed. It will not be nationally distributed until next year. No other brand has been exposed to retail sales. Yet, everyone has an opinion. Everyone already knows which system is going to be best. Yes, even though most people have not even seen a disc, they know which will be superior in quality, performance, durability, etc. I wish I were as sure! I wish the manufacturers themselves were as sure. Here are at least four of the top electronic giants in the field. They each have their own system; they each believe theirs to be superior to the others. None of them will concede anything, nor are they willing to forego their own plans to cooperate with the other companies in order to standardize the tape systems to possibly help "un-confuse" the befuddled public.

5. Editerribles

I recently attended the International Tape Association seminar at Hilton Head, South Carolina. There I absorbed much more than I had previously known, which was exactly .0002 percent of the available information on these machines. Now I know a little more (.0003 percent) and will try to impart some of it to you.

The disc player which is being test-marketed in Atlanta is the Magnavox (Phillips is the parent company) system. Seattle is their next testing ground. I witnessed a demonstration of the Magnavox system with its capabilities. I was impressed! It offers a beautiful picture. It is extremely versatile, and you can do practically anything with it: slow motion, fast motion, forward, backward, select any individual frame, show one frame at a time, connect a stereo speaker system to it for superlative sound. It has beautiful stop-motion for instruction-type discs: tennis, golf, etc. Repeat: I was impressed. This is the system which uses the laser beam rather than a stylus.

Then I was present at the surprise presentation of the Matsushita (pronounced moo-chew-sta) Company (Panasonic and Quasar) as they announced their portable simplified disc system which they state will be marketed this year. It is a small compact player which utilizes a one-hour six-inch disc or a two-hour nine-inch disc. They say it is practically as simple to play as a phonograph. In fact, their advertising shows children operating it. Again, I was impressed!

RCA did not have its highly touted stylus playing system at the seminar. But their representatives were present.

JVC's stylus disc system was also absent. However, the representatives from the company had some of the discs and components and explained the details of their system.

None of these four systems are compatible, and all of the companies are going ahead with plans to offer them to the market. Apparently, there will be no standardization compromise.

So, which system is the best? So many people think that Magnavox's laser beam system is the way to go. They say you cannot scratch the record; they say that the records will last longer; that the laser will have longer life than the stylus. These people have been listening to the advertising! These facts may be true, but I think I will wait until all the chips are in. I cannot conceive of a company the stature of RCA marketing an inferior product. I must hear what they have to say about this supposedly inferior product which they intend to sell, despite the laser. I have heard disquieting rumors that the laser leaks, that though the life of the laser may be longer than a stylus you cannot replace the worn-out laser at home. It is a shop job and an expensive one! I have heard that the RCA player will do everything the other brands will do, and will sell for several hundred dollars less than the laser type.

I am not going to form an opinion as to which video system is best until I see them all.

But, I can certainly start squirming in anticipation. Look at all the great films which will be available on disc!

Classic Images
July 1979

> *How abhorrent, how appalling*
> *From the woodwork they keep crawling.*
> *This avaricious parasite*
> *Infects us with a loathsome blight,*
> *Preying on our classic needs,*
> *The tapeworm is a vicious breed.*
> —Robert Louis Rubin

This editerrible will sound like the sort of thing I wrote years ago when I first started this publication.

Have you been ripped off lately? If not, you've been careful ... or lucky! Videotape dealers are springing up so rapidly, it is difficult to account for all of them. It appears that everyone wants to get into the act. And I mean everyone!

I have talked to many of these entrepreneurs. Most of them are legitimate business people entering a new field, with enough financial backing to buy the proper equipment, to obtain rights to the movies they are reproducing and to buy quality raw materials for processing. These are the people who can make an industry grow.

On the other hand, there are the tapeworms.

In contrast to film, it is comparatively inexpensive to get into the videotape business ... if you don't care about the quality of your equipment, your pre-print material, your raw materials for reproduction and if you have no conscience.

So, here we go with the warnings again. First of all—know the person you are dealing with! You say, "Being that so many of them are new to the field, how do we know them? How can we differentiate between the legitimate dealers and the tapeworms?"

There are general signs, not always indicative of a shady dealer, but put them all together and you have the ingredients for an unhealthy operation.

First of all, the address is a P.O. Box number. Secondly, no phone number. You check with the operator; it is unlisted. There are legitimate reasons for having P.O. Box numbers and unlisted phones, but we're only talking about ingredients right now.

Let's go further. They won't accept personal checks or credit cards—more ingredients. Another sign is if they advertise their products at abnormally low prices and do not deliver their cassettes in identifiable packaging.

If you are dealing with someone who possesses all the above characteristics, he may be okay but I would think you are taking a chance. Let him identify himself to you. Let him give *you* some credit references.

If he is selling at abnormally low prices, he is probably working with poor equipment, poor pre-print material and cheap tape. If you wish to take a chance, go ahead. You may make a good buy and get decent quality, but the odds are against you.

We have been asking the studios for years to release their copyrighted movies to the buying pubic. Now that the tide has turned and the studios are, apparently, releasing their subjects for the home entertainment market, are you accepting a slightly lesser quality duped copy to save money, thereby cutting down the sales of the legitimate tapes, and lessening the chances for more to be released? Are you?

Many honest tape dealers do business with legitimate distributors and some even discount the video tapes. However, some of the tapeworms also begin to deal with legitimate distributors and sell tapes at extremely low prices.

I talked to one of the major distributors about these people. His history of dealing with them goes something like this: They have no credit so they request a dealership with C.O.D. shipments. After a short period of business, they request credit. When it is granted, they get more credit. Then, when they are into the company for a chunk, and have taken many orders from customers, they disappear. Their phone is disconnected and your letters are returned. One of these, the distributor informed me, was out of San Jose, California.

I think you can probably (remember, I said probably) recognize a legitimate dealer if he does have a street address, he does list his phone number, he will accept personal checks and money orders, and he does not advertise his products at abnormally low prices. Another major factor (I believe) is if he continues to advertise in legitimate publications (like *Classic Images* of course) time after time. If he does develop a reputation for honest dealing, then this is the guy to go with!

The track record is that you have more chances with such a dealer than you have with others. Keep your eyes open for the tapeworms. We'll pass along any information we get on them.

Classic Images
August 1979

In the past few months I have come into contact with many collectors. After the salutations, experience exchanges and reminiscing, invariably the question arises: "What's with Blackhawk?"

As indicated in the last issue, although my office is still in the Blackhawk building I am no longer affiliated with Blackhawk Films. *Classic Images* is owned by *The Muscatine Journal,* a division of Lee Enterprises Inc. Blackhawk is owned by three individuals: president Ted Ewing and vice-presidents Carl Lange and Tom Voss.

Rumors about Blackhawk are running rampant throughout the collecting industry. I will not repeat all of them here because they are so varied and without foundation.

Because I am not a member of the Blackhawk organization, I do not sit in on their meetings. I am not included in their policy discussions and I have no say In their decisions.

But I have eyes!

Here is a company that, in my opinion, was overweight. The new owners realized that. They have pared the staff down to a bare minimum. They, too, are affected, as we all are, by inflation. So, they have decreased their overhead, their cost of doing business. Is this bad? Like all good companies, they have seen the need and have proceeded to take the necessary steps.

"Will Blackhawk make it?" is one of the questions I am asked. When I see a company which has trimmed all fat from its operation; when I see the officers of the company remove their feet from their desks, roll up their sleeves and tackle whatever operational function is lagging, whether it be shipping, receiving, order processing, or ... sweeping the floor, then I do not fear for that company. They know what is to be done, and they are willing to work to accomplish it.

A common complaint which has reached my ears: Blackhawk does not issue as many new film releases as in the past. This is no doubt true. Can you see what is happening to the market? The demand for film has diminished! More and more people are converting to videotape. Film is not the salable item it has been in the past. And, sad to state, the interest in the silents has waned to a certain extent. If you want to maintain a progressive business, you follow the trends. Blackhawk is doing this. The demand for videotape is increasing as the demand for film is decreasing. A businessman goes along with the tide. He does not stock merchandise which does not sell.

I hear, "Blackhawk's prices are too high!" Blackhawk will not issue a film (or tape) unless it is able to obtain clearly defined rights, or establish that a particular title is in the public domain. Blackhawk *buys* the rights to titles; witness the Hal Roach titles, the Lloyd titles, the Fox titles, etc. When such a purchase is made, the copyright owner usually receives consideration in the form of royalties. If you, the consumer, want a legally clear, good quality print from Blackhawk, be prepared to pay a bit more than you would for an unauthorized, dubious quality dupe.

Then, I have heard that Blackhawk quality has deteriorated. Not so! All the Blackhawk prints of the past, the Laurel and Hardys, the Little Rascals, etc. are still topnotch quality. The complaints which have come my way have been concerning the recent Fox and Harold Lloyd titles. These prints are *not* up to Blackhawk standards simply because the pre-print material obtained from the licensors was not up to Blackhawk's standards. I know, also, that if Blackhawk receives good pre-print material, the best possible resale print will be produced from it.

The company is constantly searching for better material. If superior pre-prints are available on titles currently being offered, the company will obtain them. Witness the Chaplin Mutual acquisition several years ago. Blackhawk had good prints of the Chaplin Mutuals. It was able to obtain better prints, and it spent a mountain of money acquiring them in order to give its customers the best possible material available.

To reinforce the foregoing, remember that the company has the most liberal, lenient guarantee system in the industry. If you are not satisfied with the quality of a print, send it back for credit or refund.

Then, I have heard that Blackhawk is not seeking new material. Not true! I need elaborate no further than to point at the most recent acquisition, the Gene Autry titles. Other negotiations are in progress.

Actually, the basic Blackhawk Corp. has changed little insofar as customer relations are concerned. The customers have changed! (And, I am one of them!) As we have delved more deeply into our hobby, we begin to demand more titles; because, mainly, we have pretty well creamed the market of our wants. We are not demanding more titles in videotape (ownership is comparatively inexpensive). Our tastes have changed! Step in front of a mirror, look yourself in the eye and I challenge you to say, "Who, me?" I wonder what you will be demanding from Blackhawk (and the other companies) when video discs are finally nationally marketed?

These are good people at Blackhawk. For the short period of ownership of our publication, they asked me to down play Blackhawk. They did not want this to be a Blackhawk advertising journal, as has happened to others in the past when they were purchased by distributors.

However, since there is no longer a connection between *Classic Images* and Blackhawk Films, this restriction does not apply, and I can speak my mind. If you go back to our beginnings (1962) and go through the back issues, you will find that I have always lauded Blackhawk for the quality of its products and especially for its exemplary method of doing business. No other company of its size could hold a candle to them.

Nothing has happened to change my mind!

Classic Images
November 1979

The Tape Thing!

I am getting some flack about the fact that I have been using too much space for videotape in the *Classic Images*! In fact, one reader told me in no uncertain terms what I could do with *all* the video tape!

Let me go on record, once more: I like film better than tape. There is nothing in collecting that will surpass the opportunity to project a beautiful, sharp, bright picture on a large screen and give the viewers a real show. Nor will you be able to surpass film in the use of showmanship in presenting a professional-type screening. The projected quality of a good print is superior to the tape image. And ... what could be better than that heavenly scent of fresh film?

However, can't you see what is happening to our beloved collecting industry? Can you remove your ostrich-like head from the ground long enough to take a look around and observe what is going on?

There must be a reason so many people are disposing of their films and switching to video tape. I can give you some of the reasons. Video tape is cheaper! You need only your tape player and your TV set. You need no projector, or screen, or reels, or splicer, or viewer, or rewinds, or any of the other ingredients which we oldtimers love to use in preparing films and putting on a show. The storage problem is so much simpler with tape, especially for those living in small homes or apartments. You can obtain top-rated films on tape which are not available on film, and at a fraction of film cost. You can record your own movies off television.

There are other advantages, too, but I have covered the ground sufficiently for now.

I received an education jolt a few months back. I saw disc demonstrated, and marveled at the quality of the picture, though it was still not as good or as satisfying as film. Then I witnessed a disc demonstration in which the image was projected on a large screen, approximately five feet. I was stunned at the brightness, sharpness and clarity of the picture. I would liken it to a Super 8 projected picture of similar size. The initial cost for such an outfit is high. But, if you have the money and are patient, it might behoove you to wait around a while and see what the disc people are hiding in their security dungeons for us.

Also, I read that they are working on a disc that will record!

I am adapting a wait-and-see attitude. I must see all the new equipment, the innovations in tape and disc, and the varied disc systems. Then I feel I will be better qualified to make judgment.

Right now I will repeat what I have said in the past. I predict that tape will replace film in business, in the home, and in the theater. I believe the technology is such that they will be able to develop a tape system which will blow up a good, clear, sharp theater-size image.

I believe that there will always be film and film collectors. I believe that film will become much higher in price because of production costs, raw material costs and scarcity; and I also believe that film collecting will be relegated to the position of antique collecting.

It may take 100 years, but I believe it will happen!

Yours truly, Seer Sam

Classic Images, *No. 68*
March 1980

I just can't shrug my shoulders and accept the outrageous Eastman Kodak price increases without adding my word or two about the situation.

And I can't ignore a situation which will probably drive some of the fringe dealers out of business, and force many collectors to curtail or call a halt to their film purchases.

This is not a denouncement of Eastman Kodak, as such. I realize that much of the blame for this lies with the speculators, and the manipulators of the silver prices ... and that is an important ingredient to movie film (especially black and white) and, to a certain extent, color. Also, it deeply affects all film supplies and that hits us where it hurts, because so much of it is used in the printing processes we utilize to print this here important publication.

Eastman Kodak was forced to raise their prices. However, what disturbs me is the article in *The Wall Street Journal* in which an analyst recommends the stock to investors stating that "the 'silver risk' in Kodak has been over-sated and the company will be aggressive in passing on cost increases through higher prices."

Aggressive? That frightens me. I have to draw the same assumption I have heard from many of the film dealers in my telephone conversations concerning the situation. I get the idea that Kodak's price structure is such that prices will again rise if the value of silver takes another jump. But, what happens if the price of silver goes down? Does this aggressive pricing structure leave room for lower film prices? I doubt it.

The losers in this situation will be ... the dealers and the film buyers. In an attempt to retain customers, many of the dealers are not passing on the entire price increase. They are narrowing their profit margins. How long they can do that remains to be seen. Some of the dealers are passing on only their cost increases. This also narrows their profit margins. And, frankly, profit margin is the name of the game. You must sell an item at your cost, plus a percentage of profit. That profit percentage must be able to pay your expenses of doing business. And as these expenses increase, so must profit percentages.

The film buyers are caught in the vise between their desire to own prints and the overwhelming high price of these films. If you have the money to spend, you can still get film. If not, it will be difficult to maintain your hobby. I look for many collectors to turn toward the purchase of used films. And that should be a voluminous business these days. I also look for many collectors to throw in the towel on film and turn to videotape. (This should be a tremendous surge for the videotape industry.) Some of the collectors might even get rid of their film collections altogether. This should increase the supply of used films somewhat.

What's it all add up to?

We are in a price surge the likes of which no one has ever seen. The prices keep ballooning ... and the worst part is, we don't know when, or if, it will stop. When the silver market does finally stabilize ... so shall our film industry.

Earlier, I wrote an *Editerrible* stating that I felt tape would eventually replace film in the home, business and theater. I didn't think it could happen so soon, or in such a manner. I am earnestly praying for a reversal of the current price trends so that we collectors can once again ride a placid, smooth road toward our goal of getting all the classic films we want at a realistic price.

If this is not possible, we can do what many of us have already begun ... switch to videotape.

Classic Images, *No. 69*
May 1980

In an attempt to forget the woes of the collecting industry for a short while, I have decided to write this *Editerrible* on a subject which I know has confronted all of you.

Some crass ignoramus, who knows nothing about movies, will come up to you and ask, "What is a classic movie?" How can you answer that stopper? It's been presented to me many times by collectors, film buffs and those know-nothings, the strange, alien anti-movie people.

Is there an answer? Even Mr. Webster comes up with a many-fold response. Here are some:

Webster's definition of "classic": "Belonging to the first class or highest rank, especially in art or literature, approved as a model; also of lasting significance or value."

Also Webster: "Adhering to a standard and authoritative principles and forms in art, or work generally recognized as a standard of excellence."

Also Webster: "Any well-known event thought of as being typical or traditional."

Even Mr. Webster can't make up his mind. In addition, he had other definitions to offer. I selected the one I thought apropos to the situation.

If I were to ask a Roy Rogers enthusiast to name a classic film, he would probably come up with *Trail of Robin Hood* or some such. Likewise, a horror fan might reply with *Frankenstein*; the silent film follower might say *Birth of a Nation*. *Deep Throat* would certainly be considered the classic by porno devotees. You would receive different answers from all film buffs.

So, you might say, "Very well. People interested in a certain film genre would select a film from that group as being a classic. That does not necessarily mean that people with other filmania interests would accept that selection."

So, we can adopt the attitude that a classic film might well be all the above descriptions given by Mr. Webster. But, which movies will be accepted as *the* classics by the majority of people? Who is to decide which are the true classics, putting aside personal tastes and interests?

Could we say a classic film is one accepted by the top authorities in film, such as the reviewers, the historians, the teachers? Do these people have the final word as to what is a classic? Most of them would select *Greed*, *Potemkin*, *The Gold Rush*, etc. Are they classics because people who should know claim they're classics? The *Trail of Robin Hood* Roy Rogers enthusiast would probably yawn through *Greed* and *Potemkin*.

Then, could we say it should be a "majority rules" situation. That a classic should be determined by the response of the public, by the number of people who flock to these movies, to the *Jaws*, to the *Gone with the Wind*, etc. *Star Wars*, the biggest grosser of all time, would thus be designated as the greatest classic of all time. And, if such were true, some of the other "classics" would fall by the wayside. *Greed* was a complete box office flop.

Also, would a film with universal appeal be considered *the* classic? One which can be enjoyed by any person in any country regardless of race, language, customs and living patterns?

You know, of course, this discussion could go on and on, and no one would be satisfied.

So I will offer to you the best definition of a classic I have seen. It appeared in *Dream Factory of Yesteryear*. Classics: Films that have stood the test of time, films that have enduring value, and thus are unequaled in their ability to bring joy and happiness to millions of film enthusiasts everywhere. Many of Hollywood's early achievements have become such in every sense of the word."

Amen!

Classic Images, *No. 71*
September 1980

An indicator of the trend in the collecting industry, completely ignoring the million dollar porno video cassette market, is the list of the top 50 best-selling tapes in the May issue of *Merchandising Magazine*. The first five best-sellers were: *Superman*, *The Godfather*, *Grease*, *Blazing Saddles* and *Saturday Night Fever*.

The few titles on the list which, in my book, could be classified as classic classics were: #13, *The Sound of Music*, #29 *The Graduate*, #31, *The African Queen*, #39, *The King and I* and #46, *Hello Dolly*.

Does this mean that the older classics are finished? Does this mean that the Jimmy Stewarts, the Gary Coopers, the Greta Garbos, the Jimmy Cagneys, the Bing Crosbys will be dropped by the companies because the sales have diminished? Does this mean that there is no longer an interest in the classic films of ... yes, let's say it ... *my* day?

I don't believe it!

We collectors were all part of the scramble, not too long ago, of attempting to obtain as many of the classic films as possible; classics which have withstood the test of time; classics which were a balm to the memories we retained from viewing them as younger people.

We did not collect the modern movies for several reasons. Most of them weren't worth collecting; we were steeped in the fascinating lure of the older classics; and those new modern movies were just not available in legitimate releases.

Now, all of a sudden, the latest blockbusters are here! You can purchase Class A after Class A movie, while they're still showing in the theaters, on comparatively inexpensive video cassettes; and many on *not*-so-economical-any-more Super 8 film. The doors have been opened and we are all rushing in to buy these blockbusters. It's great to be able to show in our own home, shortly after they have been released in the theaters, such movies as *Dirty Harry, Enter the Dragon, The Exorcist, The In-Laws, Foul Play* and countless others available.

But, what happens when the glamour of obtaining these late first-run movies has disappeared? What happens when that neighbor, whom we love to surprise with these new films, gets his own video cassette recorder? Will we perhaps start contemplating the older classics again, the films which have withstood the test of time, and which are popular on their own merits, not as the result of a publicity agent's efforts to brain wash you as to the appeal of his particular product?

Will we go back to the movies we remember from our younger days, which we recall with affection and nostalgia? And, yes, will we even return to the silent films which are the true treasures of Americana, portraying an era of film entertainment no other media can achieve?

Will we begin buying fewer of these late inferior publicity agent's dreams and revert to the proven classics?

I think we will!

I will!

Classic Images
November 1980

The Society for Cinephiles is unique. Our Cinecons are comprised of various types of cinematic entertainment and safaris to places of film interest. Cinecon agendas are usually jammed with continuous minute-to-minute classic programming with nary a breathing break; you seldom have time to see it all. Therefore, you must choose your program from the many offered.

Many of the collectors come to see solid back-to-back movies. Many come to be near the glamour film people who guest at the Cinecons. Many come to meet and greet old friends developed over the year. A genuine feeling of camaraderie exists.

And ... many come to buy, sell, swap ... and *shop* in the dealers' room.

Now we have come to the crux of this *Editerrible*.

There were whispers of discontent in Hollywood on Labor Day! The attendance was not up to expectations. Some dealers traveled thousand of expensive miles to participate. The rumblings we heard concern the fact that Marty Kearns' program was so full, so replete with so many good things, and so well-organized that there was little time for the Cinephiles to hit the dealers' room. Some dealers took a financial bath.

So, now, we must consider the question: How important is the dealers' room to the Cinecon?

Some will say that we come to the Cinecon to watch movies! The dealer must wager that there will be enough interest in seeing his wares that those Cinephiles will take time off from the busy program to visit the dealers' room periodically.

Some will say, "I think the dealers' room is an integral part of the Cinecon, and that is one of the reasons I attend. I live in an area in which there are no film, tape or memorabilia dealers. The Cinecon is where it all is! It gives me a chance to see and purchase the items I want!"

Some will say, "I don't collect memorabilia. In fact, I don't collect film. I come here to watch movies and I don't give 24 fps about the dealers."

Some will say, "Leave it up to Sam!"

Thanks, fellows!

As you know, I am not an officer of the Cinephiles. Therefore, I do not have the authority to speak. But since you have placed the burden on me, I will tell you what is bouncing around in my cranial vacuum.

It is my opinion that the dealers' room *is* an integral, important part of each Cinecon. Furthermore, I think that enough Cinephiles want and will utilize the dealers' room to the extent that we should give consideration to the dealers' needs, in spite of the taint of commercialism attached to it.

I think that when the programming committee establishes the activities for the Cinecon, it should consider allotting a period of time, perhaps an hour or two of each day, to schedule a dealers' room session in which no other activities are scheduled.

This will benefit everyone. In addition to the dealers, it will benefit the Cinephiles who would like to spend some time in the dealers' room, but would rather watch every film shown. Now they can do both.

Cinephiles not wishing to utilize the dealers' room can avail themselves of the various local community attractions offered; or perhaps take a little catnap to catch up on sleep lost because of those 3 A.M. viewings.

In addition, most of the entrepreneurs in the dealers' room are also film buffs. They, too, participate in Cinecon activities (such as the unheard-of relaxation to watch some films). Consequently, in many instances, when a Cinephile might be taking that time to "hit" the dealers' room, his dealer is off watching a movie and the "shop is closed."

If there would be a specific Shop Session Dealers' Room period, all the dealers would *know* that this is the moment of maximum activity; this is the time to be tending the store. They'll all be there! All Cinephiles will be aware that this is the moment all dealers will be at their tables. They'll come a-runnin'.

Here's a thought! As a promotion, some of the dealers could even have announcements made through the speaker system during the Shop Session, not unlike those you hear at the giant supermarkets. Examples: "Sam's Film House is offering a ten percent discount on all items for exactly one half-hour, starting now!" Or, "An original program to *Birth of a Nation* is on sale for $4.50 for ten minutes only."

I am sure you get the idea!

You have now heard my opinion. You will now hear a summary, which is: A Shop Session should be included as part of the Cinecon program each day. I think the dealer's room is an important part of any Cinecon, and we want to encourage the dealers to attend and display their wares by offering them selling advantages.

If you have any thoughts on the matter, I would like to hear from you.

Postscript: From a Cinephile to the dealers: "Say, fellows (or girls), why don't you put some identifying signs on your table? We would like to know with whom we are dealing. We just might be looking for you but don't know you are present because we have never met you. We have no idea whether you look like Frankenstein's godfather or Little Lord Fauntleroy. Wouldn't you like to meet your old customers?"

Classic Images, *No. 75*
May 1981

It's Not the Principle of the Thing.
It's the Money!

When the people who own the rights to the classic movies courageously began to release them on videotape, I was among those wildly cheering and heaping praises upon them. At least, we were able to get legitimate copies of our beloved movie classics. We could show them only on the miniaturized TV micro-screen, but they could be seen ... and owned!

Do not believe for a minute that these copyright owners did this out of the goodness of their hearts. They were not interested in the aesthetics of film or the conservation of these priceless movies for our American screen heritage. They realized that a profit could be made from this new medium and it was apropos at the time to exhume the films from the vaults, reproduce and sell them and thus make themselves some money.

I cannot fault them for this. You gotta make a dollar or two.

And, now that video cassette tapes have been around a while, the problem is whether it is more profitable to rent or sell tapes. There are two sides to the question. However, the copyright owners are dong a double-take on scanning the rental market. They resent the fact that they will sell a single tape to a retailer and then the new owner of this tape reaps a profit by renting the tape, permitting VCR owners to view it at a price. The copyright owners feel they should be getting (1) a larger piece of the pie or (2) the entire pie. (You'll find the rental policies of these copyright owners fluctuating from day to day as they attempt to discover a path from the morass of their indecision.) They want to make the money from these rentals. Some of them have already instituted rental programs to do this.

I can't fault them for this. You gotta make a dollar or two.

Then, these same copyright owners pounce, with righteous indignation, on the film and video pirates. It is not fair for those people to make copies of films they do not own and reap a profit from rentals or sales of the dupe films or video tapes. The copyright owners feel that any profits to be made from these films should be their profits.

And, I cannot fault them for that. You gotta make a dollar or two.

Then, I stared at the front page of the March 25 issue of *Variety*. The headline reads: Distribs Won't Pay Extra for No-Fade Stock. And, with unbelieving eyes, I read where Eastman Kodak has developed a new release print film capable of holding color for hundreds of years under the right conditions.

Kodak reports that preservation is not uppermost in values sought by distributors. The major distributors turned down the new film because of ten percent price premium and "the certainty that most prints will be chewed up in theatres long before the shades fade."

As I see it: Because of the ten percent additional costs, major distributors will not buy the new stock and do not care if the prints fade or not. They will be finished with them by fading time. So much for film preservation and the American film heritage.

Surely, Mr. Distributor, even if you are not worried about preservation, you could have at least one print processed on this new Kodak stock to preserve the color. Remember what happened when you brought your old films out of the vault to reproduce them on video tape. Some of them had deteriorated, some had completely disappeared, some had lost color, and some had been edited for television and not restored. The consequences: You were unable to issue the film as it was originally made.

Yes, I agree you can profit *now* by not paying the extra ten percent. But, can't you see your way clear to having at least that one print made from the better stock, simply to preserve the colors as they were originally photographed? You will vastly improve your public image. Even I will think better of you.

If you can't see your way clear to do this, then I can certainly fault you for it. It isn't always necessary to make a dollar or two immediately, as soon as you make your investment. However, when you have this one print made you are buying yourself an insurance policy; and, because of that, in the future you will be able to make a dollar or two ... or maybe even three!

Classic Images, *No. 77*
September 1981

The "Hoppy" Decision

On page 25 of the last issue you will find an article headed "Filmvideo Cannot Sell Hoppy Films."

The article states that the Filmvideo Releasing Corporation has been enjoined from distributing 23 of the old Hopalong Cassidy movies because, although the copyrights of the movies have expired, the copyrights on the books have not.

The court found that 11 of the films were similar in plot to the books; and though 12 were not similar, the character of Hopalong Cassidy is so well-established and known to the public it was copyrightable.

Filmvideo was ordered to turn over all their negatives, prints, tapes, cassettes and everything else used to make prints of the 23 films. This decision is being appealed ... and rightly so.

The decision has tragic, far-reaching implications which could seriously affect the collecting and home entertainment field.

First of all, if Filmvideo should lose the appeal, it could mean that anyone can buy up obscure book rights and claim ownership of films which have fallen into the public domain. Many films and tapes now being distributed by various firms would have to be withdrawn.

In this particular case, Clarence Mulford, author of the Hopalong Cassidy books, sold the movie rights of the books to Prudential Studios Corp. The Hoppy movies were copyrighted by Paramount Films. In failing to renew these copyrights, Paramount let them fall into the public domain. I repeat: The rights to make films from the books were sold. Does the court's decision mean that the film rights would then revert to the author who had relinquished these rights? Your question might well be, "Even though the books remain in copyright, how can an author reclaim the movie rights for which he has received compensation and signed over to someone else?"

Another unusual aspect of this decision (and also extremely important): For the first time in the history of the courts, the defendant is required to turn over all the material pertaining to the case. In the past, courts have stripped the rights to duplicate films from alleged offenders, but never have they required the defender to give up his legally purchased films and other material.

In this particular case, the Hoppy films were purchased legitimately from Henry Brown, owner of the films at that time. The purchased prints are not illegal, they are not stolen; they are the property of Filmvideo and, as such, should not be taken from them. These are *not* "pirated" movies.

We will watch this case closely! Several people, high up in the industry, are also scrutinizing the proceedings. Some are actively participating in the action. Filmvideo, and the industry, is not lying down and calmly accepting the decision. It is too important to too many people.

Classic Images, *No. 18*
November 1981

Does Might Make Right?

You may have read that Frank Sinatra and Liza Minnelli were suing All Star Video for using their taped television programs without permission.

Although these programs were not copyrighted, Mr. Sinatra and Miss Minnelli righteously stated, "Makes no difference. The company is still using our talents without our permission."

All Star's Les Rubinowitz felt, and was so advised by his attorneys, that the claims were without foundation. The programs were definitely in the pubic domain.

It would have been interesting if the case had gone to court and perhaps have the matter settled once and for all! However, the case will not go to court. It has been settled. All Star will no longer release the Sinatra-Minnelli tapes.

Why?

Simply because it became too expensive for All Star to pursue the matter. The preliminary expenses had cost the company several thousand dollars. Even if the court's decision went to All Star, the cost of the litigation would be prohibitive. The expenditures in such a suit could never be recovered from the sale of the tapes. And there was always that possibility that the decision could go against the company.

So, again, the people with the power of money gain their point because it becomes too burdensome for a small distributor to fight.

A fascinating thought. If the case had gone to court, and if Mr. Sinatra and Miss Minnelli had won, I believe it would have been a black day for the collecting industry. What would stop Lillian Gish, for example, from suing people issuing *Birth of a Nation* or *Broken Blossoms* or *Way Down East*? They, too, are using her talents without permission or compensation.

We have seen this situation occur and recur. Many attractive items have been removed from the collector's market because the prospective entrepreneur had insufficient funds to fight a court battle. He would receive a letter about the copyright of his particular vehicles from a claimant who had obtained some obscure literary (or other) rights. The distributor bows to the "cease and desist" simply because he does not have the money, or the inclination, to go to court.

On the other hand, the claimant, who generally has the financial means, is willing to spend the money to risk litigation because if the court goes his way, he gains the opportunity to profit from the sale of the films.

Several distributors have resisted, and emerged victorious.

Paul Killiam, for example, went to court over his right to issue *Son of the Sheik* and *Birth of a Nation*. Had he lost, there would be fewer prints of these two titles available. Fortunately for the collectors, he did not lose.

So the slogan has always been "Might Makes Right." In this case, "Might" is the guy who has the money and the accompanying clout which enables him to take the case clear to the highest court. The fellow without the money submits, surrenders, and yet another public domain film is not available to collectors.

Does this "Might" make "Right?"

Classic Images, No. 83
May 1982

Reverberations on Revelations

Sometimes when you sit at an editor's desk and smugly write your incomparable revelations and think how wonderful it is that you are able to reveal these earthshaking opinions to your readers, you forget that other people may not agree with what you say, or may draw interpretations other than the ones you intended from your words.

To use the ancient cliché, "You can't see the forest for the trees."

This has happened to me!

In the *Editerrible*s of the last two issues, in attempting to examine the predicament of Blackhawk Films, I inadvertently said a couple of things which, though not directly, may have been interpretated other than intended.

I have been told that, in extolling the virtues of Blackhawk Films and their service and transactions with customers, I did, by inference, imply that only Blackhawk gave such service.

Not so!

There are many fine film distributors out there who give first-class, A No. 1 service, who have reliable guarantees and service their customers promptly and efficiently.

Right now I feel as I did when my daughter was to be married. You check the guest list carefully to make sure you miss no one. And, invariably, you do unintentionally omit the one person you did *not* want to neglect. So, at this time, I am going to name some distributors who, readers tell me, do give good service, and if I have accidentally omitted a "good-servicing" distributor, don't get angry. Let me know and I'll name him (or them) in the next issue. I say that because the relative I missed at my daughter's wedding still isn't talking to me.

Here they are: National Film Service, Griggs Moviedrome, JEF Films, Select Film Library, Steel Valley, Glenn Photo (and you know there has to be others).

Then I have been accused of giving Blackhawk preferential treatment. In almost every issue (except this one, of course) you will find news from Blackhawk Films affecting the film collecting industry. I am right here on the spot, and can collect these items. I have pleaded with other dealers and distributors for any kind of news about their operation. And when they do give me these items, I am tickled to the soles of my feet to print them. That's the stuff which makes the *Classic Images*. I will run these items, no matter how insignificant.

However, frequently, when I do contact these dealers, I get, "Nothing new!"

So, I plead once more to the dealers. If you want equal time and space, send me the news. You will get the appropriate coverage according to the comparative importance of your news. I'll even give you a story if you are issuing a new catalogue.

I want your news. I plead for your news. I earnestly solicit your news. I can't run it if I don't get it.

I do get news, important news, from Blackhawk and I print it! Let me print yours!

Then ... I was told that I called people who complained to film companies morons; and, inferred that all complainers were morons. That did not strike a responsive chord in my cranium, so I went back to the article to see what I did write. Here it is, verbatim, "I heard many of the customer complaints and I had the opportunity to read some of the letters containing underserved vilifications written by some morons."

I don't think I'll retract that one. If a customer is unhappy with service, if there is unwarranted delay in receiving an order, then there is nothing in this world wrong with some healthy, audible complaining. But, there is no excuse in that same world for using gutter language in voicing your complaints. I have always felt that way, and will continue to do so.

If you are unhappy ... complain! Raise your voice! Go to a high plane of decibels. Let the company know where you stand. That's healthy! But, it is not necessary for verbal abuse in a manner befitting an ignoramus who does not know better. If you do use abusive language and a foul pen in your complaints, I can only think that you *don't* know better.

I rest my case!

Classic Images, *No. 88*
October 1982

Rotten Eggs Amongst Us

I have had many contacts with various clubs, organizations and other groups. The Society for Cinephiles is one of the finest groups of special interest people I know. They are from the top echelon; their tastes are the most epicurean and their friendship and camaraderie are of the best.

But, we have a few rotten eggs in our midst!

During the recent *Great Cinecon Adventure,* the people from Blackhawk Films were extremely cooperative in every respect. The company's sponsored Mississippi stern-wheeler boat ride was one of the hits of the weekend. Blackhawk maintained a continuous hospitality table in the dealer's room serving coffee and cookies. Blackhawk provided the 35mm Mary Pickford films of our ultra-successful theater viewing. Blackhawk's people helped organize the various events, helped at the registration desk and assisted in many, many ways. One example: All films offered by the AFI arrived on cores. If it hadn't been for Blackhawk, I would have been scurrying around trying to find empty 35mm reels for two features.

But, back to the rotten eggs.

Blackhawk also conducted a tour of its premises. They did not want to have a sales room for fear of the taint of commercialism. But I persuaded them to have this sales room. The place was jammed!

During the sale, some Cinephile removed film from cartons, keeping the film and putting the empty cartons back on the display table. The thievery also happened in the dealers' room at the hotel.

But that's comparatively minor. More important, someone went into the computer section at the plant and stole a printout of part of the Blackhawk mailing list.

The company has a suspicion who the culprit is. He was seen in the area. The matter has been turned over to the FBI.

We don't need people like this attending our conventions.

You can help!

It seems natural to assume that the thief is a dealer or someone who will sell the list to a dealer.

If you have been on the Blackhawk mailing list and start receiving mail from another distributor, one from whom you have received nothing in the past ... let us know. If enough of you tell us about new mail you receive, a common denominator can be established if the same name appears enough times. Remember, you must have been on the Blackhawk list; and this new dealer must be one from whom you did *not* request a catalogue or film list or anything else. If such new mail comes to you, please write to me.

Let's catch these guys. Or, at least let's make the list useless to them.

After all Blackhawk did to help us. Frankly, I'm ashamed!

Classic Images
March 1983

Don't Read This!

FBI Discontinues Investigation of Unauthorized Public Performance of Copyrighted Motion Pictures.

The item below came directly from the Cinephiles newsletter. You are not supposed to read this, because it was not intended for publication. We'll let Dave Pierce write most of this *Editerrible*.

However, here's the article, which tells about a memo from one of the major studios to its regional branches.

> We have on good authority that a major studio informed its regional exchanges this fall that due to budgetary cutbacks and an uncontrollable proliferation of video cassettes being shown in bars, the FBI has officially (but not for publication) discontinued investigations of unauthorized public performance of copyrighted motion pictures. The studio advised its representatives to redouble their own local surveillance since further redress of copyright infringement will have to be sought through the civil, and not criminal, courts.

"What does this mean? Well, not as much as it seems at first. First, as you know, the U.S. has both civil and criminal court systems. Criminal cases include those brought by the government, while civil cases, such as violations of contracts, are brought by individuals and corporations, since the issues really don't involve the state. In the case of copyright infringement, civil offenses are punishable by payment of civil damages, while criminal offenses (including those brought to trial by the FBI) are punishable by fines and/or imprisonment."

"In the past, the studios let the FBI keep track of film society, church and college schedules to look for any unauthorized shows. Since the FBI won't be dong this any more, it is possible that studios will be less likely to prosecute even if they do find out, since they will be in civil court and have to use their own money."

"Of course when it comes to the old standbys of theft, duplication and sale of copyrighted material, the FBI will still nail you to the wall but hopefully they won't be seizing prints from projection booths any more."

Now, as soon as the people involved read this, they will probably attempt to reinstate the FBI investigations. However, I feel sure that the FBI is quite busy cracking down on the film pirates who are converting all those new films to tape and probably won't bother us poor collectors who merely wish to watch some of the old classics before they disappear forever.

Incidentally, if you were a member of the Society for Cinephiles, you would receive the newsletter and not learn about things like this second-hand.

Classic Images, *No. 98*
August 1983

As our beloved classic movies on film keep getting more difficult to obtain because of price, curtailment of production and the many other reasons we have enumerated in the past, it seems the cankers of our industry are emerging from their holes in the woodwork in greater numbers ... and getting bolder.

They operate in many devious ways, but one of their favorite scams is to check the classified pages and answer that want ad in which you indicate you are searching for specific titles. One calls you and dangles an enticing item over the phone. If you are looking for more than one title, he somehow can come up with all the titles you seek. This, in itself, should arouse your suspicions. Regardless, you are so excited you can hardly hold the phone and when you hang up you immediately remit the agreed-upon price. At last you are going to get that elusive film, or films, for which you have long been searching.

Not so!

You do not receive that film, or anything else, simply because he never had it. He's banking on your eagerness to obtain these highly desirable tidbits.

It's difficult to use caution when you so avidly desire these treasures to add to your collection.

Here are a few things you can do to protect yourself. First of all, don't be so eager! Don't be in such a hurry to send your money. If you don't know the caller (they invariably operate by phone), what is wrong with asking for references? And then contact those references. Don't accept a hurry-up, high-pressure snow job.

Many of these operators have a PO Box address. Get a street address! Also, get a phone number. Then call him back to make sure it's a legitimate number.

Ask him to send the film C.O.D. At least you'll get a package.

Don't be anxious. Take your time. If he is a legitimate operator, he'll understand and go along with your investigative idiosyncrasies because he is aware that many shady characters have invaded his domain.

Now, here's the sneaky side of Sam Rubin. I am about to disregard my own advice.

I receive many calls about this situation. Here's a typical situation:

Anxious Collector: "Do you know so-and-so? He has a film I want."

Me (if I don't know the guy): "How badly do you want the film?"

AC: "I want it, I want it!"

Me: "If I want a film badly enough and there isn't a lot of money involved ... I take the gamble. If he rips me off he won't get a chance to do it again."

Let a guy offer me a print of *London After Midnight* or *The Rogue Song* and see how long I hesitate; that is, if he doesn't ask for an unheard-of bundle of boodle.

And, dear reader, that's what it all amounts to: You gamble when dealing with an unknown. If you don't wish to gamble, try some of the steps I have advocated in earlier paragraphs of this masterful piece of classic literature.

Classic Images, *No. 100* October 1983

Coincidentally, the one hundredth issue of *Classic Images* falls on the same month as my one hundredth birthday! That's the truth. My birthday is also in October. However, I do have quite a few years yet to hit 100. The Social Security office, and the many insurance companies seeking my business for hospitalization insurance as supplemental coverage for Medicare, have forcibly brought my new age plateau to my attention. And this is the month!

I am tempted to use the old cliché "A lot of water has flowed over the dam" since I began this here pearl of literary delight 21 years ago.

When the old *8mm Collector* began, Standard 8mm was prominent and popular, as was 16mm collecting.

We have lived through many changes and revolutions in our industry. We witnessed the introduction of Super 8mm with many scowls and damnations. How could they dare bring out such a substandard film in which the picture had to be cropped in order to fit it on the Super 8mm frame? And, it's still true. The 35mm frame is more rectangular to the almost square Super 8mm, and upon reduction, the picture must be cut at the side, or at top and bottom, and you do not get the complete image.

We witnessed the advent of the automatic film-chewer projectors. I wish I had just five cents for every foot gobbled up by these voracious monsters. I could retire on the income.

Super 8 magnetic sound was introduced, as was optical Super 8 sound. Super 8mm Cinevision (widescreen) was also marketed.

The new type projection bulbs added much light (at lower wattage) when they were introduced. Cut down on the heat and amount of electricity used.

Then came mylar film and the plastic film splicer which was needed because cement wouldn't work on the blamed stuff. And the film was so strong that if you had anything loose or weak on your projector ... it gave before the film. The film went on its merry way through the projector gates carrying all these parts with it.

Among all the innovations, however, that which is apparently affecting the collecting industry most is videotape and disc. You can now own films which you never dreamed of having at prices you wouldn't believe possible. You sacrifice quality with these newfangled gadgets, especially if you blow the picture up. But, what difference does that make? Rather have a poor picture at a low price than a good picture at a high price. Right?

But, so be it. The studios are releasing movies to the home market which they would never have permitted in the past. Simply because they are benefiting from the manufacturing of these movies. A step we have been advocating for years, but we were talking about film at the time.

Now, we wonder, what's in the future? We have seen the advent and subsequent demise of equipment for home movie entertainment. How long will the present videotape and disc formats last? I predict: not long! Already on the market are narrower gauge video tape cassettes. In the near future, we can look forward to recordable discs and, possibly, smaller discs. How about this wire we have heard about? Motion pictures on wire? Who knows what's coming?

One thing which is apparent from past history: For every change to smaller size and more compact equipment, we have deterioration of quality. And, because the consumer accepts these inferior pictures ... it will go on and on.

We will probably be saying before too long, "Goodbye film!" Witness: Sony is already opening up theaters using videotape instead of film.

I would say, "Don't invest in film stock ... either actual or marketable."

Happy One Hundredth Issue!

Classic Images, *No. 103*
January 1984

Did you ever start a paint job determined that you would not make a mess this time? You begin by carefully dipping your brush or roller into the paint and slowly applying it to the surface. You carefully scan your hands, your clothes, the floor, to see if any paint has dropped. If so, you wipe it up immediately.

If a large blob of paint does fall, you wipe it up. Then, another blob escapes your brush. You clean it also. Then a large blob splatters to the floor. Your hands have already become streaked with paint. Therefore, you mumble sweet nothings to yourself and say in gentle tones, "To hell with it; I'll clean it later."

Then you begin to wallow in paint. Your hands, your clothes, and the floor are all splotched with the brilliant, exotic color you so meticulously selected for the walls. It does not exactly enhance the appearance of your skin or clothes.

This has happened to me on other "just-as-messy" projects. At first I used utmost care and watchfulness, but always ended up looking like (the old cliché) "something the cat brought in."

The above has nothing to do with film or videotape other than to draw an analogy as to what is happening to the film collectors who will not dirty their hands with videotape for the many legitimate reasons which we have repeated again and again in these pages. Many are quite adamant in their refusal to have anything to do with videotape. And, having been one of them, I can sympathize. Like the painter, these diehards are not about to get involved in the videotape circus.

But some have relented. You see, at first they were only mildly subjected to the video industry publicity on the advantages of storage, economy and availability of attractive classic titles. The gentle titillation became a mild nudging as more and more companies entered the field to issue home video hardware and software. (Hardware: recorders, cameras, etc.; software: videotapes.)

The video field began to appear a bit more attractive as the film collectors became aware of the titles being marketed. Then, suddenly, the deluge! All of the major studios entered the field. Important title after title appeared on the home entertainment scene. Movies which the collector could only dream of having in the past were now available.

Consequently, the relenters, only wading at first, bought VCRs and a sampling of tape. They observed the results of the commercial pre-recorded tape playbacks; they evaluated the various classics they recorded from television; and then they plunged! Many have become rabid videotape collectors, acquiring everything in sight.

To deviate, many film collectors still resist the trend. They want to offer that large screen, brilliant quality reproduction, with better sound, in a theatrical atmosphere. And they are right—it is better! But you *can* have both. You *can* continue to show film and you *can* continue to purchase film, if you can afford it. But, why not buy the classics on videotape which are not available on film?

I am emotionally and physically in agreement about the advantages of film over videotape presentation. After all, I am the guy who resisted Super 8mm in favor of Standard 8mm for years. When Standard 8mm classic production dwindled to a trickle, Super 8mm was, suddenly, okay.

What happens, then, when you can no longer buy the classics on film? My prediction of several years ago still stands. I believe that tape will eventually replace film ... even in theaters. Film collectors will be relegated to the position of antique collectors. And, strangely enough, these antiques will be reproductions. Reproductions of the original nitrates which will have long disappeared.

Deviation completed. And now that we have (on paper) completed our analogy of a paint job and videotape collector ... what about video disc? That's like finishing your paint job only to discover that you have another room to paint.

Classic Images, *No. 104*
February 1984

There will never be a meeting of the minds between the motion picture producers and the buying public and their allies, the VCR manufacturers.

The film industry will never change its position that it is entitled to receive compensation every time one of its films is copied from television. From its infancy, the studios have adopted such attitudes and history books will show case after case in which the manufacturers of films attempted to milk every last penny from their property. Only when they felt they had exhausted all possibilities of earning a profit would they relinquish their grasp.

"Why," they say, "should anyone be able to turn on TV and record *our* movie for nothing? It's the same as going into the theater. You must pay an admission fee!"

Perhaps they are right. But the U.S. Supreme Court has decided they are not right. So, do the studios bow their heads in defeat and say, "okay, we accept this?" Nope. They will go to Congress to attempt to have the laws changed so that they *can* collect that admission fee.

They feel they gamble their money to produce a film which could possibly bomb. They take the risk. Why shouldn't they profit from the income from their own property?

The consumers and the VCR manufacturers say, "Yes, you should make a profit from your tremendous gamble. You do take high risks. You do spend millions of dollars. It is no simple chore to bring in a winner.

"As we see it, you profit from the theater income, domestically and abroad. (Don't forget you get 90 percent of the gross during the first period of showing your blockbusters.) You sell the rights to these films to TV. And the price we hear you receive should represent a tidy profit. And then you sell the rights for home video. If the yearly income figures we read in *Variety* are to be believed, you are making a profit ... and a nice one.

"If one of your films bombs, you might still recoup from TV and home video income. But, what makes you different than any other merchant of any product? Some items go, you do well. Some items die, you lose."

I am sure you are all aware of the above arguments. They are many more. So, why am I, whose head is usually buried in a book, or in editing an article, or writing some inanity for this here Illiterate Gazette, calling your attention to them?

First of all, I urge, no, I *demand* that you write to your Congressman and tell him how you feel about this matter. It will help him make his decision. The more letters he receives, the more persuasive it could be.

Then I heard something on TV which made me stop and think a bit, chuckle a bit, and wonder to myself why I had neglected to consider the fact.

With all the shouting back and forth about illegal taping, about who should derive the profits and all the other gobbledygook you have heard ... up comes the president of the actor's union and states that the actors should share in the profits of this "illegal" taping also.

Put that in your smoke and pipe it.

Classic Images, *No. 107*
May 1984

How Sad!

How sad it is!

After all these years of our hoping and praying; our cajoling and begging, MGM is finally authorizing the release of its classic silent film library to the collectors in 8mm.

I should be jumping with joy! But I consider the many years in which the studio remained firm in its determination *not* to permit the dissemination of its product to the home movie market!

And, now what a time for it to happen! Film and lab prices are the highest they have ever been.

One company ... a good company (you'll recognize the name in an instant) ... has the courage to go to the expense of releasing one of the six titles listed in the article elsewhere in the issue. I applaud its efforts!

This is probably the last dying hope for collectors to have authorized prints of these silent classics—for, if this project is unsuccessful, who would take the risk to attempting it again?

So, if you are thinking you would like to have mint, quality, authorized full-length versions of some of MGM's golden silent classics, don't hesitate. The quality is guaranteed by a company known for its excellent public relations. The prices will be set as low as feasibly possible in order to sell a maximum of prints.

If we support this company in its expensive gamble to release these silent features, there will be more! Send in that coupon!

Wouldn't you love to have all six of those titles in your library? And in the best available quality from MGMs pre-prints? Think of all the other MGM silent films just sitting there amid layers of dust, just waiting for us: *White Shadows in the South Seas, The Student Prince, The Unholy Three, The White Sister, The Wind* and on and on.

How sad this didn't happen ten years ago. Then there would have been no doubt!

Classic Images, *No. 108*
June 1984

Is CED Dead?

I have deliberately refrained from publicizing the recent RCA decision to discontinue the manufacture of its CED players because there has been so much in print! So many articles have been written; so many recriminations; so many people denouncing RCA; and so many laser competitors and users gloating. I decided to sit back, wait and see what happens, while the wolves pounced on RCA.

I am still sitting; I am still waiting; and I am refraining from discussing it ... for now.

But, I think a lot!

I can't believe that what is apparently the most convenient, the most permanent, lowest cost method of putting the film image in your home will cease to exist. Lowest cost and most convenient, everyone knows. Most permanent because there are no color dyes to turn red.

If you love the movies, and I am sure you do or you wouldn't be reading this here Illiterate Gazette, you probably realize that it is cheaper to buy and rent video discs than any other form of home video entertainment. If you want your video movies to be the best quality possible, untainted by commercials, you will want the disc.

If you wish to record off TV ... that's another story. Get a VCR! I know many people who have both!

I am fully aware of the arguments for the laser disc player. That has little to do with this discussion other than to give a laser disc owner the opportunity to proclaim smugly that I am avoiding the issue. I don't think I am. Let's say I am sidestepping, for now, the discussion of the comparative differences between the two systems. We're only taking about CED now.

There will be around three quarters of a million CED disc players sold by September. I am having difficulty believing these people will be forsaken. And, to bolster that belief, let me tell you of a juicy rumor which has reached my ears. There is a 95 percent probability that an unnamed company will announce its plans to manufacture a CED player for the marketplace at the Consumers Electronic Show at Chicago in June, or later this summer.

If you own, or are planning to buy, a CED player because they are so cheap now, and if you do not wish this particular form of home entertainment to disappear from the market, why not write to the present manufacturers and tell them how you feel? It can't hurt ... and it just might do a lot of good.

RCA has stated that it will continue to manufacture discs for three more years. I think they will be manufacturing CED discs for a much greater period of time. My left ear is twitching, and when that happens all my predictions come true.

Classic Images, *No. 110*
August 1984

You Are the Rodent in the Rhubarb

I was fascinated by the headline in *Variety*: Piracy Now 2d to Home Taping as a Copyright Menace.

They were referring to audio tape, but they might as well have added its video cousin to the discussion.

That's you, kid. The minute you purchased that VCR and recorded a movie off TV, you slipped across the line and joined the ranks of the enemy.

It makes little difference that you have spent thousands of dollars in watching the movie super productions! Despite the fact you are not copying for profit, for resale; that you only want to once again relive the precious moments from this movie which you so admire. You are a rascal. You are stealing that film right from under the magnificent noses of the studios.

Yet, it's getting tough! The studios are getting so paranoid that everyone is suspect, down to the lowly usher in the theater. In fact, the day is probably coming when you'll be frisked before entering a theater for fear you may be carrying a video camera with you and might attempt to record that momentous moving epic from the screen.

Don't laugh ... the technology is there! The cameras will probably be small enough to hide in your pocket.

I also envision a devise such as you see at airports. Each passenger must go through that skeletal scanner. "Yes, dear ... before you enter the theater, enter the scanner. We must be sure you don't have one of those devilish copying things with you."

It would be funny if it weren't so ridiculous. The technology is now available wherein you can turn on your TV and copy a film being broadcast. And you can now put a tape on one VCR and copy it with another. You are so in love with film that you would like to possess as many as you can.

But when you start recording, you are antagonizing the people who are making these powerful emotional dramas, and you have joined the ranks of their enemies. You are the rodent in the rhubarb. You are worse than a pirate.

Classic Images
September 1984

Get Off Our Writers' Backs

I get many letters from people deprecating our writers. The authors of these letters call them idiots, stupid, careless and sometimes worse, because they made errors in depicting the history or filmography of a certain star, director or studio.

Most of these letters are from people who have specialized on that particular subject and know every film, date and intimate detail in the history of the subject. Consequently, he or she can easily spot the errors.

And errors we have! If you have been with us long enough, you are acquainted with our Rubinerr department in which we take great pride in castigating ourselves.

However, our writers spend long hours compiling these articles. The information is garnered from books, magazines and, sometimes, interviews. Most of the information comes from previously published works.

If the reference articles contain an error, the writer will then unknowingly repeat the mistake. And it will probably be repeated again by some future writer who has decided to astound the literary world and write the definitive article on the same subject.

You say, "Don't stop at just one or two reference articles when researching this subject. Go deeper into the work. Get more articles!"

Good suggestion. But it depends entirely upon the subject under research. If a writer is researching an obscure character or minor player, he is happy to find any background material. But, supposing he does find additional information. What assurance has he that the additional material will be correct?

Poor George Katchmer diligently sweats over his articles. He pens every one of them by hand. He collects all the references he can find on each person who happens to be his subject of the month. George sometimes goes stark raving mad, because he finds contradiction after contradiction in these references.

Much of the material comes from the fan magazines. And, unfortunately, too many of the stars gave these fan magazine authors much leeway, permitting them to write their articles as they saw fit ... and that includes biographies and autobiographies. These writers had vivid imaginations and knew how to make an article interesting, even if it meant bending the truth a bit. Some of their hallucinations come down to us today as the gospel about that particular star, director or studio.

Witness the Tom Mix "autobiography" we recently ran in our pages. It sounded more like a motion picture scenario than a biography.

You say, "Interview these people while they are still living. Get the truth while you can."

Good idea! Problem: These people are no longer youngsters and, frankly, too many of them just don't remember! They think they do. They'll tell you what happened 50 or 60 years ago. How do you know they are giving you factual information? When you get to be the age of some of our former stars, you can't remember that much of the past.

Some incidents may be clear in their mind. But, in so many cases, the former stars have filled in the empty spots with what they believed to have happened. And, after a while, they begin believing it themselves.

You say, "Go to the studios for your information."

Here is a revelation. You cannot count on the accuracy of the information emanating from the studios. Many of them haven't kept the records, and some of them have young people who do not have the knowledge or background to find the information you might need. Many researchers have called studios for info and have come up with nothing.

And, if you do get information, how confident are you that it will be accurate?

Several years ago, I took the Universal Studios tour. At the store on the lot, I purchased an illustrated booklet about the studio. It was replete with errors. (I can't locate the darn thing now. It's buried amidst all that material I have been meaning to catalog for years.) I do remember one glaring error. There was a picture of Jimmy Cagney dressed as Quasimodo for his Chaney role in *Man of a Thousand Faces*. The caption read: "Lon Chaney in *Hunchback of Notre Dame*."

Right there I lost my confidence.

We are not the only ones to make mistakes. Some of the revered authors, researchers and purveyors of motion picture history also err ... and these, too, are repeated and passed on for future generations. I have spotted errors in Dan Blum's prodigious *Pictorial Histories of the Silent and Sound Screen*. I have been told of errors in the accepted honored books of Rotham, Schickel and Ramsaye.

So ... how do you write a story in order to get the most accurate information? You go the same route followed by George Katchmer. Round up every bit of material you can find and pray the information is correct.

If you, as a reader of this here *Illiterate Gazette*, are knowledgeable about the subject in one of our articles and spot an error, or two, or three, by all means write to us and tell us about the errors. We will print the corrections. We want them, we're glad to get them.

But, when you do send them to us ... don't call our writers idiots, stupid or careless. They are only repeating what some other stupid, careless idiot wrote.

6

The Film Fan Organizations and Conventions

Over the years, the movie industry continued to grow and television matured and rose to unimagined heights of popularity. More and more viewers were entertained by the two industries, which brought tears and laughter to the home TV programs and the giant theater screens.

The devoted lovers of the cinema witnessed another phase of their interests come to life: the movie buff conventions, during which they could enjoy the talents of the actors, the writers, the technicians, and they could meet with some of the celebrities they had come to admire. Those entertainment professionals frequently attended the conventions, to meet face to face and mingle with their fans. They enjoyed the exposure and the adulation of their followers.

More and more, the film buffs wanted to attend these gatherings to meet fellow film lovers and collectors, and to share their hobbies. Many friendships were begun, and they often corresponded and socialized with these movie addicts, who had the same likes and dislikes. Fan clubs were organized and meetings were held, some annually, and some more frequent.

The newly organized Society for Cinephiles planned a first convention at its birthplace, Indiana, Pennsylvania. News of the impending meeting was distributed to other members of the group through the pages of the *8mm Collector* and the mailing lists of other movie groups.

The number of film groups increased and their memberships grew. I had met and corresponded with some of them and gathered names and addresses from the mailing list of the *8mm Collector*.

I had met hundreds of people devoted to the classic cinema and always enjoyed connecting with them at the various conventions. I believe the Society for Cinephiles was one of the first groups of this nature.

Most of these organizations had some form of newsletter. It could be a single-page thing, or one with multi-pages. There were various size publications: Some were just newsy letters; some were small publications, produced economically by mimeograph or offset or regular letterpress printing. Some were large elaborately printed affairs.

I wanted to tell you about these groups, but there are so many good ones that it would be difficult to review them all. So I became selective and wrote to a few organizations with which I was familiar and who, in my mind, produced a quality publication.

If you belong to a film group with a newsletter or publication, and it is not included here, please don't be angry with me. There are too many of you out there!

I contacted the organizations I wished to include here. Some of the respondents sent sketchy information; some sat down and wrote lengthy, well-written histories. I argued with myself about the latter. "These are good; these are intelligent; why should it be necessary to rewrite them?" Therefore, you will find in the enclosed chapter news concerning the creation and history of selected film groups, some of them with the by-lines of the authors who deserve the credit. Look at the work they saved me! Thanks, Film Fans!

The Syracuse Cinephile Society
By John Weber

The origins of the Syracuse Cinephile Society are rather obscure, but it seems that in 1967, Phil Serling rented a 16mm projector and film and screened it in the back room of the Regent Bar & Restaurant. Phil did not know how to run a projector at that time, nor did Dr. Samuel Goldman, his partner in the venture. Luckily, a member of the audience had some experience, or else Syracuse Cinephile might have died right there.

The response to the film was positive, and the following year, the feature film *Seventh Heaven* was screened, this time at the Boys' Club, a venue which was able to provide more seating. The response was even better than that for the first film.

Phil then went a bit "big time" and rented two 35mm features for showing at the Regent Theatre, *A Night at the Opera* with the Marx Brothers and *Freaks*, the Tod Browning classic. They were accompanied by the W.C. Fields short, *The Fatal Glass of Beer*. The house was jammed for all screenings.

Realizing that there was a vast, untapped audience for these classic films, Phil bought his own 16mm projector and, with every spare cent he had, started collecting films on a regular basis. He would run a film once a month in any venue that would let him in, usually a restaurant containing a ballroom or dining room that had a large seating capacity.

In 1969, Phil heard of the Society for Cinephiles and discovered that they were having their annual convention, the Cinecon, in Rochester, New York, just 90 miles west on the New York State Thruway from Syracuse. At that convention, he met a number of like-minded individuals with whom he forged a lifetime friendship: Samuel K. Rubin, founder of the Cinephiles, and the begetter of the *Classic Film Collector* from which the Cinephiles had their origin; Gordon Berkow, Howard Kolodny, Marty Kearns, Irv Abelson and the late Lou Fazzari, inventor of the "Extend-a-Reel," among others.

In the years that followed, Phil's collection grew considerably, and with local fellow collectors Dick Rowell, George Read, Andy and Lois Eggers, Garry Canino, Mark Philp and John Weber, a strong base was created that enabled Syracuse Cinephile to be incorporated as a non-profit entity. Screenings were now held weekly in the Onondaga County Civic Center. Novelty events could now be scheduled such as the annual Halloween show, in which three classic horror films would be shown, followed by a midnight screening of *Night of the Living Dead.*

Extremely popular was the "Worse Than Bad" festival, screening films that were so bad, that they were funny, such as the Edward D. Wood "epics." Once in a while, when funds were plentiful, special guests were brought in, such as Lillian Gish, Vincent Price, Janet Leigh and Leonard Nimoy.

In 1978, Phil realized one of his fondest desires and became the host of the fourteenth annual Cinecon in Syracuse. The event was enjoyed by all who attended, and Phil wondered if it might be possible to stage an annual event on a smaller scale, such as was done in Columbus, Ohio.

Cinephile Howard Kolodny, president of the Society for Cinephiles in 1972 and sponsor of a Cinecon that year.

During one evening's screening at the Civic Center, Phil sounded out fellow film buffs Bob Oliver, Russ Thomas and John Weber about just such an endeavor. Bob suggested the name "Cinefest," and it struck the right chord.

Weber then thought that such a convention in spring would be too near the Columbus Cinevent. A convention in autumn would be too close to the Cinecon, and no one would want to come in the summer. The month of March seemed to be the only viable option. He reasoned that everyone would have a severe case of cabin fever after the long winter months, and the Cinefest would be the first convention to cure everyone of the winter doldrums.

With more than a little trepidation, Cinefest #1 was planned, in hopes that about 50 to 75 patrons might attend. The response was truly overwhelming—over 200 showed up, and there was no turning back.

In the late 1980s, cable TV and the home video explosion had, in just a few short years, greatly eroded the base of the Syracuse Cinephile audience. Where once a screening might draw over 300 people, it was now fortunate if 50 would show up. Bowing to the inevitable, the Syracuse Cinephile Society left the Civic

Phil Serling and John Weber check the credits for a film screened at the Cinefest. Oliver Hardy keeps an eye on both.

Center and returned to the "restaurant circuit." There remains a core group of about 30 to 40 regulars who still attend on a frequent basis.

Ironically, Cinefest has gone in the opposite direction, going from strength to strength, with well over 400 attendees at recent gatherings. Regulars have included such film historians as William K. Everson, Leonard Maltin, Herb Graff, Richard W. Bann, Ted Larsen, Rusty Casselton, Chris Horak and Bob Birchard. There are representatives from such great archives as the George Eastman House in Rochester, the Library of Congress, the American Film Institute, the British Film Institute and UCLA. Companies such as the Disney Organization, Turner Classics, the Rohauer Collection, Paramount and Kino Film and Video have all lent film prints. Cinefest is especially proud of its long association with Gene Autry, who lent several films from his personal collection for screening in Syracuse.

Special guests at Cinefest have included Kevin Brownlow, David Gill, James Card, Leatrice Fountain and cinema star Colleen Moore. On more than one occasion, Cinefest has screened a print which is the only one in existence, as was the case with the 1934 Spencer Tracy—Marion Nixon film *Face in the Sky*.

In 1998, Cinefest was proud to present the convention premiere of the re-constructed 1925 Arthur Conan Doyle classic *The Lost World*, courtesy of the George Eastman House. Film producing brothers Richard and Alex Gordon have provided many treasures for the viewing pleasure of Cinefest audiences. Some say that Cinefest is the best "unknown" film convention; there may be more than a grain of truth in that, as the hotel is sold out long before the convention begins.

★ ★ ★

Phil Serling's tragic death on January 6, 2002, was a stunning blow to the hobby, as he was the very heart and soul of Cinefest. The committee knew that he could never be replaced, and decided that the most fitting tribute to him would be to keep Cinefest going. That is their intent. How long they will be able to maintain the standard that he set is impossible to say, and they knew that the road ahead would not be easy. There will always be a great void in their midst, but they will always carry his memory in their hearts. That is, of course, the best memorial anyone can have, and they believe that come March, he will be somehow present, watching over the events, and finally getting to view the films from the best seat in the house!

Cinevent!
By John Stingley and Steve Haynes

When asked for a brief history of Cinevent, one of the founders, John Stingley wrote:

> To do that properly, we have to go back a few years before Cinevent began. Cinevent grew out of an earlier get-together held elsewhere.
> At that point in time, in the middle 1960s, we had been collecting 8mm movies for a while. ("We" are Steve Haynes and myself.) I had been collecting for three or four years at that time. Steve had started a bit earlier than me. We met at Ohio State in January and we discovered we had an uncommon hobby in common. We were familiar with Blackhawk Films, Entertainment Films, Griggs Moviedrome and a few other sources at that time and we had somehow discovered *Classic Images* ... uh, make that *Classic Film Collector* ... no, it was *The 8mm Collector* then. Anyway, through a reference in the *Collector*, we discovered, right here in Ohio, a dealer in 8mm films.
> Cooper's Film Rental was located in Eaton, Ohio, and Robert C. Cooper dealt in the kind of films we wanted. Not just the Castle and Ken one-reelers that the department stores carried; he stocked two-reel comedies, silent features and even some of the sound two-reel shorts and Laurel and Hardy features from Blackhawk, the only sound 8mm features available at that time. We got to know Bob pretty well, dealing with him by phone and even making trips to his house from time to time and taking new treasures back to Columbus.
> During this time, the Society for Cinephiles was having yearly conventions. They had already had a Cinecon in Indiana, Pennsylvania; another one in Baraboo, Wisconsin; and a third in Chicago. Cooper told us of his intention of holding a regional get-together in Dayton. As college students, we weren't traveling around to these other "cons," so having one nearby was wonderful news.
> To the best of my recollection, the Dayton Regional was held on a weekend in March 1967. There were only about 20 people there, but it was fantastic. All of those people with the same interests as ours! Not just strangers either. There were people attending that we had come to know through the pages of *The 8mm Collector*. Bud LeMaster, who had a regular review column on new 8mm releases, was there. Jim Fritz, who also wrote for the Collector from time to time, was on hand. Also in attendance was Samuel K. Rubin, editor and creator of *The 8mm Collector*. As icing on the cake, Stuart Oderman, master silent accompanist, was there to add his talent to the proceedings. The program was as basic as it could be. The schedule was very informal—we got to see screenings of films brought by the people who came! In addition, on Sunday, an auction was held with attendee Irv Abelson as auctioneer. A great time was had by all (or by us at least).

Cooper did another regional in 1968 that was as much fun as the first. On the phone near the end of the year, however, Bob told us he did not intend to do another regional in 1969. We were very disappointed but, being young, in the best spirit of "Hey kids, let's put on a show!," we asked Bob if he would mind our taking it on in Columbus. Cinevent was about to be born.

We were part of a group of film collectors and film buffs in the Columbus area that got together every couple of weeks. Some of these others had also attended the second Dayton Regional. We presented the idea of taking over the "Midwest Regional" from Cooper. Each of us put in ten dollars to finance the show. We sent out a one-page mailer, which we ran on a hectograph (a primitive copying gadget that used a printing surface not totally unlike very firm Jell-O), acquired a meeting room at the Neil House Hotel in downtown Columbus and we were ready to go.

Looking back on it from our perspective today, my God, it sounds so ridiculously simple. No set film schedule; we followed the precedent and screened prints that attendees brought with them, adding a few from the local members' collections. We had no dealer's room; we let Bob Cooper set up a table at the back of the film room to sell stuff while we rewound between films. For everyone else, there was the auction. No piano rental or tuning; Stu Oderman played the hotel piano just as it was. There was no advertising, program book, signs, designated projectionists, security guards, insurance, months of planning, last-minute problems, headaches, frantic pre-show setup or non-stop work during the show. Instead we would watch the films with everyone else and just have fun. Boy, that doesn't just sound like a long time ago; it sounds like it was over the rainbow!

In addition to our local group, about ten of us, we had about 20 other collectors and film buffs attending. Many of the alumni from the two Dayton shows came to Columbus. One new attendee was collector Don Poston. We had met Don in Columbus at a record store; he had a wonderful collection of (at that time) rare Douglas Fairbanks titles in 16mm, which he would present with scores assembled from various records. He would use two turntables during the screening of the film to fade from one piece of music to another with considerable skill.

With an attendance of about 30 people all told, the first Columbus Regional was considered an unequivocal success. In late 1969, we decided a second show was in order. A few of the local group came up with a radical suggestion. Why not rent some really hard-to-see silent film and announce ahead of time that it would be shown? The film these guys wanted to rent was *The Strong Man* with Harry Langdon. I was not an admirer of Langdon's comedy. I had only seen a few of his two- and three-reelers and I had not been impressed. Everybody else liked the idea, however, so we arranged a rental of the print and we sent out a flyer with Langdon's picture on it and announced the *Strong Man* screening for the show. Everyone who came to the Fort Hayes Hotel downtown for our second regional was excited by the showing of *The Strong Man*. After I saw it, I also became a Harry Langdon fan. The second show had even more attendees and was as much fun as our first endeavor.

Then, something happened. The *8mm Collector*, now *Classic Film Collector*, had run articles about our upcoming regional. Afterward, one of the writers for the *Collector*, who attended, would write a detailed article about the show, including what was shown and who attended and how much fun they had. We would provide a list of attendees. Steve and I were referred to as "Cinephiles" and the show as a "Regional Cinecon." We then received a letter from the Society of Cinephiles. Since all in our Columbus group were not members of the Cinephiles and we did not require that those who attend join the Society, they did not want their name or Cinecon associated with our show. No problem! John Baker, an attorney, jazz film collector and one of the oldest members of our local group, came up with five or six possible names for our show. I remember he called me on a Saturday morning when I had been up very late Friday night, with a list of proposed titles. Looking back 32 years, I cannot remember any of the other names except the one that I

6. The Film Fan Organizations and Conventions 93

really liked ... Cinevent. Baker, Steve and I ran the new name past the others at our next local meeting. It was unanimous. Our show was now officially Cinevent.

The next few years passed with a steady growth in Cinevent attendance and a constant refinement of our planning and presentation of the shows. We had one big advantage over the Cinecons of that time: The same people were presenting Cinevent every year. The people who elected to sponsor a Cinecon did not have the benefit of past years experience, although the people who had put on previous Cinecons were available with advice. We were learning each year from the things we did right and, even more, from the things we did wrong. We had a big "did wrong" coming up.

After bouncing around a couple of the downtown hotels for a few years, Cinevent signed a five-year contract with a hotel we had previously used successfully. For the next two years, our shows were held at the Neil House Hotel, and they were very pleasant experiences. My blood pressure still elevates when I recall year three.

We had had our ballroom space set up in theater style. We had moved in our speakers, projectors, screen and the rest. Attendees had arrived, the program started on time. Everything went well ... on Friday.

Saturday morning went off without a hitch. We broke for lunch. We took this time to straighten up the chairs and rows for the afternoon shows. While we were doing this, we observed, with extreme misgivings, bordering on panic, that another group was moving into the ballroom next to ours. They were carrying musical instruments! Upon checking with the manager, we discovered that the hotel had booked a wedding reception into the room next to us. There was nowhere else to put them or us. The afternoon screenings were a nightmare. The orchestra, which sounded to us as big as the London Philharmonic, was on the other side on one of those thin, folding partition walls. Stu Oderman tried, but his piano playing was outmatched by the waves of love songs dance music coming from the next room. At least you could still read the time cards on the screen for the silent films. The sound films didn't have a chance. It was the longest afternoon I can ever remember at one of our shows. The worst was yet to come.

At about the same time we took our dinner break, the room next to us was being reconfigured for a wedding banquet. The way they changed the wall partitions around, the access to our screening room was entirely cut off! This time I didn't go to see the manager, I told him to get up to the ballroom level and see what was happening. He was very polite, but wouldn't make any changes necessary to give us access to our room. I was not polite. Steve and John Baker kept asking me to calm down. I don't remember what I said, but, being in my mid twenties, I used a lot of language that I rarely used in business conversations.

The only space available for us for the rest of the night was the cafeteria in the hotel basement, which closed at 6 P.M. So we walked through the wedding banquet to get our equipment and moved everything down to the cafeteria. The ceiling was low; we couldn't get our screens to full height. We had to run cables wherever we could. Getting the power to the projectors was a problem. I still get upset to this day. Our attendees, on the other hand, took the whole thing with good grace and even with some amusement that I couldn't share. They realized it was not our fault. They didn't mind that the films started late and that our presentation was below our usual standards. Everything was less formal in those days anyway. It was all very friendly.

Needless to say, we broke our contract with the hotel and looked for a new home for Cinevent for the coming year, but we learned a great lesson. Thereafter, we would take all of a hotel's meeting space in our contract, even if we didn't need it. We also learned that if a bar or restaurant was attached to the hotel, we should come in on a Friday and a Saturday night to be sure that the sound of any band or group playing there did not filter into the room we intended to use for our screenings.

Co-founder Steve Haynes continues the story:

> In the years that followed, while Cinevent still frequently moved from hotel to hotel, it was usually because we had simply outgrown last year's model. As I now recall, we began our dealers' room during the Neil House days (I don't know what year for sure) and between the ever-growing need to accommodate more tables for dealers and more chairs for the screening room, Cinevent experienced steady and substantial growth.
>
> We established regular schedules for the screenings, and Jerry Clark became our first "chief" projectionist—a post he held for years. When Jerry passed away, Mike Drozewski, who had helped out occasionally in the past, succeeded him in the post and in the years to follow we added some "assistant" projectionists to the staff, so one person didn't have to do it all. When Mike decided that it was time to hang up his projectionist's hat, local member Dave Snyder, who has in recent years done much of the coordination for the film program, became chief. Dave is now ably assisted by Bob Hodge and Lance Carwisle.
>
> Sometime before the halfway point in our 35 years, John Baker introduced us to one of his fellow attorneys, Art Graves. Art turned out to be John's handpicked successor to help with running Cinevent (John had quietly planned his retirement to Florida). Art became our chief advisor (and occasional mediator!) through Cinevent 34 when he decided it was time to become a co-chairman emeritus!
>
> Music for the silent films is always a necessity and Cinevent has been fortunate to have some of the best to perform for these screenings. In addition to Stu Oderman, John Mirsalis, Robert Baker, Philip Carli, Gabrielle Thibaudeaux and David Drazin have all offered stellar support to the silent era's greats (and not-so-greats).
>
> Nearly ten years ago, Morris Everett, Jr., and Marty Davis brought their Annual Vintage Poster Art Auction to Columbus on Memorial Day Weekend, collected in the same hotel with Cinevent. Morris rightly thought that positioning the two events together would be beneficial to everyone and he was right. It was during the years since that Cinevent has regularly achieved an annual attendance of 800 attendees.
>
> The passing years have brought great change in what can be found in the dealers' rooms at Cinevent. In our early days, almost nothing but film (8mm and 16mm) and projection hardware were offered, but that quickly broadened out to include movie paper collectibles such as posters, stills and lobby cards. John and I have often said that we bought the wrong stuff at these early shows. We were mostly buying film when collectable paper was incredibly cheap. A few hundred spent over the first ten years of Cinevent could have financed our very comfortable retirements! ("Fifty dollars for a *Meet Me in St. Louis* one-sheet? Who would pay a price like that?").
>
> We have seen the amount of film available at shows sadly diminish, with 8mm and Super 8 disappearing almost totally. We've seen the enormous growth (and inflation) of paper collectibles and the expansion of home video, from Beta and VHS, through laserdisc, to DVD. However you feel about video, there can be no doubt that it has opened the possibilities of seeing some pretty obscure films to ordinary folk, not serious or obsessive enough to trek off to conventions. Add in the books, soundtrack recordings, autographs, toys and other, more peripheral movie-related collectibles, and it is easy to see how Cinevent dealers can fill 170 or more tables with goodies each year.
>
> In 1999, Cinevent presented its first annual 35mm screening, in association with the Ohio State University's Wexner Center for the Arts. The program for this occasion was the silent version of *Peter Pan* (1924) starring Betty Bronson, Ernest Torrence, Virgina Browne Faire, Anna May Wong, Esther Ralston and Mary Brian. Music for this screening was a presentation of Philip C. Carli's newly composed score for piano and small orchestra, and was performed by Mr. Carli with the Flower City Society Orchestra. The score was originally written for Italy's

Pordenone Silent Film Festival, and the Cinevent performance became a "dress rehearsal" for the recording that the same performers would shortly thereafter make for the Kino Video and DVD release. Also on the program was a brand new Library of Congress 35mm restoration of Douglas Fairbanks and Constance Talmadge in *The Matrimaniac* (1916), with piano accompaniment by Gabrielle Thibaudeaux. This screening was well-received and, each year since, Cinevent attendees have boarded the busses to the Wexner Center early Sunday morning for alternating silent and sound 35mm programs.

As Cinevent enters its thirty-fifth year, we are proud of what we have achieved and appreciate the support everyone has given us in so many ways over the years. People have only fairly recently asked us, "How long are you guys going to do this?" It's a question I don't think we can answer, but we have already talked a little about Cinevent 36!

News on Cinevent is available on the World Wide Web at www.cinevent.com

The Buck Jones Rangers

Dominick Marafioti of Rochester, New York, is a prime example of a dedicated, loyal fan to a Hollywood star; he is the National Chief of the Buck Jones Rangers of America. The organization meets annually to remember and honor the famous movie cowpoke.

Each year, Dominick has been sponsoring, practically single-handed, the group's annual convention in Rochester, which featured many of the stars of the Western films which have graced the silver screens throughout the world. He has, with his wife Marie, planned and supervised most of the work at these annual gatherings. He must now manage it alone; Marie died in 2002.

Guest stars migrate to the convention, renewing friendships with members of the Rangers and their Western movie peers. Many of these performers have formed an attachment to Dominick and his Rangers and return to participate in the activities.

Dominick founded the Buck Jones Rangers in December 1979 and has been its National Chief since then. He is well-liked! One of the conventioneers wrote to him stating that he is a legend in his own time. I agree!

On Friday, opening day of the convention, a dinner with the guests is held in the Marafioti home, and an awards banquet is held on Saturday. Golden Horseshoe-Silver Medals are presented to the honorees. The Medal is valued because it is presented to a recipient only once, making it more desirable.

Also, the Buck Jones Rangers present a Medal of Honor for achievement.

A dealer's room is available wherein members are able to purchase videos, film, stills, magazines and other Western memorabilia.

The guest stars are also situated in that room to facilitate the signing of autographs. If the guest star agrees, profits (if any) during this activity are donated to the Cancer Fund.

Films are continuously projected in two screening rooms. Feature Westerns are shown in one and serials in the other.

The Western stars and the Western fans appreciate and support the work Dominick has accomplished with his Buck Jones Rangers spectaculars.

Twenty years ago, Iron Eyes Cody, a frequent guest, had ten Iron Eyes Cody

Top: The new official Lone Ranger, Scott Shepherd, pictured with Dominick Marafioti, National Chief of the Buck Jones Rangers. *Bottom:* The author with perennial Indian screen villain Iron Eyes Cody, who frequently appeared in Western films portraying, of course, an Indian bad guy.

Peace Medals manufactured. The popular Western actor presented one to Marafioti for his dedication and his work in honoring the Western films and their actors. The back of each medal reads, "Brotherhood, Peace and Friendship." Iron Eyes' signature is engraved on the front and back of the award.

Dominick Marafioti delights in relating anecdotes from his years as "head master" of this popular movie fan activity. One of his favorites: Sunset Carson had informed him that he would be happy to guest star at the Buck Jones Festival ... *If* ... he could stay at Dominick's home. The friendly Dominick agreed.

Carson arrived and they discovered that the bed was too short for the tall and lanky actor's length. So, Dominick dredged up a stool and placed it at the end of the bed. Sunset Carson slept on this lengthened bed with his feet protruding out over the stool. A photograph of this would have been a collector's bonanza!

Sunset Carson and Bob Armstrong, guests at a Western convention.

Dominick states that Sunset Carson was a "Class A" person, and he misses him.

Henry Brandon was another of the Festival's guests who wanted to stay in Dominick's home. Unfortunately, he died a month later.

The Buck Jones Rangers of America will continue to meet annually as long as Dominick Marafioti is around. I am sure he has, or will arrange, for someone else to take over when he can do it no longer.

The spirit of Buck Jones must remain alive!

Sons of the Desert
By Savannah Furman

The Sons of the Desert, the International Laurel and Hardy Appreciation Society, was begun in 1965 by John McCabe. He had met Stan and Ollie at the

Hippodrome Theatre in Birmingham, England, when they were on tour there and he was a graduate student at Oxford. He and Stan maintained their friendship, and McCabe began doing research for an authorized biography of the duo.

The title of the organization comes from one of the best of the Laurel and Hardy films, *Sons of the Desert*, in which the Boys parody fraternal organizations while they attempt subterfuge on their wives. The song they sing at the beginning of the movie is the theme song for the Sons, and is sung with whole-hearted enthusiasm at every meeting. Each group of Sons is called a tent, to maintain the desert theme. Most of the tents use a name of a Laurel and Hardy film as their official title. The St. Louis Tent, for example, is the Babes in Toyland tent, Oasis #44.

It was while doing research for the biography that McCabe came up with the idea of forming a "real" Sons of the Desert organization, and he talked with Stan about it. In a letter to McCabe, Stan said he hoped for an organization with a "half-assed dignity from a group of serious but not too serious people, with the overriding goal being that everyone have a hell of a good time." I think we have achieved that goal.

In 1962, McCabe mentioned the idea to Al Kilgore, having already discussed it with Orson Bean. The three of them agreed to implement the three goals that McCabe had set forth as desirable. These were to encourage showing of the Boys' films, to develop a definitive list of all their films, and to establish a repository for their films.

For his brainchild, McCabe had written a Constitution, which had been added to by Stan—it's the Constitution which we still use. Al Kilgore drew a beautiful coat of arms for the fledgling organization, a proud symbol for us today. The Rev. Art Foulger-Edington, from Canada, translated the Sons' motto into Latin, to complete the coat of arms design. The motto: "Two minds without a single thought." It came from the billing for the great vaudeville team of Duffy and Sweeney, and was suggested by Stan.

The Sons' first annual banquet was on May 14, 1965, at the Three Lions Pub, Hotel Tudor, in New York, with 31 in attendance. A few years later they moved to the Lambs and entered their heyday. Many of the early members belonged to the Lambs, a private club for male show business folks and their guests. The Lambs was a magnificent facility for shows, with multiple types of accommodations including a screening room and a fully equipped Broadway playhouse. The membership had grown to over 100. The banquets, which had seating for 300, were usually sold out. Scion tents formed and their members often attended the New York tent's annual banquets. The '70s were the best of times for the New York Sons.

In 1974, the New York Sons began presenting awards to the Comedy Performers of the Year. Peter Cook and Dudley Moore received the first awards. Usually the recipient was someone who was currently performing in New York, so travel expenses could be kept low. Occasionally wires got crossed, however. Once Al Kilgore got on the phone with Martha Raye. He said, "Well, if it's not too far we'll send a car for you." She said, "Where do you think I am?" "Aren't you in New York?" he asked. She replied, "I'm in California!" Needless to say, they didn't get her. Other recipients were Dick Van Dyke, Will Jordan and Jim Henson.

Early on, additional tents were begun. These early tents included the Night Owls Tent of the Connecticut Valley, begun by Hal Stanton; the Dancing Cuckoos of Detroit, begun by Bill Rabe; the Flying Deuces of New Jersey; and the Way Out West tent in Los Angeles. The official list of the early tents, compiled by Dwain Smith, had Sons of the Desert, New York, as #1; Dancing Cuckoos, Detroit as #2; Block-Heads, Minneapolis, as #3; Tit for Tat in Canada as #4; and Way Out West, Los Angeles as #5. Bacon Grabbers, Chicago was #9 and, having been "the scene of the crime" in the movie, was the logical place to stage the first international convention.

Originally the expectation was that the Sons of the Desert would be of interest primarily to people connected to show business. New members were added by word of mouth, though the organization was featured once in *Variety*. Of course, love of Stan and Ollie, as evidenced by the letters Stan received, was a characteristic that had originally impressed John McCabe. This affection by "Everyman" led inevitably to the growth of the organization. The foundation laid by the New York Founding Tent allowed the international conventions to be successful from the start.

The New York Founding Tent had accumulated well over 20 "subsidiary" tents. The concept created by John McCabe was a fetching idea that captured the imagination; a weighty-look Constitution that was devoted to frivolity exhibited the essence of the Sons. The organization provided an outlet for people's interest in comedy and love of Laurel and Hardy. It spread by word of mouth and enthusiasm. Each tent worked independently, as they still do, but there was no link providing them with common information. That situation was about to change, however, primarily due to the efforts of Roger Gordon and Alan Garfield.

In 1974, Roger Gordon, of the Two Tars Tent in Philadelphia, with the blessing of Founder John McCabe, began the *Intra-Tent Journal* (ITJ) as a vehicle for sharing information among the tents and for disseminating information about Laurel and Hardy. Dwain Smith credits Roger Gordon with creating the cohesion of the group. He said that everyone who read the *ITJ* loved it; it made us a united organization. It also gave them a mailing list and a vehicle for contracting other tents.

The *ITJ* was a pulpit from which Gordon editorialized about the need and desire to have a national convention. In 1973, a year before the first *ITJ*, Alan Garfield had proposed to the Chicago Bacon Grabbers that they should host a convention modeled after the one in *Sons of the Desert*, which as every Son knows took place in Chicago. General enthusiasm was the result. They had, however, done all of this independently, without seeking permission or input from the New York Founding Tent. So there was this young Chicago tent agitating to hold a national convention and the *ITJ* editorializing in favor of one—the handwriting was on the wall.

In 1976, John McCabe sanctioned a National Convention Planning Committee, chaired by the *ITJ* editor, Roger Gordon. Gordon visited Chicago and he and the Bacon Grabbers agreed that there would be a Sons convention in Chicago. There were 27 tents at the time, and everyone's thinking was national in scope. No one thought that anyone from overseas would bother to come so far to a convention. The real question was, would tents, nationally, come. As Garfield said, "We could have held a convention and no one would come." In a move that would be repeated for succeeding conventions, a "historic planning meeting" was held one year prior, in August 1977. It took place in Chicago at the Ramada O'Hare Inn; representatives of nine different tents attended. At this meeting, the national and local committees met and put together the program.

Alan Garfield recalled the intent of the first convention: "I think it was just a matter of we were going to have some fun. We were going to see a lot of movies, and we were just going to get to know these other Sons." But nothing was left to chance. Directions for the registration booth staff, for example, were very explicit: "Hand delegate pre-registration packet. Hand delegate plastic badge holder. Hand delegate a paper fez. Hand delegate any other material." It was clear this was the first convention and every detail had been addressed.

An examination of the program shows that several traditions were established, which have become fixtures at the conventions. The golf tournament (the brainchild of Roger Gordon), the theater, the Grand Council meetings (two of them), banquets, celebrities, a farewell brunch, fezzes, the Grand Parade of Tents and much socializing—all occurred at Chicago '78.

The almost obligatory area explorations—a shopping trip to Chicago and a bus-boat tour—added to the festivities. There was a celebrities panel discussion and, probably unique, a film distributors panel. An auction of films, a banquet complete with wallets on the floor and a look-alike contest rounded out the days.

But almost half the time at this first convention was taken up in meetings—business meetings. Alan Garfield recalls, "Tents were getting started and they weren't sure what they were doing other than meeting. Roger had the idea [the tents] needed some guidance." On Saturday there were meetings for the newsletter editors, for tent programmers, for tent publicity directors, and a research seminar, all designed to share information and help new tents.

There was also a feeling that there should be a scholarly aspect to the group. At the first General Session, John McCabe was the keynote speaker. He set the tone for serious research and defined what the organization was about. Alan Garfield remembers, "One of the points was what kind of films should be shown at Sons Meetings—that it was legitimate to show Laurel and Hardy and basically Hal Roach–related films, but [John] did not want other films.... We just didn't know at that time, what was acceptable film. A lot of people who were joining the club were just into the nostalgia thing. They thought it was legitimate to show old movies along with the Laurel and Hardy. But McCabe was clear from the beginning that that was not the purpose.... So in that sense, McCabe had a vision that none of the rest of us had."

Roger Gordon and Alan Garfield didn't organize a convention by themselves, of course. Deep and sustained support from the Bacon Grabbers was essential. Alan, who first broached the idea to the Bacon Grabbers, agreed to head the convention and Marcia Opal, who worked closely with Garfield and Roger Gordon from the first convention committee, were stalwarts. Their ideas formed the framework off of which every convention since has operated. Joe Rooney said that at Chicago '78, "We were all strangers to each other, seeing each other for the first time. No one knew what to expect, but it was the welcoming smiles of Marcia Opal and Alan Garfield that let us know we were among *friends. And* now we are family."

As has also become customary, other Sons contributed. Bob Satterfield and

Lori Jones, from the Way Out West Tent in Los Angeles, coordinated the celebrities along with John McCabe and Al Kilgore. The New York Founding Tent volunteered to emcee the banquets, having had experience with their annual banquets. Kilgore, Tye Morrow, and Frank Melfo were much in evidence.

Smith recalled, "The first convention, though hosted by Chicago, had as much input from other tents as any of the conventions." Marcia Opal remembers, "Locally, we were working on the film program, the golf outing, the actual printed material ... we didn't even do the matchbooks. I think that Roger [Gordon] did the matchbooks."

Dan Waldron, from the Dancing Cuckoos, Detroit, saw they needed a logo. Marshall Korby agrees, "They had none. First of all, they weren't about to spend any money, and second of all, they didn't really think in terms of advertising." Waldron asked John Strainovici, who had designed the Dancing Cuckoo logo, and Strainovici designed the first convention logo.

Marshall Korby, also from the Dancing Cuckoos, suggested to Gordon that fezzes would be a popular item. Again, cost was a problem, but Sons are creative. Korby recalls, "I found an advertising company that made a paper fez that came flat.... It had a blank white spot in the front where you were supposed to put what the occasion was. I took it to the printer and I had them printed up ... and we gave them out." The Dancing Cuckoos also "sponsored" the Farewell Brunch, making it a Honolulu goodbye.

How did Alan Garfield and Marcia Opal come to be Sons? Chicago had a radio station which broadcast old-time radio programs, called "Those Were the Days." It was hosted by Chick Shaden. He had Chuck Huck and Tony DiGaudio as guests. They talked about Laurel and Hardy and forming a tent and gave a phone number. Garfield called joined, and quickly became an officer. Opal, on the other hand, couldn't join initially, because they served liquor at the meetings, and she was underage.

Having theaters running Laurel and Hardy movies throughout the convention was a no-brainer. In 1978, seeing the Boys' films was much more difficult than it is today, and many attendees had seen only a few of them. Rick Lindner said, "I remember the almost all night showing of films the best. At that time there wasn't much Laurel and Hardy stuff on video or TV.... Just being in a place with hundreds of Laurel and Hardy fans was what got me." The films and their venues were far more important to the Sons at the early conventions than they were at later conventions. Even though they aren't shown on television as much, their availability on video means that today most Sons have seen most of the films.

In 1978, film meant just that—the medium was 16mm, crisp, clean, projected onto a big screen. Most of the films at Chicago '78 belonged to Tony DiGaudio and Alex Bartosh. In addition to the films starring the Boys, films about them were screened—*This Is Your Life*, and *Laurel and Hardy's Trip to Britain*" for example. Dick Bann brought films from his extensive collection. Lois Laurel, Stan Laurel's daughter, brought outtakes from Laurel and Hardy films.

Each celebrity was introduced before her film was shown, they talked about the movies and their parts in them, and the audience could ask questions. It was a fairly intimate setting, and established another tradition for Sons conventions.

The celebrities included a number of stars who also were to become favorites.

Rosina Lawrence, with her beauty and charm, captivated hearts. Darla Hood, from *Our Gang*, participated in costume. In retrospect, her appearance was especially poignant, as she died at the early age of 46, before the next convention. Lucille Hardy Price revealed the private side of Babe, to everyone's delight. Anita Garvin Stanley and her husband Red gave out witticisms and mugged for the cameras. Della Lind, from *Swiss Miss*, reprised the song from that movie. Lois Laurel's very presence delighted the Sons. They answered questions, gave autographs, smiled, sang, danced, played golf, smiled more, answered more questions and generally ingratiated themselves forever in the Sons' hearts. John McCabe, Al Kilgore and Dick Bann were also in attendance, signing autographs of their recently published book about the Boys, *Laurel & Hardy*.

The celebrities did more than appear, as Alan Garfield remembers. "The one banquet where people were in costume—that was really amazing at that time. We just didn't know that that was going to be so nicely participated in…. One of the best was Darla Hood, who came dressed as a baby. She had diapers on and she was as funny as she could be."

Roger Gordon was also taken by the charm of the celebrities. It was, he said, "the first time I had ever met Anita Garvin and her husband Red. Anita looked like a countess in her pearls and red dress. She was a regal lady and wonderful. Red [Stanley] had led a jazz orchestra and was lots of fun."

Alan Garfield said, "For me, one of the high points was when Rosina [Lawrence] talked after the *Way Out West* film. She was very shy and wanted to hold my hand. So she got up there and I held her hand and walked her up and she just held on to my hand the whole time as she answered questions. She was, of course, this sweet, sweet lady."

John Duff also remembered the banquet. "One thing they did at that particular banquet—Joe Rooney and Mike Spack were doing a Laurel and Hardy impersonation. They started to do the last song from *Way Out West*—then they got Rosina on stage, put her in the center. They're both doing this little dance. Every time I watch *Way Out West* I think of that now."

According to a newspaper account, Lois Laurel was "called to the podium to say a few words Saturday night. After the banquet hall darkened, and the yellow spotlight hit her full, she said, 'This is overwhelming and beautiful, and I'm looking forward to meeting you all again when we meet in Los Angeles in 1980. Please, all of you, come.' At which point a whoopee cushion went off." Sons never take themselves too seriously.

From the very first convention, there were hijinks. Spontaneous or planned, simple or elaborate, they always add spice to the flavor of the conventions. The Flying Deuces of Northern New Jersey tent were the generators of many hijinks at Chicago '78. Alan Hembrough recalled, "With Al Kilgore as emcee for the Parade of Tents, the Deuces were introduced to the attendees. As Kevin Mulligan stepped forth to introduce tent members, he was confronted by two other Deuces also vying for microphone rights as well. An argument ensued and the two gave a tug to Mulligan's breakaway pants, leaving him standing in a pair of white boxer shorts covered with hearts!"

From the participant's view, Kevin Mulligan said, "Willie and Bob kept interrupting me to the point that I fed them the tag line, 'What are you guys trying to pull off?' which was their cue to pull on either side of my specially designed breakaway pants, and reveal me in all my splendor. (And what a beautiful sight it was!) I had to caution them before the skit to be sure and pull on just my trousers, and not grab onto my shorts as well, which would have left me in a rather risqué position. It was a surefire visual gag which, as I recall, went over very well with the audience.

"When I got back to my seat, I realized that I had neglected to bring an additional pair of pants to cover myself up when the function was over. I had two options to reach the elevator to get back to my room in my 'exposed' state. I could either travel along a lower floor which went by the indoor pool and would allow me to take an elevator from the basement, or I could proceed directly across the main lobby at a time when many business people were lined up to register for their rooms. Needless to say, I chose the latter and received some of the strangest looks from these bewildered travelers." If it ever was meant to be, the Parade of Tents would never be a sedate affair after this exhibit.

Though peewees were at the first convention, they were not a planned event. Marcia Opal recalls, "They [Block-Heads] brought them. We were in the ballroom ... I hit one and it went past the chandelier and then I realized this was not, probably, a good idea." The wooden peewees generated a great deal of enthusiasm and became a staple of subsequent conventions, albeit used outdoors.

There were, however, actual planned contests. One was the Babe Hardy Golf Open, coordinated by Terry Comina. Bruce Keinert, "the only drip-and-dry member of the Bacon Grabbers," won the golf tourney. Although it rained throughout, according to Kathy Luhman's convention survey report, the golf tournament "proved to be one of the more popular activities of this convention." It has become a recurring favorite at Sons conventions.

A special award was presented to Roger Gordon, Alan Garfield and Chuck Huck, the three men who worked hardest to bring a convention to fruition. It was the Billy Gilbert Nothing to Sneeze At Award.

Kathy Luhman gave an opening speech in which she, for the first time, used every single Laurel and Hardy title. At the opening hospitality session, Bob Opal played all the Laurel and Hardy songs, and Sons sang along as they got to know each other. Marshall Korby brought a rented van full of Laurel and Hardy Memorabilia. He rented a separate room and set up his own dealer's room. It was a smashing success. Paying John Strainovici a royalty, Lorby printed up 50 T-shirts with the convention logo. They sold out at once, impressing everyone with the importance of a log. An original banner from the Sons of the Desert was brought and displayed by Lois Laurel. Marcia Opal recalls its impact: "Everyone was standing in line to be able to touch it or hold it."

Bill Cubin had come all the way from Stan's birthplace, Ulverston, England. A newspaper article stated that, "Bill Cubin always reckoned that Stan ... had never received ample recognition in his home town. In 1978 he and his wife Lucy were the only Britons at the first convention of the Sons of the Desert."

John Duff recalls, "When it was over I had this melancholy feeling of 'Why can't this go on longer?'" The hotel staff had a different opinion. Rich Kaplan said, "I asked them, 'What did you think of the convention?' and they said it was the wildest convention they'd seen since the cat show when the cats got loose in the lobby!"

The first convention, in 1978, set the tone for the ones that have followed. Each convention is hosted by a tent and is flavored by the interests of the Grand Sheiks and the city in which the convention is held. Common threads are games and contests, toasts, costume banquets, dealers' room, celebrities, look-alikes, optional pre- or post- tours, the Parade of Tents and Laurel and Hardy movies. Over time the celebrities who worked with Stan and Ollie have passed away, except for the *Our Gang* kids. But the Sons who have attended these conventions have come to know each other, so that now we go to see and visit with out old friends. Seeing the Boys' films as part of a large audience is an experience not easily duplicated, and one that is growing in importance at the conventions.

The second convention was Hollywood '80, and was characterized by stars, stars, stars. All the celebrities who worked with the Boys attended; there was also an *Our Gang* reunion, with celebrities there from each *Our Gang* comedy made. It was the first time the *Our Gang* members had been together since they were filming as children. More than 150 celebrities attended.

In 1982 the convention was in Detroit, a self-contained lovefest. Many celebrities attended, as well as most of the prominent Sons. This convention became the model. Marshall Korby said, "It set the standard for what I call a traditional weekend convention.... You are in a hotel—you could be in the middle of the Mojave Desert, it wouldn't matter—you're in the hotel and *that's where everything is*."

England '84 followed. Combining several days in London with several more days in Ulverston, Stan's home town, meant a convention on the road. Rarely seen films were screened at the Museum of Moving Pictures; evenings were spent at the vaudeville-type theater. The Trivia Quiz was introduced, and it became an instant tradition. Parades down the streets of Ulverston and Blackpool highlighted the Ulverston portion of the trip. The Cumbria Grand Hotel in Ulverston made an elegant setting for our excursions.

Valley Forge, Pennsylvania, hosted the 1986 convention. Many stars, including Felix Knight, Virginia Patterson and Henry Brandon, attended. These three were featured in *Babes in Toyland*, the theme of the convention, and Valley Forge '86 was the only convention at which they were all together. They also took part in the recreation of some scenes from *Babes in Toyland*. Founder John McCabe and first celebrity Rosina Lawrence announced their engagement.

North to St. Paul for the 1988 convention, and another classic. Modeled after Detroit '82, it captured the essence of fun that is essential to the Sons. Games, rides on the riverboats, musical contests, certificates of every kind, piano wrecking and a parade—the Hopkinsville Raspberry Festival—characterized the convention. The ease and non-flappability of host Tracy Tolzmann added to the festivities.

In 1990, the Boobs in the Woods tent, from Clearwater, Florida, hosted the Sons convention. Rainy weather wrecked the beach plans, or moved some indoors, and humidity was a factor unexpected by Sons from drier and cooler climates. Still, the convention abounded in fun, with the introduction of the Midnight Madness opening of the dealers' room and an auction to raise money for the *ITJ*. A personal check written by Stan to "Hal Roach Studios" was purchased for $2000.

Las Vegas '92 was the next convention. Outstanding awards were distributed, a water park was ours for the evening, a band was imported from England to play for us, a number of new celebrities who were featured in the Boys' later films charmed us, and the usual games, costumes and gaiety characterized the convention. One unique event was an actual wedding ceremony conducted during the Grand Banquet. Hal Roach was a special celebrity; he was 100 years old at the time. He was reunited with many of the *Our Gang*ers.

The Founding Tent, New York, hosted the convention in 1994. It was, of course, like a homecoming. The Bluebird Society Orchestra performed, Laurel and Hardy Jeopardy was played, and much entertainment by Sons highlighted this convention. It was the last time that Founder John McCabe, first celebrity Rosina Lawrence McCabe, first daughter Lois Laurel Hawes and her husband (whom she met through the Sons) Tony Hawes were all in attendance at a convention.

A most unusual venue, the cruise ship *Ecstasy*, was the site of the 1996 Sons convention. A cruise convention had been talked about for a number of years; it had become a standing joke with the primary progenitors of it vigorously partaking. When the actual opportunity arose, they got the bid and *voilà*, a cruise convention. In addition to the activities of the cruise line, the Sons were able to enjoy their own brand of fun, joining a conga line in the dining room and blowing razzers at dinner. Lest we had offended other passengers, our host gave an apology to the other sea-goers the last evening, and they gave the Sons a vigorous round of applause, assuring us that they had enjoyed our fun nearly as much as we had.

Back to England in 1998, this time to Birmingham, home of Charlie Hall, one of the Boys' best helpers. The Chamberlain Hotel housed us all and (in addition to the usual fun) music, dancing, and socializing ran far, far into the night. In a note of nostalgia, the Sons had a parade in Ulverston, as we had in 1984, and spent the evening at the Cumbria Grand Hotel for the "Sons Entertain" event. We were taken on a special tour of the Hippodrome Theatre, at which site our founder John McCabe had met Stan and Ollie.

Sea-Tac 2000 was held in Tacoma, but the hosting tent was out of Seattle, hence the name. A couple of *Our Gang* celebrities came for the first time. A complete vaudeville performance was created and staged at the Pantages Theater, where Stan and Ollie had appeared on tour. It was so well-done that many Sons were tearful. The rotunda of the hotel had been converted into a backstage with sets from the various movies of the Boys. Founder John McCabe had donated many of the oil paintings done by Rosina Lawrence for auction for the *ITJ*.

In 2002 the Sons invaded Nashville. At the plush Marriott, in addition to the expected movies, cartoons featuring the Boys were run. Anticipation was evident as the audiences watched for the Boys' appearances in the cartoons. Also shown was *Revenge of the Sons of the Desert*, a documentary on Valley Forge '86. The convention celebrities were brought onto the stage of the Grand Ole Opry for recognition, and a riverboat cruise capped the celebrations.

Currently the Sons of the Desert has tents across the United States and in many European countries, especially Great Britain. Information on tents can be found at www.wayoutwest.org or by doing an Internet search for Sons of the Desert *and* Laurel and Hardy. Each local tent operates independently, and there are no international dues. Tents must subscribe to the *ITJ* to be recognized as an official tent. Tents work to spread the joy of Laurel and Hardy films, showing them at children's hospitals and retirement homes and to social groups. And every other year, for a few glorious days, we leave the world behind for the simple pleasures, the fun and festivities, embodied in the comedies of Stan Laurel and Oliver Hardy.

History of the National Tom Mix Festival
By Bud Norris

Possibly no one has been a bigger fan of the legendary movie cowboy, Tom Mix, than Dr. Richard Seiverling of Hershey, Pennsylvania. As he realized that 1980 would mark the hundredth anniversary of the birth of Mix, he decided to attempt to organize some sort of event to commemorate this date.

So Dick traveled to DuBois, Pennsylvania, Tom's childhood home, and met with the town fathers and business people to see if they would stage some type of festival. It was nip and tuck to the last minute, and Dick had to sell a car and souvenirs from his WWII service to help defray expenses, but on October 9, 1980, the Tom Mix Festival got under way in DuBois.

A small group of Mix enthusiasts joined Dick Seiverling for this event. Bud Norris, a Mix memorabilia collector since 1940, Allen "Slim" Binkley, former employee of the Tom Mix Circus, Ted and Ruth Reinhart, Western music performers, Bill Uhler, projectionist, and (all the way from Dortmund, Germany) Mix fan Kurt Klotzbach. A rodeo was booked into town. But bad weather cut attendance, which resulted in the festival losing money.

Originally, this was supposed to be a one-time celebratory event. But Dick convinced DuBois to try it again the following year. Things went better in 1981; the festival was moved back to September, where it has remained ever since. By 1982, the show was beginning to operate profitably as word of mouth spread and advertising increased.

The primary ingredients were memorabilia displays, film programs, dealers in collectibles, a parade and an appreciation banquet to cap off the event. In 1983, the Ralston-Purina Company, which had sponsored the Tom Mix radio program from 1933 to 1950, was persuaded to get involved. Ralston produced three different cereal boxes with Tom Mix's picture on them, and issued new premiums to mark the fiftieth anniversary of the radio broadcast's beginning. The festival ran an entire week this year under Ralston's support. All succeeding festivals have been three-day affairs.

The National Tom Mix Festival remained in DuBois for 10 years, when an offer that couldn't be refused surfaced. The team was invited to hold the event at the Imperial Palace Casino in Las Vegas, Nevada, in 1990. It was thought that with all the activities taking place in Las Vegas, that the Mix festival might go unnoticed. But possibly the biggest crowds ever showed up over the three days. The casino has a large collection of classic autos in its museum, one of them being the 1937 Cord in which Tom Mix lost his life. This restored auto was moved into the center of the festival auditorium as a unique centerpiece.

Representatives of the town of Guthrie, Oklahoma, attended the Las Vegas show, and convinced Seiverling to bring the festival to their locale. So from 1991 to 1994, the Mix festival took place in that authentically preserved and restored

Western town. It was also significant that Tom Mix had formerly lived and worked in Guthrie.

In 1995, the event moved once again, this time to Ted Reinhart's Western-style resort in Alexandria, Pennsylvania. Another offer arrived in 1996 and the festival moved to Peru, Indiana for one year. Again there was a Mix connection, as Peru was home town to many circuses, and Tom Mix visited there frequently during his circus days.

The years 1997 and 1998 saw the festival return once more to the Reinharts' resort, TERU Ranch, and then things came full circle as it was arranged to go back to the roots of the event, DuBois. One of the best festivals was the one in DuBois in 1999, the twentieth anniversary of the first get-together.

As of this writing, in 2002, the festival continues in DuBois, though not as it once had been. Sadly, Dick Seiverling, Slim Binkley, Bill Uhler and many Mix fans have passed away in recent years, so the event can never again be what it once was. But at least the name of Tom Mix continues to be perpetuated by the annual festival.

Only time will tell how much longer the name of Tom Mix will continue to draw attendance to the festival. His fans are rapidly dying out, literally, and new generations have never heard of him. But for a while, at least, fans and collectors have enjoyed "Mixing it up" and remembering what once was.

The Burroughs Bibliophiles
By George T. McWhorter

In the bylaws of the Burroughs Bibliophiles the organization is identified as "a non-profit literary society dedicated to stimulating interest in and preserving the works of the great American author, Edgar Rice Burroughs." As a splinter group of the World Science Fiction Convention held at Pittsburgh in 1960, 30 charter members met and elected officers of the new society. Clarence "Bob" Hyde became president (he remains president emeritus and chairman of the board in 1998), and plans were made to adopt or initiate official publications such as *The Burroughs Bulletin* and *The Gridley Wave* as well as to hold annual conventions. As with many new societies, the Burroughs Bibliophiles learned by doing, and interest in Edgar Rice Burroughs grew as his international popularity with a new generation increased and new members were recruited.

Science-fiction newsletters and fan magazines began to proliferate in the late 1930s and early 1940s, most of them amateur publications mimeographed in purple and seeking to share enthusiasms for the emerging genre. Most of these publications were distributed gratis or with nominal fees to cover mailing costs. These works frequently referred to Burroughs as "the Grandfather of American Science Fiction," but the first magazine devoted exclusively to the author and his work was *The Burroughs Bulletin*, founded and edited by Vernell Coriell, a circus performer and acrobat, who produced his magazines on cross-country tours. Coriell published his first issue in July 1947 with the blessing of Burroughs, then in retirement at Encino, California, after having served as the oldest war correspondent in World War II.

Thirteen years later, in Pittsburgh, the charter members of the Burroughs Bibliophiles voted to make *The Burroughs Bulletin* their official magazine, with Coriell as editor. The board of directors of the new society also voted to publish *The Gridley Wave*, a monthly newsletter that Coriell had already begun publishing in December 1959 and that would feature news of the latest Burroughs books, films and merchandising activity. The title of this newsletter refers to a fictional device for sending and receiving messages to and from Earth, the Earth's core and the planet Mars—a device that Burroughs' character, Jason Gridley, discovers in *Tarzan at the Earth's Core* (1923). Using Burroughs's nomenclature for other club events, the Bibliophiles christened their annual conventions "Dum-Dums," after the meetings of the anthropoid apes who dance by the light of the moon in the depths of the African jungle. Dum-Dums have been held in many major American cities, with those in Los Angeles having attracted the largest crowds; two conventions, in 1988 and 1997, have been convened at Cumbria in Northern England at Greystoke Castle. In 1998, the Burroughs Bibliophiles celebrated their thirty-seventh Dum-Dum in Baltimore, Maryland, with Gabe Essoe, author of *Tarzan of the Movies*, as the guest of honor.

The greatest and best-loved illustrator of the first editions of Burroughs' books was Chicago artist J. Allen St. John, who created memorable images for 33 first editions, beginning with simple black-and-white headpieces for *The Return of Tarzan* (1915) and ending with *Tarzan's Quest* (1936). One of his most vivid paintings that was made for *Tarzan and the Golden Lion* (1923) became the official logo of the Burroughs Bibliophiles. He also designed the masthead for *The Burroughs Bulletin*, and this has been used since 1962. St. John died in 1957, three years before the Burroughs Bibliophiles was organized, but his widow, Ellen St. John, was the club's first guest of honor at the Dum-Dum held in Chicago in 1962. An attractive blonde with delicate features, she had been the model for Jane and many other Burroughs heroines in her husband's paintings. In 1963 the Burroughs Bibliophiles honored science-fiction writers L. Sprague deCamp and Sam Moskowitz by presenting to each an engraved silver bowl adorned with St. John's "Golden Lion." The Burroughs Bibliophiles tested several different Golden Lion Award trophies before settling on the current gold-engraved plaque mounted on wood, in regular use since 1978. In 1984, a second annual award, a Life Achievement Award, was designed by George T. McWhorter for long and distinguished service to the memory of Burroughs. At the 1984 Dum-Dum in Baltimore, Coriell, known as "the father of Burroughs fandom" and in terminal illness at the time, was the first recipient of this award. He died less than three years later.

A list of Dum-Dum honorees through the years reads like a Who's Who of actors, artists, writers and publishers involved with Burroughs' works. Tarzan actors include Johnny Weissmuller, Jim Pierce, Buster Crabbe, Frank Merrill, Herman Brix, Gordon Scott, Denny Miller and Jock Mahoney. Twenty-five years after Weissmuller's guest appearance at the Boston Dum-Dum in 1971, his costar, Maureen O'Sullivan, made her first Dum-Dum appearance in Rutland, Vermont. Other well-known Burroughs artists who have been honored are St. John, Rex Maxon, Frank E. Schoonover, Frank Frazetta, Hal Foster (who set the standard for the Tarzan comics from 1931 to 1937 before leaving the strip to create *Prince Valiant*), William Juhré, John Coleman Burroughs (son of the author and illustrator of 11 first editions), Joe Kubert, Burne Hogarth, Boris Vallejo, Michael Whelan, Bob Abbett, Gray Morrow, Thomas Yeates and Joe Jusko. Authors, editors and publishers who have been honored include Forrest J Ackerman, Ian Ballantine, Lester del Rey, Donald Wollheim, Richard Lupoff, Erling B. Holsmark and Burroughs' children.

The Burroughs Bibliophiles have done more than honor famous people at conventions and publish magazines and newsletters. Their first major project was to collect short stories that had appeared only in pulp magazines and to republish them with the permission of Edgar Rice Burroughs, Inc., a family corporation that Burroughs founded in 1923 to protect his enterprises in book publishing, motion pictures and radio and television shows, syndicated newspaper Tarzan strips and comic books, and trademark merchandising of everything from Tarzan ice cream to glue, wristwatches, knives, belts and Tinkertoys. For many years the Burroughs Bibliophile reprints of *The Girl from Farris's, The Efficiency Expert, The Scientists Revolt, Beware!, The Red Star of Tarzan* and *The Illustrated Tarzan Books, No. 1* were the only editions available of these works.

In 1972 the Burroughs Bibliophiles began a new series of publications under the House of Greystoke imprint. This included works such as *The Battle of Hollywood* by James H. Pierce, *Oldest Living Tarzan* (1978), the autobiography of the fourth actor who played Tarzan and who married Burroughs's daughter, Joan. Pierce and she starred together in the 1932-33 Tarzan radio programs sponsored by Signal Oil. The most recent House of Greystoke publication is *The Edgar Rice Burroughs Memorial Collection: A Catalog* (1991) by McWhorter, who donated his collection of 70,000 volumes to the University of Louisville Library, where he is curator.

In promoting the image of Burroughs as a master storyteller, trendsetter and original thinker, it was necessary for the Burroughs Bibliophiles to find prominent spokesmen. Such advocates have been L. Sprague deCamp, who wrote an introduction to the 1986 Easton Press edition of Burroughs' first novel, *A Princess of Mars*; Ian Ballantine and Lester del Rey, whose reprints of Burroughs' works in Ballantine paperbacks are collectors' items; and Ray Bradbury, whose introduction to Irwin Porges' biography *Edgar Rice Burroughs, the Man Who Created Tarzan* (1975) is a classic accolade. Sam Moskowitz—Burroughs scholar, editor, publisher, teacher, literary agent and pulp-magazine historian—was the first to anthologize Burroughs in the mainstream press and frequently contributed scholarly articles to *The Burroughs Bulletin*. Erling B. Holtsmark, chairman of the Classics Department at the University of Iowa, is the author of two major studies of Burroughs, including *Tarzan and Tradition* (1981), which explores the classic Greek and Latin roots of Burroughs' writing. Leigh Brackett has acknowledged Burroughs' inspiration for her own Martian concepts in writing science fiction, and Henry Hardy Heins' *Golden Anniversary Bibliography of Edgar Rice Burroughs* (1964) has become a standard reference for auction houses and antiquarian book dealer catalogues. Astronomer Carl Sagan, primatologist Jane Goodall, actor Ronald Reagan and comedienne Carol Burnett have also been unexpected spokespeople.

In recent years, members of the Burroughs Bibliophiles have brought increasing public attention to the society. They have served as authorities for interviews or as writers of articles for magazines and newspapers, and they have participated in documentaries such as *Tarzan: The Legacy of Edgar Rice Burroughs*, the 1997 television biography produced by the Arts & Entertainment network and hosted by Peter Graves, and *In Search of Tarzan*, the American Movie Classics documentary televised during AMC's film festival of 32 vintage Tarzan movies. Another 1997 documentary, *Moi, Tarzan*, is being shown in many European countries, where the Tarzan myth is even more popular than in the United States.

The Walt Disney Studios produced an animated Tarzan movie released in theaters in 1999, and the commercial success of this movie added to the merchandising of Tarzan products. In summer 1997, the Palmdale Playhouse in California staged the premiere of *You Lucky Girl!*, an unpublished play that Burroughs wrote in 1927 and in which his daughter Joan was to star. In 1998, Donald M. Grant published this play, with illustrations by Ned Dameron, along with "Marcia of the Doorstep," a story about a foundling that Burroughs wrote but could not market in 1924. McFarland published in December 1996 a much-needed update to the Heins *Golden Anniversary Bibliography* by Burroughs Bibliophile Robert Zeuschner, a professor at Pasadena City College. Publication plans for new Burroughs Bibliophiles books and catalogues, including pictorial manuals for Burroughs collectibles and a complete history of the Tarzan radio shows, have been announced.

The Burroughs Bibliophiles is an international organization with headquarters at the Burroughs Memorial Collection in Louisville, Kentucky, where the magazine and newsletter are published and where the board of directors makes plans. Active regional chapters have been established in Washington, D.C., Los Angeles, Chicago, Atlanta, Cleveland and Baltimore—as well as in the states of Michigan, Florida and Arizona, and in countries such as Holland, France, Germany and Australia. Some of the chapters publish regional newsletters, such as *The Pantham Newsletter* of the Washington, D.C., National Capital "Panthans." During the last 50 years, more than 200 Burroughs fan magazines have appeared, also with titles incorporating recognizable Burroughs-inspired nomenclature such as *Amtorian, Barsoonian, Jasomian, Oparian, Erbania, Tarzine, Burroughs Newsbeat* and *Erbivore*. Some, such as *The Barsoomian Blade*, have appeared on the Internet.

For more information on the Burroughs Bibliophiles or for subscriptions to *The Burroughs Bulletin*, write to George T. McWhorter, Curator, Edgar Rice Burroughs Collection, Ekstrom Library, University of Louisville, Louisville KY 40292, U.S.A.; call (502) 852-8729; or send e-mail to gtmcwh01@ulkyvm.louisville.edu.

The Western Film Festival
By Ray Nielsen

My initial involvement with nostalgic film festivals came in August of 1977. Some months prior to that, I had met Dewey Derrick of North Little Rock, Arkansas. He was the one who told me about the Memphis festival. It had stated there in 1972 but I knew nothing of it at the time. Dewey had been collecting B Westerns for several years at this point. I had seen a news story about him on a local Little Rock television station. Although I hadn't seen B Westerns in the theaters,

I had watched them on television in the late 1940s and early '50s, while growing up in the San Francisco area.

I hadn't given them much thought for years until I saw that story about Dewey. It made me think back to my childhood and how much fun I had gotten out of watching those Westerns and serials.

I called the station and asked if it could put me in touch with Dewey. I subsequently met him and started coming over to his home to watch Westerns with him and a handful of others. It was then that I learned what I had missed over the last several years, not knowing I could have gone to Memphis to meet the likes of Russell Hayden, Lash La Rue, Eddie Dean, Max Terhune, Sunset Carson, Ray "Crash" Corrigan and other Western stars who had attended the shows in Memphis since '72. I then made up my mind that I would go there in the summer of '77.

That first show I went to was held at the Holiday Inn Rivermont, which was then the flagship hotel of the Holiday Inn chain. It sat right on the edge of the Mississippi River. It closed down in 1983 and was turned into condominiums. It still stands there.

Some of the guests who attended the show that year included Jock Mahoney, Monte Hale, Penny Edwards, Art Davis, Iron Eyes Cody, Myron Healey, Foy Willing (the one-time leader of the "Riders of the Purple Sage" musical group that appeared in Roy Rogers Westerns) and Arkansas "Slim" Andrews.

I didn't really know anything about Andrews' movie career when I met him that first day. But he looked familiar to me. Turned out he had been the host of a kids' TV show I had grown up watching outside of outside of Fresno, California, in the early 1950s. He was known as "The 49er" then and played musical instruments, told stories, manipulated puppets and showed cartoons. I had watched it many times after coming home from school in the fifth grade. He later did a similar show when he moved back to his native Gravette, Arkansas several years later. He actually commuted to Pittsburg, KS to do the program!

I had known of Healey's movie career for a long time, even though he wasn't a household name to the average person. My stepfather had grown up with Healey in Northern California and often mentioned him whenever one of his movies came on TV. When I met Mr. Healey, I told him about this and when he autographed a picture for me he made mention of my stepfather.

The first Memphis Film Festival in '72 had been organized by Packy Smith and Mitchell Schaperkotter. It had been put on at the Peabody Hotel. They did it there for another year or two, but the Peabody then closed down. It was an old hotel at the time and it must have been losing money. It stayed closed for a decade but was ultimately remodeled and re-opened. It's now the jewel it once was back in the 1940s. But it's too expensive for the pocketbooks of the average old movie fan, so the festival never went back there.

After those first couple of years at the Peabody, Smith and Schaperkotter took their show on the road to Nashville, Tennessee, for a couple of years. Smith lived there and it was more convenient for him. But there were some Memphians who were unhappy about the festival moving from Memphis. The most notable of these was a guy named Jim Rorie. He worked as a ticket agent for Delta Airlines. He also had some friends in the same business who also liked old Westerns. They got together and decided to put on a festival of their own in Memphis. This was probably about 1975. I'm not sure. But they were the ones who'd put on the show I went to in '77.

For reasons not known to me, Rorie and his crew did not put on a show in Memphis in 1978. I was disappointed since I'd had so much fun at the earlier one. Then I heard another collector named Harry Thomas was going to put on a show in St. Louis in '78. I went to it. It was put on in an aging Ramada Inn there. I don't remember everyone who came that year, but if my memory serves me, they included Don "Red" Barry, James (*Rin-Tin-Tin*) Brown, Kay Aldridge, Smith Ballew, Hank Worden, Rand Brooks and more. I actually get some of the names mixed up because there was a second show in St. Louis the following year that I also attended. I may have transposed some of the names.

Other names that come to mind, who could have been at either show, include Yakima Canutt, Victor Jory, Leon McAuliffe (the steel guitar player for Bob Wills and the Texas Playboys, who had appeared in several Westerns with Wills and Russell Hayden), Jimmy Ellison, Jennifer Holt, Terry Frost, Edgar Buchanan, Marshall Reed and Myrna Dell.

Rorie and his crew did revive the Memphis show in '79 but I chose to go to St. Louis instead since St. Louis had many more guests attending. The only one I can remember who went to Memphis that year was James Best. Harry Thomas gave up the St. Louis show after '79 and moved back to Tennessee. I think Rorie gave up again after his show in Memphis failed.

That meant there would be no shows in 1980. At least as far as we knew. There was several of us here in Arkansas who didn't want to see that happen. We contacted Jim Rorie and asked him if there was any chance we might try another show in Memphis. We went to him because he knew something about putting shows on and we didn't. All we knew was that we wanted a place to go to watch old films and meet celebrities who were in them.

Ray Nielsen, *Classic Images* columnist and television personality, who showed interviews with screen stars on his television show and repeated them in his monthly column, "Ray's Way."

About a dozen of us got together

in Rorie's home. We agreed to try it again at the Rivermont in 1980. Meanwhile, unbeknownst to us, some of Harry Thomas' friends also thought there was a void and got together with some people in the Charlotte, North Carolina, area to start a show there.

My first real involvement in putting on a festival came in that summer of 1980. I was still in the Navy Reserve then and earlier that year I had been on training duty in the San Diego area. On my weekend off, I ran up to Los Angeles to meet with Yakima Canutt, who I'd met the previous summer at St. Louis. I stayed in his home overnight.

I also made some telephone calls from his home to people I was trying to recruit for Memphis. One was George O'Brien. The other was Joel McCrea. I was successful in getting O'Brien to Memphis. Mr. McCrea said he'd try to come but ultimately didn't make it.

There's a side bar to that story. I had interviewed Mr. McCrea many times over the phone when I was working with public television in Arkansas. I had made other attempts to get him to Memphis but things just never fell into place. Several years later, after he had passed away, I was able to convince his widow, Frances Dee, to come to our show.

I was communicating with her through her son, Peter. In one of our many conversations, he said to me that he had something at his dad's ranch that he thought was meant for me. He had a lobby card and photograph that were autographed to "Ray." Peter didn't know who I was when he first saw them, so he didn't know who these articles were meant for. It later dawned on him. He then had them sent to me. The lobby card was from *Union Pacific*. Receiving that autographed card and picture was one of the biggest thrills of my life.

The next weekend I was free from Navy duty, I went out to a resort in the Salton Sea area of California. That's where Charles Starrett had a vacation home. I had communicated with him by mail and arranged a meeting with him there. It was there that he agreed to come to Memphis. I couldn't believe it. In my first try, I was able to lure two of the biggest B Western stars in the history of the genre to come to our show; George O'Brien and Charles Starrett. I can't remember everyone else who attended that show.

Jimmy Wakely came in the last day to replace Eddie Dean, who had become ill. Cecilia Parker, who had acted with O'Brien in a film or two, was also on hand. So was Monte Hale. I remember he brought a friend with him who I wasn't familiar with. An old stuntman buddy. Turns out this guy had just gotten into acting and had a major role in a film that had just come out called *Comes a Horseman*. His name was Richard Farnsworth. Pat Buttram was there and emceed our banquet.

The 1980 show was a success and we continued on at the Rivermont until it closed down in the winter of '83. Earlier that summer, we had what was probably our biggest success. That was the year Clayton Moore attended our show. He was a huge hit and enthralled everybody. He was still under legal restraint at that time from wearing his famous mask because the owners of the Lone Ranger character didn't want him stealing any thunder from Klinton Spilsbury, the "star" of the Lone Ranger movie that was coming out at the time. Mr. Moore had to wear sunglasses instead. Some of the others who attended that year included Harry Carey,

Screen star George O'Brien at one of the film conventions.

Jr., John Russell, Richard Webb, Jock Mahoney, Pat Buttram, John Agar, Sunset Carson, Anthony Caruso and Henry Brandon.

After the Rivermont closed down, our group was left in limbo. We no longer had a place to put the show on. We had to do some hotel-hunting fast and it was a little late in the year to be making deals for the summer. We finally landed a contract at what was then the Hyatt Regency Hotel (now Adams-Mark). But the only dates they could offer us were over the Fourth of July weekend. We had no choice but to take them. Jim Rorie and his Delta boys were pulling most of the strings at this point. I helped recruit guests and did some panels, but had little or nothing to do with the financial arrangements.

Jim was a party guy and was mostly in this for that end of it. He tended to go a bit overboard on the spending and went hog wild in '84. We had a lot of guests and several hangers-on that were all being paid for. It proved to be too much and caused us to go into quite a bit of debt. That broke the organization up and we reorganized for '85. But '84 did provide us with some memories, not all of them good.

That was the year former Dead End Kids and Bowery Boys star Huntz Hall attended. He turned out to be the most infamous guest we ever had in the history of our festival. I say that because he was extremely difficult to deal with. He was very temperamental and demanding and was egged-on by his shrewish wife. He also ran up huge bills at the hotel, which took us a long time to recover from. Others who were there to witness all this: Doug McClure (who left early because he was trying to stay away from alcohol and saw too much of it at our place), William

Campbell, Marc Lawrence, Victor French (who had a bit of a wild streak that also left us open-mouthed at times), Fred Scott, Monte Hale, Sheb Wooley, Lew DeWitt (formerly of the Statler Brothers), Johnny Russell (from the Grand Ole Opry) and Gene Evans. Gene made his first of many visits to Memphis that year and became like family to us. He lived not too far away in Jackson, Tennessee, and came whenever he could. It was his close association with Jack Elam and director Burt Kennedy that ultimately got those two to Memphis in the mid–1990s.

After the '84 break-up, the *new* Memphis board managed to put on another show in '85. It was also at the Hyatt Regency. I think that was the year we had a trio of B Western leading ladies: Vernie Hillie, Beth Marion and Marion Shilling. They were all delightful! Others who attended that year (and these names sometimes blur together with guests from other years) included Sammy McKim, Jimmie Rogers (the younger son of Will), Fritz Feld, Will Hutchins, Billy Benedict, Junior Coghlan, Anne Jeffreys and Marie Windsor.

We did one more show at the Hyatt in '86 and I may be mixing up guests names from '85 when I mention performers such as Macdonald Carey, Guy Madison and Forrest Tucker. I remember Tucker was brought off the plane in a wheelchair when we met him at the airport. He could walk but was battling cancer at the time and just wanted to take it easy. When we got ready to take him to the hotel, he asked us to take him to a liquor store first! He used to say he'd spilled more liquor than most people had drunk; but he had eased up by this point and was content with some special brandy he wanted us to get. He usually had a glass of it with him most of the time but seemed completely sober.

That makes me think of the only other infamous guest we had, Elisha Cook, Jr. He was that great little character actor from *The Maltese Falcon*, *Shane* and so many more. We didn't know until he arrived in 1981 that he was a hopeless alcoholic who stayed drunk about 90 percent of the time he was there. He was so bad off we had to lock him in his room at one point. When the awards banquet came, we didn't even place him on the dais because we were afraid he'd fall off of it.

Bruce Furman, a nice young guy and film collector who later died in a traffic accident, led Cook up to the podium from the audience to get his award. Cook was drooling on himself when he approached the microphone. Emcee Pat Buttram took out a handkerchief and wiped Cook's chin for him.

That was one of the low points in our festival's history. Huntz Hall's ranting and ravings in the hotel lobby probably topped the list and right behind Cook's antics was the night former stuntman, bit actor and "comedian" Russ McCubbin sprung an off-color lounge act on us at the banquet in front of the likes of Audrey Meadows, Efrem Zimbalist, Jr., Elena Verdugo, Terry Moore, Edd Byrnes, Beverly Garland and others. It was in poor taste and we had no idea he was going to use that kind of material. Some of us had our faces in our hands and we apologized profusely to the women. On top of that, we had to evacuate the hotel during the meal because someone had set off the fire alarm with a big cigar. We had firemen with yellow slickers running hoses through the lobby while we stood out on the street!

The Hyatt underwent some remodeling in '87 and they broke their contract with us to do it. We again were faced with finding a new hotel and ultimately settled on what was then called the Memphis Hilton. With a couple of forays in-between to the Crowne Plaza and to the Hollywood Casino in Tunica, Mississippi, the Hilton is where we've spent the better part of 15 years. But it changed its name a few times after that! It was later known as the Memphis Airport Hotel, the Best Western, the Sheraton Four-Points and, most recently, the Holiday Inn Select.

That first year we were there provided us with several memorable moments from the awards banquet: Monte Montana throwing a rope around Janet Leigh; Eddie Dean singing as good or better than we'd heard him in films from 40 years earlier; Mexican singing star Tito Guizar (who'd co-starred in a couple of Roy Rogers films) showing us why he was so popular in his native country; and Jerry Van Dyke bringing the house down with his comedy act. He did this despite the fact that the air conditioning went out in the middle of his performance. He sweated up a storm (as did the audience!) but everyone was still howling.

I only have time to go into one other thing. The Memphis festival started out as a B Western and serial show. It remained that way for a number of years. But as similar shows sprung up in Charlotte, North Carolina; Knoxville, Tennessee; Asheville, North Carolina; Rochester, New York; Lone Pine, California; Sonora, California; Phoenix, Arizona; Williamsburg, Virginia and other locations, it became increasingly hard to justify our emphasis on these genres. Many of the stars from these films had passed away and the ones that were left were going to all of these other shows too. This made it difficult for us to attract fans because they now had several choices, some of them much closer to home, where to go.

There was disagreement within our own organization about what to do about this. It created rifts between some of us that ultimately led to a parting of the ways. Our organization had once boasted close to 30 board members! By the

Mr. and Mrs. Eddie Dean. He was a frequent guest at the Western conventions.

early 1990s those numbers had dwindled down to a handful. Those that were left agreed that we were going to have to broaden our appeal if we were to survive. We tried doing that for several years and brought in people who had nothing to do with B Westerns. Names like Stella Stevens, Kim Hunter, Bruce Gordon, Jeremy Slate, James MacArthur, Kevin McCarthy, Dwayne and Darryl Hickman, Aneta Corsaut, Betty Lynn and Johnny Sheffield come to mind. These names and others all fitted into the nostalgia mode, but didn't have much to do with our old Western themes. We probably lost some fans because of this but gained new ones.

The year 2002 marked 30 years since the first Memphis show had begun. We decided to round up as many guests who had worked in B Westerns as we could as a way of remembering where we came from. We thought we might win back a few of our old Western fans in the process. Although we had a great time and all the guests were wonderful, we didn't have the size audience we'd hoped for. We'd probably lost that B Western core long ago to the likes of Charlotte and the now-defunct Knoxville because so many of those die-hard fans lived closer to those cities than they did Memphis. With the economy being what it is and people getting older, there just isn't as much desire to travel long distances to see the few B Western personalities that remain.

We intend to come back in 2003 but we will not have a solid Western theme. We'll still show many of them and they'll always have a warm place in our hearts. The economic realities of the times dictate that we'll have to be somewhat more diversified if we're going to be able to continue. I'll close with a list of some other names I can think of who have been to previous Memphis conventions:

Buddy Ebsen, George Montgomery, Jeff Corey, Ben Cooper, Ben Johnson, Anne Francis, Ann Rutherford, Dale Robertson, Linda Stirling, Eleanor Stewart, Rex Reason, Robert Pine, Ed Nelson, Rick Jason, Fred Foy, William Windom, Debra Paget, Coleen Gray, Morgan Woodward, A.C. Lyles, Kenneth Tobey, Richard Anderson, Peggy Stewart, Pauline Moore, Walter Reed, Bob Terhune, Frankie Thomas, Jan Merlin, Joan Leslie, Spanky McFarland, Louise Currie, Troy Donahue and many, many more. Between 1972 and 2002 there were only a few years that no festival took place in Memphis. I think that may have been in 1974, '75 and '78. Each year there was an average of ten guests. If you put a pencil to it, that would probably come close to 300 guests in all that time!

★ ★ ★

Classic Images, *No. 160*
October, 1988

Cinecon 24

There are still stars in my eyes as I reflect upon a fabulous Cinecon 24.

I will carry the memory of it with me for many years, and I want to thank Dennis Atkinson, Jim Limbacher and all of the people who worked to make this one of the most successful of all Cinecons for the honors they bestowed upon me. And for the amount of work they put into it.

The Society for Cinephiles honored me with a plaque. That in itself was gratifying; but to be introduced by such pros as Leonard Maltin and Herb Graff, who said so many nice words about me, was a thing to remember.

Great silent films, many not seen for years, were beautifully accompanied by the likes of Bob Vaughn on the organ and Jon Mirsalis on the piano. Compelling early sound films were avidly devoured by the Cinephiles as they watched their favorites cavort on the screen.

Here are some of my own Cinecon thoughts and impressions ... I kept no notes and I'm doing this from memory. You may well be reintroduced to some Rubin-errs in this here literary masterpiece.

Left: The music of Jon Mirsalis will always be remembered. He sits down at the piano and, when the room darkens and the screen lights up, he takes control. He manipulates your emotions as the story unfolds in front of you. Jon's accompaniment is an integral part of the program. The movies would not be the same without him.

Pianist Robert Vaughn, one of the chief accompanists at the various silent screen convention presentations, who received the Cinephiles Award in 1981.

The Beloved Rogue, shown at a previous Cinecon, was once again offered to the Cinephiles. But what a difference! This was a 35mm print projected on the large screen at the Temple, accompanied on that mammoth organ by Bob Vaughn. What a thrill it was to see it again under such circumstances. It was a goose pimpler!

For the first time at a Cinecon, Cinephile Art Stephan accompanied one of the 16mm silent classics projected at the hotel screening room. It was a superlative job.

I gloried in seeing one of Will Rogers' silent features, *Jubilo*. In our continuous habit of watching for stars in bit parts in earlier films, we spotted Guinn "Big Boy" Williams as an onlooker in Will's big fight scene.

John McCabe's presentation on Jimmy Cagney was fascinating and effective. Marty Kearns and Herb Graff offered their always enjoyable film programs.

It was great seeing so many tried-and-true Cinephiles at Saginaw. I believe I had the distinction of being the only person present who has attended all 24 Cinecons. I even gave up my fiftieth high school class reunion two years ago to attend Cinecon 22.

Pioneer John C. Black of Shawano, Wisconsin, was there. He attended the first Cinecon in Indiana, Pennsylvania. He's the attorney who drafted the articles and bylaws for the Society of Cinephiles.

I enjoy going to the Cinecons. It is now my pleasure to finally be able to watch some movies instead of being anchored to a table in the dealer's room peddling my papers (*Classic Images*).

Classic Images, *No. 180*
June, 1990

Each Labor Day, as Cinecon Time approaches, I lapse into a lethargy of a sort and dream of events of past Cinecons and what could happen at the next Cinecon. This year we go to Hollywood for the fourth time. Each trip to the glamour city has been a highlight of the year for me. This will be the twenty-sixth outing for us.

For the uninitiated, let me tell you a little about Cinecon. Each year a group of film nuts, the Society for Cinephiles, meets in a different city over the Labor Day weekend. Instead of a festival or confab or convention ... it's a Cinecon.

What do we do?

We watch movies! We see rare classic films, many of which have not been viewed since their original release.

We have guest stars! In Hollywood, as in other cities, we get to meet top classic film personalities: stars, directors, authors, producers, animators, cameramen, etc. I have no idea which film bigwig will brighten up our Cinecon this year. Knowing *Entertainment Tonight*'s Leonard Maltin, who is chairman of the event, I am certain there will be enough filmmaking people to satisfy the most dedicated of our members.

In the past, we have had such guests as Myrna Loy, John McCabe, Colleen

Popular screen star Myrna Loy in 1976; she was presented with a Cinephile Award.

Moore, Johnny Hines, Patsy Ruth Miller, Cullen Landis, Roy E. Eitken, George O'Brien, Joe Franklin, Eleanor Powell, Jane Withers, Marian Nixon, Ben Lyons, Esther Ralston, T. Marvin Hatley, Hal Roach and Jackie Coogan, to name a few.

Each year there is also an Awards Banquet honoring guests or members.

We wheel and deal! There is always a sizable dealer's room in which the Cinephiles can buy, trade, or sell movie memorabilia, books, films, videotape or anything else related to the classic cinema.

We make friends! The Cinecon is round-up time for that tight-knit group of classic film devotees who are organized into the Society for Cinephiles. It is the time we again meet and greet the many friends made over the years. And we do make friends. When you can get together with people of like interest, who understand your thoughts and emotions of the classic screen, you have to become friendly. Since the first Cinecon at Indiana, Pennsylvania (Jimmy Stewart's home town), I have met many, many people with my cinema addiction with whom I can talk and would introduce as my friends.

If you have a love of the classic films ... you will be entranced by the Cinecon. You will see silent films presented in such a manner that you will be mesmerized and forget you are watching silent movies. They are screened as they were presented in the theaters years ago, with the proper musical accompaniment, offered by fine organist Bob Vaughn and versatile pianist Jon Mirsalis. In fact, we are often able to watch actual 35mm presentations in theaters accompanied by the giant organ originally installed in these old movie palaces.

Such presentations, appropriate background music and theatrical atmosphere enable you to completely enjoy the presentation of a vintage film.

In the past, the usual weekend-long programming consisted of 50 percent silent films and 50 percent early sound movies. We have watched many movies which were not available for television: classic features, short subjects, obscure movies and any other celluloid presentation which would satisfy a bunch of film freaks such as us.

Classic Images, *No. 193*
July 1991

The Great Cinecon Adventure

The above is how we advertised Cinecon 18, which my wife Lois and I sponsored in Davenport, Iowa, in 1982. It was a financially successful and satisfying Cinecon, marred by only a few unpleasant episodes. It pleased practically everyone and left a pleasant taste in the mouths of the Cinephiles.

But it was accomplished only with the help of a million people. You cannot run a convention without help. Even at the very first Cinecon at Indiana, Pennsylvania, which I detailed elsewhere, so many contributed efforts put it over.

The final profit figures could not have been realized without the support of the great people at Blackhawk Films. Lois and I had our hands full, but our friends from Blackhawk and the Davenport community helped pull us through. There were trials and tribulations of every nature!

Blackhawk's contribution to Cinecon 18 was immense! They all pitched in physically and financially. They insisted "No publicity!" Well, the old Blackhawk is gone, and I can now give them the credit they deserve.

The plans: Hold the Cinecon in the largest hotel in the city, the Blackhawk; have the usual program of great films which were almost always available to the Society for Cinephiles; give the women something to do while their husbands were enjoying the films and activities; have a 35mm Mary Pickford program in the local theater palace with its organ; present the annual Cinephile award posthumously to Kent Eastin; invite Buddy Rogers as guest star; and show the Cinephiles some good old Davenport hospitality.

Quality classic films poured in from George Eastman House, the American Film Institute, Bill Everson, Gordon Berkow, Marty Kearns, Kit Parker Films, Ron Hall, Dave Mruz, Jon Sonneborn's Reel Images, David Shepard, Richard Bann, Jack Oakman, Murray Glass' Glenn Photo Supply, Ed Hulse, Images Film Archive and probably others I do not recall.

The 35mm films came from the Mary Pickford Company (time has erased the actual name of the company from my mind) and the AFI. Larry Urbanski brought (and operated) his 35mm portable projector so we could screen that size in the hotel.

During our preparation, the Blackhawk people really pitched in! First, they arranged to obtain the 35mm Mary Pickford double feature to be held in the local theater. They also arranged for Buddy Rogers to make a personal appearance, to be honored, and to introduce the Pickford films. He cancelled out at the last minute when the Queen of England requested that he attend an affair in that country. He thought that was more important than a Cinecon. Wonder why?

The 35mm film shipped to us from the AFI arrived ... on cores! Who would have 35mm reels? Blackhawk would! Tom Voss, vice-president of the company, placed the 35mm film on reels. During the theater showing, the projection booth was situated way up on top of the peanut gallery in back of the theater. You needed an oxygen mask when you reached those heights.

Tom carried those monumentally heavy 35mm cans, containing the two features, up seven flights of stairs to the projection booth. It took more than one trip. When the show was completed, he carried them all the way back down. He also had arranged to get the two features from the Mary Pickford company. He handled the entire transaction, including the return of those heavy cans.

Lois planned a delightful trip for the women to Galena, Illinois, a town known for its many antique stores and historic Victorian homes. Blackhawk offered to sponsor a stern-wheeler riverboat drive. We assumed that only the wives would want to take this ride so we scheduled some delightful screenings for the same time. But, it didn't work that way! Everyone wanted to take the boat ride on the Mississippi! The screenings were practically deserted as a mob of Cinephiles climbed on the boat. Blackhawk paid for all these admissions, three or four times as many as originally anticipated.

An innovation: The Blackhawk people set up a hospitality table in the dealer's room with cookies and coffee. All the women involved in the Cinecon baked the cookies; the hotel was to supply the coffee. Unbeknownst to the Blackhawk people, as no financial arrangements had been made, the hotel charged 50 cents for every cup poured. The final unexpected bill was $800. The Cinephiles and the dealers are coffee drinkers!

Came time to arrange for the theater. The rental price was high, around $1500 if I remember correctly. The huge theater organ was being maintained by the local organ society, and they charged us $300 for its use. There was an additional $75 charge for the union projectionist. Before making the decision to rent the theater and the organ, I talked it over with Ted Ewing, president of Blackhawk, who said that he would guarantee up to $2000. So, I went ahead with the theater project. We charged all of two dollars and filled the theater, giving us a good profit.

How did we fill the theater? We threw it open to the public! The city newspaper, *The Quad City Times,* a division of Lee Enterprises, which is the parent company to *The Muscatine Journal,* publisher of *Classic Images,* permitted us to have three huge ads, almost one half-page each, in their daily newspaper ... no charge. We were able to really ballyhoo the Mary Pickford story with its Bob Vaughn theatrical organ accompaniment.

Allow me to digress a moment to relate a humorous incident in the theater. After the people started entering, someone reported to me that there was no toilet paper or towels in the rest rooms. I approached the manager. He said, "It wasn't in our arrangements. You are supposed to supply those." I argued, "It's too late now; people are coming into the theater."

He said, "Well, you're a pretty good guy, didn't give me a hassle. I'll put them in." He was big-hearted. I believe he returned the ones he had probably removed when we rented the theater.

We felt we must have liability insurance for the weekend. Upon contacting insurance agencies, I discovered it would be almost prohibitively high. I discussed this with Carl Lange, vice-president at Blackhawk, who was financial manager and controller for the firm. He arranged for us to get a rider on the Blackhawk liability insurance. We paid for it, but at a fraction of the cost if we had arranged it ourselves. More Blackhawk help! And, a good thing! We ruined a 35mm print from the AFI and had to replace it. The insurance covered the cost, which was more than the cost of the insurance.

We wanted a printed program for the Great Cinecon Adventure! And we did get a beautiful professionally printed program; and we also ended up with professionally printed tickets! This was because Ted and Carl approached, separately, two printing companies with which they did a substantial amount of business and persuaded them to print these for us ... no charge! Another Blackhawk care package for the Cinecon!

We wanted to get an organ for some of the hotel screenings. One of the local organ stores had a "theatrical sound" electric organ. The owners were friends of the Eastins and were persuaded that the publicity would be good for them. They let us use the organ ... no charge! Then, Carl had a fishing buddy friend, in the kitchen cabinet business, who had a large truck or two hanging around. Carl twisted his arm and, presto, the organ would be delivered to the hotel and returned to the music shop ... no charge. Another valuable Blackhawk assist!

Ted Ewing accompanied me in making hotel arrangements. He was the one who helped calm my ruffled feathers when the hotel took away one of our promised projection rooms in order to let a big shot in town have a wedding rehearsal dinner. The hotel said this was arranged a year ago, which we knew was a lie. They gave us a substitute room on another floor, spoiling our plan of having everything on the same floor.

This was the foundation for the Sam Rubin Cinecon Creed: Don't trust the hotels when you are making arrangements! Get it all in writing!

Gene Fernett, esteemed author and *Classic Images* contributor, attended Cinecon 18 and supervised a seminar on antique projectors. Herb Graff (of *New Yorker* magazine article fame) presented his usual top-quality humorous address at the annual banquet. The highlight, to me, was his comment that we must have raided the old people's home to fill the theater. He saw a plethora (he loves to use that word) of canes, walkers and wheelchairs. He did have a point; many senior citizens of the community took advantage of the opportunity to see Mary Pickford films in a theater once again.

What did we show? *Poor Little Rich Girl* and *My Best Girl*!

If you had the fortitude to read this far in the article you are now aware that it took many people to operate Cinecon 18. Who were all these people?

Here they are: From Blackhawk, president Ted Ewing and wife Jennifer; vice-president Tom Voss and wife Beverly; Carl Lange; and head of Eastin-Phelan Corp., Bob Evans and wife Mary Ellen. Bob also helped us by arranging to get the straw hats with which all Cinecon workers were identified. Jane Eastin and daughter Jill were also on the list of volunteers.

From the Davenport community, Jack Hummel, Erwin Peterson and Elmo Hutchison handled the 16mm projection; Elmer and Leah Levin, Betty Lund and

Charlotte Griggs worked at the registration desks, as did Jane Eastin and wives of the Blackhawk officers.

Davenport Mayor Chuck Pearl, a film bug and neighbor of the Rubins, gave the opening welcoming address at the annual banquet. Also helping from Davenport were Marty and Mary Kay Phelan. Marty was the financial expert during the heyday of Blackhawk with Kent Eastin before the company was sold to Lee Enterprises in the mid–'70s prior to the Cinephile award presentation, Marty spoke at the banquet, relating his experiences with Kent Eastin and Blackhawk and telling us what we already knew, what a fine man Kent was. Mrs. Kent Eastin (Jane) and daughter Jill were present to accept the posthumous honor. Oh yes, Sam Rubin was also given an award.

We filled our allotment of rooms at the Blackhawk hotel and arranged for a special room rate with another friend, Larry Satin, who co-owned the Clayton House Motel, a block from the Blackhawk Hotel. We filled many of the motel rooms. In gratitude, the motel provided a large bus which provided service from the two hotels to the scheduled tour of the Blackhawk Films building. No charge!

Blackhawk conducted this tour of its building, a huge, converted brewery, and also held a sale of film and associated products. Most of the Cinephiles went on this conducted tour through all the levels and hidden recesses of this ancient building.

It was here, unfortunately, that one of the blotches of the Cinecon occurred. While all of the Blackhawk people were busy guiding Cinephiles or managing the sales room, one of the conventioneers who had a video mail-order business slipped into an office and stole a Blackhawk mailing list. The Blackhawk people soon discovered the thief because, weeks later, after the incident, Ted Ewing's father-in-law, who was not interested in film, received a mailing from the company. His name, which had been on the Blackhawk list because of his connection, had been misspelled on that listing. The mailing piece from the other company was addressed exactly as it appeared on the Blackhawk labels. There were other similar incidents of people who also received the company's mailing, which could be connected to Blackhawk because of peculiarities in the addresses.

It is my understanding that Blackhawk contacted the company, but I am unaware of any action taken.

Also, during the sale, several films were stolen. The culprit removed the film from the box and left the empty containers. Because of the M.O., it is assumed that this sly operator was also the one who filched some film from the hotel dealer's room, again leaving empty cartons. These incidents cast a pall over the entire proceedings.

Upon reading the preceding hodgepodge of words, do you get an impression that we had a lot of help at Cinecon 18? We did! Lois Rubin slaved; the Blackhawk people and friends from Davenport sweated; and many Cinephiles donated their time and efforts to the cause! Everyone pitched in!

So, while this was going on, what did Sam Rubin do? He sat back, gave orders and told everyone else what to do.

It was a breeze!

Classic Images, *No 205*
July 1992

Cineventing!

What a great feeling to be attending the annual Columbus Cinevent.

Meeting so many of my old friends was a contrasting, soothing balm combined with an exciting time. I thoroughly enjoyed each and every conversation with these people, most of whom I have known for years.

Next to the annual Cinecon, the Cinevent is one of the oldest of the currently active gatherings for movie collectors.

The Cinevent was born years ago when Mr. and Mrs. Pterodactyl were chittering and chattering as they flew around wondering what piratical dinosaur had stolen those rare films from their aerie in the big prehistoric stone-econ. The next one will be the twentieth-fifth gathering for the group.

The convention is a prime example of what can be done when the same people cooperate and operate the meeting every year, namely, Art Graves, John Stingley and Steve Haynes, who have continued chairing and sharing the responsibilities so long that each knows his personal task and is able to function efficiently, avoiding the many pitfalls which face a novice in running a convention. They plan ahead!

Our congratulations to a great bunch of people: the three musketeers and all their helpers, including the projectionists, the pianists, the wives and everyone else who participated in the event. They all knew their tasks.

Back to the Cinevent! Part of the thrill to me was once again sitting at a dealer's (son Jay's) table and talking to the Cinephiles as they approached. Sitting directly across from me was editor Bob King and his lovely wife peddling *Classic Images* as I had done for so many years. Bob is doing a superlative job with the publication (as you all can see), and I glow with pleasure as each issue comes my way; I see the manner in which he is assembling and editing it. *Classic Images* should expand and grow like it never has before.

Bob has the help of those two wonderfully talented and efficient girls, Carol and Marlene. Carol has been given the opportunity to do more with her artistic talent than when I was at the helm. For example, she does the covers ... and they look good. She never had the chance when I was around. Selfish Sam wanted to do everything; I liked to play with the pictures, artwork and articles in assembling each issue.

Then ... there's Marlene ... of the nimble fingers, which fly over the computer keyboard, so much so she reminds me of a hummingbird whose wings beat so rapidly you can't see them. Marlene typed so fast I sometimes wondered if she had fingers; I couldn't see them. But, better than that, she does her work intelligently and, despite the speed, she spots and corrects misspelled words, grammatical errors and anything else that might aggravate the many scholars and critics who read *Classic Images*.

Ray Courts amazed me. He was the only dealer in a huge room completely surrounded by stacks and stacks of 16mm film. And he told me that he has warehouses full of film. There was more film in that room offered by one dealer than I've seen at any convention. He had hundreds of titles.

Which leads me to one of my unintelligent predictions. The conventions today offer more video cassettes than film. The price of film, except for some rare titles, is falling. Here's Sam Rubin's insane prediction: The price of used film will continue to fall as video continues its popularity. Then it will level off. As more dealers are forced to discontinue selling film, the classic reels will become more scarce and will be relegated to the category of being antiques. Then ... the prices will go up again! In about five or ten years, remind me of what I said and see how crazy I am.

I am fully aware of the controversy concerning the consecutive Cinecons held in California. It all comes down to the basic problem: We're not professionals! Some Cinephile in an area of the country, other than western, must volunteer to sponsor the convention. Because I have been unable to attend recent Cinecons, I do not know if any Easterner or Midwesterner has made that offer. I assume not. I am hoping the matter can be resolved Labor Day. If a sizable group of Cinephiles wish the Cinecon to be held in its area, someone must offer his, her or their city and indicate willingness to do the work. From the conversations I have heard, it is apparent that some would like a change, mostly because of the cost and the length of travel time for such a distance.

Cinecons are fun; Cinecons are a great experience! Let them continue to be so! At each Cinecon, a vote is taken as to where to meet the following year. Someone has to take the horn by the bull and volunteer to sponsor a Cinecon.

A few more comments about Cinevent. I met many of my old friends in Columbus. I hesitate trying to name them because of my faulty memory, and I would not want to miss anyone. Right now, I have trouble remembering my own name.

As I was sitting at Jay's table, I felt a lack of something important, a kind of vacuum. Something did not feel right, and I couldn't pinpoint the problem. And then, like a flash from the blue (or green or red), it came to me. I did not have a camera! There was no longer a need to take all those pictures for *Classic Images*. Frankly, it never even occurred to me to take a camera with me. Shows you how I have deteriorated.

That's one of the joys of retirement. It was always a hassle snapping pictures, making sure they would be developed in time for the next issue, planning the page of photos and, more important, trying to remember the names of everyone I photographed.

Classic Images

Film Convention Lament—1996

Here I sit, crying in my beer (root beer, that is; I don't like the taste of the other stuff) contemplating and lamenting the changes in our film conventions.

And they *have* changed! The dealer's rooms, generally, are larger; but the tables do not have quite the same merchandise on them as in the past. Formerly, many tables were loaded with film, mostly 8mm and 16mm. Now, you see little film and much video-related material. There are exceptions! Ray Courts, for example, in recent years has rented a separate room or suite and displays mountains of boxes containing film with desirable titles—so many more than he displayed in other years.

There are still scads of movie memorabilia, but the really old stuff has become scarce; and the prices have changed a bit. Someone squirted helium on the vintage lobbies, one-sheets and other movie display material, and the prices are headed skyward, towards the moon ... or beyond.

New and used film equipment has become more scarce as demand has withered. The second-hand stuff has become relatively inexpensive. You can go home with several used 16mm projectors for the price formerly paid for a new 8mm projector ... which "you can't hardly find no more."

The filmcon attendees have become younger. I attribute their interest in classics to the more frequent showing of vintage films on TV; they are learning to appreciate the "old flicks." Many of the older attendees are still around, but they *are* older. I have difficulty recognizing some of them (and remembering their names). Seems like they're all aging ... except for me, of course.

And the stars! Remember all the scintillating, glamorous, famous film personalities who attended our cons? We still host some of them; but, so many of the people we loved and revered and who did attend our conventions are no longer with us. Most of the ones who remain and come to visit with us bring their wrinkles with them. It is not easy for us to watch them on vintage films, see how young, vibrant and handsome they were; then emerge from the screening room to face these same people, now aged, almost unrecognizable, and witness the ravages of time.

It is difficult and downright embarrassing when one of the old stars comes up to you and introduces himself, or herself, "Hi, I'm...." You haven't recognized that person; you've only seen 100 of his or her movies. To paraphrase Walt Disney, "Honey, I shrunk your fans."

I won't soon forget the shock of seeing a slow-moving Douglas Fairbanks, Jr., at a Cinecon several years ago. This just couldn't be the dashing, hyperactive, evil Rupert of *The Prisoner of Zenda*. He's still handsome, in a much more mature way, and has maintained his sense of humor. This was proven by his remarks after watching one of his old, rare films which, unfortunately, was shown with foreign dialogue.

I have attended few of the conventions in recent years after my retirement, because of a combination of personal tragedies, the cost and, sorry to say, a loss of some interest. The only auctions I have witnessed were the professional memorabilia sales in which the older collectibles were sold at inflated prices, as has happened to other rare antiques and artifacts.

I miss the type of auction which was a feature of past Cinecons, wherein dealers and collectors attempted to get rid of items they were unable to sell earlier. I have a fond memory of such an auction when Gordy Berkow, sitting in the audience, bid on an item he, himself, had placed up for sale.

What is truly sad to me is each year at the Cinecon there were always two or three people waiting to present a bid for the right of sponsoring the next one. They were prepared with sales pitches to the Cinephiles, extolling the virtues of their cities and their facilities for such an event. It doesn't happen any more!

We still have the old reliable classic film events, which go on year after year, run by the same people in the same city. I'm referring to the Cinevent, the Cinefest, the Cinesation, Memphis Film Festival, Western Film Festival Knoxville Film Festival, and festivals for Tom Mix, Buck Jones, Roy Rogers and on and on. They are always exciting. You visit old friends and you meet new friends.

The films screened at these events have not changed as drastically as the rest of the hobby; but, nevertheless, they have changed. So many of our beloved classics are now shown on TV; so many more of them are available on video cassettes. Many titles are no longer considered "rare."

In the past, we went to the conventions to watch films unavailable for viewing elsewhere. This has not changed, but the selection and availability of the rare films has changed. We've seen most of them. In fact, we are now repeating many of them at the collectors' gatherings.

On the plus side, film libraries, aware that we are sincere film lovers, knowing we contribute to preservation, are liberal about permitting us to view their new acquisitions. It is always exciting to hear of the discovery of a rare classic in some foreign country or, in some cases, buried in barns or attics, or film libraries, or even covered with dirt in an old abandoned swimming pool. Or perhaps an avid collector has died, leaving behind his one-of-a-kind classic rarities, which he has hoarded and kept secret all these years.

Yes, the hobby has changed; the convention picture has changed; the equipment and formats have changed ... and the people have changed. Like the tools of the trade, the collecting pioneers are becoming more scarce and are mired in the aging process.

Unfortunately, so am I. The hair becomes more sparse, the stomach gets larger, the vision deteriorates and the mind begins to disappear.

I must go back to the beginning of this article and read it. I have forgotten what I am writing about.

Classic Images, *No. 311*
May 2001

Broodin' 'Bout Cinecon

As editor emeritus of that distinguished publication *Classic Images,* I was sitting in our home-office-sitting-room-bedroom-den-enlarged-clothes-closet with my emeritus butt parked on the emeritus chair with my emeritus feet placed on the emeritus desk. What was I doing? I was broodin'! Broodin' 'bout what? Broodin' 'bout Cinecon.

The 1999 convention of Cinephiles was a well-attended, delightful, A-1 Cinecon. Held in Glendale, California, it boasted a fine film program and top-of-the-line guest stars. The various Cinecon functions were aptly presented by Bob Birchard and an efficient, active committee.

So why was I brooding at this late date? I was brooding because of my less than plentiful contribution to that quality event. In fact, said contribution was practically non-existent. Whose fault was it? My fault!

I was to be honored as founder of the Society for Cinephiles on its 35th anniversary; therefore, at that time, I began to form a mental image of an acceptance speech.

"Let me forget the past," I muttered to myself. That past consisted of a number of appearances before an audience. On each occasion, when the time arrived for me to address the Cinephiles, my tongue turned into a cork screw, my gums became powder dry and my teeth suddenly loosened, almost to the point of falling out. I was only able to mutter a few words and anxiously seek a place to sit down out of the spotlight.

So there I was, preparing an acceptance speech, a short one, because I knew that those fabulous guest star honorees, basking in the adulation of their fans, would follow me and deliver a lengthy, fascinating barrage of words to keep the Cinephiles on the edge of their seats.

Therefore, I prepared a mini-acceptance speech, expecting to offer it during the proceedings. Unexpectedly, I was the very first one to be introduced. Dazed, my mind entered its customary stage of having everything vacuumed from it, leaving nothing but scattered thoughts. I was able to mumble a few choice words thanking the Cinephiles for the honor, completely forgetting my prepared acceptance speech.

So, I brooded! Then, like the proverbial flash of lightning, an inspirational thought entered my cranium. "Although it's some time since that fateful event, why not deliver my unheard message to the readers of this outstanding publication, *Classic Images,* now! Among them are many members of the Cinephiles!"

Now, to you few readers courageous and curious enough to struggle through thus far, please enter my time-reversal chamber and return with me to Glendale, Labor Day weekend 1999. I have just been introduced and have received the award. The entire audience is sitting there, mouths agape, awaiting my earth-shattering words.

★ ★ ★

Sam's Acceptance Speech

"President Bob, officers and members of the Cinephiles and honored guests. Thank you! Thank you for this highly valued and important award! Thank you for your continued interest in the Cinephiles and the classic screen! You have my deepest appreciation for extending this honor to me.

"I see many familiar faces among you; but I do miss the faces of those who have passed away. I am extremely lucky to still be here to enjoy this fine film program and to meet and greet the many friends I have made over the years since that first Cinecon in Indiana, Pennsylvania (Jimmy Stewart's home town), on Labor Day weekend 1965.

"I do not intend to take a lot of time and go into the details of that first Cinecon and its many fascinating features. I know you will be disappointed, but there are many talented and experienced speakers waiting to follow me.

"However, I must make this one observation of comparison. There were about 40 people attending that event which was held in the Holiday Inn. The previous night, I, my family and several local film buffs went to the Inn and plastered the high walls of the banquet room, top to bottom, with rare one-sheets, window posters, 11 × 14 lobby cards and 8 × 10 glossies, mostly from silent films!

"We left them there overnight, unguarded! Without apprehension we returned the following day and not a single one was missing. Questions: Could that happen today? Oh for the good ol' days!

"Once again, I want to extend my appreciation to you for it, this honor; I shall cherish it!"

★ ★ ★

Here's Sam again, back in Florida (the election capital of the world). Right now, that very same Cinephile award is proudly displayed on our television set in our family room. Anyone watching a TV program at our place must see this prestigious recognition.

Thanks, Cinephiles! I am no longer brooding!

The California Cinecons

The *Classic Images* Rubin Era came to an end! The Cinecons, sponsored by a group of dedicated California Cinephiles, continued to be held!

This group's efforts turned the annual affair into a mecca for film-starved Cinephiles as they looked forward to meeting their fellow film fans and some of the most revered actors still living in that hallowed Hollywood scene.

Writing about the California conventions is Mike Schlesinger, one of those dedicated Cinephiles. As we often hear on television, "in his own words," as he surveys the Hollywood Cinephile Cinecons....

The California Cinecon 26
By Mike Schlesinger

The 25th Anniversary Cinecon was held in Cleveland in 1989. And, as was sometimes the case, there was some doubt about where next year's event would be held. But a new face was in attendance: Randy Haberkamp, who ran the Silent Society in Los Angeles, and was ready to propose Hollywood for 1990. It had been a full decade since the last Cinecon in Tinseltown, and he had assembled a sizable staff, headed by UCLA archivist Jere Guldin, to help him pull it off. The attendees readily agreed to go back to SoCal.

Mike Schlesinger, active Cinephile.

Cinecon 26 was a huge success, although there was some grumbling about the Hollywood Roosevelt Hotel, which often seemed to be staffed by Mack Sennett's people, a situation that never really improved. (When Haberkamp noted that the very first Academy Awards ceremony was held there, veteran Cinephile Richard Roberts retorted, "Yeah—and they never came back!") Still, being in L.A. meant access to more stars and more archival prints (the Blossom Room was large enough to accommodate 35mm) than usual, and when Haberkamp, Guldin and Co. offered to do it again, there was unanimous approval. Cinecon 27 was equally marvelous, but two years was enough for Randy.

Then a ringer appeared. Ed Hulse, who had run outstanding Cinecons in New York in 1979 and 1985, announced that he was moving to L.A. and volunteered to take the helm for 1992. Several of the local folks, including Bob Birchard and myself, agreed to stay on; and so it was L.A. for a third year—though with so little opposition, a few of us began to wonder if we'd begun to plant roots in L.A. And with more stars and more 35mm archival prints than ever before, Cinecon was slowly transmogrifying from a convention into something resembling an actual film festival.

Cinecon 28 was another smash, and Hulse and his posse were readily endorsed for another term. However, Ed suffered some personal problems during this year, which caused him to step down and eventually move back to New York. Birchard and the others picked up the slack and the show proceeded smoothly. But by this time, people were enjoying L.A. too much, and though four years were more than enough for the group, no offers of other cities were forthcoming. Birchard agreed to take charge, and many of us hoped that Cinecon 30, being an anniversary as well as the fifth in a row in L.A., would be a kind of closure, and that we could get back on the road. Ironically, several veteran Cinecon attendees had begun drifting away, complaining that it had somehow been "hijacked" by the California people; however, none of them offered to take it off our hands!

But it was not to be; the thirtieth was just as excellent as the previous four. Noteworthy guests included Burgess Meredith and cinematographer John Alton. Although there were a few rumblings about Phoenix and Kansas City, no formal offers were tendered. Birchard and his group were exhausted, so Haberkamp and Guldin, having had three years to recoup, stepped in to helm Cinecon 31. It was another outstanding show, chiefly memorable for guest star Sylvia Sidney, who proved to be as hilariously cranky in real life as she was on-screen. Other guests that year included Ann Miller, Janet Leigh, Francis Lederer (at 97, the oldest guest to that time), Audrey Totter, Gloria Jean and directors Richard Fleischer and Robert Wise.

Cinecon 32 proved to be a groundbreaker: the first (and to date, only) one run by a woman. Margarita Lorenz volunteered to take the helm, with yours truly pitching in. Guests that year included Fay Wray, Virginia O'Brien, Karen Morley, Lois Collier, George Montgomery and directors Stanley Kramer, Abraham Polonsky and Edward Bernds. With such a lineup of celebrities and great films (almost entirely 35mm at this point), it was another triumph. But who would be willing to shoulder the responsibility now?

Then, during the business meeting, an entirely new face popped up. His name was Kevin Charbeneau, and he had assembled a team that was ready to take on

Cinecon 33. Moreover, he had an ambitious plan in mind: Cinecon would move to the Red Lion Inn in Glendale, with 35mm screenings in the historic Alex Theatre just down the street. Although there were some pockets of dissent about leaving Hollywood, most people agreed that seven years of the Roosevelt was enough, and they were ready to try something new.

The Red Lion was a modern, well-run facility that everyone loved; the trade-off was that the Alex was about eight blocks away. Though shuttles and busses were made available (and many attendees had cars), it often seemed that attendees would have to walk to make a show on time. Still, the opportunity to watch these rare films in a beautiful old movie palace was irresistible. Guests that year included Donald O'Connor, Ray Harryhausen, Kathryn Grayson, June Havoc, director Ronald Neame and Anne Jeffreys, among others.

However, there was one other guest there, and her presence made Cinecon 33 the most infamous of them all: Leni Riefenstahl. The notorious German filmmaker had made appearances in the U.S. before *sans* incident (notably the Telluride Film Festival), and Kevin Brownlow arranged for her appearance. Unfortunately, Charbeneau gave the "exclusive" to *The L.A. Times'* Kevin Thomas, not realizing that Thomas had had it in for Cinecon for some time. At the banquet (which that year was on Saturday rather than Sunday), he had Thomas seated next to Riefenstahl (whom, it was decided, should not sit on the dais), and they chatted all evening.

The next morning, this headline appeared in the times: "Nazi Filmmaker Honored in Glendale." In a completely fallacious and slanted article, Thomas described the Cinephiles as some sort of secret society that had gathered 1,000 strong (actual attendance at the banquet: just under 300) to honor Hitler's mistress. No mention was made of any of the other celebrities, nor did he acknowledge that Riefenstahl received no award and did not speak. (Despite their lengthy conversation, he couldn't offer a single quote. He also failed to acknowledge a panel discussion on the Blacklist; apparently seven Communists don't equal one Nazi.) The result was instantaneous: Some people who had received her warmly suddenly flip-flopped. (One person even demanded his money back when he was waiting in the autograph line!) They were only a handful, and had it ended there, it would have passed quietly. But the next day there appeared another *Times* article, in which various Jewish leaders were grilled about the situation and obligingly denounced Cinecon as "anti–Semitic," even as they admitted they'd never heard of the organization. (The fact that the Cinephiles' membership contains a considerable number of people who are Jewish, gay or both didn't seem to matter.)

Then came the business meeting Monday morning. Despite the required badge, several people who were obviously outside agitators and not attendees managed to slip in, and they turned the normally boring session into a screaming match. By the time things had calmed down (more than an hour later), Charbeneau was so shaken by this turn of events that he withdrew his offer to run Cinecon again. Birchard stepped in to take over the reins, and the rest of us joined in, too. However, the fallout continued for some time; a *Hollywood Reporter* staffer, with the scent of a Pulitzer in his nostrils, kept digging for months trying to find some dirt; he failed, of course. (Ironically, six months later, Riefenstahl appeared onstage at Radio City Music Hall to celebrate *Time* magazine's seventy-fifth anniversary, side by side with the likes of Mary Tyler Moore, Tom Cruise, Walter Cronkite and John

Glenn. There wasn't a peep of protest, not even from *The New York Post*.) The story eventually faded away, but still pops up every now and then, as when Riefenstahl turned 100, but it still left a lot of wounds, not all of which have healed—although Thomas has since made peace with Cinecon and is now one of its strongest supporters.

Since then, Cinecon has remained in the hands of Birchard and his team, including (but not limited to) Robert Nudleman, Danny Schwartz, Marvin Paige, Stan Taffel, Critt Davis, Jere and Sue Guldin, Ruth Silny and yours truly. Cinecons 34 and 35 remained in Glendale, with a non-stop flow of great guests and remarkable films. The year 1998 featured Sydney Chaplin, Jane Withers, and a reunion of the surviving members of the Watson family. Marsha Hunt and director Andre DeToth reunited for a screening of *None Shall Escape*, while Evelyn Keyes and Claire Trevor did likewise for a gorgeous color print of their 1943 Western *The Desperadoes*. Then 1999 offered Howard Keel (with an incredibly rare screening of *Annie Get Your Gun* that helped trigger its release on DVD), Ann Savage, Rhonda Fleming, Herbert Lom and a pair of legendary writers: 97-year-old Curt Siodmak and Frederica Sagor Maas—at 100, the oldest guest in Cinecon history.

As the new millennium arrived, change was again in the air. The Red Lion Inn was sold to Hilton, which had another client that wanted the hotel for Labor Day Weekend. So Cinecon returned to Hollywood—but things had changed. The Egyptian Theatre had been restored and reopened by the American Cinematheque, which was willing to let us have the theater for the entire weekend. Moreover, an enormous new complex was being built at the intersection of Hollywood and Highland, including a brand new Renaissance Hotel. It would not be finished in time for Cinecon 36, so back we went to the Roosevelt.

Because of the late change, the banquet facilities at the Roosevelt had already been booked, so it was decided to replace the banquet with an informal picnic in the Egyptian forecourt. This eliminated the head table and gave attendees a better opportunity to mingle with celebrity guests. The program was stellar, as always, with both the Mont Alto Orchestra and the Maria Newman String Quartet accompanying silents in addition to the usual pianists. Guests included Eddie Bracken, Jan Sterling, Barbara Hale and legendary cartoon voice artist June Foray.

In 2001, the Renaissance opened, and Hollywood finally had a first-class, luxurious hotel for its visitors. The picnic was such a success that it was repeated; guests included Jane Russell, Eddie Albert, Kevin Brownlow, director Joseph Newman and, in what proved to be his final public appearance, Budd Boetticher, who appeared with UCLA's print of the rarely shown *Seven Men from Now*. (Sadly, another intended guest, David Swift, fell ill and had to cancel; he too passed away shortly after.)

Cinecon 38 may have had the best film schedule yet, including 35mm prints of the seldom-seen *Bulldog Drummond Strikes Back*, *Journey's End* and *The Cohens & Kellys in Hollywood*. Guests included Robert Stack (with a camera-neg print of *Badlands of Dakota*, which he confessed he'd never seen; co-star Ann Rutherford presented him with his award), Mickey Rooney, Beverly Roberts producer Stanley Rubin and director Ken Annakin; the latter came with his 1948 comedy *Miranda*, and received his award from its star, Glynis Johns. The banquet returned, and was held in a splashy club in the Hollywood/Highland complex.

As of this writing, the planning of Cinecon 39 is well underway; those roots have long since set down in L.A., and with sister conventions in Syracuse and Columbus still going strong, there now doesn't seem to be any hurry to hit the road again. With the proper combination of theater and hotel now established, Birchard & Co. have had their workload reduced somewhat, and function as a smooth-running, well-oiled machine (though some of us might dispute that). How much longer can it run? As long as there are films that haven't been screened, guests that haven't been honored and Cinephiles willing to see them ... perhaps forever.

Join Us!

The Society for Cinephiles was originated for the advancement and appreciation of the vintage films; for the preservation of such films; and as a vehicle to enable the members to get together once a year for this fascinating display of rare films.

The history of the Cinephiles has been told many times in the past. However, I do want to mention two off-shoot conventions. Each year in early spring (March or April), the Syracuse Cinephiles, headed by Phil Serling, have their own Cinefest, patterned much after the Cinecon. Featured are rare films, guest stars and a dealer's room.

Each Memorial Day weekend, film addicts from Columbus, Ohio, sponsor their own Cinevent. This differs from the other two only in that there is no attempt to have guest stars. Instead, the capable group headed by Art Graves, John Stingley and Steven Haynes promotes a giant-size dealer's room which attracts hundreds of dealers and collectors to make this one of the most important of buying, selling and trading events.

I did not intend to go into such detail on past Cinecons when I first hefted my typewriter to the table and started poking the keys with my thumb. This is supposed to be a soliloquy ... so I will soliloquize.

Picture this: I am lying on a sofa and I am daydreaming! Gee, I can't wait for the Cinecon. It has been such a wonderland for me each year, especially those held in Hollywood. I'm looking forward to meeting and matching lies and experiences with all the Cinephiles again. I anticipate another round of studio visitations and wandering into the many movie memorabilia stores. I am wondering who the guest stars will be, speculating as to what films will be shown; and just immersing myself in a series of images and conjectures about our anticipated fourth visit to Hollywood.

Now that I am no longer editor of *Classic Images,* I wonder if any of the nuts living in Hollywood will approach me and prate about their particular obsessions as they have done in the past. I have been cornered by many eccentrics, and I have heard some weird stories.

I remember how I was impressed by the rooms at the Hollywood Roosevelt. Now that they have been remodeled, they must be a sight to behold. I hope, however, that they also changed the mattresses. They do wear out!

I am looking forward to seeing old friends again. Their names and faces are flashing through my mind right now. I will make no attempt to list them ... there are too many. And … these days, I forget … and I may omit someone and would pound my head against a projector for days.

I remember when my son Jay and I were on a tour of the various sets. I was introduced as Mr. Rubin, a publisher from back east and given the red carpet treatment, including sitting in the director's chair during the filming of a *McCloud* episode. When I returned home, my hat wouldn't fit. I was considering conducting an autograph session.

Alex Gordon took us on a tour of the 20th Century–Fox studio which I will never forget. I especially enjoyed the *Hello Dolly* set and meeting and talking to Eddie Albert in his studio trailer dressing room.

The Universal tour was delightful; I'll probably take it again. I understand it has been expanded. I don't think I'll forget the last one. I purchased a descriptive book at Universal's gift shop. I was astonished at the many errors such as a still of Jimmy Cagney as the Hunchback of Notre Dame from his *Man of a Thousand Faces* captioned "Lon Chaney as the Hunchback." I did not expect blunders like this at the studio where the original *Hunchback* was filmed.

Also at Universal, the Frankenstein Monster grabbed hold of me when I wasn't looking. I pleaded with him, but he removed my head.

I'm considering the possibility of going to Disneyland again. I've been there twice and to Disney World once. They were magnificent … both of them! I received my greatest thrill going through the prehistoric jungle with its animated dinosaurs at Epcot.

I am also thinking with great delight of our escorted tour by Dave Shepard through a studio in the company of those wonderful people Kent and Jane Eastin. And I'm thinking of Steve Barkett, a young man who attended the first Hollywood Cinecon with us. He screen-tested for a part in a movie … and landed the job. He later produced his own film, *Aftermath,* a sci-fi fantasy starring himself, his wife and son.

With sorrow, I am also dwelling on all the celebrities who have died since we enjoyed their company at the Cinecons. Names which come to mind as I daydream are Ed Finney, Johnny Hines, George O'Brien, Eleanor Powell, Colleen Moore, Roy E. Aitken, Beverly Bayne, Leatrice Joy, Bob Clampett, Jack Oakie, Richard Arlen, Sam Jaffe and so many more.

I could lie here all day and think of past Cinecons. But, right now, in my retirement, I tire easily from all this rest. So, I'll go to sleep and dream of Hollywood.

Meanwhile, if I have whetted your interest enough to want to go to a Cinecon with us, you must join the Society for Cinephiles. Come meet film buffs from all over the U.S., Canada, and some foreign countries.

7

Film Collectors and Collecting

Classic Images, *No. 162*
December 1988

Lo!

Lo, the poor apartment house movie collector!

If he is a serious classic film collector, the continued developing technological and other advancements in the field are slowly throttling him!

I know, I'm one of them! How many more of these luckless people are out there?

What can we do? What is the solution to this stifling situation other than moving to larger quarters?

I've got the bottle of cyanide sitting here beside my desk, alongside a recently honed knife, six bottles of sleeping pills and a fancy (not Yancy) derringer.

Listen to my tale of lo ... ah, er ... woe!

Back in the late 40s, when I was living in a spacious house, I blissfully discovered the wonderful world of classic film collecting when I became aware of the fact that many of my favorites of the silent screen were available on 8mm.

I ran to the store and purchased a screen and a projector. Then I sat down and ordered my first classic film, *The Lost World,* of course.

The insidious collecting bug had struck! I became an instant addict! As finances permitted, I ordered films right and left, accumulating quite a few.

Attendance at the Cinecons made me realize that a silent film is not a viable entity without musical accompaniment. So I purchased a reel-to-reel tape recorder and began accumulating sound tapes to accompany my silents. I was soon buying blank tapes in quantity as I attempted to make a track available for every one of my silents.

Naturally, I purchased a second tape recorder in order to copy tapes. I was swapping musical background tapes with other collectors.

Then, I discovered 16mm.

I really didn't discover it. I became aware of it. I was able to obtain a decent projector, which opened up the field to me. I began collecting 16mm, always aware of that common denominator of my other purchases ... "as finances permitted."

Of course, after obtaining so many 16mm titles, it behooved me to get another projector so that I could use true theater showmanship by not halting a show to stop and change reels. (I had already purchased a second 8mm projector for the same reason; then an 8mm sound projector as Standard 8 sound films became available.)

Ah, those were the good old carefree days of living in a house with a huge basement and practically limitless storage space.

So ... Super 8mm arrived. Not wishing to discard my standard 8mm projectors (they had become staunch, trusty old friends), I bought a Super 8 projector and then added a sound projector, as finances permitted.

I continued to accumulate film in all three sizes, as they became available, and when I could make some good buys, and (as usual) as finances permitted.

Video was a comparative newcomer when we moved to Davenport, Iowa, with my piles of film cans, reel-to-reel tape boxes, my editors (oh yes, I purchased them too), my splicers, my tape recorders, my six or seven projectors and the various and sundry which always accumulates with pack rats such as I.

We moved into a condo, no less, without a basement, without extensive storage space. We converted an entire bedroom into a crowded film room.

Classic Images was part of Blackhawk Films at the time. Being a member of the Blackhawk family, my eyes bulged at the shelf after shelf of used film, and my ears fluttered when I heard the price for which I, as an employee, could purchase these films. So I purchased and I purchased ... afp (as finances permitted).

The bulging film room became bulgier. *Now* to show a film, it was necessary to drag my equipment into the living room and set up a screen for my shows. This was difficult to assimilate as I had everything set up in the basement of my previous existence in good ol' Indiana, Pennsylvania.

Well, as the writers write, "The end was not yet in sight."

Video struck!

Naturally, as finances permitted, I acquired a VCR. Then the avalanche of video cassettes descended on me. I was in the fortunate (unfortunate?) position of being able to buy the darn things at a low price. I received review tapes from various companies which I was permitted to keep. I bought blank tapes in quantity for my own recording. The mountain of cassettes climbed as not a week went by that a new one (or more) was added to the collection. The stack of tapes approached the size of Mt. Fujiyama.

At present, as all collectors, I want to buy more equipment, more films, more tapes, but I have been stifled by the vast mountains that surround me as I sit here in my film bedroom contemplating my next move during these luxurious retirement days.

I think of all the other collectors who are probably in the same situation. I know of some; I have been to their apartments.

I have seen closets converted into projection rooms; I have seen films stacked in hallways; I have seen bathrooms crowded with film cans; I have seen tables made from film cans; I have seen living rooms succumb to the pressure of all the tape and film and equipment which cluttered it.

And I have seen many divorces in our collecting industry as a result of this vicious, insidious disease which has struck us.

So I sit amidst my piles of movie and video equipment and film cans and tape boxes and all the other flotsam, too numerous to mention, and I carefully weigh the advantages of each of the lethal weapons I have placed beside me.

Eureka! In a flash of mental inspiration the solution has arrived ... for myself and all the other afflicted apartment dwellers.

It's simple! Just go out and buy a room stretcher!

Classic Images
July 1988

My FBI Scare

There are many horror stories rampant in our collecting hobby about visits from the gentlemen of the FBI, checking for copyrighted films; and, if found, gently removing them from the possession of the collector.

We know now they were mostly looking for the guys who were actually illegally duping those films. But the people who owned questionable prints shivered and cowered in fear of such a visitation.

I doubt there is a collector who does not possess some print in 8mm or 16mm for which copyright ownership could be shaky. When film collecting began, we bought these films in complete ignorance that they were being made illegally. The studios didn't care about these old silent classics. Not until they realized that the old silents could be worth a lot of money did they forsake their outrageous policy of destroying negatives and started thinking about preserving the films which they now stated were our American Film Heritage,

Of course, we knew about that American Film Heritage long before the moguls created the facade of inventing the phrase. We could go into the subject for pages, but we have done so in the past. This article is about *my* visitation from the G-man.

I was in the furniture business when I initiated the *8mm Collector* 26 years ago. I published it, and its successor *Classic Film Collector*, for 16 years as a hobby in our location at Indiana, Pennsylvania, doing the work in my spare time.

I was ill and remained home one fine day when the telephone jangled and one of the girls from the store said, "Sam, there is a gentleman from the FBI here to see you. He wants to come down."

I swallowed my heart, which had leaped into my mouth, and told her to send him down. Now I was really sick. What could I do? I knew there were a few titles, acquired years before, which were certainly questionable. It was too late to hide them. Should I go down and kiss them goodbye? I was so fond of them.

I was hoping he would have an accident on the way to my house.

He arrived! This time the doorbell jangled. It was an excruciatingly painful sound! The FBI agent entered and introduced himself. As all good agents do, he showed me his identification card and got right down to business.

"Mr. Rubin, you have a subscriber in Australia who has not received his issues of *Classic Film Collector*. He claims he wrote and received no answer."

The girls later claimed they could hear my sigh of relief in the store, which was ten blocks away.

At that time *Classic Film Collector* had grown to the point that it became a burden to produce in my limited spare hours. Friends had taken over the circulation. They maintained two copies of the mailing list; one was kept in an office and one was kept at home in their trailer.

One night they brought the list from the office to their trailer home to update it. While the two lists were in the trailer, it caught fire and both lists were destroyed. We mailed the next issue from an old list I possessed. Details of the fire appeared in that issue, requesting people to update us on any changes and to inform us if they knew of anyone not receiving their issues.

Naturally we weren't able to contact all the new subscribers and apparently the Australian was one of the recent new comers whose name and address was lost. Also, we had received no letters from him.

I explained this to the agent, showing him a copy of the issue describing the fire. He thanked me, took the issue with him and left.

I collapsed!

That was the last I heard of it. We, of course, took care of the subscriber from Australia since we now had his address from the FBI agent.

I vowed never to have a fire again!

Classic Images, *No. 173*
November 1989

Home Theaters

Any bona fide movie collector worth his salt has but one ambition: to project his beloved films in a home theater, simulating as much as possible the atmosphere of a regular theater.

Construction of such a theater would be hampered only by space available and finances. Without those obstacles, there is no limit to the extent to which a collector would go in the development of his own home theater.

Because of this innate desire of all collectors, Sam Rubin included, living in an apartment is hell. But, I have covered that territory in the past.

Now I would like to talk about some of the home theaters I have seen and admired. My observations will be tainted by the hate and jealousy I feel for the owners of these home "palaces" for having the unmitigated gall to have such wonderful projection sites.

In my travels I have seen quite a few of these rooms which gave me the "greenies" and which caused me to (cliché) eat my heart out.

The first I remember was up in Wisconsin during the Baraboo Cinecon. John Schellkopf invited the Cinephiles to his home. He had a small (two or three rows of seats) theater in his basement. And what a theater!

John obtained his equipment from a theater that had closed. His projection booth, behind a huge glass window partition, contained two 35mm full-size projectors, plus facilities to use the smaller film size equipment. There was plenty of room for film storage ... and for movement in the projection room. The theater seats were plush! The CinemaScope screen stretched across the wall. Speakers were installed on each side of the screen, and a curtain which covered the screen was operated by remote control from the projection booth. Drool!

At the time, John had contact with a local 35mm film rental service and was able to bring current films home and watch them on that blasted beautiful screen in that aggravating, ulcer-causing home theater.

John has since moved to California, and I have often wondered if he took his miniature dream theater with him. Its memory remains with me.

★ ★ ★

Many Cinephiles have been to the home of Gordon Berkow, who is fast becoming the dean of film collectors.

Gordy, who has a tremendous library of film classics, can project them in his unique home theater. His projection booth has been made from a closet facing the screen. He has an unusual arrangement in which his projectors are stationed vertically, one higher than the other. He stoops to thread one; he goes up on tiptoes to thread the other.

Gordy has a large screen against the wall that will accommodate either a regular or widescreen picture. Rows of theater seats give one a feeling of authenticity. But, even if you don't get that feeling, the rarity of the film you are watching will counteract that.

★ ★ ★

For the most luxurious film watching of all, I must refer you to Paul Ecenia in Florida. This is the most recent home theater I have seen. Paul must have noticed me turning green with envy as I was extolling its beauty.

Paul doesn't worry about projection rooms. He projects from a table in his theater. He, like the others, has a large screen at the end of the room.

It is a giant room of necessity because down the length of each side are row upon row of cans of films on shelves. And, now the crowning touch, the most luxurious of all theater watching, professional or amateur: There are eight or nine huge, plush, permanent-type recliner contour chairs in front of the screen. You wiggle into the recliner and you are practically horizontal as, in complete relaxation, with your feet elevated, you watch the reels unwinding. Paul is only able to screen good movies in his theater. If he doesn't, his audience will really go to sleep.

Paul has built a miniature theater atmosphere for which he can be proud. The walls are completely covered with one-sheets, lobbies, 8 × 10s (many autographed) and even some stills of Paul and his lovely wife Rita, both of whom were in show business. Paul, as many of you know, sang on stage and was in several films.

That night I batted my head against the wall!

These weren't the only home theaters I have seen. There are many of them out in collector land. But the preceding three are examples of what can be done. I repeat ... all you need is the space and the money.

Classic Images, *No. 222*
December 1993

The Fanatics

Having been away from the collecting scene for some years now, and as I am a bit ignorant about the classic movie market, I am beginning to run short of ideas for this here column in this here publication which I used to call the "Illiterate Gazette" when I was editor. (Which it ain't any more; you can read and understand it. Bob King is doing a good job.)

Because the "ritin'" ideas are becoming more infrequent, when I do get one I immediately put my thoughts on paper before they leave me forever. This time, inspiration came while I was in the shower. So, if you see any drops of water, I didn't take the time to properly dry myself.

I have always loved the classic films; the people who acted in them; the people who made them; and the people who have collected those vintage treasures and the related memorabilia. I have talked to hundreds of classic buffs over the years (and throughout the world) and have found them, on the whole, to be a friendly, affable group of people.

However, as in all hobbies, we have our fanatics. I am thinking of the type of person who has mentally attached himself to a classic star, becomes infatuated with the actor or actress and can think of nothing else in this world. He or she eats, sleeps and dreams about his or her particular favorite movie personality.

So, let's talk about one of these fanatics. Let's call this lunatic Rainy Featherbrain, and let's call the star Stormy Weatherbrain.

To get to the crux of my ensuing remarks, suppose *Classic Images* runs a biographical piece about Weatherbrain, saying he was born on July 6th, 1888, at 4 A.M. Featherbrain becomes highly incensed and writes a letter. "How can you say he was born at 4 A.M. when everyone knows he was born at 3:59 A.M.?"

Ol' Rainy knows *all* there is to know about ol' Stormy, who has been deceased for a good 20 years. Rainy has thoroughly researched the life of Stormy. Now, being that Stormy is no longer with us, where did Rainy get his information? From books, magazine articles and such. Of course, Rainy has taken the information which appeared in these articles about his dearly beloved Weatherbrain as the absolute gospel.

If he had read those articles more carefully, he may have found discrepancies on the Stormy facts. (Ask George Katchmer about that!) Most of those artifacts, and the information contained within, were disseminated by press agents who all had vivid imaginations; and had no compunctions about inventing incidents involving the famous people they were representing. You will find distortion after distortion as these agents used their own craniums as reference books, mostly to give their employers exciting private lives.

A good case in point is the Tom Mix story. The famous film star was actually born in Pennsylvania, but many writers locate his birthplace as Texas. New writers to the field perpetuate this information because, in researching the star, they refer to past articles containing such misinformation.

Rainy, of course, is ignorant of this. If he read it in a book or magazine, it must be true. Stormy Weatherbrain was born at 3:59 A.M. ... for sure, he thinks. His only reference: those books or magazines containing the misinformation, which might have originated in the press agents' inventive minds.

Another angle: I have previously written of this, but I don't think it would hurt to refresh my memory (perhaps yours too). Let's suppose that Stormy is still alive and Rainy has obtained that dreamed-of, wonderful moment: an actual interview with his favorite person. Stormy tells him, "I was born at 3:59 A.M.!" A sigh of ecstasy is released from Rainy. At last he is vindicated, his information is correct; it came from the great man himself.

I say, in that famous, educated, high-toned language for which I am famous, "Baloney!" How could Stormy remember that? In fact, how can any of these aged stars remember what happened over 50 years ago, especially the exact moment of their birth? I can't ... and I'm over 50 years old. I know that because I have a calendar. Those people can't remember these things! So where do they get their information? From the same articles Rainy has read. In fact, to their immense delight, they have read these articles over and over again and have begun believing them ... and repeating that information as having actually happened. Many of the stars begin believing the hallucinations of their press agent.

As I said earlier, I love the classic films, the actors and actresses, the producers and directors ... and the collectors. I even love Rainy Featherbrain, because he, too, is infatuated with the early films. I don't like his fanaticism, his stubbornness and his unwillingness to believe that maybe some of these writers, and the stars themselves, could be mistaken.

And, speaking of fanatics, I cannot forget the wild glare in the eyes of the autograph seekers when they discover one of their favorite stars nearby; and I will always retain the memory of the wild-bull rush of these collectors as they descended upon that star in the hopes of pressuring him or her into signing an autograph.

I abhor it; I do not do it. I respect the privacy of the stars, even if some of them love that sort of thing!

Classic Images, *No. 228*
June 1994

The Film Collecting Metamorphosis

Here I sit amid gentle lapping waves in my retirement surf; they nibble at me like a swarm of minnows in an obscure pool in the forest. I stretch in utter contentment except for the many waves of thought which insidiously continue to enter my mind. And, you know what I am doing down here in my residence in Palm Harbor, Florida? ... I'm *thinking*!

Yes, I'm thinking ... and my mind reverts to the beginnings of our movie collecting hobby; how it has changed throughout the years; how it has undergone a complete aging process (like many of us); and how it is now a completely different animal than when we started.

No better proof can be shown than to tell you that I am typing this vital, important message on a word processor (my typewriter gave up the ghost), and I am earnestly struggling to learn how to use the blamed thing. This may be hopeless!

But, let's return to my thoughts on the metamorphosis of our collecting hobby. I, as many other collectors, started with standard 8mm. My first purchase was the five-reel version of *The Lost World*. The collecting bug's stinger pierced me, and I have been at it ever since. I remember that I paid $5 a reel for the feature, at that time a lot of money (for me). My memory also returns to that general time period when, on a trip to New York, I entered a shop, Abbe Films, which sold used 8mm and 16mm films and equipment.

I was able to buy 8mm features at $2 a reel. I recall seeing 16mm in the shop and regretting the fact that I was into 8mm only and felt I couldn't afford 16mm. Certain titles at $10 a reel appealed to me. One of them I almost purchased, even if I didn't have a projector: William Boyd in *His First Command*. I resisted, and to this day I'm sorry. However, I did load up on 8mm.

I recall the exhilarating scent of the acetate when I opened a shipment of my latest purchase of a new film subject—the most tantalizing odor in the world. Pure essence of everything enticing to my ears, nose, throat, brain and every other part of my being.

Then Super 8mm was introduced. We purists lauded the larger screen image but resented the loss of a portion of that image. Inasmuch as the picture was squared off from its rectangular shape, some of the picture (very little) had to be sacrificed for the larger projected image.

But, we were forced to accept it when Standard 8mm production lagged. We bought new equipment to accommodate the revolutionary Super 8mm.

When video began to make inroads into our hobby, we were determined never to switch. "Look at the loss in sharpness; look at the shrinking of size in the projected picture. The image on the screen does not even approximate that which is thrown from a projector."

We would never succumb to the unappetizing lure of the video image. (Look at the lines!) But reality attacked, and when we realized how much less expensive it was; when we realized that so many more of our beloved classics were available in this format than in any others; when we realized we could increase our collection a hundredfold with rare, otherwise unavailable titles, we did indeed succumb.

We sat back and watched the shrinking classic film market as fewer and fewer film prints were struck, due, of course, to inflation and its accompanying higher costs of raw materials, plus the diminishing demand because of the much higher prices manufacturers were forced to ask.

Many of us, of course, also collected 16mm, paying higher prices but getting a much larger and sharper image utilizing 16mm's ability towards the longer and brighter throw. Much of 16mm could be projected in a small theater.

As prices began to climb, the number of 16mm collectors also began to diminish. They also weakened in their firm resolve to resist the temptation of video's low comparative prices and the greater selectivity of titles. This was a greater sacrifice than that made by the 8mm collectors because of the superiority of the 16mm projected image over 8mm.

A paradox: Now, strangely enough, 16mm collectors who attend the various collector shows and conventions may be able to make some remarkable purchases. As the demand for 16mm went down and the dealers' 16mm inventory did not, many prices were also lowered.

One incidental factor: The influx of used 16mm prints which were made to be shown on long distance flight airplanes (now supplanted by video) brought comparatively new color features down to startling low prices. I have seen new recent vintage color 16mm features selling for as low as $25; prints for which we would have previously paid anywhere from three to six hundred dollars, possibly even more, according to title, length and quality.

There were, and are, classic film enthusiasts who collected 9.5mm and other oddball sizes. Some even collected 35mm, being able to purchase discarded theater prints for amazingly low prices, simply because there were comparatively fewer people who favored that size.

Invariably, most collectors had home theaters, attempting to emulate the pros. Some had plush seats, stereo sound, large screen, projection booths and everything else to simulate a theater atmosphere ... including popcorn! Video changed some of that!

Video discs arrived. Two major systems were introduced. One used a stylus, similar to a phonograph needle; the other used a laser beam. The "needle" system was short-lived; the laser system persisted and is still popular today. The disc offered a comparatively larger and sharper projected image.

Those who have read my ramblings and ravings at previous times know that I have covered most of this material in the past. However, I am merely trying to encapsulate all this in my own mind. I don't remember what I said in the past (I am too lazy to look it up) and, besides, I don't even know where I placed my head this morning! Also, there might be one or two of you who have not read my past inanities.

Frankly, having been out of it three or four years, I am not completely up-to-date on today's collector market. I have joined the Film Artifacts Society and have become a loyal and enthusiastic Artifact. (Our posthumous, honorary star member is Art Acord.)

But, I do know a few things. First of all, there is a completely new breed of collector. Today's collector can buy an unlimited number of attractive titles at amazingly low prices, as compared to what we had to "shell out" in the past. He can buy the old, revered classic, and he can buy recent movies.

I think the quantity and quality of the titles he collects is limited only by the amount of money he is willing, or able, to spend; and, the storage facilities he has to accommodate all the videocassettes (or discs). I know one collector who, at last count several years ago, had 14,000 titles in his collection.

Another factor: Anyone can dupe a tape! So, if you are unable to obtain an original cassette, someone will probably copy it for you. Some charge for this service, some may accept the price of a blank tape; a friend may do it as a favor.

As is true with film, you must have an original master for the best copies. If you copy and recopy from other copies, the quality weakens with each generation. So you can get good dupes and you can get bad dupes.

So, now we have thousands of collectors! Many kids can afford to start a collection; they can obtain almost everything on video. The shocker to many of us

The author with former screen star Colleen Moore, who starred in silent and sound features.

"oldtime" collectors is that the studios are actually releasing these tapes themselves—sometimes simultaneously with the actual release of a new film. In some cases, they are making more money from video sales than from the theater proceeds.

Some of these studios are the same ones which used to burn their old original material (thereby, of course, destroying much of our film heritage which everyone is talking about today). These same people suddenly realized that these old movies might be valuable. Then they started the huge (humongous?) campaign towards film preservation and actively pursued the "dupers" who had the temerity to copy some of those wonderful "treasures" which they previously discarded. (There I go on that old theme again!)

They did this shortly before the video era was born and even enlisted the aid of the FBI to track down these "film pirates." Today they would have to hire six or more armies of agents, because we're all duping now! However, they're not worrying too much about it. They are selling videos of their films themselves, working from original prints of negatives (making much better quality videos than the "pirates") and, in many cases, able to offer them at lower prices.

Now, young man or lady, if you have the desire to start collecting the classics, now is a good time. However, one thing you must keep in mind (much as we ancient collectors had to remember) there is always something new on the horizon. There is talk about changing to a higher definition video system, as used in European countries. That system has more dots, or lines, to a frame, thereby offering a sharper image. You will be able to project it onto a larger screen. There are videos already being shown in theaters overseas.

If the TV powers do decide to switch, we will once again have to buy new equipment (hardware and software) in order to utilize the new system.

For all you diehards who have Standard 8mm equipment, Super 8mm equipment, 16mm equipment, videocassette equipment, video disc equipment and any other equipment (including the defunct Betamax), you will now, according to my understanding, have to retrench once more and buy still additional equipment to handle the new video format.

For my last searching inquiry now, I can only paraphrase that famous Shakespearean movie personality, Bugs Bunny, "What's up *next*, Doc?"

Classic Images, *No. 161*
November 1988

But!

In my 26 years at the helm of *Classic Images*, I observed, and was part of, the mutating, ever-changing classic movie film collectors' field. Each time a new dimension was added to the sphere (new film size, new equipment, sound, color, etc.), it seemed there was yet another innovation on the horizon.

And, there was always a *but* when something new appeared.

With each addition or change, it became apparent that classic film collectors were forced to sacrifice some quality in their movies in order to include the innovation in their collection.

Just for the fun of it, I'm going to take a general look at this phenomenon without delving into specifics. And, in doing so, I am deliberately ignoring the less popular, odd, substandard sizes, such as 9.5mm and 20mm, which were short-lived and did not make as great an impact on the classic movie collectors' scene.

At first there was 35mm!

There weren't too many collectors out there then, and there was not much product available for the home. The equipment was bulky, impractical and dangerous, what with nitrate film and carbon arc projectors. A few portable projectors were developed for the traveling showmen, but they came later when there were light bulbs of sufficient brilliance.

And people didn't have the money to spend on such nonsense at the time.

There were some 35mm toy projectors available, accompanied by small reels of bits of film of the famous stars of the period. I even had one of these myself.

And then ... 16mm was introduced. The 35mm theater people said it would never work. When you reduced the size of the film by half, you would lower the quality of the projected image when blown up to theater size.

But!

16mm did work! The quality of the 16mm projected image was, perhaps, on a long throw, not quite as sharp as a 35mm enlargement of the same size, but it was satisfactory. It could easily be used in small theaters.

The 16mm equipment was not as bulky as the 35mm. The 16mm projector could be used more efficiently for travel shows, schools and, of course, in the home.

This was the infancy of the classic movie collector field. Even in the midst of the Depression, some movie fans were determined to own prints of some of their favorite movies, which were then obtainable on the market. Films were being offered for sale to educational institutions, road show people and even to the general public.

The motion picture industry was not worrying about collectors, copyrights and residuals at that time.

Then ... Standard 8mm was developed.

The 16mm collectors, who were growing in strength, ridiculed it. "This is a toy," they said. "You can't get a good, sharp image with any kind of long throw. How can you show to a large audience?"

But!

This was the real beginning of the classic film collectors' market, which rapidly expanded as thousands joined the field. Sure, you sacrificed picture quality and large audiences, but the price was right. The average person could afford this equipment and film, of which more and more was being made available to the general public. Some of the movie titles were authorized for resale, many not.

Some of the 16mm collectors began adding 8mm to their libraries because of the lower price and the availability of films they couldn't purchase on 16mm. They could own many more titles and show a decent projected picture to fairly large groups of people ... perhaps not theater-size audiences, but enough to satisfy their ambitions to be showmen, of putting on a theater-like program.

Then Super 8mm was developed!

Again collectors were up in arms. "Super 8mm is fine," they said. "You get more image on the same size film, and consequently, a larger picture on the screen. However, in order to accomplish this, the rectangular frame of the original picture must be squared off, and you lose part of the image. In some cases, even the titles are partially cropped. It won't work!"

But it did work! Super 8mm continued to be made and the market grew; more and more titles were offered in that size. Even though the purists felt they lost some of the image from a reproduced classic movie, collectors flocked to super 8mm.

Standard 8 was being phased out. Some sold their Standard 8 titles, but most retained the films and equipment; purchasing Super 8 equipment to handle the new size. Some manufacturers helped by developing projectors which handled both sizes, thus eliminating the need for a second projector.

Some collectors retained 16mm, standard 8mm and super 8mm.

Then, along came video.

"How can it work?" the purists asked. "You lose so much of the quality of the projected picture. It is not as sharp and you are restricted to the size of the television screen. You lose the thrill of putting on a show; setting up a screen, threading your projector, adding your musical accompaniment if necessary, and showing to a decent size audience." Then they added, "No one can tell us how long a videotaped image will last. Will I go back to my videotape in ten years and find the image gone? I would never buy it!"

Video took off! New collectors entered the fold, unaware of the difference in quality. Film collectors began accumulating video because there was a vast quantity of titles available which were unobtainable on film.

Sure, quality was sacrificed; but the cost of film skyrocketed as the cost of video plummeted. Unless you were well-heeled, it became practically prohibitive to buy movies on film of any size. 16mm was still the most expensive of the collector sizes, but the cost of Super 8 was approaching that of 16mm. Standard 8 had practically disappeared from the scene altogether as some major manufacturers stopped making Standard 8 stock. Simultaneously, the demand for Super 8 was also receding.

So, many of the diehards, who would never buy video, capitulated, their quality standards forgotten. Some sold off their film collection; some retained the film and added video, in its various forms, to their library.

I know collectors who have 16mm, Standard 8mm, Super 8mm, video disc and videotape in their collections, all requiring varied and diverse equipment.

Now we see that 8mm video is making inroads in the collectors market. Now collectors are saying, "It won't work. The image isn't as sharp as VHS; we'll have to buy new equipment. I can't see it taking the place of VHS or Beta [already fading]. It will never go!"

In comes DVD, chest stuck out and accompanied by ear-bursting fanfare. They acclaim, "*This is it!* Look how much you can get on one disc. Look at the quality! It is not necessary to rewind! There is no needle! This looks like the ultimate in video discs."

So, off we go to the video store and purchase more equipment! It is necessary to dig through your closets and drawers to find a shoehorn, which you use to deftly fit the new equipment into a space beside the old.

"It's great," you shout. "I didn't have to buy a new television set." The quality is just about as good as you can get on film, some better!

Classic Images, *No. 218*
August 1993

Classic Film Potpourri

I received a call from Harrison Fisk a few years back, which started me thinking (that's a rare occurrence).

Harry had just returned from a theater screening of Fairbanks' *The Mark of Zorro*. He was a bit distraught about the quality of the picture shown (most of us have better prints in our collections). I reported a similar experience with Flynn's *The Adventures of Robin Hood* in these pages last year. It appears that a terrible, substandard print of *Zorro* was shown in that theater. Some of the original scenes were missing, the projection was exceedingly poor, and the print shown had much to be desired. Harry's experience sounded like my *Adventures of Robin Hood* adventure. One (I'm the one) wonders where they get these terrible prints to show in a theater.

Harry also remarked that this theatrical version had a different ending than those he had seen in the past. I think I can throw some light on that subject.

I do not know if the practice still continues, but, in the past, the studios sometimes made two versions of their movies: one for domestic consumption and one for the European market. I can't answer why they did this, but I do know they did.

I once had a print of Chaplin's *The Circus* from Europe. The ending differed from the one distributed in the USA. Also, many of the scenes were dissimilar.

Harry also complained to me (as I, too, grumbled) of the inferior sound on the classics when shown on video and in the theater. So, I am vindicated somewhat. I am *not* the only one with this difficulty. I now have company in the aural department.

Harry and I also discussed the absence of news in the media of FBI raids on the homes of collectors. They are apparently not happening any more. Why should they? Practically everything is available on video cassettes now. Also, I am sure the studios are not prodding the officious gentlemen of the FBI (we used to call them G-men) to pursue those poor unfortunate collectors who had the temerity to possess one of the studio's films which was still under copyright.

I think another reason is that the copyright of so many of the classics have, by this time, expired, and the taint of illegality can no longer be associated with the possession of these films. And, anyways, what's the use? Most of the collectors are not buying the classics on film any more. Practically everything can be obtained in fine quality reproduction on videotape at a fraction of the cost of film.

Now they can enjoy the old classics in front of their television sets without the bother of hauling out heavy equipment, the annoyance of threading the film and the inconvenience of starting or stopping the film in case of interruption, such as a phone call (or a visit from the FBI). Besides, you don't even have to turn the lights out.

You *do* lose quality when you display your collection on video, but you do gain peace of mind, much convenience ... and you save mountains of money, even if the picture quality is not exactly up to your standards.

Our collecting world has changed ... but we still enjoy the *old* classics, most of them more than the majority of the modern movies.

Face it, Sam, you're getting *old* too!

Classic Images

Rarity or Quality?—1997

In recent years, my Classic Clinic column was devoted to reviewing silent film videos. After as much thinking of which I am capable, I have reached the conclusion that I was remiss in my evaluation of these movies; in trying to emulate the movie critics and the film award groups, by attaching unusual names to these various levels of opinion.

I had established a system of titles for lauding or criticizing each video screened. Those "clever" names were SAMMY, PG, TOL, SS and ECH: each were to describe my reaction to the movies viewed, much in the manner of the professional reviewers.

I hereby state I was wrong.

Here's why! A movie critic has his eye on storyline, acting, photography, direction, musical background and such. I, too, have been looking at these features and absent-mindedly forgetting that I am writing for *collectors*! Collectors *are* interested in all the above, but he or she needs to know, considering the age of the original films, the quality and the availability of each video.

Of course, quality is of prime importance; but is quality the only criterion for a collector in purchasing a video of an aged film? I say scarcity and availability is also a requisite in a collector's attempt to obtain some rare jewel which is difficult, or impossible, to obtain.

Example: Suppose someone discovers a complete print of *London After Midnight*. It had probably been stored in some remote hayloft, or bird's nest, or abandoned swimming pool, and no doubt suffered deterioration. He has the movie duplicated and is now in possession of a rare, highly desirable bit of film history, which will drive the Chaney fans bonkers. He has the only extant print of this collector's treasure.

"No one else has this," he exults with pride. "I am the only person in the world possessing this movie and no one else is going to get it!"

One of his dear friends, upon discovering its existence, begs the owner to let him make a video copy of the film. After hours of mental torture, the owner agrees with the admonishment, "Don't let anyone else copy it."

His very dear friend agrees and keeps his promise until a very dear friend of his, to whom he owes favors and who owes him a bundle of money, asks to have a copy of the video. He is quite reluctant, and agrees to have it done *if* no further copies are made.

Then that very dear friend also has a very dear friend who discovers he has the film. The cycle continues and results in a score of more videos of *London After Midnight*. Each owner shows the film, proclaiming, "*This* is the only print!"

The point I wish to make is, that each time the next generation of the video is duped, as with film, a bit of the quality disappears. This would make little difference to the average collector, if he can get his hands on a video of this supposedly "lost" movie.

He can't wait to screen it for unbelievers. *London After Midnight* is lost, they all think.

A Lon Chaney enthusiast wants to own *all* of Chaney's films. He would kill to get a print of *LAM*. Even if he is unable to obtain a quality video, a lesser quality will do until the day comes when, he hopes, he can locate a better print.

I think you have realized my vital message. Although quality is important, rarity is also a prime requisite.

Classic Images, *No. 166*
April 1989

Collecting Autographs

I have met and respected hundreds of movie collectors of films, tapes, lobbies, magazines, books, memorabilia and ... autographs. I am a collector of films and tape myself. This hobby helped initiate the old *8mm Collector* 26 years ago.

I do not collect autographs, but I can certainly understand the desire to collect them and the pride of ownership in having them.

I have several mental blocks which prevent me from collecting autographs myself. If I should meet a celebrity in my travels, I feel that I am invading that individual's privacy by approaching him, unsolicited, and asking for an autograph.

Secondly, ever since my days in the Army, I have heartily disliked standing in line. So, come convention time with the celebrities seated at a table signing autographs, it is abhorrent to me to get in that line so that the revered star can sign a picture or a magazine or a napkin, or whatever comes to hand.

I don't think I would get in line for an autograph even for bragging purposes to prove I saw a particular star.

I am repelled by the fanatic autograph collectors who will go to any length to get that signature. There is a wild look, a fanatical glare, a desperate drive in these people. I have witnessed it often. I have also seen the same look on shoppers in front of a store, waiting for the doors to open on a big sale in which tremendous unheard-of bargains have been offered. They are afraid there is only one of the particular sale item of their interest and are determined to be first in line to get it.

My advice: Don't get in front of such people. They won't see you! A buffalo stampede is mild in comparison.

Some years back, during the National Film Society Festival in Washington, D.C., I came in contact with some of these fanatic autograph collectors. Rita Hayworth was the guest star. The Society also honored some kook named Sam Rubin. (But none asked for *my* autograph.)

It was rumored that Gene Kelly was to make an appearance. Gene actually was coming to visit Rita Hayworth. However, he did not want the hassle of meeting the public; he wanted a reunion with Rita to renew old acquaintances.

Alice Becker (Levin), who was on the Society committee, was to escort me to the hospitality room to meet Rita and to have my picture (with the award) taken with her. (Of all the photos taken in that room that night, mine was the only one which did not come out.)

Alice told me that Gene was arriving at the rear of the hotel. She asked me to go with her to meet him and bring him up the back elevator.

Meanwhile, roving groups of autograph hunters were scrutinizing the entire hotel for possible entrances where Gene might appear. I saw heads poking around every corner.

Gene arrived at the rear entrance. Alice and I met him, as did several wild-eyed autograph seekers. As they approached, it was comparable to facing a band of hungry cannibals storming towards dinner.

Gene, gentleman that he is, signed his autograph; and then we went up to the hospitality room.

I have autographs, though I do not seek them. Those in my possession were given to me without requesting them. Some were sent in gratitude for an article written, in thanks for a favor, or at the request of a third party.

I can recall only three exceptions where I was involved with autograph-seeking and all were unpleasant, mostly my fault.

We went to see and hear Gene Krupa at a Pittsburgh supper club. Gene, wandering around between shows, sat down at our table and ordered a drink. We talked

Alice (Becker) Levin with the author as he is presented with the National Film Society Award at that group's convention in Washington, D.C.

a bit and my wife Sissy asked him if he would autograph something or other (probably a napkin or menu); she wanted to take it home for our daughter. Gene laughed, "Oh, c'mon, you want it for yourself." And she did. I vowed, "Never again."

Jane Withers attended one of our Hollywood Cinecons. I thought it a great idea to get her autograph for my daughter and my granddaughter. So, I took a couple of postcards (stupid me) and asked Jane to address them in her handwriting, giving her the addresses. Congenially, she did. Then I asked her to write a message on them. She did not get angry at this effrontery, but she was irritated and complained to the chairman who was nearby. Feeling about the size of a gnat's elbow, I apologized and withdrew, vowing, "Never again!"

The grand old lady of the cinema, Lillian Gish, attended a recent Cinecon in Minneapolis. Son Jay, who was unable to attend, asked me to have Lillian autograph an oil painting of her. Breaking my vow, I got into the autograph line.

I watched Lillian arrive and sit at the table. She appeared dazed. She was surrounded by her entourage. Her manager, I presume, was telling her, "Don't write too much, just sign your name." Dictating the actions of the star.

No doubt he was being solicitous of her and wanted to save her strength, but I felt like a brutish intruder when I put the painting in front of her for signature. A deep feeling of compassion and sorrow came over me, and I wished I were in two other places.

I vowed, "Never again!"

Classic Images, *No. 312*
June 2001

Book Review: A Silent Siren Song: The Aitken Brothers' Hollywood Odyssey—1905–1926

Now, here's a book! This one will be dear to my heart for many a day! It's the tale of the careers of the Aitken Brothers, who practically invented Hollywood. It details the ups and downs of the famous brothers' "odyssey," relating the many contacts they had with a large number of fabled actors and directors of the silent screen in its infancy.

The Aitkens, who produced, financed and owned the rights to the most famous of all screen epics, *The Birth of a Nation,* introduced so many actors to their adoring public. Authors Al P. Nelson and Mel R. Jones have much to tell about the people who thrilled the audience during the infancy of the movies and, in detailing the lives of Harry and Roy Aitken, they bring in the Society for Cinephiles and some of their members. Plus (and I quote) "one particular relationship," whose name I will reveal in a few paragraphs.

The prolific authors of this book detail the rise and fall of the two brothers: Harry, the enthusiastic, aggressive promoter who swarmed all over their problems with enthusiastic fervor, and Roy, more reserved, taciturn, who usually went along with any of Harry's ideas.

The Waukesha, Wisconsin, pair was involved with practically every facet of the early movie industry including early Nickelodeons and theaters, film exchanges and production, employing many of the actors and technicians of the day, many of whom became household names under the Aitken banner.

Five hundred fifty of these actors, with selected credits, are listed in this book. Here are a few I recognized: Mary Pickford, Douglas Fairbanks, Fatty Arbuckle, Charlie Chaplin, William S. Hart, Syd Chaplin, Chester Conklin, Dorothy Dalton, William Desmond, Minta Durfee, Louise Fazenda, Dorothy and Lillian Gish, Raymond Griffith, Edgar and Tom Kennedy, Harold Lloyd, Fred Mace, Hank Mann, Mae Marsh, Tully Marshall, Charles Murray, Owen Moore, Mabel Normand, Jack Perrin, Wallace Reid, Mack Sennett and his Keystone Cops, George Siegmann, Ford Sterling, Roy Stewart, Mack Swain, Blanche Sweet, Constance and Norma Talmadge, Conway Tearle, Ben Turpin, Henry B. Walthall, H.B. Warner, Kathlyn Williams and Clara Kimball Young. D.W. Griffith was the most famous of the directors filming for the Aitkens.

The authors tell us that the brothers founded various studios of the early screen era. Among them: Mutual, Reliance, Keystone, Majestic, Epoch, Triangle, Fine Arts, Kay Bee and Equity.

They entered the film business with little or no money and were in the same condition when their careers ended. With insight, the authors have delved into the working of the minds of the two Aitkens, detailing how they handled success and adversity, and faced their adversaries, the opposing (enemy?) studios headed by such giants of the film industry as Laemmle, Lasky, Goldwyn and Zukor.

Now comes the revelation, the most fascinating part of the book as far as I am concerned. The authors make mention of a relatively unknown film buff: He's the guy who's writing this here article! I quote:

> One particular relationship developed between Aitken and a Cinephile named Sam Rubin, who operated a furniture store in Indiana, Pennsylvania. Rubin published a mimeographed periodical for movie buffs known as the *8mm Collector.* Next it was re-titled the *Classic Film Collector,* and then it became *Classic Images.* Whatever the name over the masthead, the periodical contained the same content: news about silent and sound film companies, movie buffs and their collections, reminiscences of movie pioneers, and other film matters. Of course, Rubin asked Roy to write a lengthy recollection of his and his brother's long and distinguished movie career. After the article was published, Roy received a number of letters from old silent movie friends he had not heard from in years and he made new friends. It seemed that Cinephiles everywhere wanted to correspond with Roy Aitken of Waukesha, Wisconsin.

Perfectionist, which I am not, I must make one correction in the foregoing paragraphs: Our publication was never mimeographed. From day one it was always produced by the offset method of printing. The early issues may have looked like mimeographing; but the offset method was easier to use, was more versatile and more attractive ... and a lot let messy to work with.

I did not remember the Roy Aitken article which, the book mentions, appeared in the *8mm Collector;* and I could not find it in the index; so, I painstakingly (literally) searched back issues until I located it. That was a tough job!

In those early days of our publication, finances were limited. A flood of top-grade articles was pouring in. In order to print more of them without adding pages, I decided to reduce the type in order to make room for additional material in each issue. In those days, when I was much younger, I had no trouble reading the resultant tiny print. Things have changed. Now, with these aged eyes, those small letters are no longer in my visual range. I had to dig up my magnifying glass in order to make them legible.

I guess all the readers were younger then. The only complaint I remember receiving was from Stan Laurel who, upon receiving a copy of *8mm Collector,* swore and said that it was like reading stuff printed on the head of a pin. Today, I finally agreed with him!

Roy Aitken's article appeared in issue #9 of *Classic Images,* September 1964. It was titled *"Birth of a Nation* Story Coming!" It contained excerpts from letters Roy had sent to me. All of the letters were a kind of preamble to the publishing of that book.

The article contains interesting stuff. I've excerpted a couple of paragraphs for you to enjoy! This is Roy Aitken writing: "I recall the many times I would listen to a story [Griffith] wanted to produce for us. We were always pressing him for better material from his directors (you know, while he was in charge of our Fine Arts studio in Hollywood he had as many as eight or nine directors under him and was supervising each production) so probably the story was written by a more noted author and the price would be higher and he was selling us on the idea. But, he made you listen. No doubt he was producing it as he was telling it.

"They (we) were both young. Neither had any amount of cash with which to start the show. I knew how to operate a machine, having had considerable experience in Chicago the year before with our own Nickelodeons. My brother and I had one on State Street and four others scattered about town. Operators were scarce then. No one knew much of anything about this new business. So I had to learn and operate and hire and teach new material."

Roy talks about starting new Nickelodeons: "The experience of getting him [a cousin] started in no time at all (three or four days) was a strain, not only on me but his party and his family too. This would take too long to tell of because I want to go on and briefly speak of my cousins. I got them going and taught them how to operate and watch film. They told me later that when banana oil ran out, they used spit to hold the films together. When business was bad, they would go behind the theatre in the alley and shoot off a 22 caliber pistol, using blank cartridges."

Hope you enjoyed the above Aitken paragraphs as much as I did. I, of course, was fond of the section containing information about the Cinephiles. It names several people with whom I was familiar: Kent Eastin of Blackhawk Films, Mike Kornick, Clark Wilkinson and Raymond Plopper.

As you may have surmised, I thoroughly enjoyed this trip back to early film history. Being that the authors included me in it, I may even autograph it to myself.

A Silent Siren Song has an attractive dust cover with pictures of the Aitken brothers. It is printed by Cooper Square Press. It has 38 illustrations. For ordering, contact Rowman & Littlefield Publishing Group at 150 Fifth Ave., Suite 911, New York, NY 10011.

Classic Images, *No. 212*
February 1993

"Nitrate Won't Wait"

I think many of you know that Tony Slide, who did the book reviews for *Classic Images*, is from England. I first met him when the Cinephiles invaded that country some years ago.

It was one of the most delightful episodes in Cinephile history, as any of those who made the trip can attest. I was absolutely delighted with the quiet manners, the courtesy and the friendliness of the English People.

Tony was no exception. He invited my wife and me to lunch to an East Indian restaurant where I was introduced for the first time to food cooked with curry. I hope I was able to conceal that I disliked the taste of the stuff ... and still do.

Tony has been a perfect gentleman with each and every one of our contacts; quiet, unassuming ... a pleasure to be with ... and overwhelmingly knowledgeable.

Tony edited a classic movie buff publication in England called *The Silent Picture*. It was printed on glossy paper; a delight to behold and to read. It contained fascinating stories on the classic movie people.

You may have heard that Tony has come up with a book which makes my efforts look pitiful. He has written the definitive preservation book entitled *Nitrate Won't Wait*, subtitled *Film Preservation in the United States*.

Now, what about the book? It is intelligently written and is easy reading because Tony has a way with words.

I think the description of what this volume contains can best be served by giving you the titles of the chapters and letting you decide its worth for yourself in your quest for information on the preservation of our American Film Heritage.

The Introduction explains the nature of nitrate and why it "won't wait" and some of the history of the decomposition and other causes of nitrate's demise.

The first chapter, entitled "Early Years and the Museum of Modern Art," deals with the history of the volatile, vanishing nitrate: the whys and wherefores, and the introduction of preservation at the Museum of Modern Art in New York.

The second chapter deals with Newsreel Preservation and the National Archives, dwelling, in detail, on the attempts to preserve the massive amount of newsreel footage shot during the nitrate years. And "massive" is a mild description.

The Library of Congress is "taken on" in the third chapter. Here Tony explains how many of the films were preserved on paper strips instead of celluloid and the steps taken to transfer them to more durable material.

Chapter 4 gives us film collectors our due, indicating how collectors helped to save so many of our classic movies. Here you'll also see pictures of some of the well-known collectors, handsome as they are! He also has much to say about George Eastman House in this chapter.

Chapter 5, "The Fifties and Sixties," delves into the biographies and activities of the better-known archivists in the country. Here are names you have read before in this publication: Eileen Bowser, Richard Griffith and Kemp Niver, to name a few.

Tony goes on, in subsequent chapters, to deal with such items as the AFI "rescue list" of titles; preservation of specialized films; new areas and methods of preservation; a lengthy chapter on colorization; the problem of stock footage libraries; and goes on to tell of activities in preservation into the '90s, some of which you have read in previous columns of mine.

Tony goes into further detail by listing addresses of the various archives, the Commercial Libraries and the Video Libraries. He also describes what is happening overseas with preservation.

In short, Tony Slide covers the entire field of film preservation. If you are at all interested in the subject of saving our classic movies, I must revert to an old cliché (which I have strived to avoid!) ... Tony Slide's *Nitrate Won't Wait* is a "must." I unhesitatingly recommend it!

Tony's book, *Nitrate Won't Wait*, is printed by McFarland & Co., Inc. It is available from Classic Images' Books, Books, Books, PO Box 809, Muscatine, IA 52761.

Classic Images, *No. 210*
December 1992

Acetate Won't Wait!

With the help of Jan-Christopher Horak, Senior Curator of Film at George Eastman House, we are able to present this enlightening information about the film deterioration problem. I met Chris at a Hollywood Cinecon and he was not cooperative.

He did not prepare me for the mass of material which has been written on the subject and submitted to the Office of Preservation, National Endowment for the Humanities. Also, I was not prepared for some of the technical aspects of the multipage report. To one, as myself, having only a BA degree, I would need a Masters in science to understand some of the technical aspects.

I was muttering to myself until I got to the summaries, which covered the situation in a manner I, or anyone else, could understand. So, I am presenting those summaries exactly as submitted.

They do offer a surprising and somewhat horrifying aspect of the length of life of the so-called "safety" film in which we have had so much confidence while we were vilifying nitrate.

So, I'll re-title this column: "Nitrate Won't Wait ... Neither Will Acetate." Read and be dumbstruck ... or is struck dumb?

Take special note of the conclusions at the end of the article.

PROJECT SUMMARY

The project "Preservation of Safety Films" was a three-year research effort to explore the influence of the storage environment on the deterioration of the plastic supports of cellulose acetate photographic and cinematic films. Acetate degradation is becoming one of the most serious issues facing photographic and cinema archives, which catastrophic losses having already occurred, and many more threatening. Staggering costs of duplication are projected in order to preserve film materials. This project sought to measure the rate of deterioration in the major types of safety film, quantify the role of temperature, humidity and their interactions, and to improve preservation by putting forward recommendations for optimum storage conditions.

Because the principal underlying mechanism for degradation (acid-catalyzed hydrolysis) was reasonably well known, the project relied on accelerated aging experiments directed at practical considerations of storage, rather than chemical analysis of reaction products. The scope of the project was very large, involving well over 25,000 individual film samples, representing not only the major types of acetate films, but also cellulose nitrate and polyester films for comparison. A variety of physical, chemical and gelatin emulsion properties were measured. In many cases, it was possible to use a mathematical model known as the *Arreniuss Relationship* to predict the behavior of films under various storage conditions. This technique allowed the relative stability of films to be easily compared and made it possible to quantify the benefits of low temperature and low humidity storage.

KEY PROJECT RESULTS

1. All of the cellulosic film materials, including all the acetate safety films and at least one sample of cellulose nitrate, have the same general behavior with respect to deterioration—they can be expected to deteriorate at the same general rate if kept under similar storage conditions. Accepted beliefs that nitrate will necessarily degrade faster than acetate, and that among safety films, that diacetate is much worse than triacetate, are not supported by the data.

2. The age of materials and their storage history are the key determinants of their state of preservation, not the type of cellulosic plastic involved. Rather than speak of a nitrate problem or diacetate problem, we should consider them to be aspects of a larger cellulosic plastics problem which requires a coordinated overall preservation strategy.

3. Deterioration is strongly humidity dependent. The data showed that lowering the RH of the storage environment from 50 percent to 20 percent RH will prolong the life of the film from three to ten times, depending on the property measured. IPI has proposed to ANSI and ISO that the recommended RH range for storage of film be 20 to 30 percent.

4. Deterioration is also strongly temperature dependent. Lowering the storage temperature from 68 degrees F to 37 degrees F will increase the overall predicted life of film by a factor of ten times.

5. Optimum storage conditions for film include both low temperature and low humidity. Indications are that the benefits are additive, i.e., that the combination of low temperature and low RH is better than either alone.

6. Acetate film which has been properly processed and stored under reasonably benign conditions (20 degrees C, 50 percent RH) will likely remain in good condition for a century or more. Storage at higher temperatures and RH's will shorten its lifespan, sometimes dramatically. On the other hand, low temperature/low RH storage can greatly extend film life. Such conditions may be the only practical way to preserve the large amounts of film which are still usable but are already beginning to degrade.

7. Another significant influence on the course of degradation is the extent to which acidic degradation products are trapped in the film or allowed to escape. Because the reactions of deterioration are acid-catalyzed, once deterioration begins storage circumstances which trap acids in the film lead to faster overall rates of degradation.

Conclusions: Implications for Preservation Strategy

1. Because of past and present poor storage, increasing amounts of acetate safety film will deteriorate in cinema, microfilm and still photography collections during the next several decades. Much of this film will be lost because the will or resources necessary to duplicate it will not be available.

2. The historical progression of nitrate film deterioration over the previous 50 years approximately predicts the course of acetate degradation over the next 50 years. It is difficult to accurately estimate the overall percentage of film which will degrade over that time period. Just as considerable nitrate remains in good condition in 1991, much acetate film will still survive in 2041. Many individual collections, however, will experience near-total loss because they were composed of films of similar origin and storage history.

3. Preservation planning now should emphasize a balanced approach which combines duplication and improved storage. In the long term, improved storage is by far the most cost effective and satisfactory solution. While the lower the temperature the better, formidable capital costs, operating costs and handling difficulties are associated with cold storage. The most important new element in preservation planning is the realization that safety films are more sensitive to poor

storage than previously thought, requiring better conditions, careful monitoring and active collection management. This project has quantified the benefits and penalties associated with high and low temperatures and humidities.

4. With new understanding of the nature and magnitude of the safety film deterioration problem, many practical issues now present themselves for consideration and investigation. These include the lack of practical methods for surveying the condition of collections with respect to acetate degradation, many issues regarding the design and materials of enclosures and cans, and numerous questions about how to design and build improved storage vaults.

8

Dealers and Distributors

Here is a series of essays on companies that manufactured, sold or distributed classic home movies, then were forced out of the film business by video, rising costs of reproducing the vintage celluloid classics, supply and demand, or a myriad of other reasons.

There are also some question marks here. Having been retired for a decade and not participating in collector activities, I am not sure of the status of some of the companies. I do believe my information is correct.

Blackhawk Films

It was a memorable time in the life of this would-be editor! For 27 years I had assisted in the management of our Star Furniture Company, in Indiana, Pennsylvania, with active partners Jimmy Levine and my brother Irvin (Daidy). It was a family business founded when I got out of the Army in 1945 at the end of World War II; and I thoroughly detested it.

I hated: the long hours (we remained open six days a week); the constant haggling over price with potential customers; the stolen time which prevented me from being with my wife and kids; and the endless meetings with various and sundry organizations, which I had joined because "it was good for business to make these contacts." And I was a good member, attended meetings and was active doing my share of the functions of each group.

Tragedy hit! Within a short period my wife died, Daidy died, and Jimmy Levine died. A Rubin meeting was called for all the partners, seven of them, to decide what action was to be taken.

I was asked if I wanted to continue operating the furniture store. Because both my kids were now adults, I did not hesitate with my emphatic negative reply. So we decided to sell the Star Furniture Co.

Now, I must go back in time to explain why I am relating this crisis of mine before I get into the story of Blackhawk Films.

I had been interested in the motion pictures since I was a teenager. I had amassed a huge collection of films, magazines, photos and other related memorabilia. And, because I had a passion for journalism, I had established a news bulletin in practically every organization to which I belonged. In 1962 I had started the *8mm Collector*, a publication for film buffs. I had always secretly desired to make journalism my profession.

I worked on the *8mm Collector* in my spare time. It grew so rapidly that it was taking practically all of my after-store hours. The subsequent increase in circulation and apparent interest in the publication helped me decide to sell it, if I could arrange to go along with it as editor.

I had changed the name to *Classic Film Collector* because so many of the readers collected movie memorabilia and other film sizes than 8mm.

Friends of mine, the Gene Friedlines, ran a business called Contact, Inc., which handled printing and related functions. They agreed to manage the circulation of *CFC* for a percentage of the profits.

I just surprised you! Yes, I was making a profit, albeit very little because, as a classic movie enthusiast, I bartered advertising for films and collectibles! And these advertisers were peddling items I desired. This circulation arrangement was a giant relief for me! *Classic Film Collector* was jamming me into a corner, causing me to neglect my family, our business and my friends.

Therefore, I sold it to my first choice, Blackhawk Films, for one dollar ... *if*.... I went along as editor. It was not quite the bargain it appeared. The company agreed to fulfill all the outstanding subscriptions! This came to a tidy sum. Regardless, I would have probably paid *them* to complete the transaction, I so wanted it!

What did I know about Blackhawk Films? I had been dealing with the company for years. There were never any problems and I had nothing but praise and respect for their business methods. I was highly elated to be joining the firm.

The Blackhawk operation was located in Davenport, Iowa, in a two-story building which had formerly been a brewery, built around 1857. It is on the historic register. The two floors were located as any building's two floors ... straight up! However, this structure had three basements where the brewery's vats were located. In order to tour the Blackhawk property, you went up two and down three!

The lowest level consisted of two long brick arch-ceiling "caves." Apparently the barrels of beer were stored there. Blackhawk found the cool caves-tunnels to be an excellent safety film storage area.

The company owned, or had the rights to, more than 1,500 movies. Because they were quality reproductions of vintage classic films, these prints were popular to the many collectors and film buffs. Included in this group were almost 100 early D.W. Griffith productions, films of Charlie Chaplin, Douglas Fairbanks, Mary Pickford, Laurel and Hardy, Harold Lloyd and many more of stars of the early screen.

These films had been cleansed of all flaws that could be removed, and new negatives and master positives made when necessary. Sharp remade titles were added along with appropriate background musical accompaniment on some to make them the best quality available.

Blackhawk made quite a coup in obtaining the rights to Harold Lloyd features, which were on the top of practically every collector's want list and were otherwise impossible to obtain.

Kent Eastin and Marty Phelan owned the Eastin-Phelan Corporation, which distributed the popular Blackhawk films. Eastin had founded the company as Eastin Pictures in 1927. When Marty Phelan arrived in 1947, they divided responsibilities. Eastin managed the business with the general public; Phelan headed the commercial department, which sold the Blackhawk product to schools and libraries. He, with his business sense and aptitude, added much to the company's image.

Blackhawk was a mail order business, which at times sent out as many as 100,000 catalogs per month.

Kent Eastin was deeply interested in railroads and added railroad slides and movies to the Blackhawk catalogue. From the late '60s to the early '80s, color slides were an important part of the business. Slide sets covered a wide range of interests: railroading, travel locations around the world, flowers. insects, animals, art and events such as the Tournament of Roses parade and other annual celebrations.

In 1968, Eastin-Phelan purchased the black-and-white still collection owned by George Jessel. The collection contained 100,000 glossy photographs from movies dated 1915 to the mid–30s.

In the late 70s', film sales began to sag, initially because videotape came on the scene. In addition, Blackhawk was forced to raise prices of film due to a giant jump in raw film prices, which was caused by a huge increase in the cost of silver used in the manufacture of black-and-white film.

Eastin-Phelan sold the corporation to Lee Enterprises, a large media company with offices in Davenport.

In 1979, Kent Eastin retired. He died in April 1981.

After two years, Lee Enterprises sold Blackhawk to a trio of knowledgeable people.

Ted Ewing, who was well-qualified, became president of the new company. He graduated from an important managerial position at Sears. He knew the intricacies of sales, management and the functions of running a mail order business.

Vice-president Carl Lange continued with his familiar chores: in charge of operations, accounting, data processing and all office functions.

Vice-president Tom Voss, who began his career with the Eastin Pictures Co., was now an owner. He was now head of all the functions with which he was familiar, and had supervised for many years: film duplication and manufacturing.

An addition to the officers, David Shepard went along with the new company. David had taught at Penn State (my alma mater). His position had been assistant to Kent Eastin. He was placed in charge of film acquisitions and production.

In about 1976, Blackhawk Films began selling Betamax videotapes of Hollywood-made movies. Then the company set up its duplicating line to copy its films on to videotape.

With the advent of the new-ownership, Blackhawk opened video rental stores in the area. They were located in Muscatine, Iowa City, Bettendorf and Davenport, Iowa, and Geneseo and Rock Island, Illinois.

It was a good life during my stay in the Blackhawk building. My office remained there throughout all the turmoil which was to come. I was treated as part of the family by a group of wonderful, caring people.

I was there when Super 8mm film arrived. Many of the collectors graduated to this new format even if it meant the acquisition of a new projector and all the necessary equipment needed in order to utilize the new size.

The Blackhawk operation expanded to include this new film to its inventory. Its customers were advised of this in articles in *Classic Film Collector* and news items throughout the country and, of course, to their customers in the company's catalogue.

The company's relationship with its customers did not change! They were all treated fairly and liberally on sales and returns. They accepted all returns for any reason! There were no problems unless that rarity when one of them took advantage of the policy by frequently returning films, video and other merchandise for no good reason, obviously abusing the privilege. Such persons were cut off and notified that they would be denied returns for any reason.

I must tell you about an incident which happened during my early days after I had moved into the Blackhawk building. On the first floor was a substantial used film department with racks of used 8mm Blackhawk titles.

I browsed and discovered some titles I did not have in my collection. I asked one of the fellows who worked the department for the price of these desirable films. He quoted a price so low that I immediately put my eager hands on a cart which was in that part of the building.

I began piling cartons of 8mm films on the cart. I could not let these highly desired Blackhawk titles escape me while I was in the position to buy them at these terrific prices. One of the girls saw me doing this.

Shortly after, Carl Lange appeared. "What are you doing, Sam?"

"I'm selecting titles I wish to purchase." I told him the price I was quoted by one of the fellows, apparently the manager of the department.

Carl laughed, "You can't just go to the shelves and pick out film for yourself. You must go through the order department. Besides, the price you were quoted was our cost. You can't buy them at that price. Your price will be 15 percent off the retail price. You didn't know what you were doing."

I looked at Carl and I also laughed, "I knew what I was doing; *he* didn't know what *he* was doing!" Reluctantly I put the boxes back on the shelf. Later I selected some titles I wanted for my collection.

Prior to my days at Blackhawk, I had founded, with the assistance of film collector Tom Seller, the Society for Cinephiles, which met annually over the Labor Day weekend. You will find complete information on the group in another section of this book.

After my arrival in Davenport, I offered to sponsor that meeting, which we had named Cinecon, in that Iowa city on the Labor Day weekend of 1982. Blackhawk threw its entire staff into helping plan this event. The Cinecon was comprised of a yearly meeting and three days of screening rare classic movies; a huge separate room filled with tables of collectible films, videotapes, posters and movie memorabilia offered for sale by dealers and members; and a meeting for election of officers and to decide on the location of the Cinecon for the following year.

Blackhawk helped finance the '82 Cinecon and suggested new activities for the annual meeting.

Examples: a boat ride on the Mississippi and a program of 35mm (theater-size) classic movies in a local theater.

Because of the company's support, interest and participation, that particular Cinecon has always been considered as one of the best and most successful.

I was there when Super 8 arrived. Many collectors of Standard 8mm graduated to the new format at that time. That meant, for them, acquisition of a new projector and all the other necessary equipment in order to utilize the new film size. The Blackhawk catalogue, which all the collectors loved, was expanded to include Super 8. The catalogue, which was received by several thousand movie buffs and collectors, listed thousands of titles; it, too, grew with the new product.

After Super 8, along came video. Again, the company had to revise its inventory to include the new items and their accompanying side products. Film sales decreased as video sales increased.

Then video discs arrived. The two major systems were RCA Selectavision and Lazer Vision. The company felt it could not do justice to two video disc systems. The officers decided to stock and market the RCA product. Wrong choice! It was the Lazer system that took off! The RCA disc faded out of the picture and caused a drop in Blackhawk's profit picture—one of the reasons they decided to sell the company.

I liked what one of the newspapers said about Blackhawk: "Pioneer in preserving the legacy of the film industry's earliest achievements."

I talked to many film buffs and collectors attending the various conventions. Invariably they had only words of praise and respect for Blackhawk Films.

I had moved from Indiana, Pennsylvania, to Davenport, Iowa, into the Blackhawk Films building. The *Classic Images* operation was then shifted to *The Muscatine Journal*, Muscatine, Iowa, 30 miles away. I was permitted to maintain my editorial office in the Blackhawk building in Davenport.

Each month I would occupy that office for two weeks, writing and planning *Classic Images*. I would then go to Muscatine the latter part of each month for the physical production of the publication. It was thrilling for me to watch it come off the press—like a dream come true.

Blackhawk Films is no longer with us! Decades of diminishing interest of movies on film because of the video revolution and the consequent availability of the classic films on videotape, with greater selection and lower prices, had changed the entire movie collecting hobby. Because of the company's inability to compete with the studios, which were now releasing their classic movies on videotape, the officers decided to sell the company while it was in a profitable position. Everyone could cheaply reproduce film and video at a much lower price, and practically everyone did!

In 1985, Republic Pictures purchased Blackhawk and proceeded to move the operation to Hollywood. The grand old brewery building was vacated. Some months after the transaction, a railroad car jumped the tracks and banged into the unoccupied previous home of Blackhawk, causing considerable damage.

There is something ironic, or possibly poetic, in this incident occurring after the building had been vacated by the major purveyor of railroad pictures.

The damaged end of the building has been rebuilt and looks good.

I was still living in Davenport when the accident occurred. I decided to take a nostalgic trip to the location. In horror, I witnessed the amount of damage resulting from the incident.

I felt like crying!

I had 12 beautiful years in Davenport and Muscatine, Iowa. I was happy doing the work I loved. I was given carte blanche in the production of *Classic Images*. I was in a dream world!

My wife, Lois, also loved writing and was a great help to me. She wrote a monthly column on books, reading and writing about the movie industry.

Top: The Blackhawk Films building in Davenport, Iowa, a short time after the railroad car crashed into it. *Bottom:* Jay Rubin (left) and David Shephard (right) at David's house in Tyrone, Pennsylvania, before his stint with Blackhawk Films.

Lois and I met many wonderful people and lived in an atmosphere of friendship, peace and serenity.

Addenda

I am indebted to Tom Voss and Martin D. Phelan, former owners of Blackhawk films, for information included in this article.

I kept in touch with Tom, who was a gold mine of information, and contacted Marty in Florida. Marty sent me fascinating information on the birth of the firm. So much so that I decided, even if there are minor differences or contradictions from the details which I dredged out of my memories, to run his material as received. It makes for interesting reading.

The following is from Marty, who is so much more qualified to present facts on Blackhawk than I am:

> As you have said, in 1927 Kent started, under the name of Eastin Pictures Company. During high school, he had worked in theatres in Galesburg, Illinois, and became a film buff. Originally, he rented 16mm sound features to so-called "roadshowmen" who barnstormed very small towns putting on film shows in town squares, etc. They were paid by the merchants of the town to attract trade to their stores.
>
> As audio-visual education came on the scene, he added classroom film to his inventory and began to rent to elementary and high schools. This grew amazingly as, at the time, schools had no money with which to buy such films. Their only source was through rentals.
>
> Then World War II came along. Kent was commissioned in the Navy (a film bureau of some kind) and the business stagnated.
>
> After WWII, Kent reactivated the business and found it growing almost beyond control. He was then located in the Putnam Building, a downtown office building, on multiple floors. It was a mail order business in a totally unsuited location. Further, Kent found that his lack of business familiarity was limiting him.
>
> As for my association with the company, Kent and I had known each other during the war. Prewar, I had been a mail order executive with Montgomery Ward. As a Reserve Officer, I was called to immediate active duty and was assigned to the Rock Island Arsenal. Kent and his wife, Jane, were very hospitable to us as they were still living in Davenport (prior to his Navy duty).
>
> The war ended and I went back with big companies as a merchandise man (Butler Bros.—which controlled the Ben Franklin chain)
>
> One day the phone rang. It was Kent—who wanted to know whether I wanted out of the big town, big company field. His thought was that he loved film and the handling thereof. Also, he had some background in printing and advertising. But, he needed someone who knew mail order operations and business procedure. Would I take that responsibility?
>
> I was particularly desirous of getting out of big cities as we had a young son. I wanted him to grow up in a better environment than the big cities offered. So we agreed, and my wife and I moved to Davenport in July of 1947.
>
> Shortly thereafter (I've forgotten when) we changed the corporate name from Eastin Pictures Company to the Eastin—Phelan Corp. We broke our responsibilities as agreed. To improve our operations, we moved from the office building to a two-story rental structure.
>
> As the '50s developed, we found that our classroom rental business was deteriorating. Schools were buying their own films. In essence, we were paying taxes so

that schools could use tax money to eliminate such concerns as ours. Not a healthy situation.

During that time, the rights and/or the negatives to silent films could be bought for very little. They were considered to be "just old movies." Kent, as our resident film expert, came up with the thought that "the silent motion picture is an art form which will never be repeated" and that the acquisition of rights and copying materials could prove financially advantageous. We began acquiring without any clear plan as to how the stuff was to be used.

As our rental film business evaporated, our inventory of used and surplus prints grew. To sell these prints without affecting our basic company, we created Blackhawk Films. It was a trade name only—never a corporate structure. In effect, it was a clearing house. But, it had a catalogue issued regularly. To begin to get revenue from our silent film investment, we added 8mm and 16mm copies to Blackhawk's offerings.

Kent looked for a lab that could duplicate both 8mm and 16mm prints for us. Dave Bonine had just such a lab in Clive, Iowa. He had been doing commercial film printing but was eager to grow and willing to do some minor investing in equipment. Eventually his entire activity was limited to duplicating for us.

About this time, our lease expired on the rental building and we acquired the old brewery with which you are familiar. It was actually built around the turn of the century (before refrigeration) and the tunnels, which you remember, were kept to cool the beer. Being underground, they maintained a constant temperature. The tunnels, Kent thought, would be an ideal climate for our old negatives.

After some experimentation, Dave Bonine came up with a technique for duplicating. It involved a glycerin-based solution, which could be sprayed on the negative just as the frame was passing through the aperture of the copying machine. This so covered scratches that they became virtually invisible. He also developed a rubber roller control that permitted copying from materials with damaged sprocket holes. The result was that our prints were close to mint in quality.

The demand for 8mm prints grew. They were an alternative to TV. As there were reportedly in excess of 10,000,000 8mm projectors gathering dust in the closets of the USA, the ability to see one's own selection was not too inconvenient and was inexpensive.

Based on our experience with direct mail demand, we offered 8mm and 16mm prints to a few selected public libraries. To our great satisfaction, their circulation proved sizable.

To handle this new area, we created a separate corporate entity, calling it the Eastin-Phelan Distributing Corp. Bob Evans was brought aboard as sales vice-president of that division. His efforts were successful to the point that there were, in the late '60s, upward of 900 public libraries offering our materials. (Subsequently, Bill Gottlieb joined Bob in a sales capacity.)

During this same period, we discussed with Sears the possibility of a specialty catalogue, which would consist of Blackhawk's offerings. The orders resulting would be forwarded to us for filling. A percentage return would be paid to Sears. Sears agreed and the catalogue were issued.

One of the Sears buyers involved in that plan was a bright young man whose name was Ted Ewing. And Ted Ewing became sufficiently attracted to Blackhawk so that he came aboard.

It was at this time that we began discussions with Lee Enterprises (and with McGraw Hill and others) about the sale of the companies. We had reached retirement age. One of the sticking points in these discussions was the lack of successors for Kent and myself. Kent brought a young man from the American Film Institute as his backup. Ted Ewing was mine.

Lee had visions of using our companies as a base from which they could build distribution of whatever form of video disc/tape proved successful. However, they were basically a newspaper company. Growth possibilities in the newspaper field, though, became more rewarding, so that Lee really did not pursue their video strategy.

Classic Images, *No. 179*
May 1990

The Shepards

David and Kimberly Shepard's Film Preservation Associates has rescued the Blackhawk Films Collection from oblivion.

Not only have David and Kimberly rescued the collection, they are reviving it: improving an already quality product by adding material which had been removed by Blackhawk; by reprinting some of the material; and, in some cases, replacing the Blackhawk titles with the original titles.

Some of you purists who have been so happy with the Blackhawk product may have to consider ridding yourself of the print you own to replace it with the new improved print. After all, you will no longer have the best print available on some of the Blackhawk subjects.

In addition to bettering the films, the FPA is adding new titles which were in the Blackhawk Collection but never released; and, also re-releasing titles which the revered Davenport, Iowa, company had originally advertised and then removed from the market a short time later.

Examples of new titles being offered are: two silent feature classics, C.B. DeMille's 1915 *The Girl of the Golden West* with Mabel Van Buren, Theodore Roberts and House Peters; and the 110 minute, longer-at-24-fps British version of Pabst's *Pandora's Box* starring Louise Brooks, with English titles. Both prints will be struck from 35mm originals.

Among the new shorts is *All Teed Up* with Charley Chase. To be released in the fall will be another Chase, *Whispering Whoopee,* and *The Spanking Age,* an "Our Gang Comedy." Other yet-unreleased silent Chases and Our Gangs are among the Hal Roach titles to be offered in the future.

There will also be a new version of Laurel and Hardy's *Pack Up Your Troubles.* This release will be ten minutes longer than the original Blackhawk offering. The silent Chase, *Crazy Like a Fox,* which was originally available in 8mm only, will be processed in 16mm. A new silent short, also to be scheduled: *The Professional Patient* with Mr. and Mrs. Sidney Drew.

Among those titles which Blackhawk released near the end of its existence and which were never highly advertised are two "Our Gang Comedies": *The First 7 Years* and *Free Eats.*

Videotape rights for the Blackhawk products have been licensed to KING Video, which intends to bring out a large part of the library in video. Laserdisc video rights have been licensed to Image Entertainment, who have scheduled 25 releases from the Blackhawk collection during the next two years.

David has asked me to mention that and Blackhawk reproductions and restorations sold by anyone else are not only without consent from FPA, but are also taken, in many instances, from old 8mm and Super 8mm prints. These prints are poor indications of what the licensed videos taken from Blackhawk negatives and fine grains will look like.

Kino has already released Blackhawk's *Phantom of the Opera* and *The Spiders.*

What about these Shepards?

David and Kimberly are both alumni of Blackhawk Films, having worked there during the golden years in the 1970s. They are intelligent and knowledgeable and have a reverence for the classic films, especially the silents. Knowing the Blackhawk product, they are aware of the strengths and weaknesses of the Blackhawk prints and are in a position to do something about it.

I first met David Shepard a million years ago, before his Blackhawk period, when he was teaching at Penn State (my alma mater). He lived in a frame cabin in a wooded area in Spruce Creek, Pennsylvania, about ten miles from Tyrone, Pennsylvania. Ah, Tyrone, Pennsylvania! Tyrone had a paper mill which emitted an odor with effectiveness for miles around. Approaching Tyrone was like entering the fringe of a sauerkraut jungle.

David informs me that the odor did not reach Spruce Creek, one of the "prettiest places on earth." But I like to talk about it!

I drove up to Tyrone with my son Jay, approximately 75 miles away. Kevin Brownlow was visiting David at that time.

I have never met two people more dedicated to the preservation of the silent film than David Shepard and Kevin Brownlow. Whereas my former contacts had mostly been film enthusiasts who enjoyed the art of the silent films and the thrill of collecting them, these two were actually involved in preservation; David was with the American Film Institute Archives for five years and four years with Blackhawk Films, in charge of product development. And, of course, Kevin, who was to become world-renowned for his reconstruction of *Napoleon* and other early features and his BBC-TV series on Chaplin, Keaton and Lloyd.

One incident I will not forget is their demonstration of the inflammability of nitrate film. Kevin held a length of nitrate, touched a match to it and ... *poof,* it was gone!

Jay and I witnessed some film rarities on that visit. David kept his collection in a dirt floor fruit cellar, which was protected from moisture by a dehumidifier.

David, over the years, has collected a tremendous library of rare classic films. His collection is now divided among the UCLA Film Archives, the University of Southern California and the Wisconsin Center for Film and Theater Research. Some of the films were donated, and some were sold outright. Several hundred titles are simply on deposit. He, of course, has complete access to them.

After leaving Blackhawk, David went on to the Directors Guild of America in Hollywood. He was there for 11 years and then returned to teaching at the University of Southern California School of Cinema and Television. When Republic Pictures purchased Blackhawk and when it became apparent they had no intention of seriously distributing film, David approached the company to purchase the Blackhawk Film Library. He also purchased much of the Blackhawk equipment.

The Film Preservation Associates sells the Blackhawk product in 16mm only. However, it has sanctioned the release, to date, of some 20 Super 8mm prints through Roger Williams' Front Row Movies, PO Box 756, Slidell, LA 70459. Phone: 504-649-0707.

What about quality control? The FPA does its own printing, thus is able to control lighting, contrast, etc. With David's expertise and dedication, a superior product is practically guaranteed. Independent labs are used to develop the negatives and the positives.

The FPA plans to release approximately 50 Blackhawk titles quarterly. Two groups have already been offered earlier. A third group has recently been announced.

16mm is not dead! Many 16mm collectors have elected to go the cheaper, smaller screen video route. But the true 16mm collector is a rare breed. He will not quit; will not surrender his prized prints, and will not accept the inferior quality and size of the video picture.

Despite the acclamation of video collectors about the wonderful quality of the picture on the small screen, a side-by-side screening would easily demonstrate the difference.

My own feeling has always been that it's better to own a fair or poor print of a rare title than to not have it at all. Contrary to others' feeling, it's my creed, much to the disgust of my son, Jay, who is a perfectionist.

Consequently, many of us have video already, but as an adjunct, not a replacement for film. Quality-conscious collectors are not giving up their films; some of them are obtaining video titles which are not available on film. But, if a desired title can be purchased on 16mm, it takes priority over any other collector format.

Now ... how do you purchase these new-era Blackhawk prints?

FPA is the exclusive 16mm distributor of Laurel and Hardy comedies produced by Hal Roach Studios from 1926 to 1941. In addition to reviving the Blackhawk collection, the company also offers a specialized film printing and restoration service.

Do they have a catalogue? Sure!

To paraphrase the old cliché about the weather: David and Kimberly Shepard are not only talking about preservation, they are doing something about it!

Classic Images, *No. 164*
February 1989

A Trio of Distributors

When film collecting was in its infancy, a small group of people were prominent in making rare silent classics available in 8mm and 16mm. Three of them, who seemed to always come up with rare title, earnestly sought by collectors were John Griggs, William Donnachie and Ed Finney.

They were widely diverse individuals. Griggs, a former actor, was a flamboyant, bombastic, outgoing person. Donnachie was a dour, frugal Scot. Finney was friendly, subdued, and played an active role in Hollywood production. They had in common their efforts to bring rare films to the collectors.

John Griggs was the first to issue Doug Fairbanks' *The Thief of Bagdad* to the home market. Its success prompted him to bring out other titles. He was a first-class showman and businessman. He produced a quality product and developed a substantial following among the collectors.

I was headed for a business trip to New York. John lived across the river in New Jersey. He invited me out, and I took an extra day to visit with him.

A scene I will never forget: When I arrived, John had three teenagers (around 13 years old) stand up in formation and salute me. One of the kids was Leonard Maltin, whose name you all know.

John welcomed me into his home; screened rare silent films with outstanding organ accompaniment; had me to dinner where I met his rarity of a fine wife, Mary; and took me to New York while he recorded a radio commercial. He also took me to the famous Players Club (or Masquers, I get the two confused), personally escorted me through the rooms of the famous building and introduced me to some celebrities, one of whom was the original "Vagabond King," Dennis King. Indelibly impressed on my mind was the viewing of death masks of famous actors.

What a wonderful person ... and what a personality. John Griggs reminded me so much of his favorite actor, John Barrymore.

Our relationship continued until his death. His film business, Griggs Moviedrome, was taken over by Robert E. Lee, who still runs the firm, and his famous Essex Film Club. He screens classic films for the members in a small theater in the rear of his home. He puts on a great show!

★ ★ ★

The story differs with Bill Donnachie. Bill was difficult to get to know. He issued highly desirable rare silents with such titles as *Ben Hur, The Three Musketeers, Robin Hood, The Kiss* and many others. They were, mostly, still under copyright, and he was taking a risk.

He lived near Philadelphia. My wife and I were taking a trip in that direction, and I decided to pay him a visit. I couldn't find his place. Later I wrote to him, and his answer was to the effect that he could see no reason for us to get together.

So there!

Despite that, our relationship continued on a pleasant, but distant, basis.

I do not remember ever talking to him on the phone, except the time he called me in an extreme state of anxiety. He had been raided by the FBI and wanted to get a good attorney. I recommended the few I knew in the area.

He was quite agitated and fearful, and the shock of the visitation affected him tremendously. In fact, it was instrumental in killing him. He died of a heart attack.

★ ★ ★

Many of us knew and admired Ed Finney.

Ed Finney was the producer who introduced Tex Ritter to the movie world. But we Cinephiles knew Ed Finney as a knowledgeable distributor who was on the same wavelength with other film collectors.

Much of the rare material on the market is a result of the efforts of this man, especially the films of Johnny Hines, who was Ed's personal friend.

I remember Ed best from our first Hollywood Cinecon, Labor Day weekend, 1968. Another man, a minor actor in the field, who claimed Fay Wray as his godmother, had agreed to sponsor the Cinecon. He did little or nothing, and Ed took over with the assistance of Cal Dobbins and Tom Seller.

And how Ed took over! That was a Cinecon to remember! What with studio trips, Grauman's Chinese, tours of the stars' homes, visits to the book stores and the many other attractions Hollywood had to offer, Ed brought a host of stars to that Cinecon, the likes of which we have not seen since. Most of them have since died. In attendance were Johnny Hines, Clair Windsor, Minta Durfee Arbuckle,

Edith Thornton Hutchison, Betty Bronson, Donald Reed, Mary MacLaren, Gertrude Astor, Spencer Gordon Bennet, Johnny Roth, Leo G. Carroll, Babe London, Gaylord Carter, Arthur Miller and Lita Grey Chaplin.

Ed did something which I will not forget. He escorted my wife Sissy and me to the Magic Castle, an experience of a lifetime.

Ed was one of the giants of Hollywood ... and of the collecting field. He is missed! I know he would have been extremely happy at the thought of VCRs and video cassettes because then he would be able to get more of his beloved classics into the hands of the people who appreciated them.

All three of these men are gone, but their impact on the classic film collecting field continues. Their rare prints are still around. They are now rarer than ever, and command high prices.

Classic Images, *No. 33*
January 1990

More Distributors

HARTNEY'S MILESTONE FILMS

No longer in business, Hartney Arthur's Milestone Films holds a tender spot in the hearts of most collectors, for its activities in its short tenure (about a decade) in the 8mm film scene. Hartney's Milestone Films is *not* to be confused with the Milestone Films operating today.

Hartney Arthur began the company in Connecticut, issuing a few titles at a time. But, what titles! He produced material collectors could not purchase elsewhere. He released titles which titillated their souls; titles most collectors believed to be still under copyright and unobtainable. Perhaps they were still under copyright, but issue them Hartney Arthur did! We conjecture that he made some sort of arrangements for reproductive rights.

Not only did he issue these rare movies to collectors, he produced a quality product competitively priced. He kept careful watch over lab production and made sure that the best possible prints were obtained from the preprint material available to him.

Here are a few of the titles: *Faust,* Fatty Arbuckle's *Leap Year, White Gold, The Last Outlaw, Paths to Paradise, Smouldering Fires, The Vanishing American, Salvation Hunters, Straight Shooting, Joyless Street, Waxworks, White Hell of Pitz Palu, The Night Club, The Most Dangerous Game* and *That Certain Thing.*

Hartney Arthur was a gentleman and a good businessman. No legitimate complaint went unanswered. He established a reputation for his quality product, speedy service and exemplary business methods.

It was a sad day when the burgeoning video giant forced Hartney to close up shop.

We miss him!

Select Films

Most collectors are familiar with Select Films, which operated a film rental library and a sales room from its retail location in New York City for many years. The company sold films from many distributors, including the luscious titles from Griggs Moviedrome.

However, in the 8mm field, Select exclusively had the Regent Films with which many collectors were familiar. In the library were hundreds of shorts from the stalwarts of the silent film comedy ranks and such features as *Beyond the Border* and C.B. DeMille's productions of *Risky Business, Made to Love, Eve's Leaves* and *Sunny Side Up*.

The last I heard (several years ago), the company is still operating from the same location ... but, it's all video. To my knowledge, the Regent titles have not been converted to video.

Select Films, another victim of the big change!

Film Classic Exchange

An integral part of the classic film collecting scene for many years, Film Classic Exchange, headed by Charles Tarbox, continued operating until his death some few years back. His business, like all the others, dwindled, but he remained at it and literally "died in the saddle."

I knew Charles (never Charlie to his face) for many years. He was quite unpredictable. He had a strange philosophy towards a quality product. His standards varied. Some of his material was excellent, some good, some unacceptable. You always said a little prayer before opening a package from Film Classic Exchange.

If you received an unsatisfactory product from Tarbox and requested remedial action and talked to him like a gentleman, you would probably have your problem corrected. If you did not take the gentlemanly route and uttered a few mild blasphemies, your problem would *not* be corrected ... ever. Charles could be stubborn, not reacting to threats or promises of violence, or any other action.

Despite this, Film Classic Exchange had a considerable business with collectors during its many years of operation, chiefly because of the rarities of the titles which Tarbox issued.

Located in Hollywood, Tarbox managed to obtain exceedingly rare early silent movies including films of Mary Pickford, Keystone, Broncho Billy, early Harold Lloyd ... and so much more. Some of his features included *Gypsy Blood, The Man from Beyond, Primrose Path, Last Days of Pompeii, Tillie Wakes Up, Robinson Crusoe, Spartacus, Six Feet Four, Shadows, Legend of Sleepy Hollow, Wolf Tracks, Back Fire* and *Riders of the Law*.

Following the death of Charles Tarbox, JEF Films purchased the inventory of the company with the intention of weeding out the lesser quality material and reissuing the better quality titles.

The industry lost one of its pioneers at the death of Charles Tarbox.

Nick Florentino

Nick Florentino made a valiant effort to enter the classic film field. He was not with it for a long period of time, but during his short regime as a vintage film distributor, he manufactured a quality product at a competitive price and delivered what he advertised.

His titles were not exactly blockbusters, but they were rare items relished by the silent movie collectors. Some of them were *The Forbidden City, The White Sin, The Mad Whirl, Hawk of the Hills, Dangerous Hours* and *The Phantom Flyer* and such shorts as *Man from Tia Juana, Feast of Ishtar, Making of Broncho Billy, Big Boobs and Bathing Beauties, Dunces and Danger* and *In the Tennessee Hills*.

Nick, who lives in New Jersey, is still an active collector, but has long departed from the distributor scene.

MINOT FILMS

From way up in Maine, Minot Films made quite an impact on the vintage film collecting scene for the short period in which they were involved with it. They issued titles which caused many a collector to drool. Some of them, we feared, were still under copyright, but the company fearlessly went ahead with them.

Thus, many collectors grabbed such titles as *Uncle Tom's Cabin, City Lights, Modern Times, What Price Glory?, Sunrise, Tumbleweeds, The Wizard of Oz, Blood and Sand, Way Down East, Capitol Punishment, Mademoiselle Midnight* and *Heart of a Siren*.

The first name of the founder of the business escapes me; I think it was Charles Minot. You can correct me on this. Minot died, and his business apparently died with him. Collectors have puzzled over the whereabouts of the negatives.

Perhaps some of you out there can shed more light on Minot Films.

CINE SERVICE VINTAGE FILMS

Bandleader Bill Bissonnette decided to enter the film manufacturing business and issue classic 8mm and 16mm prints in silent and sound. He plunged into the field, acquiring tons of material and equipment.

He created quite a stir in the industry producing a quality product and issuing new titles with astonishing speed and regularity. Many wondered how he accomplished it.

Bill threw himself into the business and was able to obtain pre-print material on many rare and desirable titles; he was building a respectable clientele for himself.

Then, gangrene set in! Bill had over-extended himself in his rush to become a giant. His creditors closed in on him, and he was forced into bankruptcy, owing many people. His operation was closed and his material sold at auction.

The last I heard of Bill, he was again leading a band.

NILES FILMS

Bill Nagy operated Niles Films. He had a sizable catalogue of film releases and was becoming well-known in the industry.

His quality was erratic. At times, one would receive a good print from him but, sad to state, quality deteriorated in others.

When the video monster began making inroads into the film business, Bill was able to sell his Niles Films. The name of the purchaser eludes me, but they apparently were unable to improve on the quality and were forced to close down.

There are many Niles prints floating around, but the knowledgeable collectors are wary of them.

RED FOX AND CANTERBURY

Two companies who joined the film manufacturing ranks late in the market, while 8mm was still in demand, were Red Fox and Canterbury.

Red Fox, the larger of the two, had a sizable library of 8mm titles, mostly sound subjects. Ron Knorr, head of Red Fox, manufactured a quality product. He distributed Westerns, cartoons and comparatively recent sound shorts and features.

He negotiated for the rights of the copyrighted material he manufactured and came up with some attractive titles, including some highly desirable MGM features.

Red Fox is still in business, at the time of writing this article—in the video business. Ron's 8mm business went the way of 8mm. It just melted down to a dribble, until the company decided to do away with that portion of its operation.

Les Brooks' Canterbury Films entered the market with a splash. He featured mostly sound shorts and cartoons. He also manufactured some public domain features, mostly sound films.

He was doing quite well at the beginning and then, like the others, ceased production when interest in film vanished with the burgeoning of the video industry.

PARKCHESTER FILMS

Jim Acitos' Parkchester Films was a boon for the collectors of 8mm silent Western features.

In the 1960s, he began offering silent Western titles, which brought many of the almost forgotten cowboy stars to the home movie screens. His catalogue was loaded with features starring most of the better known silent actors, and some of the more obscure ones.

Some of his titles included: Bob Custer in *Arizona Days*, Art Acord in *Fighters of the Saddle*, Art Mix in *Below the Border*, William Desmond and Helen Holmes in *Blood and Steel*, Hoot Gibson in *Fight It Out*, Harry Carey in *Border Patrol*, Tom Tyler in *Canyon of Missing Men*, Leo Maloney in *Perfect Alibi*, Ted Wells in *Across the Plains*, Fred Church in *Stacked Cards*, Lefty Flynn in *Golden Stallion* and Jack Hoxie in *Riders of the Law*.

So, Western collectors ... some of those Parkchester prints are still out there!

UNITED ARTISTS 8

For a short while in the 1960s, it appeared that a new star would grace the 8mm collector scene, a distributor for one of the major studios, United Artists 8.

UA8, through urging from the pages of *8mm Collector*, and other sources, announced a plan to reproduce some of their highly desired classic films on 8mm, working from the original material. It seemed too good to be true.

But, true it was, for a short period. The company released three of its titles with some of the sharpest, brightest quality 8mm to ever appear on the market: John Barrymore in *Don Juan*, Richard Barthelmess in *The Patent Leather Kid* and Colleen Moore and Gary Cooper in *Lilac Time*. Owners of these scintillating originals from UA8 probably still have them in their possession. Who would want to dispose of them?

Apparently these releases did not generate the expected sales volume and the company discontinued its efforts to reproduce the features.

Dupesters did obtain prints of these three UA8 features, but their efforts did not approximate the quality of those original prints.

I know of one 16mm collector who swore he would never buy 8mm; then he saw a print of *Patent Leather Kid*. Presto ... another convert! He became the owner of an 8mm projector.

It was a thrilling experience to have a major studio release its silents to the collectors ... even for such a short period.

Entertainment Films

Entertainment Films made a splash in the early 1960s when it entered the 8mm production market. One of the pioneers in the field, it made its debut with fanfare and began producing 8mm silent titles which made the average collector drool.

Early on, the company produced quality prints of *The Mark of Zorro* and *The General*. Then, in the years to follow, it offered such attractive items as *The Iron Mask, Thundering Hoofs, The Leatherneck, Son of the Sheik, Way Down East, The Cat and the Canary, The Cabinet of Dr. Caligari, 10 Days That Shook the World, Metropolis, Merry-Go-Round, The Yankee Clipper, Raffles, Road to Yesterday, Eyes of Youth* and *Hell's Hinges*.

I have no way of knowing what actually happened, but deliveries from the company began to take longer and longer. There were quality complaints, most of which I understand were resolved. Then, a series of broken promises about deliveries followed.

My feelings are that the company over-extended itself and fell by the wayside because of it. Phil Alcuri, who headed Entertainment, attended several Cinecons and was extremely cooperative with collectors in the early stages of its existence.

Too bad! They had a good thing going!

I.K. Meginnis

Irving K. Meginnis (Mac) had a short fling in the 8mm productions game; a delectable, quality product emanated from his Washington, D.C., location.

Mac had a product to be proud of and the collectors liked what they saw. He was one of the first to issue a quality 8mm *The Lost World*. It was a good one! He also produced William S. Hart's *Square Deal Sanderson* and numerous shorts including early Lloyds, Tom Mix, Melies and Mac Linder.

Mac attended the first Cinecon in Indiana, Pennsylvania; in fact, he was the main speaker. He met many of the collectors and grew to know them well, learning first hand what they wanted to see. He has since attended some of the Cin-events held in Columbus, Ohio, every year.

He retired from the 8mm film manufacturing business just a few years after he went into it.

But ... it was good while it lasted!

Norward Enterprises

In checking back to some of the very old *8mm Collectors* and *Classic Film Collectors*, I noticed several ads from a short-lived company, Norward Enterprises.

Three attractive titles, in addition to others, appeared on their listings: Lon Chaney's *Nomads of the North*, William S. Hart's *Man of the West* and Paul Wegener's *Asylum of Horrors*.

This concludes my little foray into the world of 8mm distributors who closed up shop. I am sure I have not covered them all! I am just as sure that some of you people out there have information on other firms I failed to mention. Why not send it to me in care of Classic Images?

Classic Images
April 1990

Distributors ... Still Active ... Maybe

I have been away from it for years, so you cannot accept all this as the gospel truth. Here are some companies who were in business when I retired. I can only assume they are still operating.

THUNDERBIRD (MORCRAFT) FILMS

Thunderbird Films was operated by Tom Dunahoo. He departed from the scene and Dermit Morgan took over. He changed the name to Morcraft Films.

When I left the scene in July of 1988, 8mm and 16mm films were still available from the company, albeit a large portion of its business had apparently shifted to video.

The company issued a large multi-page catalogue. Tom had apparently decided to garner the classic film market and acquired a multitude of titles. He had his own lab and could control quality. And, in most cases, the quality of Thunderbird prints was good (depending, of course, on the condition of the pre-print material).

For example: his *Birth of a Nation* was tinted, printed on color stock, and was, apparently, a version containing scenes not included in prints offered by other firms.

I believe film production continues and I believe you can still receive a catalogue from Morcraft listing hundreds of classic titles available on 8mm and 16mm.

In order to find out if I know what I am talking about, write to Morcraft at 837 Caheunga Blvd., Hollywood, CA 90038.

GLENN PHOTO SERVICE

Murray Glass has been operating Glenn Photo Service as far back as I can remember. I believe he is still in business. Like the others, he has entered the video field with his Glenn Video, and also operates the EMGEE Film Library.

Up until the time I entered the ranks of the deliberately unemployed, he was still offering 8mm and 16mm vintage classics for sale.

Murray delights in finding rare, obscure titles which are dear to the heart of the serious vintage film collectors. Unfortunately, in recent years, I get the feeling that the enthusiasm has been a bit dampened by the influx of video and the diminishing film sales. He has joined the video ranks, but his heart is still in film.

Proof of this is the fact that he purchased the Ed Finney inventory of silent classics after Ed's death. Included were films of Doug Fairbanks, Sr., Johnny Hines, Gloria Swanson, William S. Hart, Charles Ray, Wallace Reid and others.

A wily businessman, Murray operates his film business in the proper manner, giving decent service and acting on complaints immediately. In all the years I was at the helm of *Classic Images*, I do not recall a single complaint against Glass.

Assuming that he still issues a catalogue of rare film titles, why not write to him? 6924 Canby Ave., No. 103, Reseda, CA 91335. Website: http://emgee.freeyellow.com/ Email: mglass@worldnet.att.net Phone: (818) 981-5506

Enrique J. Bouchard

Argentina's audacious Enrique J. Bouchard is still offering rare silent classics to the dedicated 8mm collectors. When I say rare, I mean R-A-R-E!

He manufactures and openly advertises blockbuster silent film titles which none of the domestic distributors could offer, when they were still in business.

This is only a conjecture, but apparently there must be a thing about the material not being protected by copyright, or anything else, in Argentina. It is my only conceivable solution to the dilemma of how Bouchard can keep selling and advertising these desirable rarities.

Most of his titles cannot even be bought on video in the open market. We're talking about *Ben Hur* (which MGM did release on video cassette), *Underworld, Robin Hood, Greed, The Penalty, Three Ages, The Cameraman, Our Hospitality, Battling Butler, The Kid Brother, Hot Water, For Heaven's Sake, The Pilgrim, Sunnyside* and many others.

Of course, video has also become a part of his business, and he has recently come up with such delectable video titles as *Four Horsemen of the Apocalypse, The Saphead* and *The Unknown* for his listings.

Enrique J. Bouchard is the complete gentleman and operates a friendly, efficient business. In the many years he has advertised in *Classic Images*, there has never been a complaint on his business methods.

European Market

Other than Derann Films, which has a tremendous library of classic films, I have been out of touch with the European market, insofar as determining which companies are still manufacturing and selling classic titles on film.

In the past, our Maurice Trace, who helmed the British Collecting Scene, kept us up-to-date on these people and annually surveyed the market.

Derann apparently features more of the comparatively recent sound films, downplaying the silents and early sound to a certain extent. The company is distributing top-rated sound classics legitimately, negotiating for and obtaining the home movie film rights to these titles.

You'll find a large selection of desirable movies in their catalogue. For further information, why not write to Maurice in care of *Classic Images*. And, don't be in a rush for a reply. Maurice lives in the British Isles.

I regret that I have been away from it long enough to have no knowledge of the overseas products available.

Reel Images

In the case of Jon Sonneborn and his Reel Images, I must plead a bit of ignorance since I have departed from the active reporting scene. The last I heard, John was still offering film titles in 8mm and 16mm. Why not drop him a line: 600 Main St., Monroe, CT 06468.

Jon, a collector, has had a variety of titles in his catalogue. His service has reputedly been good.

JEF Films

JEF Films was a comparative johnny-come-lately in the field, entering the market after some of the other distributors had already quit.

The company, at the time I departed the scene, had a sizable catalogue of classic movies on film. In addition to its own titles, JEF had acquired the Film Classic Exchange inventory after the death of its owner, Charles Tarbox.

JEF Films is operated by the Aikman family: Elsie, Don and son Jeff. Having never seen any of the company's product, nor having any reports on same, I am unable to evaluate the quality of the films the company reproduces.

National Cinema Service

In business over 50 years, Bill Flohr's National Cinema Service has been servicing the 16mm collectors with a large inventory of features and shorts.

Bill states he has over 700 brand-new public domain features and hundreds of shorts. He also maintains a large inventory of used films.

Bill's service, in the many years he has been operating, is above reproach, and he does much repeat business with his customers. They keep coming back for more ... a good sign!

A simple request will bring his catalogue to you: PO Box 43, Ho-Ho-Kus, NJ 07423.

Festival Films

Former Cinephile President Ron Hall has been operating his Festival Films for over a decade. Ron has an interesting catalogue of 16mm classics, which include silent and sound features, and a listing of foreign made films.

Ron has earned a reputation for good service and for handling quality prints. He does much repeat business selling to schools, libraries, etc., in addition to collectors.

He issues a periodic catalogue. Write for one: 2841 Irving Ave. S., Minneapolis, MN 55408.

9

People!

In my various sorties into the past, I have discussed, and will further discuss, people with whom I have come in contact over the two-and-a-half decades of publishing *8MM Collector, Classic Film Collector* and *Classic Images*.

It was mentioned to me recently that most of the people who have emerged from the keys of my typewriter were good guys—gentlemen to the point that I almost lionized them. I was asked, "Didn't you run into any of the rapscallions of the industry?"

Answer: "Sure have!" However, right now I prefer to write about the people who bring me pleasant memories. Sure, I've had plenty of contact with the vultures and scavengers of the collecting industry. I have no desire to recall them in these pages. Let them stew in their own obscurity.

Perhaps I may change my mind someday and write about some of the scams perpetrated upon the collectors. But, right now, I feel good about the past, and to repeat an appropriate cliché, "Let sleeping dogs lie!"

Now, I'm dredging up memories from 26 years of editing the three above-mentioned publications before I retired to catch up on 50 years of lost sleep. Here are a few of the people who left an indelible impression with me.

Harry Bloom

Good old Harry Bloom (I think he's old). He will probably read this if he still receives *Classic Images*. I have never met Harry. Harry, who lived (perhaps he's still there) in Baltimore, has presented me with many memories ... some pleasant.

While publishing the earlier versions of *Classic Images* years ago, I advertised that you could write for a free sample copy. Postage was cheap at the time. Harry would send a postcard with a message printed in large block letters, something like "Send me a free copy of *Classic Film Collector*."

Inasmuch as I was doing everything myself, I would let the sample copy requests accumulate until it was time to mail the next issue, so that it could all be done at once. Consequently, the response time to such requests was a bit sluggish. After a short period I would receive another Harry Bloom printed card, "How long does it take you to mail out my free sample copy?" Naturally, because I had my hands full with a full-time furniture store and an expanding publication, I didn't respond and sent him his sample copy later with the others.

Next issue ... another card asking for a free sample ... and, a subsequent card asking the reason for the delay.

I am a bit dense, but eventually I caught on to the fact that he would continue asking for free samples as long as I was willing to send them. So, to fill the following request, I sent him an earlier issue. Of course, Harry was incensed and requested the latest issue.

I squeezed out a bit of time and wrote to him, telling him the price of a subscription and then tactlessly telling him not to bother me any more about free copies.

I believe he did subscribe at one time. He may even be a subscriber now. However, some time later, the request for free copies began again. You could not ignore Harry Bloom. He kept writing those cards with his inimitable large block letters requesting action.

Harry has been a devoted reader. After the sample copy price went from "free" to $2, he continued to request them and sending the money. Sometimes the girls sent him the latest issue; sometimes, earlier issues. Whenever a new girl would take over circulation, she would receive a refresher course on Harry Bloom.

When I retired, Harry was still with us! I have a mental image of Harry Bloom. Someday I would like to meet him ... and talk over old movies. He is probably quite knowledgeable. I would like to meet him face to face; after all, we have had a lengthy correspondence.

★ ★ ★

Years ago, when I was trying to run a furniture store while publishing *Classic Film Collector* as a hobby in my spare time, I would get visitors. I would invite them to my desk, and we would discuss old movies. Some came just to meet and visit with me, others came with a purpose.

One day a collector, who was a well-known producer of experimental or impressionistic films, arrived. He gave me a 50' 8mm film he had produced—a movie of a butterfly's wing. That's it. 50 8mm feet of a butterfly's wing! And, reputedly, the film has been acclaimed. And this collector is exceedingly well-known in the field; his name has appeared in various books and journals.

He loved Buster Keaton at the time and told me that he had seen one Keaton film 70 or 80 times. Each time he watched it, he would learn something or would see something he had not perceived before.

Now, here was my kind of guy! Although I can get everything I want to see out of a Keaton movie after three viewings (sometimes one or two), he earned my respect!

While he talked, he would remove a pint bottle from his pocket and put it to his mouth.

"Well," I thought, "if he wants to drink, let him drink." Until ... I took a good look. He was spitting into it. I don't remember if he was chewing tobacco or was just spitting. Perhaps he was ill. All I do remember is that it sickened me.

It still does.

★ ★ ★

Lt. Col. Oscar Estates began sending articles and illustrations way back in the early days of the *8mm Collector*. He was a knowledgeable, talented man. His articles were top-notch, well-researched and ably written. His artwork was beautiful ... above reproach.

We corresponded and became friends. When my wife and I, with friends, drove to California from Indiana, Pennsylvania, we stopped in San Antonio to visit with him. He wined and dined us, and we had a most pleasurable visit.

He continued to submit articles and artwork ... until...

One of our advertisers submitted an ad, indicating he was selling prints of *The Lost World*. I searched my files for an illustration and came up with a dinosaur Oscar had drawn. I inserted it in the ad.

When the issue was distributed, I received a phone call from Oscar: "You stabbed me in the back!" It was about the *Lost World* illustration. I tried to explain what had happened, not dreaming he would object to its use. I tried to apologize; he would not listen.

This happened years ago. I have not heard from him since.

★ ★ ★

Many of my collector friends have died; I could write in depth about them.

I could write for hours about Cal Dobbins, the most congenial, friendly person you could ever meet. A real film buff ... and a fine artist. I loved his work, which was so reminiscent of the cartoons of yesteryear (Cal collected these cartoons and comic strips). My all-time favorite Cal Dobbins work of art is hanging on the wall over my desk.

Mike Kornick was the epitome of the serious-minded collector. He attended all conventions and had a huge collection of movie memorabilia. Everyone liked Mike! In addition to his love of the classics, Mike's main interest was collecting obituaries of the stars.

How about likable Harold Kinkade, who would be recognized by all the Cinephiles? Harold's forte was the Westerns, but he liked all vintage films. He began a small business of selling or bartering films ... and then, later, videotapes of vintage movies. He sold tapes manufactured by other people who did not wish to advertise the rare, sensitive titles they were reproducing. Many collectors obtained some desirable titles through Harold.

Or, how about Jerry Clark? Affable Jerry was another serious collector; he was also in the film

Harold Kinkade, popular Cinephile, who was a regular attendee at the various conventions.

rental business. In addition to being a collector, Jerry was also a top-notch projectionist, and you would often see him at the projectors at the various film conventions.

There were so many of these great guys! And, there are just as many top-notch people still attending our conventions.

Classic Images, No. 159
September 1988

George Katchmer!

The name means nothing to millions of people in this and other countries who are unfortunate enough not to be classic film buffs.

The name will mean nothing to some of the unfortunate classic film buffs who do not read *Classic Images*, the publication of which I was lucky enough to be editor for 26 years.

But, to readers of *Classic Images*, the name George Katchmer attached to a biography always signified a fascinating glimpse into the lives of silent screen actors who brightened the film scene during those hectic early days of Hollywood. They recognize him as a man who has contributed so much to their knowledge and appreciation of the classic film scene.

Readers of *Classic Images* know George Katchmer as a retired football coach from Millersville State College, Pennsylvania, who grew up in the coal mining town of Arcadia in western Pennsylvania. They know that the young George so idolized the early film stars that he sometimes walked miles to the nearest theater to see them on the screen.

They know that his love for these popular stars never diminished over the years as George continued to write about his favorite people in the pages of *Classic Images*. Those of us who talked to George over the phone and at film conventions found that he was always ready to discuss any aspect of the early movies and was proud of his personal collection of film.

They know, by the thousands of words which have poured from his pen, that George can ably express his feelings about his heroes of the silent screen. He is especially fond of the westerns. Mention Jack Hoxie, and his face lights up!

Now, here are some facts that perhaps they don't know. In my mind's eye I can see George Katchmer at his spacious desk starting to write one of his biographies. I say "write," because that's exactly what I mean. George does not type. That tremendous output of articles were, and continue to be, handwritten.

The arrival of one of George's articles would bring excitement: "Wonder who George wrote about this time," and "I wonder if he did it again?" "Did it again" refers to the fact that George Katchmer frequently had afterthoughts following the penning of a page. With each afterthought, George would place a large asterisk at the spot in which the additional material should appear. Then, if there was room at the bottom of the page, he would insert the material. If there was not room at the bottom, George would turn the page and write vertically in the margin. And, if there was not enough margin, he would flip the page to add his secondary thoughts to the other side.

My wife, Lois, was a tremendous help to me as we constantly fought the battle of the deadline in getting *Classic Images* ready for the press. We were always too busy to type George's articles. So editing corrections were made right on the sheets of handwritten pages and then turned over to Marlene Hanifan, who fed the material into the computer terminal. When I handed Marlene one of George's handwritten chronicles, she would look up at me with the soulful eyes of a hurt kitten, sigh, and say, "Okay!"

George Katchmer has thoroughly researched all of his articles. He has amassed large amounts of material in his constant quest for information. He has had much help in his probing of the past from his sons, Michael and John, and 100 percent moral support from his wife, Pauline. Film buffs such as Mrs. Peter Smith, Bob Robinson, Tom Fulbright, Anthony Phillips, Gerald Hamm, Charles K. Stumpf, George Geltzer, Marvin Kravitz, Lary Byrd, Richard E. Braff, William C. Wilson, myself, and many others contributed toward the gathering of material for his biographies.

In the preparation process, George has agonized over many of his chronicles. His major irritation is that the facts, as written by biographers and publicity departments about his favorite people, never jibed; often, pertinent facts about these figures from the past would not agree. He would find three or four different birth (or death) dates for the same person. Much of the material written about the stars of yesteryear arose from the imagination of publicity writers—and they did have vivid imaginations!

George found many contradictions in his research. Harry Star went to Harvard; Harry Star went to West Point; Harry Star never went to school; Harry Star was self-educated. To ferret out the true story, George would peruse a multitude of references about the same person. When the same data was repeated in several articles, he would have to assume that it was the correct information.

However, he was to find out that once a fictitious item was printed concerning a particular star, it would be picked up by future biographers who would repeat the information in their own articles, thus perpetuating the same misinformation.

George could have been responsible for spreading misinformation; but he carefully researched his material to avoid it. The reader can assume that most of his material is as correct as careful scrutiny could make it.

Another major irritant for George Katchmer is the fanatical film buff who narrows his or her interest to one or, possible, a few stars. This fan, over the years, has gathered every possible bit of information about his particular favorite. This collector knows everything about the star's career, every intimate detail of that star's life.

So, along comes George Katchmer to write an in-depth article on Harry Star, accumulating his material from the articles he and his helpers have researched. In the biography he states that one of Harry Star's toenails was green. This causes an upheaval in the life of Mac Cumulate, whose idol is Harry Star and who knows everything there is to know about Harry Star.

Mac Cumulate writes a blistering letter to *Classic Images* saying, in effect, "George Katchmer is a blundering idiot who should research his items more carefully. Everyone knows that one of Harry Star's toenails was purple, not green."

Justifiably, such a letter would turn George Katchmer purple. He felt it wasn't necessary for him to receive such a letter from this Harry Star fanatic. He did not mind the correction for, Heaven knows, he could see where such an error could result from so much contradictory material that passed through his hands. But he deeply resented this extremist's language in pointing out the error.

Writing film biographies has been George's life in these retirement years. What a legacy he is leaving for classic film buffs! He has been able to convey his information in an interesting manner and has already captured a large following of the classic enthusiasts who immediately turn to his articles upon opening the pages of *Classic Images*. More, who have been unaware of George up to this point, will flock to his banner after reading this book.

George has captured the fast pace and excitement of the people of the silent screen!

Classic Images, *No. 215*
May 1993

The Toy That Grew Up

How many of you remember the television series *The Toy That Grew Up*?

It was produced and introduced by Cinephile Robert C. Seipp in August 1962. The series was one of the first, I believe, to seriously approach the silent classics and to present them in an authentic manner, complete with musical accompaniment, *sans* the usual ridicule and wisecracks we were accustomed to seeing and hearing on the tube.

The series lasted a decade.

Bob conceived the program in 1960. He acquired, researched and cleared copyrights for over 100 silent pictures; 90 percent of the films were acquired from private collectors.

Bob researched the background material and wrote scripts for each program, which were then produced with organ accompaniment by Hal Pearl, who had played for the silents at the Archer's Midwest Theater in Chicago in 1927.

Seipp, an authority on the era of the silents, also collects old phonographs, phonograph records, transcriptions and cylinders. His record library numbers over 75,000 and includes many historical recordings of such famous people as Theodore Roosevelt, William Jennings Bryan and many turn-of-the-century entertainers.

The silent film series was popular among Cinephiles. Such classic features as John Barrymore's *The Tempest* and *Dr. Jekyll and Mr. Hyde*; Buster Keaton's *Steamboat Bill, Jr.*; Emil Jannings' *Variety*; Rod LaRocque's *Captain Swagger*; Florence Turner's *East Is East*; Mabel Normand's *The Extra Girl*; Conrad Veidt's *The Cabinet of Dr. Caligari*; John Hines' *Burn 'Em Up Barnes*; Ken Maynard's *$50,000 Reward*; Fred Thomson's *Thundering Hoofs*; Colleen Moore's *Orchids and Ermine*; Lon Chaney's *The Phantom of the Opera* and *The Hunchback of Notre Dame*; Boris Karloff's *The Bells* and many other titles offer a sampling of the type of films which were the backbone of the popular program.

I was pleased to see Bob at the Hollywood Cinecon in September. He informed me that he is not sitting still. At that time he was working on a project for the Smithsonian Institute, a special on World War I for cable and a TV special on Bobby Breen.

In an attempt to get a complete collection of his *Toy That Grew Up* series on videotape, Bob is now searching for such tapes. He does have some of the original programs recorded, but is anxious to acquire the others.

Classic Images, *No. 221*
November 1993

The Accompanists

As you well know, there never was a "silent" film. From the very beginning, there was always musical accompaniment with the silent "flicks" (how I despise that word!).

Be it piano, organ, violin; be it duet, trio or full orchestra, the background music always increased the enjoyment of the film. And if the players were accomplished musicians, they added an immeasurable quality to the film, making even the lowliest "B" movie a bit more bearable.

I have come in contact with many of the people who provided the background music for films shown at our various conventions. I am about to write concerning a select few. Select only from the standpoint of my personal contact with them. Heaven knows there were, and still are, many fine accompanists in the field. I can only talk about my personal experiences with a few of them. If you are a piano, organ player or other musician and are not mentioned here, it's only because I have had little or no personal experience with you. Don't get mad! I know you belong to a highly sensitive group!

Take Stuart Olderman, for example. A fine pianist! I notice he is still playing and is advertising his services. I consider Stu a personal friend, and we have corresponded. He was once a Cinephile and played for many of our screenings, adding so much to those films with his performances.

"Dutch" Campbell! There's one name most of you never heard. Dutch lived in Indiana, Pennsylvania, birthplace of *Classic Images* and the Society for Cinephiles. Dutch was a good friend; we knew each other well, having met years before at a Lions' meeting. (Yes, I was once a Lion!)

When I began showing silent films in the area to civic organizations, the county home and the local University of Pennsylvania at Indiana, Dutch played for me ... and would never take a cent for his work because he so enjoyed it.

He always told me he couldn't read a word of music. I didn't believe him because, at one time, he had played for Fred Waring ... and knew all the Pennsylvanians. And Fred Waring did not hire musicians who could not read music.

Dutch would sit at the piano before the screen and accompany a movie he had never seen. He could instantly change tempo and mood and adapt his playing to coincide with the action being projected in front of him. He was a marvel! When he died, I mourned for him as a good friend and a *great* piano player.

9. People!

Gaylord Carter! This column is being written in June, long before the next Cinecon. However, it may not reach you until the annual meeting is history; but Carter is scheduled to be at the convention. Once you hear his famous touch on the organ keys, you will know why he is in such demand, and it will be difficult to adjust your senses to listen to others. He is an artist. He has a hairline sensitivity to the action on the screen and has the ability to adjust his music ... and to bring tears to your eyes.

I first heard Gaylord's organ magic at the home of John Griggs, founder of Griggs Moviedrome. John asked me if I wanted to see *Beau Geste.* Did I! He screened it for me in his viewing room, and there is where I first heard the wizardry of Gaylord Carter (on tape, of course). John presented me with a copy of the tape, and when I reached home I was able to listen to it for many hours. Later I was able to get an 8mm print of the film and thrilled over and over again at that same Carter music.

How about the versatile Bob Vaughn? He has played for the silents at many of our conventions. Bob is at home on organ or piano. He does, however, favor the organ. Bob has come through with many brilliant scores to enhance the enjoyment of the movies. Like many accompanists, Bob prefers to view the film first and then prepare an appropriate score. He has come up with some thrilling movie music; he is able to follow the action on the screen without the obvious hesitation, which sometimes occurs whenever there is a change of pace. Bob has played professionally for years, much of the time spent in the Castro Theater in San Francisco, his home town. However, he has traveled thousands of miles to add to the Cinephile's enjoyment as they, too, traveled many miles to attend the various conventions just to watch the classic films and to enjoy the company of fellow enthusiasts and appreciate Bob Vaughn's quality accompaniment.

I remember the scintillating music John Muri added to our screening of *The Vanishing American* at an early Cinecon. I was fortunate to be able to get a tape of that performance, and it never failed to cover my skin with goose pimples when I listened to it.

To deviate from live accompaniment, I like to remember the first time I attended John Hampton's Silent Theater in Hollywood during our first Cinecon there; the feature was the thrilling *The Volga Boatman* with William Boyd. He had dual turntables in the projection room. He used them both, shifting records between the two to enable him to offer appropriate background music for the various scene and location changes. To me he was doing a miraculous job of always having the right music for a smooth transition as the film's pace changed. I don't know if he was a musician, but I do know he was an artist in his ability to provide the proper musical background for the silent films.

Jon Mirsalis! I'll always remember the music of Jon Mirsalis. He sits down at the piano and, when the room is darkened and the screen lights up, he takes control. He manipulates your emotions as the story unfolds in front of you. Jon Mirsalis' accompaniment is an integral part of the movie; it wouldn't be the same without it.

As mentioned earlier, there are many fine musicians out there accompanying the screening of silent films; I rarely had extensive contact with others than those mentioned above, and I am not purposely neglecting them.

My credentials? I play a mean kazoo and have become adept at pushing the ON and OFF button on tape players.

Classic Images

The Impactors!

There are many people out there who had great impact on our movie collecting industry. Initially we'll discuss two whose influence will be felt for years to come: Kalton C. Lahue and Forrest J Ackerman.

One of the most revered and respected authors in the classic film field is Kalton C. Lahue.

Lahue is no longer active in the field, but his books on the very early days of the screen have guided many a researcher in his quest for information and are an integral part of the cinema collecting scene.

His books have been carefully researched and he traveled far to gather material for them. They have been an important reference source for so much of the material that has appeared in *Classic Images* and its predecessors, *8mm Collector* and *Classic Film Collector*.

We became acquainted in my early days of film collecting. In fact, Kal added prestige to the very first issue of *8mm Collector* with an article about collecting slides.

I will never forget the first and only time we met.

I was busy with a customer at the Star Furniture Company in Indiana, Pennsylvania, where I spent my first 32 post–World War II years, eking out a livelihood. One of our salesmen informed me that some people wanted to see me. Looking up, I saw a young man, casually dressed, with his wife and baby. I waved at them and said, "I'll be with you in a few minutes."

When I finished with my customer I went up to them and he introduced himself and his wife. "Kal Lahue," I intelligently exclaimed, "I didn't know it was you!"

"Who did you think it was?"

"Some bum," I blurted with my usual display of tact and thoughtfulness.

He laughed ... thank goodness!

We had a great time as he visited with me. I showed him my collection. He found some stills and lobbies he could use in his books. You'll see my name in a couple of them.

Kal is no longer writing books on the early screen. The last time I talked to him, some years ago, he told me that he had completed his goal. He had written all the film books he had set out to, and was entering another field. He became editor of a magazine on motorboats. As far as I know, he is still at it.

Kal, if you're still out there and have the chance to read this, I want to thank you for your contributions to our classic film collecting field. Your work is deeply appreciated. Now that I am retired and can look back, I can see just how important your work was. It still is! Thanks!

FORREST J ACKERMAN

To those not into science fiction and fantasy, the name Forry Ackerman may mean nothing. But, to those who are knowledgeable about that classic literature genre, Forry is Mr. Science Fiction; he is the number one fan in the country.

Forry has (had?) an unsurpassed collection of science fiction and fantasy; the books, the magazines, the artifacts, the everything. Situated in Hollywood, he amassed thousands of items. He filled his basement, he filled his living room, he filled every room in the house with his collections. When he reached the bathrooms, he and his lovely wife had to move ... and turned the house into a science fiction museum.

National newspapers and magazines carried the story of the huge auction of his material.

For years, Forry was editor of *Famous Monsters of Filmland* magazine, a publication which approached the horror movies with a tongue-in-cheek attitude. It had a multitude of illustrations and the magazine was a treasure trove of material for those interested in vintage sci-fi and fantasy. And, it also kept up to date on the modern scene. *Famous Monsters* approached much of its material from a humorous angle utilizing atrocious, unforgivable puns.

Forry was an avid admirer of Lon Chaney, Sr., and devoted much space to the famous actor. Because he devoted many pages to the older films and illustrated them with so many rare photos, I began reading it and became addicted. Now, the older issues are collectors items, bringing in fancy sums.

Forry was familiar with *Classic Film Collector* and we developed a mutual admiration pact. He ran several reviews of *CFC* and we devoted space to *Famous Monsters*.

Once he wrote in one of his issues that he and his wife were planning a tour of the country and if any of his readers would like to have him visit, to drop him a line. I firmly believed he would not put Indiana, Pennsylvania, on his travel schedule. Regardless, I wrote that he would be welcomed there.

He must have received five million requests, but he did answer that he would stop in Indiana and visit with us.

When he and his wife arrived, our first meeting demonstrated what a gentleman he is. All of my film and paper collection was in the basement. So, after dinner, we descended to the Rubin inner sanctum. I was willing to show him some of my collection, but it wasn't to be.

I had made some enormously clumsy sci-fi movies with my kids. *Jay of the Jungle* and *Pioneers of Space* starred my son Jay and daughter Jo Anne, with other kids. The films were as amateurish and inept as inexperience, poor equipment and little knowledge could make them. Each lasted an hour.

Against my wishes, my family insisted that we screen them. Forry Ackerman and his wife sat through these without a complaint, and even lauded them. I said to myself, "These are fine people to endure this."

What endeared him to my kids: Forry put out his hand on which was a ring, "This is the ring," Forry proudly stated, "that Bela Lugosi wore in *Dracula*."

It was a pleasant visit, and they left us with a warm feeling of friendship.

Later, during one of our Hollywood Cinecons, we visited his Ackermansion.

After seeing the vast amount of material in the Ackerman collection, I further realized how generous it was of them to stay and tolerate my infinitesimal gathering of bits of material.

Forry Ackerman is not the Ackermonster he likes to declare himself. He deserves the respect and adulation he receives.

10

The Stars

Classic Images, *No 223*
January 1994

Mason ... Perry Dead or Alive?

TV's Perry Mason, Raymond Burr, died in 1993; but will Perry Mason die? I don't think the powers of the movie and TV industry will let this popular character die. Like the legendary Tarzan, I think Perry Mason, attorney supreme, will continue to outwit the murderers on the big and little screen for years to come.

Before Raymond Burr assumed the role, I can recall two other actors who portrayed Mason in the movies: Warren William and Donald Cook. When Burr's original one-hour TV series ran its course, Monte Markham assumed the role with little success.

When I first came in contact with Perry Mason, I thought Warren William was the ideal, living image of the famous lawyer. Then, on TV, Burr assumed the role. Erle Stanley Gardner, originator of the character, was quoted at the time as saying that Burr fitted his image of the fighting barrister. I, too, changed my opinion after watching Burr on the small screen. He, to me, also became the epitome of the lawyer; Raymond Burr *was* Perry Mason.

When the weekly one-hour *Mason* series was terminated, Burr again took over the Mason role in perhaps 30 or so two-hour versions. He now had a beard and, with his illnesses, was often forced to appear with a cane. Burr was a large, chesty man. During his acting career, his weight went up and down like a yo-yo. He had difficulty controlling it. He was thin in many of the early Masons, but became quite portly and was heavier in the two-hour shows. But, whether stout or thin, Raymond Burr *was* Perry Mason!

I have read much of Erle Stanley Gardner's work. I have most of his mystery books! He was a prolific writer, not only with the Perry Mason stories, but he made other characters famous. He even wrote Westerns, adventure, science fiction and who knows what else! Gardner was a regular contributor to *Argosy, Detective Fiction Weekly* and other pulp magazines. He also appeared in some of the slick publications.

He wrote a series of books under the pseudonym A.A. Fair, introducing the characters of Donald Lam and Bertha Cool, private detectives. Bertha, originally head of the detective agency, was a tough, hard-as-nails, solidly built, buxom female. She hired the down-and-almost-out Lam, a short, gutsy fellow with the brains of an Einstein. The books were written in Lam's first person. He soon bulldozed himself into a partnership. They took on many bizarre cases. Cool continually lost her "cool"; and Lam, just as continually, "cooled" her down.

Gardner wrote superbly. He grabbed your attention from the first word. You hated to put his books aside. I spent many a late night in bed reading "just one more chapter" into another chapter; and, suddenly, I had reached the end of the book.

Gardner discovered a weakness in the law in his first Lam-Cool novel, in which a person could commit murder and legally get away with it. It was so effective that later the laws of California were changed to plug up those loopholes that Gardner discovered.

He originated many other characters: Terry Clane; D.A. Douglas Selby, a fighting district attorney; Gramps Wiggins, a wise old reprobate; Bob (I think) Zane of the "Whispering Sands" Western series; Major Brane; Lester Leith; Sheriff Bill Eldon; and countless other personalities. I own, or have read, all of Gardner's material that has appeared in book form and in the *Argosy* pulp magazine. I missed much of the material he submitted to *Detective Fiction Weekly* and some of the other pulps.

His science fiction stories were superb. His Western tales were excellent.

Television affected Gardner's writing! I am aware of two incidents in which television set the tone of his characters, and Gardner changed the description of those characters in the books to coincide with the TV versions. There were probably more! The original Perry Mason was a pugnacious, stormy, fiery character; quick to lose his temper, ready to fight, and defied all the odds in protecting his clients. Burr's Mason was toned down from that original portrayal of the world-famous attorney. He often underplayed the role. Gardner started to present a more pacified Mason in his novels. Though the attorney still went to great lengths for his clients if he believed them innocent, he did so in a more subdued fashion.

More noticeable was Gardner's description of Police Lt. Tragg. At the beginning, Tragg was described as a suave, tall, thin, smooth-talking man. When Ray Collins assumed the TV role, the Tragg of the novels became a gruff, more elderly, rougher person—descriptive, of course, of the TV player's physical characteristics.

There were probably other character changes as TV continued to exploit the attorney, making him famous. Though TV affected Gardner's writing, it did not affect his thinking. He had a way with words; and he, as a former attorney, knew the law and could think up intricate, legal situations of which the average author would be incapable.

When I talk to people about Perry Mason, they say, "He never lost a case!" But, he did! I can recall one; there may have been others. Mason was defending a client who gave him the wrong name. From the very beginning, Mason was defending the wrong person, and it was not discovered until the end of the novel.

As you seldom find with many "series" authors, everything was not always on the same monotonous track and pattern with Erle Stanley Gardner's writing. His situations were always unique, many of them unexpected. I'm thinking of one unusual incident when Perry Mason finds himself alone in a room with a gorilla.

The dyed-in-the-wool TV fans all mourn the passing of Burr, who incidentally was also *Ironside* on TV, and portrayed countless villains prior to his Perry Mason life.

As sure as I am sitting here bruising my fingers on these blankety-blank typewriter keys, Perry Mason will not die. There will always be a Perry Mason!

I'll miss Raymond Burr. And, there will never be another Erle Stanley Gardner. I have mourned him since he died some years back and will always remember that he's the one who invented Perry Mason.

Classic Images, *No. 163*
January 1989

Memory of the Stars

It's a thrill to see so many luminaries of the classic screen while we are attending film conventions. We have had our share of them at the various Cinecons. Because of the proximity of the stars and because so many of them were still living then, our first Hollywood Cinecon was the apotheosis of such a convention. A large group of Hollywood people, some of whom are no longer with us, attended.

Such appearances are mutually beneficial. The stars, many no longer active, meet their admiring public and conversely, the admiring public gets to meet the movie people who have given them so much happiness and entertainment.

I have heard many of the speeches with which the stars addressed their audiences. I have listened to quantities of television interviews, and I have heard many older stars ramble on and on about their past.

And, sometimes I wonder!

I'm kinda ancient myself now, and I have difficulty remembering what happened 30 and 40 years ago. Even some of the memories of early Cinecons have eluded me.

I am firmly convinced that the stars of the early years do *not* remember! I feel that much of the verbiage they push out are words from their publicity agents of yore, merely reiterating what the agents have written. They have repeated the stories so often that some of these stars begin to believe the publicity.

I shouldn't generalize. No doubt the majority of the stars do remember incidents from the past, even though I wonder how they can retain all this when I have so much difficulty reviving the past in my mind.

A prime example: Lillian Gish, that grand old lady of the screen, has repeated in her interviews the fallacy that "Mr. Griffith" did not do retakes. Every scene, especially in *The Birth of a Nation*, was shot only once. The actors had to know their parts and do them correctly the first time.

This sounded great and added to the respect and admiration accorded the great director. However, at one of our Cinecons, we were treated to an entire reel of outtakes from *Birth of a Nation*.

So, my sordidly suspicious mind starts gnawing at me. "How many more of these reminiscences of their past lives are not quite true?"

VISIT TO THE STUDIOS

I keep referring to the Hollywood Cinecons, not that the other Cinecons were lacking in quality. But, those held in the film capital of the world had a touch of the glamourous, the ethereal and the exciting which no other city could offer.

New York, Chicago and even Davenport, Iowa, were thrillers ... but, of a different variety.

Perhaps Hollywood was so stimulating because that's where the movie's glamour years began. There is so much to see and do which is related to our mutual interest, the classic films.

I must tell you about our personal trips to 20th Century–Fox. There were two of them at different Cinecons. Alex Gordon was at 20th Century–Fox then, and he graciously took the time to take us on a trip through the studio. We were especially impressed and thoroughly enjoyed our visit to the *Hello Dolly* set with its elevated train and its New York Street.

Most memorable was our luncheon with Alex at the 20th Century–Fox Commissary where we rubbed elbows with the likes of Rock Hudson and other stars. And where I discovered that a Reuben sandwich at the 20th Century–Fox commissary, at that time, was comprised of turkey and ham, neither of which I eat.

Another of our tours through 20th Century–Fox was arranged by Mort Zarcoff. (I've since lost track of him.) He arranged for my son Jay and me to visit the stages where they were shooting.

The first two were disappointments. The *M*A*S*H* set was closed to visitors because they were having a meeting; it looked like a story consultation. We did get to see the tent and operating room sets.

Disappointment number two: We were halted prior to entering the *Baretta* set by the sign, "Working with animals ... No Visitors." It was apparently parrot day. If you remember, Baretta had a pet parrot.

We next went to the *Switch* set. Robert Wagner was not there, but Eddie Albert was shooting at the time. The introduction: "Mr. Albert, I would like you to meet Sam Rubin; he's a publisher from back East." (Big shot that I am!)

Eddie invited Jay and me to his trailer. We sat and talked for about 15 minutes. Eddie Albert: a real gentleman and a trouper.

Next stop was the *McCloud* set. I do not recall the name of the director, but our introduction to him was the same. "I would like to have you meet Sam Rubin; he's a publisher from back East."

"Oh, yes, Mr. Rubin. You are welcome to watch us shoot. There are no unoccupied chairs, so why don't you sit in my chair?"

So I sat in the director's chair as they shot a scene for *McCloud*. This scene, with Dennis Weaver and Don Meredith, had a fascinating fight scene. That business you see about substituting doubles in the fight scene is true.

We were introduced to Weaver and Meredith, who appeared to be happy to meet this big publisher from back East.

Needless to say, it was quite a thrill for us.

Other studio trips were arranged for us later by Dave Shepard, who at the time was with the Directors Guild, and Steve Barkett. During the latter trip, Lois accompanied me, along with Kent and Jane Eastin, who attended that last Hollywood Cinecon.

Steve, if you recall, was the Cinephile who came with us to a Cinecon and managed to get screen-tested and won a Hollywood job. He had recently completed a feature, *The Aftermath*, which he produced, directed and starred.

My biggest thrill was to see the happy look on Kent Eastin's face as we watched scenes from *The Aftermath*, which were shown to us on a Moviola. I had never seen one, and I don't think Kent had seen one this size.

Yes, those were happy trips to "Filmland," California.

Classic Images, *No. 253*
July 1996

Jimmy Stewart Museum's First Birthday Party

Much time has passed since the opening of the Jimmy Stewart Museum in the famous star's hometown, Indiana, Pennsylvania, which is also the birthplace of *Classic Images*.

My son Jay, who is president of the museum, invited me down for the anniversary celebration, which also occurs on Jimmy's birthday. The guest star was June Allyson, who had starred in motion pictures with the Indiana native; most memorable to me was *The Glenn Miller Story*. She is also a friend of Stewart.

Audrey and I were returning from our trip to Italy. Audrey went to Long Island to visit her children; I came to Indiana, Pennsylvania, to visit my family and attend the birthday party.

The celebration was a delightful affair with June Allyson receiving the Harvey award, which will be presented every year by the museum. She arrived with her husband, David Ashrow; they made a charming and delightful couple. I was fortunate to be invited to a separate dinner with Jay, June and David. And, for the first time in years, I became star-struck.

In the many years during which I was publisher and editor of *Classic Images*, I met countless Hollywood stars. Many of them were pleasant and friendly; many were arrogant, standoffish, condescending; and, horrors of horrors, some charged for their autograph. And many people paid them for that bit of ink scribbling.

June Allyson was, by far, the sweetest, most pleasant of all the stars I had ever met. She was constantly smiling, she was sincerely friendly to all, even to some avid autograph hunters who thrust a stack of stills in front of her for signatures. She was affable, easy to talk with, and a delight to be with. She increased her number of fans by everyone who was there.

June Allyson, unlike many of her peers in "senior movieland," has taken care of herself physically and mentally. She has retained her beauty and looks and acts just as she did when she was starring in the many films which earned her fame. If I sound like a star-struck teenager, that's how I feel.

June Allyson, everyone in Indiana loved you! David, you have every right to be proud of your lovely wife. There is only one June Allyson. There were many present who envied you.

It was a wonderful, memorable Jimmy Stewart birthday party. And, that's coming from old man Sam who is usually unbelieving and skeptical. Now, like Wendy and Peter Pan ... I believe!

Classic Images, *No. 331*
1994

The Two Dougs!

I enjoy working crossword puzzles. It gives me satisfaction to be able to finish one. But, I've been having trouble lately. All these wizards who concoct the brain-twisters now use the names of modern-day entertainers: movie stars, playwrights, TV performers, etc. They put me in a bind because, as I have admitted in the past, I am not up on the current entertainers. Only a limited number of them are familiar to me.

I admit that I am probably in the minority, and I ought to awaken and join the rest of the world, but my mind is still steeped in the past. Ask me about Mary Pickford, Tom Mix, Lon Chaney, Charlie Chaplin, Harold Lloyd and even Rudolph Valentino, and I'll probably have an answer for you. Ask me about Douglas Fairbanks, Sr., and you'll see my face light up. You'll be bombarded by happy rays that emanate from me, and you will see me come to life at the mention of his name.

Doug! He was my favorite, and I'm sure it's true with many other aged movie-goers. His acrobatics, his agility, his effervescence, his energy and his filmatic bravery all captivated me ... and all the other kids I knew. I never lost my infatuation for Doug. I have always enjoyed his films.

I remember my first Fairbanks movie. It was in 1924, and I was but six years old. The film: *Robin Hood*! Thirty or forty years later I still remembered scenes from the silent blockbuster when I was once again able to view it.

After *Robin Hood*, I never missed a Fairbanks film. Most of his later pictures were historical swashbucklers. I went through the gamut of such pictures as *The Black Pirate, The Gaucho, The Thief of Bagdad* and *Don Q., Son of Zorro*. When he aged and was not quite as agile and athletic, I still enjoyed his work with such "late in his career" films as *Mr. Robinson Crusoe, Taming of the Shrew* (with wife Mary Pickford) and *Around the World in 80 Minutes*.

When I began collecting movies, I caught up on his career, obtaining most of his earlier films, including the unforgettable Fairbanks tradition-breaker *The Mark of Zorro*, which made me an instant Zorro fan and elevated the word Zorro into my "favorites" dictionary.

I began to read everything about Zorro, including the first Zorro novel, Johnston McCulley's *The Curse of Capistrano*" from which *The Mark of Zorro* was made. I followed the Zorros: Tyrone Power, Guy Williams, John Carroll, Reed Hadley and all the others.

I was able to obtain a quality print of his famous D'Artagnan role in *The Three

Musketeers and also the later sound sequel *The Iron Mask*, which is the only Fairbanks film I can recall in which he has a death scene. I'll always remember the reunion in the sky (after death) of D'Artagnan and the Three Musketeers.

Like Zorro, everyone wanted to play D'Artagnan. There were numerous films featuring the famous swashbuckler. Offhand, I can recall Walter Abel, Don Ameche, Gene Kelly, Michael York and Warren William. There were, of course, others. Even the Ritz Brothers got into the act by playing substitute Three Musketeers to Don Ameche's D'Artagnan.

I was introduced to, and enjoyed, many of Doug's earlier movies, including *The Lamb* (his first), *American Aristocracy, Flirting with Fate; Reaching for the Moon* (and later, the sound version with Bebe Daniels), *His Majesty the American, Down to Earth, The Man from Painted Post, The Americano* and so many others. Most of these earlier movies were shot with modern backgrounds.

I even enjoyed seeing Doug in a cameo "sit down" appearance in Marion Davies' *Show People*.

Doug Fairbanks has always been the prototype of the ideal cinematic hero to me. I never fail to watch one of his films when the opportunity arrives.

Then Doug, Jr., came upon the scene! I felt, at first, that he was a fine actor but was emulating his dad in many of the swashbuckling roles he portrayed. He appeared in many modern dress parts, but I enjoyed him most in those historical swashbucklers. My thoughts were prejudiced when I said, "He's imitating his dad." My second thought was, "I don't think these roles are imitation." I opined that he was creating his own swashbuckling image and personality in such movies as *The Prisoner of Zenda, The Corsican Brothers, The Fighting O'Flynn,* and *Sinbad the Sailor*.

I enjoyed all those films and was thrilled to see him in person at last year's Cinecon in Hollywood.

So, there's a Doug Fairbanks in my past, in my present and in my future. I will never miss a chance to get another look at a screenplay containing some Fairbanks "derring-do" whether it be Senior or Junior.

Classic Images, *No. 167*
May 1989

Name Dropping

Like all people who have departed from the active scene, I have many memories. And, like all people who no longer participate in the production of the very thing that made them happy and constructive, I remember many of the important people with whom I came in contact over the years. Some were major film stars, some were character actors, some were distributors, and some were collectors.

So, following the path of other retirees, I'll devote a few chapters of this milepost of inanities to some name-dropping.

COLLEEN MOORE

On top of the list is that wonderful actress who had one blue eye and one brown eye (I may have the colors mixed) ... that elegant lady of the screen, Colleen Moore.

One can't get much "eleganter" than Colleen Moore. She was a guest at our first Chicago Cinecon and, years later, accepted an invitation to the Syracuse Cinefest.

I was placidly sitting in my home in Indiana, Pennsylvania, when I was awakened by the alarming jangle of the telephone. The voice: "Mr. Rubin, Colleen Moore is in Pittsburgh and would like to meet you."

After determining it was not a joke, I gathered my family, jumped into the car and hied into Pittsburgh (55 miles away)

We arrived at her hotel room where I was informed that she had just written her autobiography. We spent a delightful hour with Miss Moore as she told us about her life and the writing of the autobiography. She also stated that she was looking for some of her films, especially *Flaming Youth*.

When it was over, we parted with an autographed copy of the book and a kiss for each of us by that gracious lady. We all fell firmly and deeply in love with Colleen Moore.

And ... she didn't forget us! In later years, at Syracuse, she loudly stated to everyone concerned: "Where is Sam Rubin? I want to see him."

I was lucky enough to be able to put her on to some of her films ... and to a reel of *Flaming Youth*. She graciously permitted me to have a copy of her 16mm print of *Irene* made; and that's one I treasure!

I was saddened by her death and only regret that we were never able to take advantage of her invitation to visit her at her ranch in California.

Mel Torme

I have had the privilege of meeting Mel Torme several times, one of them at the National Film Society Convention in Hollywood. I want to tell you about the first time because, you see, Mel Torme is a real gentleman ... and, to sweeten it, a film collector.

The advertisement read that Mel Torme would appear at Pittsburgh's Holiday House Supper Club. I knew Mel was a film collector, and I was familiar with his great talent. I wanted to see him.

A party of six of us went to the Holiday House. I took several copies of *Classic Film Collector* (predecessor to *Classic Images*) with me. I suggested to the other two couples that perhaps I would be able to visit Mel in his dressing room. They scoffed and ridiculed me; they laughed and snickered, "No stranger gets to visit the stars' dressing rooms at the Holiday House."

We were shown to our tables. I handed the waitress the copies of *Classic Film Collector*, requesting her to give them to Torme and to ask for permission to visit with him.

The scoffing, ridiculing, laughing and snickering continued!

The waitress returned saying, "Mr. Torme would like to see you."

The scoffing, ridiculing, laughing and snickering ceased!

My wife Sissy and I prepared to go to Mel's dressing room. "Sam," came the earnest plea from the scoffers, ridiculers, laughers and snickerers, "see if you can get us in too."

When we were ushered into Mel's room, he greeted us like the gentleman he is. I learned that he was familiar with *CFC*; he purchased his copies at Larry Edmunds Bookstore.

We spent a half hour with the kind of warm, friendly collector talk of which you are all familiar. We bragged about what we had and what we wanted to add to our collections.

Mel told me about an article on World War I aviation films which he had written for a national adventure magazine some time before. He gave me permission to run it in *CFC*. Unfortunately, I was never able to do so, because I was unable to get permission from the publisher.

"Mel," I interrupted, "there are two couples at our table who are dying to come in to see you. May I bring them?"

Gentleman that he is, Mel said, "Yes"

The other two couples arrived. One of the men was smoking a large, vile cigar. Mel exclaimed, "Oh, no. No smoking here ... my throat!"

Then the girls began: "Oh, Mel, I enjoy your singing so much. I saw you here, I saw you there" ... etc., etc.—the inane chatter all celebrities detest.

The effect was as if a huge, wet blanket had descended on the room to smother everything that was warm and congenial.

The meeting was definitely over! A warm farewell from Mel Torme did not make me feel any better about the situation.

We wended our weary way back to Indiana, Pennsylvania, where I got out a sledgehammer and smashed every window in the house in order to ease my vexation. It didn't work!

Classic Images, *No. 165*
March 1989

Stan

One of my prized possessions is a recorded telephone conversation in which Stan Laurel talks about the *Classic Images'* predecessor *8mm Collector*.

It's a gem! But, before I reveal it to you, it must be prefaced with a few introductory remarks.

When the *8mm Collector* was first started in June 1962, I had a mailing list comprised of a limited number of collectors' names I had received from other people. I had decided, before starting to publish, that I would use only funds on hand. The greater the sum of money to arrive, the larger the issue.

The publication did grow; the amount of material submitted for publishing grew disproportionately, causing the one recurring problem which never ceased until the day I retired: too much material for the available space.

So, in order to get more material in each issue, I reduced the size of the type ... considerably. I did get complaints. Stubborn as I am, it was some time before I saw fit to enlarge the type. (Stan Laurel was instrumental in forcing this upon me.) However, at that time, I established the policy of squeezing as much material as possible into the available space. That policy never ceased!

Now, let me introduce you to Mike Polacek from the state of West Virginia. (Huntington, I think.) Mike was a fanatical Stan Laurel devotee. I have not heard from Mike for years. I heard from several sources that when Stan Laurel died, the heart went out of Mike, and he discontinued his Stan Laurel activities. It's hearsay only, I can't vouch for it.

Anyway, Mike came to visit me in Indiana, Pennsylvania, one fine day. We had a scintillating talk about Laurel and Hardy. He even managed to pry some L & H lobbies from me.

I asked Mike about the possibility of a Stan Laurel interview. Following his suggestion, I wrote to Stan.

Mike was an engineer at a TV or radio station. He would call Stan regularly and record the conversations. Some time after our meeting, he sent me a copy of a tape in which he and Stan discussed the *8mm Collector*.

The following is an excerpt from that tape, reproducing only the portion pertaining to the *8mm Collector*. Usually, I edit conversations or interviews because superfluous words and much repetition so often occur in them. However, I have left everything in this conversation to retain the flavor and enable you to read what Stan Laurel really felt about the *8mm Collector* in his exact words.

★ ★ ★

Stan: Hi!
Mike: Hello, old buddy!
S: How are you, Mike? Glad to hear from you.
M: How's everything with you?
S: Oh, pretty good ... about the same. Y'know, some days good, lousy in others. We have a hell of a heat wave here.
M: I saw that in the paper ... and you wrote to me.
S: Brother, it is really murder.
M: I told you, send some of it down here.
S: Yeah, I wish I could. You're welcome to it.
M: We could use it. Of course, it's not too bad in the daytime, about 70. In the evening it gets chilly and frosty.
S: Where?
M: Here!
S: Oh, back there!
M: Yes, back here ... it's getting to be about that time of the year.
S: I got a letter from [hesitation] ... Sam Rubin. He sent a kind of questionnaire.
M: When I was up in Pennsylvania, I stopped in to see him.
S: Yeah, you told me.
M: He said that he got a letter from you.
S: I told him, I'm not up to writing anything.
M: I told him that "I'm pretty sure you can ask what questions you want, and I'm sure Stan can help you on that."
S: He sent me a kind of questionnaire, and I answered what I possibly could, you know.
M: He wants to do a big article on you.
S: I told him he needed bigger type in that paper.
M: See, he is actually running in a hole with it. He's an old movie collector.
S: Well, no wonder he's running in a hole with it. People can't read the goddamn thing. I mean, Jesus, what's the use?

M: Well, the first one he had started with fairly big print.
S: I'll bet he can put the Lord's Prayer on the top of a pin.
M: I know what you mean. He's only had 60 some subscriptions to it.
S: At least a typewriter would be better than that.
M: That's what you call photo-offset printing.
S: I know, but he better get something people can read, for Christ's sake. You can go blind trying to read that bloody thing. It's ridiculous.
M: A lot of times I have to use a magnifying glass to read some of the stuff.
S: It's ridiculous. I mean, Jesus, you can't put out papers with that type of print.

★ ★ ★

The taped conversation then went on to other subjects. The questions and answers appeared in one of our issues at the time.

To increase my mortification, I played the recording at one of the Cinecons; the audience was comprised of Cinephiles, most of them were subscribers who were aware of the difficulty in reading the tiny print. Upon hearing the conversation, the audience broke out laughing, emphasizing the fact to me of which I was already aware. The type in the *8mm Collector* was too small.

I took appropriate steps!

11

Flashbacks

Some hard-to-accept truths about silent films come to you when you reach my venerable age and you are retired. You realize that the number of people who actually experienced the silent films during their original release is becoming fewer and fewer.

Today, other than the brilliant London Thames revivals with orchestra and their subsequent U.S. performances and the rapidly diminishing group of repertory theaters in the country and a limited number of available silent film videos released, the closest you can come to an actual reproduction of a vintage silent screening is a presentation at a film convention.

I am thinking specifically of the Cinecon, the Cinefest and the Cinevent wherein silents are often shown in theaters with organ or piano accompaniment. Silent films are always a feature of the screening programs at these conventions.

Even there, you may not get the ultimate silent film program if the projector being used is geared only for sound speed. Then the action on film is subsequently speeded up from that originally intended. If the projector can be geared to silent speed, then you will get a true reproduction of a silent film program of the '20s ... if you are able to obtain a quality print to illuminate your screen.

Silent film buffs have heard the same inane responses when the subject comes up. "Oh, I remember silent films ... Charlie Chaplin and Harold Lloyd." Baloney! I doubt that statement!

Those who claim to remember Harold Lloyd can recall only the image of the famous comedian hanging from a clock and only because that particular scene has been reproduced so often in the newspapers, magazines and books that even our grandchildren recognize it.

As for Chaplin, they recall him from seeing his many imitators and from the countless times he was shown on TV at sound speed, putting the action on "fast forward," with scratched and splicy film. The Chaplin shorts were shown on *Howdy Doody* and other kids' programs. What a horrible way for our kids to be exposed to Chaplin and the other talented comedians.

My memories of the silents go back to 1924. I remember scenes from the first movie I ever saw, Doug Fairbanks' *Robin Hood*. When I saw the film again, about 20 years ago, I recognized them.

I still remember how frightened I was at the showing of *The Phantom of the Opera*. I covered my eyes when Chaney's face was revealed ... some people screamed.

I still enjoy the *Phantom* after countless viewings. But, now I keep my eyes open and enjoy the artistry of Chaney's makeup with his skeleton-like visage. The *Phantom* has become an old friend.

Of course, the silent movie which impressed me the most was the classic *The Lost World*, which, as many of you know, was instrumental in the founding of *Classic Images*. I have written enough about that in the past.

We eased our way into the talkies in my small hometown. First we had films with synchronized music; then some with part dialogue; and then they all talked.

I was enthralled by the early talkies. As an avid movie fan, I tried to see every film that came to town—impossible with three theaters. Those I did see were marvels to me. However, when I view them today, so many of the early sound films do not stand the test of time—not nearly as much as the silents.

The Jazz Singer is a marvel. But, *The Jazz Singer* is a silent film with only the songs (and one short dialogue scene) with sound.

At first viewing years ago, I loved *Just Imagine, Sunnyside Up, The Vagabond King* and *Hollywood Revue*. I have been fortunate to be able to view these four again.

Sunnyside Up remains a delight to me. It still retains its charm. *Hollywood Revue* is disappointing. It was made in 1929, and the studios were feeling their way with the musical revues. It was great then, but stilted and not as much fun today. MGM brought out most of their big guns; there were superior skits with Laurel and Hardy, John Gilbert, Norma Talmadge and so many more, plus a rousing finale with the favorite, "Singin' in the Rain."

My greatest disappointments were *Just Imagine* and *The Vagabond King*. I idolized both musicals; they had given me so many fine memories. The memories were squashed with recent screenings.

Just Imagine is a science fiction musical. The dialogue is stilted, the musical numbers awkward, including an inane song Frank Albertson sings about a fly. A recent viewing deflated my memories of El Brendel being shocked by lightning on a golf course in 1930 and returning to life in 1980. He even took a trip to Mars. Maureen O'Sullivan made one of her first appearances in the film. There are some good special effects including the city of 1980 as envisioned in 1930.

For years, some of my favorite tunes to hum and sing in the shower have been the wonderful tunes from *The Vagabond King*, especially "The Song of the Vagabonds." You know ... "Sons of toil and danger," etc. The stars were Jeanette MacDonald and Dennis King. What could be better? Dennis King, direct from Broadway musicals, projected his voice in proper stage manner so that everyone could hear him. He brought his stage histrionics with him. The stagey performance did not gel when I saw the film at a Cinevent. Too much unnecessary "stage presence" and the dialogue did not ring true.

I never thought I would be bored at a re-viewing of this illustrious musical. But I was! Although I enjoyed the music and singing as much as I had in the past, the film left me cold.

So much for memories of the past. I am happy that so many of the silents still exist for the expressed purpose of giving me enjoyment. How I loved a second, third and fourth look at such stalwarts as *The Big Parade, What Price Glory?, Lilac Time, Birth of a Nation, Son of the Sheik, The Beloved Rogue, Don Juan* and so many, many more.

Yes, I'll take a good old silent over a poor old sound film. It took a few years for the actors to modify their talents to catch up to the progress of the sound movie world. But, when it happened, dialogue became an effective tool for an improved presentation of a motion picture.

Even the two most famous holdouts for silent films finally succumbed: Charlie Chaplin and Lon Chaney.

Classic Images
May 1996

Going to the Movies in the '20s

There are some good movies being filmed today, and there are many with which I am unhappy. I see excess violence and gore. I witness and hear voluminous obscenities as the moviemakers (as always) continue their campaign to lure people to the theaters for shock treatment.

This practice started from the very inception of motion pictures. Even the first commercial movie, *The Kiss*, just a short scene of a couple kissing, shocked some people, seeing such outrageous behavior outright for the first time in public. Others were *Nosferatu, The Phantom of the Opera, Dr. Jekyll and Mr. Hyde, The Wolf Man* and countless films of their ilk with subsequent, inevitable sequels. In the past, most of them at least had satisfactory endings when good triumphed over evil, and the audience usually went home happy that the bad guys and the monsters had been aptly punished.

I'll not dwell on this subject. Instead, I am going to relate some of my experiences going to the movies some decades ago ... and I do mean decades!

I plan to explore the attic of my head, sift through the many cobwebs there and try to remember some of the fun of going to the movie when I was younger, much younger. I will return to the days when I lived in a small town in Pennsylvania where the most popular kid, the theater usher, had the unprecedented luck of being able to continually watch the current film programs, which usually had a run of only a few days (sometimes only one). Week-long exhibitions were practically unheard of.

I will return to the time when "Going to the Movies" was the only game in town. It was a time when I entered a theater in 1925 to watch Lon Chaney's original *Phantom of the Opera* and cowered in my seat at the famous unmasking scene. This was true horror stuff to me, and I walked home looking from side to side to make sure I wasn't being followed by some other gruesome phantom.

There were three small theaters and one large theater in town. The large theater, off the main street, screened the latest "A" first-run releases. One of the others we labeled "The Ranch House" and it showed only Westerns and other "B" films, along with news, a short and a serial. The other two screened some "B's" and mostly second run "A's."

Each week my dad would give me 15 cents to go to the show. Ten cents went for the theater admission; the remaining nickel bought a chocolate nut sundae.

We kids always went to the Saturday matinee, at the Moon Theater (The Ranch House). Some of the popular cowboys were Tom Mix (of course), Bob Steele, Ken Maynard, Wally Wales, Buddy Roosevelt, Fred Thomson, William Desmond, Bob Custer, Tom Keene, William S. Hart, Pete Morrison, Rex Bell, child actors Buzz Barton and Frankie Darro and so many others. We all had our favorites.

As today, some had little or no use for certain designated cowpokes. I will never forget passing the Moon one day when one of the kids vented his disgust at the current offering. To the entire world he shouted, "Fred Humes! Peeoo [phew?]. He stinks." That early film critic influenced me, and I did not attend that performance.

My greatest disappointment occurred one Saturday when a Wally Wales film was scheduled for the Moon. A chapter of the William Desmond serial *The Ace of Spades* was also to be shown. I was looking forward to seeing the program when one of my friends informed me of a feature playing at the Star Theater, up the street, home of the second-run "A's." "It's all about a guy," he stated, "who wears a mask and goes around fighting duels and robbing stages."

Here was a dilemma! Should I go to the popular Wally Wales and the next chapter of the serial which I had been following, or should I go and see this exciting new guy who sounded like my kind of film hero? I mulled over this important decision and finally decided to give up Wally Wales and William Desmond in favor of this latest example of a derring-doer.

I walked into the Star and sat through the entire program in utter disgust and frustration. It was a love story! Some nobody guy named Rudolph Valentino in *The Eagle*! To make matters worse, I had to pass the Moon on the way home, just as the movie ended. The kids poured out of the theater with enthusiastic shots of joy. "That was great! Wally Wales was terrific; and they found out who the Ace of Spades was!"

I blindly stumbled home and, if I had been much older, would probably have contemplated suicide. What a catastrophe! That, my friends, was when I discovered that everyone has different tastes in movies. That was when the seed of mistrust of film critics was planted in my brain.

Fred Thomson arrived! His films, at the time, were released by one of the major studios, Paramount. And, much to our surprise, they were shown in the large theater in town, which normally ran the first run highly publicized "A" films. He became almost as popular in our group as Tom Mix.

During my collecting years, I searched for Fred Thomson Westerns. This fact may have changed, but the only extant title at that time, to my knowledge, was *Thundering Hoofs*. It had an unforgettable scene in which Fred's father dies. He had apparently been living alone and, in the absence of humans, his horse buries him! Match that, you *Star Wars* fans.

There are so many memories in my mind about the silent film era. Once in a while, during a program, the film would break, or the operator would forget to renew the carbon for the powerful carbon-arc light, or some other show-stopping calamity would occur. You never heard such commotion: yelling, foot-stomping, hand-clapping, until projection was resumed. We were unruly and impatient with that guy up in the projection booth. Who did he think he was, interrupting the show like that?

How about the incentives and premiums which they used to entice you into the theater? They started giving out cards (some the size of baseball cards, some smaller) of movie star pictures. We were all collecting them. Perhaps that's when the collecting bug bit me. We were all trying to get a complete set. We traded cards with each other. This was possible because often you were handed a duplicate at the box office.

Another ploy! They would draw numbers on the stage, giving away pieces of china and dinnerware. The ladies went for that! There were other premiums but, unfortunately, I can't remember any of them. They were all designed, however, to draw us away from radio's *Amos 'n Andy, Myrt and Marge, Jack Armstrong, Little Orphan Annie* and such.

Most of the time the theaters were crowded and you often had to stand until the first show was over. When people in the audience streamed out, just as many streamed in. Exception! One day in the summer, the theaters were always practically empty. The circus had come to town. That was a banner day! The schools closed, and all the kids were free to go to the circus grounds and watch the tents go up, with the help of elephants, of course.

We could witness the always exciting circus parade with its clowns and other performers, the animals and, of course, the calliope; and then attend the afternoon or evening performance. We would always wheedle money from our parents on circus day for popcorn, peanuts to feed our faces and the elephants, and the purchase of the various circus souvenirs.

I can remember the Sparks and the Downie Brothers circuses. Our town was on the route of one or the other, and we were able to see a circus every year.

It was a memorable time for those who lived it. You could approach a theater and hear the waves of sound as the audience responded to the successful efforts of the hero: the fights, the chases, the escapes from dangerous situations.

In those days there were few anti-heroes. The good guys invariably came out ahead, and the bad guys received their just come uppances!

The good guys, usually in Westerns, had sidekicks for comedy relief. Many of the film's serious moments had an accompanying snicker or laugh as the hero's "pal" would grimace, or take a pratfall, or do something stupid ... often while harassing the villain.

We who still remember the silent films will recall the antics in the "Our Gang" comedies. They were later called "The Little Rascals." We were young enough to empathize with what was happening to this lovable gang of kids. Years later, we were fortunate to have Spanky McFarland as a dinner guest in our home.

What vividly comes to mind with fondness is the derring-do of Richard Talmadge as he climbed, jumped and fought on buildings, bridges, cliffs and everything else dangerous, much in the manner of the ever-popular Douglas Fairbanks, Sr., who was noted for his acrobatics and effervescent activities.

We also remember the exquisite timing of master comedian Harold Lloyd. He, too, went through extraordinary gyrations in dangerous situations, but his were for comedy effect; each gag was choreographed and timed to the fraction of a second.

My few words do not even scratch the surface in describing the action on the silent screen. And, never doubt, it was practically all action.

There was always musical accompaniment from the very inception of motion pictures. No matter how large or small the theater, there was always music to create a mood for the action on the screen. In some cases there was a single piano or organ (the larger the theater, the larger the organ); in others, musical combos. In major theaters, there were full-fledged orchestras. They all provided the musical background. No one had ever heard of a laugh track; the audience provided the laughs for comedy situations. And, unlike the laugh track, the merriment exploded only when something funny occurred on the screen.

When a theater received a silent film for its program, it was often accompanied by a musical cue sheet, indicating the type of music apropos to the mood of the film's action, often naming the pieces which should, or could, be used. Also, with some major productions, complete musical scores for large or small orchestras (and even piano or organ) would arrive with the film when the theater received it.

And, don't forget the slapstick pie-in-the-face antics of the comedians, their pratfalls and their many irreverent pranks as they committed mayhem with everyone, including themselves.

Today we tend to forget that most of the silent films were photographed, and then projected, at 18 frames per second. The action on the screen moved at a natural pace, unlike the speeded-up behavior we see when the films are shown today with projection equipment geared for the 24 fps speed of sound films. When you see the silent film players frantically dashing around, don't forget you are not seeing the action as it was originally shot and projected. This type of frenetic "goings-on" can turn the uninformed person into an unhappy viewer with a misconception of how the silent films really were.

Here is something which should make you groan. The advertising material (posters, ad mats, glossy photos, lobby cards and such) were all purchased by the theaters. A few of the movie houses retained and stored these displays; others trashed them. Today we call that stuff "memorabilia." Think of the thousands of dollars (today's value) that went into the incinerator. Stop gnashing your teeth!

SOUND ARRIVES

I'll never forget when sound was introduced in 1926. At first, a short subject, demonstrating this marvelous invention, was distributed. I still recall that guy on the screen, facing the audience, singing "I Wish I Were in Peoria." I think the short was entitled, *When the Movies Found Its Voice.*

The first feature with synchronized musical background, *sans* dialogue, was John Barrymore's swashbuckler *Don Juan*. Next came the feature usually touted as the first "talkie." Al Jolson's *The Jazz Singer* was actually a silent film except for the songs and one short scene when Al talks to his mother while playing the piano, and his father, Warner Oland, angrily enters and demands he stop playing that sacrilegious "jazz" music in his home. All the remaining dialogue was captioned on the screen. Incidentally, a young Myrna Loy appears as a chorus girl.

The first all-talking picture arrived! Cullen Landis and Helen Costello starred in *Lights of New York*. The "talkies" were here, and all the theaters scrambled to install sound equipment, some of which remained in use for many years. And the sound, at times, left much to be desired.

Many stilted (by today's standards) musical revues came into being. Because the sound cameras were enclosed in a soundproof chamber and, consequently, were clumsy and almost immobile, the photography was confined to close-ups and long shots with little or no zooming.

It may surprise some to know that the song Gene Kelly made so famous in *Singin' in the Rain* appeared in an early MGM musical which had just about every star on the company's lot in the cast. They sang the famous rain song in a scene in which practically the entire cast was present, all wearing raincoats. The film: *Hollywood Revue of 1929*.

Even Buster Keaton sang in that one, and John Gilbert proved he did have an acceptable voice in a scene from *Romeo and Juliet* with Norma Shearer. A young Jack Benny was the emcee. Lon Chaney was represented only in a song in one of the skits, "Lon Chaney Will Get You If You Don't Watch Out."

Two early musicals enthralled me when they were first released: *Just Imagine*, a journey into the future; and *Vagabond King* with Jeanette MacDonald and Dennis King. Years later, I was able to view them again, and they failed to stand up for me, especially my favorite, *The Vagabond King*. Apparently MacDonald and King had been recruited from the stage and acted as if they were still playing it "live," projecting their voices, always facing the camera, and over-emoting.

Unrelated: it was 1927! We kids, with the rest of the world, were excited about Lindbergh's famous flight to Paris. The rumor came to us that Lindy was in town at the local newspaper office. We dashed madly to that newspaper office. Lindbergh was indeed there! He had been there for years! He was an employee of the publication. Someone had "put us on." In the parlance of those medieval times, someone was "pulling our legs." The only flying he ever did was "in a rage" when someone sicced a bunch of kids on him.

I've had fun writing this article. Now I am awaiting word from film buffs correcting the errors I may have made. Don't forget, without volumes of reference material, I am doing most of this from memory, which is getting so bad I'm going around and asking people, "What's memory?"

Classic Images, *No. 202*
April 1992

Movie Critics and Camera Angles

My subjects, ladies and gentlemen, are: *movie critics* and *camera angles*. Starting with a head filled with Iowa corn, Las Vegas chips, Arizona cactus and Florida citrus, there is little room for any other material in my minuscule brain, so I probably won't have anything important to say. But, important or not ... you know me, I'll say it.

Movie critics ... I hate them!

On the surface, it appears that a movie critic has that dream job. All he has to do is watch a film, go home and write about it ... and even get paid for having all that fun.

I can mentally see one of these critics in a theater. His eyes are directed toward the screen, but where is his mind? Is he really involved in following the story? I don't think so!

Here's what he (of she) is thinking: "That's an interesting scene! How am I going to describe it so it doesn't sound like repetition of all my other reviews? What different adjectives can I use?" He is thinking more about what he's going to write and how he's going to say it, rather than completely digesting the film and clearing his mind of everything else which might enhance his enjoyment of the action on the screen to be able to really evaluate it. I have no faith in movie critics. They have their own taste in film fare, and I have my own idea of what makes a good film.

I am finally, after many years, attending the movie theaters again, watching some of the current films—meanwhile trying to identify the current crop of stars who are completely unfamiliar to me in name and face.

I went to see Sean Connery's *Medicine Man*, despite poor critical reviews. I thoroughly enjoyed the movie. What do you say about that, Mr. Critic?

I go to a movie to enjoy myself; I become completely absorbed in it. Sometimes I cry!

You'll find real movie fans among the Western enthusiasts and collectors. Observe the number of Western film conventions held. Some of these Western buffs "eat up" every cowboy film shown ... if the convention has only one screening room. However, some have three and four screening rooms; one must then be selective as to what oater one watches. Some of these conventioneers have traveled far (sometimes thousands of miles) to see the likes of Roy Rogers, Gene Autry, Tom Mix, Hopalong Cassidy, Lash LaRue, Charles Starrett and all the other stars of the horse operas.

I wonder what the critics would say about one of Fred Thomson's pictures which is still in existence: *Thundering Hoofs*. Fred's father dies, alone, and the horse buries him! That's pure Western entertainment.

How about the mystery, sci-fi and horror fans? They would probably gag at some scene about which a critic might rave.

I'm just reminding you, Mr. or Mrs. or Miss Critic, that everyone has different tastes. Remember, also, even if you have watched the same trite, clichéd plots and scenes countless times, others have not. Also, many people like to see the same sort of action over and over again. Witness the long-lasting popular TV series, especially the soap operas with the same characters who often relive identical situations in various episodes. How about the ubiquitous car chases? They're as common as the horse pursuits in the old Westerns.

I've also given thought to another phase of the critic's life. Many studios have their very souls tied up in a particularly expensive film and want to publicize this so-called "block buster." They will go all out wining and dining the critics; taking them to exotic locations; treating them royally; presenting gifts and souvenirs; offering special reviews of the film while inundating them with studio publicity and production facts; and even having them meet the stars.

How does all this affect the review of the film? I think it would be difficult to knock a film made by people who have so befriended you.

After all, a critic can make or break a film; there are thousands of people who believe every word the critic has written. The critic's word is *the law*! If a critic does not like the way an actor picks his teeth, the fans will be watching for that disgusting scene and be equally upset about it. So many fans form their opinions from the words of the critic; after all, he's a pro.

Advise to the critics from a weary-eyed old time (long time) movie buff: When you're in the theater, stop thinking of how you are going to astound your readers with your vast knowledge of the English language and your innovative descriptive techniques. Why not just sit back and enjoy the show and write about it later?

A bag of popcorn might help. Or, better yet, take someone with you and hold hands. That will definitely enhance your perspective.

CAMERA ANGLES

Remember when movies used to tell a story? They still do but, oh, how differently. It seems to me that many of today's directors are more interested in camera angles and unusual effects in their attempt to unfold their plots.

Whatever happened to the "Fade-in" and "Fade-out"? Of course, they are still used, but are often ignored. You are watching a scene; suddenly you are somewhere else viewing different action, with no logical transition or explanation.

One example: While you are watching a scene, the telephone rings. Don't worry if there is no phone in the scene (the characters may be wallowing in lava at the bottom of Mount Etna, or some other Mount). The tinkle of "the bell" is from the next scene. The phone is answered by someone, perhaps hundreds of miles away, who is involved in the next piece of action. The characters in the previous scene never hear the bell, even if it's jingling while they are in the process of some vital histrionics.

How about the close-ups? I think it was D.W. Griffith who invented the film close-up. What an effective piece of moviemaking it is! You can actually see the scars, blemishes (and some wrinkles) on the faces, despite the makeup. Some directors like the close-up so much so, it seems that's about all they use. All you see are close-ups. Some films have so many, you sometimes wonder what the actor or actress is doing with his or her hands. And ... are they wearing shoes? Mr. Director, close-ups are fine, but show us some of the action.

One of my favorite "Oh no, not agains" is the slow motion shot. It was designed, of course, to slow down the action. Slow motion is fine, but some directors will take an *action* film and at certain points, when the action gets really active, they switch gears into slow motion and the piece of action, which should be accelerated, is lowered and you must gnaw on your fingernails for a longer period.

Example: The villain is thrown through a window from the 30th floor, and it takes half the film for him to land.

I will admit that this is good technique and quite effective, but it's overdone, especially on TV. Perhaps some of the directors are using this process to slow the action and increase the running time of the show to fit the time slot.

Then, did you ever try to read the credits on a TV movie, especially at the end? I'm not referring to the cast, directors, producers and such people. They get the *billing*; they're always listed with large type and the viewer is given plenty of time to read the names. But I feel sorry for the rest of the people involved. I'll bet they sometimes have trouble finding their own names, the letters are so small and flit by with lightning speed.

And, lastly, I am always surprised to see that one of the actors of a TV show is also the director of a particular episode. In most cases, it's the star who probably used his star clout to get that job. I have heard that most actors would like to direct; they feel they can do so much better than those inept characters who tell them how to act.

Nothing wrong with a star directing a show. Only thing (and there are some exceptions) so many of them are bad-bad-bad! Some of the actors have directed top-shelf episodes; but many have also come up with low blows to the watcher's sensibilities.

Take this advice from someone who doesn't know what he is talking about: Stick to acting where you already have it made!

Similarly, I ought to stick to watching the films and TV shows and refrain from writing stuff like this.

Classic Images, *No. 264*
June 1997

TV Potpourri

I am, and have been, disenchanted with some of the TV shows. I admit there are too many to watch. I also admit there are many new shows I haven't even tasted. I also admit I am unqualified to make such a verdict and am also unqualified to write this particular column. But, I'm doing it anyway.

Even though I am retired, my viewing time is limited because of the unbelievable amount of activities one gets involved with when one finally reaches that point when one no longer has to look at a time clock.

Therefore, when one is able to find time to sit in front of a TV, one sticks to a comparatively few of the new drama series (notice I didn't say "one" of the new drama series) and one watches many of the reruns he enjoys.

And, to answer your unasked question, we have more than one TV. Audrey and I have different tastes.

I avoid the talk shows and the sitcoms. I am repelled by most of the talk shows because I hear so many, to me, foolish, inane questions and answers. Celebrities on these shows actually answer these questions, smile and make them sound important.

If there are two or more celebrities on the same show, they probably hate each other but hug and kiss at the onset and also at the end of the program.

Then, in recent years, the hosts and hostesses are getting desperate and are introducing many lurid situations for shock value. Many people eat this up!

The sitcoms! Again, I am not really qualified to criticize them because I have avoided them. The few I have monitored are composed of situations designed to entertain you and include an endless series of one-liners accompanied by a laugh track which is supposed to make you think everyone in the audience is laughing, even if the show is not being shown to a live audience.

Everything is funny, if you believe the laugh track. I find myself laughing ... at the laugh track.

Example—Actor: "What is your name?"

Answer: "John Smith" [laughter]

The serious stuff we have been watching are some of last year's winners: *Chicago Hope, ER, NYPD Blue, The Commish* and *Law and Order*. I particularly enjoy seeing reruns of winners from previous years: *Murder She Wrote, Matlock, In the Heat of the Night, Perry Mason, Mike Hammer, Columbo, Banacek, McCloud* and *Quincy*. (*Dr. Kildare*, where are you?)

Do you think I am partial to medical and mystery dramas? Where in the world did you ever get such an idea? I watch other shows occasionally, perhaps once a month, if they appear promising.

I even go to a few movies if they sound interesting. I do not particularly enjoy the smut and gore which is running rampant on today's screen. I'm the guy who walked out of *Pulp Fiction* after listening to about ten minutes of continuous profanity.

Referring to newspaper articles I have recently read, seems like I am not alone in my feelings about the unclean trend of some of the modern films.

Back to the tube? I particularly enjoy watching for stars and extras of the past as they appear in minor roles on TV shows and series. Having been able to watch only an infinitesimal fraction of the programs, I can only report on the few I have seen (and remember). I know there are so many more.

A few examples: I spotted George E. Stone in an extremely minor role as a court clerk in the *Perry Mason* series. He would swear in the witnesses and then disappear.

How about Jackie Coogan? I saw him several times, bald head and all! Once he was a bartender.

Eddie Quillan was walking a dog in one mystery drama.

I remember seeing Ruth Roman, Kathryn Grayson, Margaret O'Brien and Bob Steele, all appearing as extras in the twilight of their careers.

Not only do I get a charge out of watching these older actors, it's fun to watch some of the more recent stars as they appeared on early TV at the start of their careers.

How about Burt Reynolds and Dennis Weaver on *Gunsmoke*?

In watching these old programs, you see actors on the way up ... and you see actors on the way down. How delightful ... and then, how sad! *All* of these people have given enjoyment to a multitude of movie and TV fans.

I'll conclude this nostalgic mishmash with a couple of quiz questions ... for young and old.

For the young: How did daytime serials get the name soap operas?

Answer: The daytime serials, which started on radio, were invariably sponsored by companies which sold soap. (I haven't watched them in years, but this may still be true.)

For the oldtimers, here's a toughie. It can win you some money at the bar where you spend so much time.

Question: Who was the first actor to play Tarzan on the screen? (If you say Elmo Lincoln, you're wrong!)

Answer: In the 1918 film *Tarzan of the Apes*, an unidentified baby, at the beginning of the picture, was the first Tarzan. The second actor to play Tarzan was

Gordon Griffith, who had the role as the ape man as a boy in the same picture. The third actor to portray Tarzan was, of course, Elmo Lincoln.

If I can stop thinking of what we are going to have for dinner, I may come up with some more of this dumb stuff in a future column.

Classic Images, *No. 206*
August 1992

Rumblings and Grumblings

I opened the pages of that rare and unusual publication, *Classic Images*, and saw my name listed as Editor Emeritus. "What's an Emeritus?" I asked. Are they calling me names because of all the garbage I've been writing? I was about to take umbrage with the *CI* staff when I decided to call my good friends Mr. Funk and Mr. Wagnall for a definition. I quote: "Emeritus. Retired from active service, partially because of age, but retained in an honorary position."

I did a double take on that "partially because of age" bit, and I planned to take the Funk and Wagnalls to task until...!

In a couple of days following this literary masterpiece, I will be going into the hospital for a prostate operation. I don't recall any young people having such a procedure. So, at last, I am "partially" convinced that I am growing older.

Only "partially," remember. I surely don't feel my age, and I still have young men's thoughts. Only thing is, I have trouble remembering them.

I wrote about the Cinevent, and what an exhilarating experience it was to me. Here comes some of the "grumblings" from this month's "stumbling" effort. In the past, when I was editor of *Classic Images*, many people would come up to me at the conventions and get into lengthy discussions about various film topics. The conversation always leaned towards subjects in which they had a personal interest. In fact, most of the dialogues were actually monologues as they spouted their own ideas, opinions and convictions on their favorite subject. That did not bother me because I enjoyed talking (and listening) about film. I always felt you could learn more by listening than by talking. However, this year at Columbus, some of these same people passed me by with merely a nod of the head, or a "Hello, Sam," and continued their vital, important path to someone with willing ears who might be able to give them publicity, or help them, somehow, in the pursuance of the favorite obsession of their own small, limited world (either information-wise or collecting-wise).

Don't get me wrong; these are rare specimens. Most of the collectors went out of their way to approach me and sincerely welcome my return, and joined with me in interesting and sincere discussions.

And, talking about talking, I encountered a few surprises down here in Florida retirement land. I look around and see so many prehistoric people like myself, and sometimes I even get to converse with some. I am so used to exchanging words with people knowledgeable about the classics that I am a bit dumbfounded when, during a conversation, such names as Harry Langdon, Lupino Lane, Lloyd Hamilton, Mabel Normand and even Yakima Canutt come up, and no one knows of whom I speak. Of course, they all know Charlie Chaplin! Perhaps I ought to start a course on the silent classics and revive these people's memory.

The above paragraph is one of the reasons I have little feeling of aging. I remember Charles Farrell, Syd Chaplin, Lila Lee, Priscilla Dean, Cullen Landis and many others if I could think of their names. Of course, I have seen their films much more recently than these ignoramuses, and I have personally met many of the movie people.

This will be the shortest column I have written since the days of our troubles with the dupers who were peddling poor prints years ago. This will also disprove the theory that I have diarrhea of the typewriter.

I'm stopping now!

Classic Images, *No. 195*
September 1991

Show Biz

I have been wanting to tell you about my experiences in various phases of show business, which is the mother and father of the film entertainment field. These all go back to the early days of my life in Indiana, Pennsylvania, before and during the beginnings of the *8mm Collector* and *16mm Collector*, predecessor of *Classic Images*.

I was quite active in community affairs, belonging to the Lions Club, Kiwanis, Boy Scouts, Red Cross Blood Program, the local synagogue and ... the PTA. There were never enough hours in the day with my stint in the "long-houred" furniture store and my outside activities.

I have a fault: If I belong to an organization, I will be active. I cannot be just a member, attending meetings and doing nothing. So, with almost every one of the above activities, I would open my mouth too quickly, too wide, and would usually find myself in a predicament which I could have avoided by keeping aforesaid mouth closed.

The first one that comes to mind concerns Rubinoff.

Remember Rubinoff and His Violin and his many appearances with Eddie Cantor? My wife Sissy was distantly related to Rubinoff. Third or fourth cousin ... or something.

The Kiwanis Club, in search of a money-making entertainment event, scheduled Rubinoff and His Violin for an appearance in Indiana. It was to be in the local high school auditorium.

When I heard the news, I puffed up and started bragging, "He's a relative!" I must have been a bit brassy, because in no time at all every member of the club knew that Rubinoff was a relative.

It reached the point where I uncovered the old cornball I had been using for years when meeting new people: "My name is Rubinoff, with the 'off' off."

The big day of the show arrived! The club had sold many tickets and, of course, Sissy and I were looking forward to it. That afternoon I was called to the phone in our furniture store.

A voice, with heavy accent, asked, "Mr. Rooobeen?"

"Yes."

"This is Rubinoff. I hear you are related to me."

I explained the relationship. He said, "Oh, yes!" He remembered Sissy. He invited us to dinner before the show. We went to his motel, the Holiday Inn. He was a gracious host, and Sissy and he had quite a conversation about family.

Meanwhile, I noticed that members of the Kiwanis Club were in the dining room. I waved; some came over, and I introduced them to Rubinoff. No doubt about it, I was puffed up. When we left the dining room, I noticed that my hat had become smaller.

We filed into the auditorium; I waved at friends and fellow Kiwanians, a big grin on my face. As the curtain rose, I was sitting upright, edged forward in the chair, making sure everyone saw me.

Rubinoff came out on the stage and made an introductory speech before he began his performance. In heavy gutteral accents he said, "You people of Indiana, Pennsylvania are very lucky tonight that you are able to see Rubinoff and his violin for only $2 admission. I am worth more ... and usually get more!"

The peculiar noise my neighbors heard was a groan from Samuel K. Rubin. I edged back, as far as I could, into the seat, and started to sink down so that people couldn't see me. I tried to make myself as small as possible.

When the performance ended, I crawled out of the auditorium ... and I mean crawled.

That incident should have taught me to keep my mouth shut! It didn't; there is more to come!

Classic Images, *No. 196*
October 1991

Sam the Lion!

The Lions' Club in Indiana, Pennsylvania (Sam Rubin and Jimmy Stewart's home town) was quite active. Shortly after World War II, the club had a large group of exuberant, active doers ... most of them fairly young and boisterous.

The Lions' Club, as you may know, is dedicated to service to the community. In performing such service, it was usually necessary to raise funds.

Indiana is the county seat of Indiana County. The town has an annual county fair which is held in a rather large facility containing show grounds, barns and a race track.

Some Lion had the idea: In order to keep people off the highway during the Fourth of July holiday, why not have a carnival and celebration, including auto races and wrestling at the fair grounds? All this to be preceded by a parade.

It was a tremendous success. The first time we tried it, we were terribly undermanned, never dreaming of the crowd we would attract. I had a brainstorm—get a pick-up truck, fill it full of huge tubs of soda pop on ice and set it in the large field surrounding the race track where people were picnicking. I opened my mouth and suggested such an activity.

"Good idea, Sam. You do it!" So, under blistering sun, all day long, I gradually broke my back bending over, opening pop bottles. I learned to hate the sight of a pop bottle.

We made a considerable sum that first Fourth of July celebration, and it became an annual event. Then, several years later, I opened my mouth again at a meeting! "We Lions have this parade every Fourth, why don't we get a lion's costume and have a Lion identifying mascot march along with the parade?"

"Good idea, Sam. You do it!"

I called one of the costume suppliers in Pittsburgh (55 miles away) and arranged for a lion's suit. It arrived ... to big for me! With the ingenious (!) use of rubber bands we adjusted the length of the legs so that they wouldn't flop over my toes.

The Fourth of July arrived ... absolutely the hottest day in two centuries. I muttered to myself as I donned the lion's suit prior to entering the parade, "You and your big mouth!"

I cannot understand why real lions elect to remain in that hot African climate. It was blistering inside that suit. The sun's rays poured down unmercifully as I gaily skipped and frolicked in front of one of the bands. I left a trail of sweat behind me.

It was fun, albeit hot fun. I enjoyed going up to people I knew and surprising them, calling them by name ... perhaps saying vile things to them. They were unaware who was behind those slavering fangs!

I'm sure I lost several pounds in that parade, and I was truly wrung out when it was over. And, after that, I still participated in selling refreshments at the fair grounds. I would *not* be capable of repeating that performance today. But, at that time I was full of pep and vinegar.

Once more, however, I swore, "I will never open my mouth at a meeting again!" Especially after the club decided that the lion's costume was a tremendous success and they should continue doing it ... with Sam as the permanent lion!

In addition, I was getting active in Scouting with son Jay, and that was one of the reasons I departed from the Lions' Club. Several years later I decided to join the Kiwanis club, which was less active ... I thought! That was another mistake.

The Blood Bank

It was shortly after World War II. I was married and living in Indiana. I had been stationed in the South Pacific during the war and had occasion to see the good work of the Red Cross overseas. I became friendly with some of the local Red Cross people. The supervisor of the Indiana chapter told of the formation of a Red Cross blood bank and how difficult it was to get people to donate blood.

I opened my big mouth again!

"Why don't you get some television performers from the pioneer station KDKA in Pittsburgh, have them come here in person and charge a pint of blood for admission?"

"That's a great idea, Sam. Will you do it for us?"

I had forgotten that "mouth" promise I had made to myself ... and now I was to become a promoter!

My wife Sissy was distantly related to Harold Cohen, who was then drama editor at the *Pittsburgh Post Gazette*. I called for an appointment and we met to discuss the situation. He approved, thought it might be innovative ... and perhaps even a good idea! He said that he would contact the performers for us.

He was as good as his word ... and arranged for a group of well-known TV personalities to donate their services and come up to Indiana for a show. Then the publicity started. We deluged the community with blurbs: newspaper, radio station, posters, speakers. We disseminated all sorts of juicy items about the great variety show with "your favorite Pittsburgh TV personalities." We arranged to rent the local high school auditorium, which sat about 1200 people.

On the evening of the show, Sissy and I had a cocktail party in our home for the entertainers. Then we all went to the auditorium and waited for the people to arrive. We waited ... and waited ... and waited.

When the show began, there must have been all of 100 or 200 people in the auditorium for 1200. The place looked absolutely barren.

I can only attribute the failure of the show to the fact that people were not yet educated to the fact that donating blood was painless, harmless ... and so helpful and necessary. I can think of no other reason: The performers were well known in the area and the publicity was ample.

The performers were troopers and put on a good show. I can imagine they were saying, "Never again!"

Sam Rubin was also saying, "Never again" ... and spicing the remark with something about ... "my big mouth!"

Classic Images, *No. 197*
November 1991

The PTA!

I have always felt that the Parent Teacher Association is a wonderful organization. I think it could be so much better if some of the parents would not use it to grind their own axes. If they could only view the group as an instrument to help all the kids and all the parents to have contact with the teachers and to cooperatively mingle, sanely discuss the problems, and sit one-on-one with the teachers to determine what would be best for *all* the kids, not just their own little monsters.

The above has nothing to do with this column, but I had to let out a little steam, which has been simmering in my mind for years.

The PTA produced one of my first contacts with show people of any kind. Neff the Magician, home town product of Indiana, Pennsylvania, was fairly well-known and had been on the road for years. He had retired, but a friend had prevailed upon him to give a show in the local high school auditorium for the PTA benefit. He was to be paid his usual fee.

The subject was brought up at one of the meetings I was unfortunate enough to attend. The PTA president asked for ideas. Completely ignoring my vows to keep my mouth shut, I arose and offered my opinion as to what should be done in the line of promotion, the gathering of ushers and everything else about which I had had no experience at all.

"Those are some great ideas, Sam. Will you be the chairman?"

I met Neff. He was truly one of the better talented old time showmen; I knew this after I saw him perform ... but, I'm ahead of myself. He was seasoned and experienced, and when we discussed the show, he gave me many innovative ideas about promoting it.

What made this so memorable and horrifying: While I was rounding up committees to take care of the many facets for putting on such a show, Neff was also active. He informed me, after the fact, that he had put an ad in the local classified section of the newspaper, the *Indiana Evening Gazette*, words to the effect: "Wanted, girl to be burned alive. Top pay." The ad gave his name and a place and time for applicants to meet with him. He was getting a good price for his performance, so I thought nothing of the ad. If he wanted to pay the girls "top wages," that was his business. He called me and asked me to come to the meeting to meet the girls. I thought that was a pretty good idea, never having interviewed potential showgirls before. I was even looking forward to it.

Sure enough, a small group of girls answered the ad, which had asked them to be burned alive. Neff took me aside, "Sam, I want you to talk to these girls. Explain to them that this is a charity show and that none of the people working on the show are getting paid."

I felt like a mortar shell had landed on me.

Because I was dumbstruck and didn't want to jeopardize the show, I stood before the girls and, to my everlasting shame, spit out those fateful words during what must have been the most embarrassing situation of my life.

Some of the girls walked, a couple stayed ... and Mr. Neff, the great magician, had his free assistants. It was then that I again vowed, "Never again will I open my mouth at a meeting!"

The show, incidentally, was a success. It was a good show; Neff was a pro. The PTA made money, and I lost many pounds of faith in my "fellow" show people!

Minstrels!

With deep humility, I must report that I was again faithless to my vows of silence! Again ... a PTA meeting! They were going to hold a minstrel show. Of course, this was years ago; and such shows were common.

"Sam," I sincerely said to myself, "stay out of it!" So, I volunteered nothing ... except when they wanted someone to write the publicity. Right up my alley. I volunteered; it was to be nothing ... I thought!

They started to rehearse the show with their volunteer performers. I attended a couple of rehearsals to get publicity background material. One of the end men failed to show for the rehearsal, so I volunteered to read his lines that night.

Using my best Southern accent, I placed the right amount of emphasis, with the proper timing, on the key words and punchlines. The next thing I knew, they were laughing, and one of the chairmen said, "Sam, you are so much better than the other guy; why don't you take the role?"

"It's happening again," I thought. Everyone was looking at me with his or her best "it's for the good ol' PTA" look, and I succumbed.

I have always had difficulty performing in front of people. I enjoyed being in the background and telling other people what to do. This time I was to be on display and on the receiving end.

I decided to write my own material!

The night of the show I was dressed as a fat woman (with plenty of padding) and sang my home-grown song. I was terrible! Later on I looked at some of the pictures taken that night and discovered I also looked terrible!

Then, once more, I promised myself, "Never again will I open my big mouth at a meeting!"

Classic Images, *No. 199*
January 1992

Sam the Shill!

When I was a kid, still in high school, I had an uncle who worked with a traveling carnival at times and, at times, worked games of chance in amusement parks.

I liked him! He was personable! He knew kids and could always keep us happy with his humor and cheerfulness. And, there was always this mystique surrounding him. Carnivals were truly lands of magic in those days.

One day my mother gave us the tremendous news that Uncle Lou was coming to our small town as manager of a traveling carnival! Excitement! I obtained VIP status with the neighborhood kids immediately!

The carnival finally arrived ... a real flea bag! But, I didn't see it as such. It was fairyland. My uncle arranged for me to take all the rides and see all the shows *free*! I was the envy of the block.

This was to be the first and only time I was to see a geek! The dictionary defines a geek as "a carnival performer whose act usually consists of biting off the head of a live chicken or snake." This geek used a rabbit! He bit off its head and succeeded in thoroughly turning my stomach.

I don't know if carnivals still have geeks, but I vowed I would never take another peek at a geek.

Didn't Tyrone Power play a geek in the movie *Nightmare Alley*? I deliberately passed up the film for that reason and was never sorry.

My uncle had his permanent residence in Cleveland. When he finally married and settled down, he confined his carnival activities to the Cleveland area where I journeyed every year to visit cousins. I always managed to find time to see and talk with Uncle Lou.

Uncle Lou had a "game of chance" at Cedar Point, an amusement park on the shores of the lake at Sandusky, Ohio. He invited me to spend a few days with him. I was thrilled! The game my uncle operated consisted of wooden balls immersed in water flowing down a trough. The mark, after putting his money on a number on the counter, would pull one of the balls out of the water. My uncle would inset a steel tool into the side of the ball, pushing out a metal tab with a number engraved on it. If the number matched the one selected by the customer, he won a prize.

I never did find out exactly how the thing was fixed, but I think it had something to do with the amount of pressure he used in pressing the metal key into the ball, thus controlling the numbers to be exposed.

But, I deviate again. My story has to do with the time when one of the operators across the way had attracted a crowd to his stand with his spiel. He was running a number wheel. You have all seen these wheels. The wheel, of course, must land on the number which you selected in order for you to win one of the beautiful prizes on display—attractive, desirable items to tempt people to risk their money.

My uncle saw the crowd and gave me a nickel (that's all it took in those days). He said, "Take this and put it on a number at that stand!"

The operator of the stand saw me coming, and he shouted to everyone concerned, "Okay, folks, place your bets!" I went up and placed the nickel on my favorite number (at that time), nine. I had not seen the signals passing between that operator and my uncle.

The wheel spun and stopped on nine. I shouted with joy! I had won! The people around me were envious. I selected a radio that was on display.

I took the radio, walked around with it to some of the other stands and then sat down on a bench to inspect my prize. It was an empty case. The works had been removed or had never been there!

Disappointed and angry, I returned to my uncle who took a look at the stand across the way which had now been cleared of people. He said to me, "Take it back!" Sadly, I returned the worthless box to the stand owner … and then it hit me! I didn't know the word then … but I had become a shill!

Later I learned that all the merchandise on the stands in that park was "rented" at the beginning of the season and returned when the park closed. I also learned that if stands at a traveling carnival or amusement park had beautiful, expensive prizes, you had about as much chance of winning as you had of digging up a million dollars from a truck garden.

I never shilled again; nor did I ever place money at one of those stands again! This was all during the Depression. I have no way of knowing if the carnival stands still operate in the same manner. But, I did learn to stay away from the stands with expensive-looking prizes.

If you feel like gambling to win a prize, try the ones offering items which, apparently, you could buy for a few bucks! You might even win an inexpensive doodad!

Lions

We were playing ball in an empty lot in Indiana, Pennsylvania. We had a team that went around and played various church teams in the area. I was permanently glued to the second base position; they wouldn't trust me anywhere else.

We heard a loud sound, like the roar of a lion, near us. It was a frightening sound! We looked around and could see nothing. We continued playing; the roar recurred.

There was no circus in town; it couldn't possibly be a jungle cat. We were hundreds of miles from the jungles. We investigated. Near the edge of the playing field was another large lot and a ramshackle shack at the end of the lot

We crept near the shed and, as the roaring continued, we grew nervous. I crept up to the shed and lifted a canvas covering. Sure enough, in the back of the canvas were iron bars, and behind the bars, a lion ... a real, live lion!

As they used to say in the old days, "We skedaddled!"

Later, upon investigating, we learned the lion belonged to a man named Christie who toured the country with circuses, billed as Christie's Lions. (We only saw one!)

The moral of this story: "When you go out to play softball, watch out for the lions!"

Classic Images, *No. 171*

Academia

It has frequently irritated me to hear college faculty members talk about academia, their academic world. There is no sane reason for this idiosyncrasy. But so many of the higher "educators" to whom I have spoken invariably use the word academia.

It's probably inane for me to even mention it. They have earned the right to use the term when discussing their own professions.

Perhaps I feel they are divorcing themselves from the rest of the world and perhaps placing themselves a step above the average fellow.

Kick me! I know I'm wrong, but I just wanted to get it on paper. Many wonderful educators have impressed me with their knowledge, tact and wisdom. Conversely, I have met some who were egotistical nincompoops, devoid of kindly feelings toward anyone not involved in their world of academia.

The crux: few know that I, Samuel K. Rubin, was a member of academia at a large Eastern university. After a semester, I think they discovered their mistake and neglected to invite me back. During my lengthy tenure at the head of the class, there were a few incidents, frightening at the time, hilarious in retrospect. And, I discovered that those in academia can lead difficult lives in the classroom.

My son Jay was a student at the university. He had a brainstorm and proposed that he teach a course on the silent film, utilizing prints from our sizable collection of classics. Thus, the school need not spend money for film rentals and the course could become quite lucrative.

The university officials liked the idea and approved it. It worked! The school also paid less money to Jay, a student, than a regular faculty member would have received.

The subject of the course: "History and Appreciation of the Silent Film."

HAAOTSF was an evening course. There was one hour-long lecture and two or more hours of film screening and discussion. Approximately 100 students enrolled for the course.

When Jay graduated, he suggested that his dad could continue with the course; he was qualified. They liked the idea. When I went in to see the people, I was asked one question: "What's your Social Security number?"

I was in!

It would be easy, I foolishly thought. Jay had the course all prepared. All I would have to do would be to read his notes, project a film and discuss it.

Naive Sam Rubin went to his first class.

Remember, here was a man (me) with no previous teaching training or experience, facing 100 knowledgeable, sophisticated college students who apparently delighted in torturing faculty members. The lecture room was an amphitheater; 100 malevolent gargoyles were staring at me.

I was reading the notes on the history of the film. A student's hand shot up. "Mr. Rubin?"

"Yes!"

"Why are you reading all this material to us? Frankly, it's boring me."

I turned red, green and purple; I was dumbstruck, then I stammered, "I'm sorry if I'm boring you. Perhaps you would like to take another course." Apparently, I had accidentally hit upon the proper squelcher.

Other students muttered obscenities at the kid. Some shouted, "No, he's wrong."

The student came to the desk later to apologize.

Mid-course!

A student approached me before the class started. "Mr. Rubin, I have missed the last three classes and the dean told me that I could continue with the course if you approved."

I didn't care. I had told the students at the beginning of the semester that I would grade the course from the test results. I told him so. "By the way," I asked, "where were you?"

"In jail."

Twilight time! The final classes!

One student approached me before class started, "Mr. Rubin, I have a thing about final examinations. I don't like to take them. Can you give me a project or something else so that I won't have to take the exam?"

I explained that I, too, always had a horror of final examinations. But, I had to take them ... and so would she.

Understandably, I was not asked to repeat the course the next semester. The officials and I had independently arrived at a mutual decision without contact between us. I would not ask to repeat the course, and they would not ask me to return.

I made my decision because I had never learned to project my voice and had trouble communicating with the class. I also had difficulty coping with students who were taking the course for easy credits and probably had more in-depth knowledge of film history than I. After all, we people in academia are independent!

Classic Images, *No. 287*
May 1999

The Awakening

It happened in a doctor's office! I already knew I was behind the times, but I still hadn't realized the world had passed me by.

I had a computer and couldn't handle its multitudinous functions, so I sold it. I switched to a word processor when my typewriter spewed its last electric clunk. I couldn't handle it either.

I still have it but use it as a typewriter (this article is being brilliantly generated on it), unable to utilize its versatility and its many advantages: its "robotical" functions calculated (they say) to make life easier for a writer.

I also had trouble with the instructions. The aforesaid were written by an alien electronic age wizard (an egghead) who was unable to lower himself to the level of us ignoramuses who couldn't understand his terminology, his use of technical words (perhaps commonplace to him) that would confound Einstein.

Unlike cheese or wine, I don't get better with age. Riper? Perhaps!

Now, back to the doctor's office. You know how it is in these modern medical facilities. First you sign in, as if you were planning to spend the night in the bridal suite of a hotel. You're actually signing for waiting room admission. You sit in the waiting room and wait to be called.

After an interminable wait, a technician enters and escorts you to a tiny room and interrogates you medically and then you wait some more for his majesty, the doctor.

In some offices you are escorted again to another waiting room to, once again, wait for his (or her) royal highness. It becomes a weighty proposition.

So, in each waiting room you pick up a magazine, most of them dog-eared, with coupons clipped. Sometimes you need several magazines.

It happened in the midst of one of these "waits." I picked up a copy of *Multimedia World*, began to read and discovered I was in a foreign land and had become an outdated dinosaur. I knew the film collecting world had outdistanced me, but opening the magazine introduced me to a technical age of marvels.

I did feel like a yokel while attempting to digest the pages of that publication. I couldn't comprehend the language. There was a galaxy of words which had no meaning to me. Examples: Pentium pro, pc, single board, spin control, browser, netscape, web sets, wash board and so many more initials, words and phrases.

I read some of the articles *sans* understanding.

What tremendous advancements this new technology has made, especially in the movie and TV fields! To me, the innovations are not as blatantly apparent in the modern film and TV productions as it is in the field of TV commercials. What wizardry I see when I watch the commercials, no doubt all computerized. And their magic message must be handed to you, literally, "in the blink of an eye."

In theatrical films, there is an attempt to make the animation and other special effects appear as natural as possible. Not so with the commercials! It seems there is no effort to naturalize the action. In fact, it is my belief they go to extremes for weird, unusual effects, taking advantage of all the modern technology this computerized world offers, to forcibly catch your attention and keep it. If you can remember some of these selling ads, they have succeeded.

I'm not about to attempt to describe some of these innovative commercials. You have all seen them; perhaps you have said, "How did they do that?" I truly marvel at these marvels which would have taken weeks to produce in the past but can now be accomplished in a fraction of the time.

I am unfamiliar with today's animation technology. But, in the past, to animate an inanimate object, it was necessary to move the article a tiny bit and shoot a single film frame of it. Then, move the object another tiny bit and shoot another frame. Each minute bit of additional movement required another frame.

Thousands of separate frames were required to make artwork, puppets or other still objects come alive in simulated lifelike movement in an animated feature.

I'm completely ignorant as to the computerized techniques in today's animation; but I do know it is making inanimate objects move and look natural so much more efficiently and with a greater savings of time than in the past.

The animated action today is limited only by the imagination of the filmmakers. I'm astonished by what I see on TV and on the big screen, and I enjoy the results. I only hope I'm around in the future to see what additional strides these wizard have made in the manufacture of these "moving" films.

As I said earlier, this Rubin is sandwiched between the film and TV world of yesterday and today. I am determined to become acquainted with the modern terms and expressions in this (to me) new world. I think, perhaps, I may have become contaminated with these terms and may turn into a "terminologist," whatever that means.

Meanwhile, I think I'll go back to that doctor's office and look at that magazine again. I may even steal it; they'll never miss it!

The Chaplin Mutuals ... Remastered

If you are a silent film enthusiast you probably own, or have seen, all 12 of these Chaplin Mutual shorts. I have! However, no how were the others of such quality. I sat, enthralled, as I watched the latest versions of the 1916-17 two reelers and attempted to find words to describe them. Such would have been inadequate, so I'll let Kino speak directly to you with their gift of handling the English language. We are told that the "Chaplin Mutuals—Remastered" are "an eye popping compendium of the comedic master's shorts, significantly and digitally restored." You know those sweet melodic words never came from me. I would have said, "This is good stuff!"

Included is detailed information such as: "There are several versions of the Chaplin Mutual comedies available on video (including an analog Kino version from 1984), but recent years' advances in video technology have made this the right time to remaster these 12 short films for an all-new edition. Film scholar and restoration producer David Shepard's first step was to create a master from the best surviving 35mm pre-print elements (rather than from old prints long circulated in the marketplace) and transfer the films at the visually correct speed. The 35mm negatives—the remains of the original nitrate-base camera negatives and other early generation material—were then mastered digitally, eliminating much evidence of age and wear.

"The process known as 'Digital Vision Noise Reduction' cleaned the image of many little black and white flecks. Scores of hours using other recent technology were spent electronically 'painting out' film damage such as splice lines, flaked emulsion, and punch marks.

"Michael Mortilla, composer of the acclaimed score for our earlier release, revised, re-orchestrated, and rerecorded his music in digital stereo for this new edition.

"With the combination of unbeatable original materials, superior film-to-tape transfer, and painstaking image repair, these films are far superior in picture quality to any video edition previously seen. Roger Ebert once said that 'in my life I've never seen a Charlie Chaplin short that didn't look as if somebody hadn't dragged it behind a truck." The revelations of these new tapes may be compared to those awaiting an astigmatic person putting on his glasses for the first time. One reviewer who compared this new version to the prior releases claims that *The Chaplin Mutuals: Remastered* 'is a true advancement in quality—as if a fog has been lifted from the screen.'"

Nuff said!

The comedies are compiled into three tapes, each lasting an average of an hour and a half. Tape one contains the 1917 *The Immigrant*, *The Adventurer*, *The Cure* and *Easy Street*. Tape two has the 1916 *The Count*, *The Vagabond*, *The Fireman* and *Behind the Screen*. Included on tape three are the 1916 *One A.M.*, *The Pawnshop*, *The Floor Walker* and *The Rink*.

Appearing with Chaplin in this group of releases are the oft-seen faces of co-star Edna Purviance plus Eric Campbell, Frank Austin and Henry Bergman. You are all familiar with the stories (or you should be!). To me, they seem as fresh as they were when first released, before I (and most of you) was born!

With Chaplin's talent, and his razor-edge sense of timing, he is able to wring laughter out of practically every movement on the screen.

If you are a Charlie Chaplin collector or enthusiast, here's what you ought to do: Check the papers for the next film convention or the next yard sale, or put an ad in *Classic Images*. Get rid of the one you have and grade up to these new quality releases! You won't be sorry!

Classic Images, *No. 217*
July 1993

Is It Me?

I've suddenly started to attend the movies in a theater again ... and somehow, it isn't quite the same (including the price of the popcorn). I have also started to watch some of the later movies on the tube; and they also, to put it mildly, somehow are not the same. I'm not enjoying myself.

I have been delighted with only a rare few of the modern films. And, of course, I don't recognize the performers!

So, I must ask ... is it me? Am I the only one? Or, are you also experiencing the same difficulties becoming attuned to the modern movie scene.

First of all: these multiplex theaters. One operator keeps track of the many projectors being utilized at the same time. How can he pay close attention to focus ... to sound ... to when those large platters (replacing reels) run out of film? I assume they have automatic devices to control such situations, but much of the projection I have seen has been way below a movie buff's acceptable standards.

How about the sound? Is it because I am older or do you also have difficulty understanding some of those garbled noises? I admit I have lost some of my hearing, but I do not believe it is causing my ears to misinterpret what's entering them. I expect them to start flapping any day now.

And, have you noticed how fast the young people talk today? Their mouths travel at 5,000 lip smacks per second. I have difficulty following their speech unless I can see their faces and watch their non-stop ultra-speed mouths. And, even then, I sometimes have difficulty catching all the words.

I'll repeat ... "Is it me?" Should I go to see an ear doctor ... or, perhaps, a shrink?

Worst of all ... the language. I will never understand why a director or writer must resort to such foul language. I understand they are striving for realism, but that doesn't keep me from wincing when I hear obscene conversation. How easy it would be to have the characters effectively say the same things without having to resort to obscenities. There are enough words in the dictionary. (Or, perhaps, the writers can't read.)

I know you are waiting for me to say this. How about the way members of the audience talk in the theater today, with utter disregard of the feelings of their neighbors; those people for whom they are ruining the enjoyment of the film? I'd like to investigate this mace spray which is recommended for personal protection. Perhaps it will work on the movie magpies.

Because of all of the above, I do not watch many movies in the theater or on TV unless it is a classic or if it has a story which particularly appeals to me. Or if it is released by such a company as Disney, when I know the chief object of the film is to entertain me, not to shock me.

In the past, during the earlier, ancient film age, except for a few movies, there would always be a satisfactory conclusion: The Frankenstein monster would have been killed (even if he would be revived in a future picture); Dracula would have a stake run into his heart; the gangsters and mobsters would have received their just due; marriage disputes would be resolved; and the comedians would make you laugh without resorting to one-liners. In most cases, you would walk out of the theater with a good feeling.

T'aint so any more.

So, now I'll repeat ... is it me? Or is it you too?

Classic Images, *No. 204*
June 1992

Thirty Years!

It took a call from *Classic Images* editor Bob King, while I was meditating (napping) on the patio of the apartment in which I live, to alert me that this was the 30th anniversary year of this here publication which I used to call the "Illiterate Gazette," but which has become quite literate without me.

I should have remembered the anniversary. Remember the big deal we made at our twenty-fifth?

Bob thought I would like to write something for the thirtieth anniversary issue. My first, almost automatic, response was to say, "I'm sorry." However, Bob did get my mind to wandering about the past 30 years of film collecting and the many wonderful people I have met during that period. "And don't forget," I muttered to myself, "this is your baby." And, I continued to mutter, "This is your chance, Sam, to start crawling out of that shell which has been suffocating you."

So, here's that vital thirtieth birthday message from SKR.

Title: "How Things Have Changed!"

This is not going to be one of those, "I remember when" things. This is going to be one of Sam Rubin's serious commentaries on the film collecting industry.

I remember when (you knew I was lying) because of the love of the classic films, so many of us with collecting souls started garnering Standard 8mm titles, graduating to Super 8mm because Standard 8mm became almost non-existent (thanks, Mr. Kodak), trading up to 16mm and then, finally, going into video.

I'm the guy who said there is no greater thrill than opening that newly arrived carton containing your latest film acquisition and reveling in the excruciatingly wonderful aroma of the recently developed celluloid.

I'm the guy who said that there is nothing in the world like threading a projector, darkening a room and sitting back, with an audience, to enjoy one of the classics which gave us (and still does) so much pleasure! What an exhilarating experience to watch one of the old silents, projected at the proper speed, with an appropriate musical background.

I'm the guy who said you could enjoy a film so much more if you have an audience to appreciate it with you. When other people are watching, the comedy is funnier, the mystery more mysterious, the Western wilder and the romance steamier. I still believe that!

How much easier it is to slip a cassette into your VCR, sit back, relax and watch a movie on the tube. Sure, the picture is not as good, but you still enjoy it. And, you don't have to lug all that equipment. So what if your video tape has been reproduced from a CinemaScope film and, at times, you can't see the people talking, those who happen to be at the extreme ends of the screen. The scenery between the actors (whom you can't see) is beautiful, isn't it? That door between those two invisible actors may possibly be made of solid oak. Isn't that fascinating? And, don't you love those introductory titles and scenes from a CinemaScope film converted to video? All the words and characters escaped from the third dimension, and they're riding off into the wild blue yonder on a tangent.

Also, what difference does it make if your videotape was copied from a TV version, which was expurgated (I always like to think of it as "purged") in order to fit it into a particular time frame. They can't have cut out too much important material (it says here); it still plays well. You couldn't have missed too many important scenes. It would have been sacrilegious to have infringed on the time of a commercial.

And, here's a real advantage you have. They have been able to add color to so many of our beloved black-and-white classics. Sometimes a face may become purple, but so what? You're seeing it in living color!

I may have related this in the past, but I want to digress just a bit and recant. Some young cousins (teens) came to visit us in Iowa. I offered to show them a movie and handed them my video list. They checked the titles; if there was interest in one of them they would question, "Is this in color?" If the answer was negative, they did not want to see it!

So, there may be more merit to this colorizing business than you and I know. The young people want their screen fare to be in color. Might as well colorize them all. We oldtimers won't be around that much longer.

How many of you remember Sam Rubin's historical diagnosis of the quality of the projected picture from the various film sizes? Remember, I said, "With each innovation in film format for home movies, you have a loss of quality on your projected picture." The quality pyramid started with 35mm, the best. Then 16mm was introduced which still projected a good large picture. Not as good as 35mm, but still good enough for larger audiences. Then, they invented Standard 8mm, fine for a short throw, fuzzy with a long throw. After that came Super 8mm; the picture was squared off from its regular rectangular shape. It gave a bit sharper picture on a long throw, but you lost part of the picture, usually one or both sides. Finally, video tape, the most convenient of them all, with the worst picture. So, with each change you lost quality. Try projecting your video picture to the same size as a projected film picture and compare them!

I close my case!

I was with a mixed group recently and, knowing of my interest in film, they directed the talk to the classics. Several of the people collected videotapes.

I was amazed to hear them talking about that rare videotape they managed to get. They were forced to pay a high price for it, but they had to have it. It was reminiscent of how we used to brag about bagging a rare film. I know that I am not with it these days, but it is difficult for me to visualize boasting about a rare tape that anyone with decent equipment (or poor) can copy! And, the possibility remains that the rare video find could have been a dupe.

But!

Didn't we act the same way with film ... and still do?

Let us remember that it was through the efforts of film collectors like ourselves that today's video collectors are able to obtain some of these classics. Unfortunately, in the past, many of the studios had never heard of preservation and shamelessly neglected their old films and had no desire to save them. They took no protective steps, and consequently many of the classics are gone forever. But, those same studios now rave about the valuable old films to which they hold the rights. They have a treasure trove and always knew it (they say). And ... worth lots of money (they say).

I am *not* against video tape. I have hundreds of them. My films and projectors are no longer in my possession. If I want to watch something, it will be on video.

No doubt I have gotten lazier in my ancient years. I do enjoy watching video classics.

I have been away from the field for many years, and no doubt there have been innovations of which I am unaware—but I wonder if anyone has come up with the answer to the question which has always troubled me. How long will the image on a videocassette last? Is there a point where the picture will begin to fade or deteriorate or completely disappear?

Keep in mind what has happened to many of the color film prints in our collections. They are now a beautiful, scintillating *red*! Anyways, kids, that *is* color, not black and white.

Thanks for reading this far. And, happy thirtieth anniversary to *Classic Images*, the best film publication in the world. Ask the guy who founded it.

12

Wondering and Wandering

Classic Images, *No. 40*
November 1990

Now presenting, in encapsulated form, the trials, tribulations and traumas of Samuel K. Rubin as I travel to the Stone Ages and in between, to relate some of the memorable incidents which occurred in my lifetime of enthusiasm for the classic films. Some of these will be humorous (to me); some will not. Because of my less-than-perfect power of recall, I may repeat some anecdote on which I have written before. However, I will relate them, as usual, in my straightforward, unbiased manner. I am honest!

I Am Honest

I have had countless dealings with many people in the past, dating back to the time when Columbus was trying to find a name for his newly discovered land. I have trusted many; and happily, almost 100 percent have trusted me. I have done my utmost not to betray that trust.

In holding conversation and preparing to deal with people with whom I have had no previous contact, I always alert myself when I hear one particular phrase. If this newcomer tells me, "I'm honest!," I immediately throw up my guard and mutter to myself, "Forget this guy. Honest he ain't!"

I can recall no exception in my initial dealings with anyone, backtracking even to my furniture store days, to the fact that all who make such a proclamation are to be feared; be careful when you deal with them.

Sam says, "Beware of anyone who states, "I am honest!" Please note the end of the first paragraph of this opus.

First Projector

Imprinted indelibly in my memory is my first projector, a 35mm Keystone, capable of handling, as I remember, 100-foot reels of 35mm film—a projector not meant for professionals!

This was during the Depression. My daily allowance was five cents. We kids in the family had to work. Each of us, as we grew older, inherited one job in our family-owned store which was handed down from the older to the younger kid in line. We had to come to the store every day and bale the accumulation of cardboard and paper. The paper baler, in the basement, was an upright piece of obstinate, extinct equipment in which you stacked the paper, pressed it down by means of a long, wooden handle, then threaded metal strands of wire around the bundle, pulling them tight. The resultant bales were around 100 pounds each.

Here was the kicker! Our pay: the amount of money the local scrap dealer would give for the bale. The price sometimes went up to 40 cents a bale. But, when Sam aged enough to assume the duty, right in the middle of the Depression, the payment on a 100-lb. bale was five cents. And, according to the scrap dealer, a friend of the family, it was a donation because he felt sorry for me. There was practically no demand for the used cardboard and paper.

So, I saved my nickels, the ones my father gave to me and the ones I earned by my labors, and accumulated enough to buy the Keystone projector. I am sure it cost under $5. It arrived ... with one reel of film. I was in ecstasy. The film contained clips of a Tom Mix movie.

I turned it on for the first time and was extremely disappointed with the amount of light this toy threw on the screen. It must have been a 40-watt bulb. This would never do. How could I show my friends a picture as dark as this? (Even at that time the thrill of displaying movies to others was inherent in me.)

I arrived at a decision. Again, I saved my nickels and purchased a screw-type base 500-watt projection lamp which would fit into the socket of my Keystone. Then I scheduled a showing of the Tom Mix film (all of three minutes) with some friends in their home. I proudly brought my projector and the film, set it on a table and carefully inserted my newly purchased projection lamp.

I cautiously threaded the film, displaying my infinite knowledge of such things, made sure all was in order and had the lights turned off.

And then I turned the projector switch. A brilliant flash of light erupted from the projector ... and immediately disappeared while I watched, with horror, the projected image melt on the screen. The film melted; the lamp, of course, blew, the wiring on the projector burned ... and I melted.

I as never able to use the projector again and was unable to buy another until years later when I purchased one of the small Universal 8mm projectors which were so popular in the late '30s and early '40s.

Never again would I try to insert a lamp in any projector other than that of the wattage designated for that equipment.

Rita Hayworth

I had my picture taken with Rita Hayworth! Therein lies a tale! It was during a National Film Society convention. I knew that Rita Hayworth was to be honored at the awards banquet. I did *not* know that Samuel K. Rubin was also to be honored at the event.

No one took the trouble to notify me. In fact, everyone took many pains, in collusion with my wife Sissy to keep me uninformed.

So, now we are at the annual awards banquet. It is just about time to proceed with the awards. I feel the urge to go to the restroom. Our table is on the opposite side of the room from the door leading to the restrooms.

I rise and walk across the enormous banquet room in front of everyone. As I make my way to the other side of the room, I notice the officers at the speaker's table are a bit agitated about something and are holding a hurried, whispered conversation. People at the other tables are apparently anxiously watching me.

"Gee," I say to myself, "a guy can't even go to the toilet without causing a disturbance." When I return, I notice that all these same people are now smiling. I am so happy that I have given them a good performance.

As soon as I sit down at our table, my named is called; and I, surprised, go to the table to receive an award. It is an unexpected shock to me. When I return to the table, Sissy is laughing. "They were all worried about you. It was almost time for your award, and you were leaving."

Apparently, they were asking each other "Where's he going?" If they would have asked me, I would have told them.

Rita Hayworth received her award; and, after the banquet, in the hospitality room, I stood next to hear, each of us clutching our awards, as our picture was taken.

One of the many hundreds of pictures taken at the National Society Convention that day, and that's the only one which did not come out!

Classic Images, No. 42
December 1990

The Old Fart!

There were many memorable moments at Blackhawk. My tenure there was among the happiest days of my life. I enjoyed what I was doing ... and so liked the company and the people working there.

One incident, which I thought hilarious, was when the company had hired a girl to, among other duties, assemble and write the Blackhawk catalogue, that famous, attractive booklet anticipated by every collector of film who dealt with the company. It always contained a complete listing of films with lengthy descriptions of the new titles. Our incident has to do with one of these descriptions.

Blackhawk was releasing a new Wheeler and Woolsey film, *Cockeyed Cavaliers*. Noah Beery, who had a beautiful singing voice, was in the cast, portraying a lecherous old man lusting after a young girl.

The new advertising manager wrote a description of the film stating that "Noah Beery, an old fart, lusted after a young girl."

The catalogue was printed, and officers Ted Ewing, Carl Lange and Tom Voss were leisurely looking through the pages when one of them caught sight of the statement.

Repairmen had to replace the roof the next day. Things like that did not *ever* appear in a Blackhawk catalogue.

Needless to say, whether for this reason or not, the girl was not with the company very long. Ted, Carl, Tom and myself enjoyed a good laugh over the situation—these were the same guys I would sit down with and swap dirty jokes.

But ... never in the catalogue!

More Blackhawk

For years, when a new issue of *Classic Images* came off the press, I would give each Blackhawk employee a copy. Although none was a collector, some of them read it avidly. Others, I knew, did not.

However, I continued to give them each a copy of the current issue, dreaming that each of them took it home to read and distribute among their families and friends. Thus, I was making new friends for *Classic Images*.

I maintained this dream ... until ... one day I was walking through the shipping room and discovered some *Classic Images* on the piles of discarded newspaper which were used to stuff packages being shipped to the Blackhawk customers. They were using my *Classic Images* as package stuffers!

It had to be the best stuffing they ever used! "Besides," I said to myself convincingly, "we might get new subscribers from the people who received the packages."

And, lo, my children, thou believer of miracles ... that's exactly what happened! We did get new subscribers from this promiscuous, uncalled-for, inhuman package stuffing.

Cheese Story

While at Blackhawk, I would go out to lunch with some officers and employees. Kent Eastin would frequently join us. It was a congenial group. We would vary our menu by going to different restaurants.

One time, we went to the local Steak and Shake. I had just had some dental work and was told to stay on a soft diet for 24 hours, so I ordered a milk shake and a cheese sandwich. The waitress looked a bit puzzled at the order, and I saw her walk up to a man who, I assumed, was the manager.

She returned, "I am sorry, sir, but we do not have cheese sandwiches. However, we do have grilled cheese sandwiches."

I looked at her in amazement and laughed; we all laughed. I said, "Okay, bring me a grilled cheese sandwich. By the way ... don't grill it."

Telephone Story

In the same vein: there was a fine French restaurant in Muscatine, Iowa, where *Classic Images* was and still is printed. It was about 30 miles from our home in Davenport. Lois and I planned to have dinner there and decided to call for a reservation. Not knowing the number, I called information and asked for the number of the Muscatine Hotel.

After an unusual delay, the operator said, "I am sorry, sir, we have no Muscatine Hotel listed."

"You must have," I insisted. "It's been there for years."

The operator: "I'm sorry, we have no Muscatine Hotel listed. However, we do have a Hotel Muscatine."

Classic Images, *No. 187*
January 1991

Classic Contributions

From the day I first started, *8mm Collector*, forerunner to *Classic Film Collector* and *Classic Images*, there was never a time when I wanted for editorial material for each issue. And, conversely, there was never enough advertising.

From the very beginning, I was deluged with material from amateur and professional writers. At first I refused none of them, running everything that came my way. After all, if someone else wrote the article, it would not be necessary for me, in my tight time schedule, to research and, consequently, pen the material.

In the beginning, I printed all the nostalgic "I remember" articles submitted. Then they began to sound monotonously the same, and I had to return some of them.

Then, many of these so-called literary contributions were downright illiterate. Some of these I returned and others, depending upon the reader interest in the subject matter, had to be completely edited, consuming many hours, to be put in readable shape.

Film enthusiasts all wanted to write concerning their love for film, their personal experiences in attending the theater, of their contact with the movie celebrities.

A local merchant, a young man in Indiana, Pennsylvania, approached me: "Sam, I have a terrific movie script which I have written. I would like to have you read it." When I did, I was astounded at his complete ignorance and lack of understanding of the written word. He had penned the script in longhand, displaying no knowledge of grammar, punctuation or spelling. He was going to submit it to a studio, designating which actors and actresses were to portray each part, ignoring the fact that these stars might work for different studios.

And ... it was a terrible, hackneyed plot!

I let him down as gently as I could, suggesting he get a professional writer to help him.

On the other hand, I received literate, well-researched articles on every phase of the classic screen. And, even then, I would be forced to turn some of them down because of subject matter.

One example: A female college student had a brilliant notion concerning that "old saw" about *King Kong* which has been around so long. No doubt she probably heard it from some pervert but thought it was her own idea and decided to elaborate on it.

She wrote that *King Kong*, from beginning to end, was a subtle epochal bit of sex cinema, probably elaborating on Robert Armstrong's final fade-out statement that "Beauty killed the Beast." The producers, she asserted, went out of their way to insert sex symbolism throughout the movie.

She went on to select obscure happenings in the film, translating them into symbolic sex acts. The topper was when she indicated that the Empire State Building scene of Kong's famous ascent was a phallic symbol.

I'll bet RKO, Cooper, O'Brien and everyone else concerned with the production would have had second thoughts if they had heard all this nonsense.

"Perhaps," they would have said, "we wouldn't have killed Kong. It would have made a great sequel, *Kong's Other Wife!*"

The Great Publisher

I was the great publisher! It only took a few compliments on *Classic Images*, to titillate my ego. But, there were times when some incident causes the opposite effect.

An example I will always remember: Lois and I were to visit son Jon in his Pittsburgh apartment. He had some student friends, avid film enthusiasts, who would love to meet me. They had taken courses at one of the local universities. I agreed. "Why not?" I prepared to bask in further adulation.

John's friends arrived at the apartment and immediately began to discuss their love of the classic film, especially of *film noir*, which some smart alec professor had introduced to them.

"*Film noir?*" I asked, hearing the expression for the first time. "What's that?"

Immediately the air grew chilly, and I could hear their thoughts as if they were spoken. "What kind of stupid, ignorant know-nothing is this guy?"

I now know what *film noir* is—I wonder how many of you know what it is? I wonder if the producers of these movies realized they were making *film noir*? No doubt the name was dreamed up by some historian, researcher or teacher who needed a title for that particular genre of movie. (It could even be one of those nincompoops who filled those particular students full of *film noir*.) If the producers were aware that they were making *film noir* ... they might have added more "noir" for further effect.

Religion

They say you shouldn't talk politics or religion in a publication if you want to keep your friends. To this point, I have deliberately avoided both topics. That policy comes to an end ... right now!

To me a truly religious person lives a good exemplary life, attending his church or synagogue, giving to charity and living by the Golden Rule. This religious person does *not* spout religion on all occasions, informing others how religious he is, and how important he is to his church or synagogue.

I ran into many (more than I like to remember) of the "self-proclaimed" "religionists" during my 32 years in the furniture business. I had people enter the store and inform me how important they were to the religious community. They bragged about their accomplishments, how the church could not run without them; some were self-proclaimed deacons.

I learned! I learned that when a person spouts religion to you, he's after something; in my business it was always a discount. I also learned to stay away from them. They cannot be trusted; their word means little.

They are using religion as a crutch to obtain their own needs.

Unusual People

I met many unusual people during my tenure as editor and publisher of *Classic Images*. They perhaps tend to congregate around me because I am a good listener; and, in my position, I was a warranted, solid film buff who would not ridicule them for their dreams and schemes.

Years ago, in Hollywood, I was cornered by one of these people. He checked to make sure no one was listening. "Sam, I have some important information for you. Could we meet for lunch?"

I agreed, thinking that perhaps there would be a good story here; the guy was nervous enough. My wife and I met him at an obscure restaurant not far from the hotel.

He looked around furtively to make sure mine were the only ears to receive the message and then handed me this explosive announcement, "I took a picture of Pearl White's grave!"

I tried to look excited, "Yes, that's interesting."

It developed that Pearl White was buried in England (or was it Paris?). It was not permitted to snap pictures of her grave. That wasn't going to stop him. He went to England to the cemetery, climbed the wall, and got the picture!

It was a great achievement!

Classic Images, *No. 188*
February 1991

Flea Markets

You can pick up many items of value at flea markets. I have, at times. That is why I keep going to them. (Out west they are also called swap meets.) In the past you could some times pick up movie items at reasonable prices.

But, things have changed a bit! These flea market entrepreneurs think that everything related to movies is valuable. Because of the law of supply and demand, I can understand asking high prices for rare, old pieces of memorabilia such as the very early fan magazines.

But look at the prices some of them are asking for glossies. My biggest shock was to see one dealer who had poor dupe 3 × 5s and 5 × 7s. They were dark, a bit fuzzy and unclear as only duped pictures can be. He wanted $5 apiece for them.

Maybe I should have hung around to see if he sold any. If he could actually get such prices for that junk, maybe I can become a flea market tycoon. I could start copying some pictures myself (I have plenty of them ... rare ones) and initiate Sam's Super-Duper Junk Picture Shop.

There's money in it!

Mexican Lobbies

Someone out there did it to me! Several people have, but I am talking about one specific instance.

At one of the conventions, I had some Spanish language 11 × 14s. I had no table and didn't want to fool around with them. I approached a dealer to see if he was interested. He answered in the negative, but he did have some Mexican customers and might be able to sell them for me.

I agreed. He was to sell them for a commission. I do not remember the details since this was a long time ago.

I never heard from him again. No doubt, he has attended other conventions, but I can't confront him because I do not remember who he is. He may have even sold me some pictures since then ... the dirty crook.

On the other hand, he may have forgotten who I am.

Now he knows!

Young Collectors

Remember how avid you were when you first stared collecting? It was the most important thing in the world. I have had contact with many of these enthusiastic youngsters, and I am glad ... and I am sorry ... for them. "Happy" to see such enthusiasm, glad they are accepting this healthy hobby for their particular interest; and "sorry" because they'll never have enough money in these times to pay for the really rare material which is becoming so much more difficult to find.

I remember one young man. He was so eager to meet me. His mother brought him to the office, and I encouraged them both to continue with his interest. He was so anxious and eager.

I met him again at a later time at one of the conventions. "How are you?"

"It's great," he said. "This convention is every bit as good as you said it would be. I have obtained some wonderful material."

I asked him if he was staying at the hotel.

He answered, "I was, but I checked out. I spent all my money on movie material, and I'm sleeping in the car."

English Swap

I have nothing but admiration for the English collectors. I met so many of them on that historic Cinephile trip to England some 15 years ago ... and liked them all. I discovered them to be knowledgeable and friendly; and some, I learned, were quite frugal.

One of the English collectors, knowing we were coming, wrote and asked me to purchase a film book for him, one which could not be acquired in his country. I agreed, purchased the book and brought it with me when we went to Britain.

Upon our arrival, he looked me up. When I told him I had the book, he handed me an old book, probably a rare collector's item, which had nothing to do with film. Would I like to swap the book I purchased for his old book?

I was surprised and had difficulty finding the right words. I thanked him so much for the generous offer, the book was doubtlessly valuable, but I had no interest in just any old book, and would like to have my money.

He paid me, and we both walked away happy.

TV Interviews

There is always trouble with TV interviews. Back in Indiana, Pennsylvania, my son Jay and I were to be interviewed on the Pittsburgh public TV channel. We drove in (60 miles one way) and were subsequently interviewed.

We returned home. Later we received a call: The tape had been accidentally erased. Could we come in again?

We did!

In Davenport, Iowa, Ted Ewing, president of Blackhawk, and I were to be interviewed on the local public TV station in conjunction with the Cinecon to be held in that city.

We discussed the interview with the interviewer before the cameras started to roll. We had brought several reels of film from which typical scenes were to be shown. One was Fairbanks' *The Thief of Bagdad*.

The first problem was that no one took the trouble to review the reel but selected a scene haphazardly, a long distance shot of the Sultan's troops marching. It was difficult to see and did not show Fairbanks at all. And, of course, we talked about Fairbanks and his screen personality on the show. Unfortunately, the viewers were not able to sample Doug's pep and vitality which we discussed.

The guy was asking us all kinds of questions about the Cinecon, and I had requested that we also talk about *Classic Images*. I was bound and determined to talk about *Classic Images*. Time was passing, and until now he had not mentioned our beloved publication. So when he asked me a question, I answered by saying that much of this material appears in that great publication for film buffs, *Classic Images*, which is published locally.

Following the next question, I said that I was editor of *Classic Images*, which has been carrying stories of the Cinecon.

He bristled. He was so angry. During intermission he said to me, "If you mention *Classic Images* once more, I won't bring the subject up at all."

Eventually, much against his will, he did ask about *Classic Images* ... and I had my chance.

I wondered about him! Later some of the crew, unsolicited, approached us and said that this interview was one of the most interesting they had ever held and that he was a jerk (I had already determined that). He always had problems with his interviewees.

That made me feel better. I was also pleased, weeks later, to hear that he was no longer with the station.

However, I will never forget the look Ted Ewing gave me when I began the *Classic Images* repartees. He had difficulty refraining from cracking up!

Classic Images, *No. 189*
March 1991

Jack LaRue, Where Are You?

I don't think I was ever as intense about the classic film field as many of the newcomers to the hobby. I love and appreciate and admire the classic films as much (and probably more) than they, but I never reached the point where it became an obsession, a driving force in my life. I was always able to drop my film activities to engage in some other interest.

But I enjoyed seeking these young people take hold of the hobby. Years ago, at the Cinecons, a group of younger collectors, who had already been in the hobby for a lengthy period, engaged in a fun name-dropping caper. They would declare they were forming a Grady Sutton Fan Club, or a Franklin Pangborn Fan Club, or such. And then pretend that these character actors were planning to attend this session of the annual Cinephiles meeting, the Cinecon.

The knowledgeable collectors, who knew these kids, knew what they were up to and that these actors would not appear. It was all a put-on and a running joke among the perpetrators.

However, some of the young newcomers to the field were ignorant of this. When told that this or that character actor would appear, or was already in the audience, some of the newcomers would scurry around trying to locate him or her.

To my deep shame, I would occasionally join in on some of these charades. During one of the Cinecon meetings, believing that everyone knew me, I arose and announced that I was Jack LaRue.

Later on one of the younger collectors came up to me, "Are you really Jack LaRue?"

I never did it again.

Adventures in Publishing

As you may have surmised, in reading some of these literature masterpieces, I am enjoying my retirement. On many occasions I get into the prone position, stretch out my legs and just ... muse (sometimes snooze).

At this moment, I am recalling my adventures in publishing *Classic Images*: the trials, the fun, the tribulations, the fun, the headaches, the fun, the miserable people and the wonderful congenial people, the fun and the problems at the conventions and with the advertisers. And, did I mention the fun? It was a complete joy to me turning my hobby into a profession and doing the things I wanted to do during my 12 years in Davenport, Iowa. There aren't many people so privileged.

Adventures in publishing? There were many. I had a lot of fun with the ubiquitous typographical errors which cropped up more often than I wished. I called them Rubinerrs. Seems like we were always rushing to meet the deadline. Under such a situation, we couldn't take the needed time for really careful proofing.

Take for example the incident when I wanted to praise one of our contributors for his detailed coverage of one of our events. To describe his superior efforts,

I wrote that his coverage was "more than adequate." The typist somehow missed the "more than," and his work ended up being just "adequate." It was corrected next issue, but I had some harrowing moments explaining it.

Contributors

As many of you know, *Classic Images* has always been a hobby publication, by and for hobbyists. None of the contributors get paid, including S.K. Rubin before he went to Iowa and turned pro. It was, and still is, a labor of love from the editor, Sue Laimans, down through all the contributors. Every piece of artwork and written material is contributed without pay. Seeing the material in print has been sufficient compensation for most of the people. I know that because it is always a thrill to see something I write appear in glorious black-and-white on newsprint paper.

Because these guys and gals contributed their work does not mean that headaches did not occur. There were plenty of them!

F'r instance! Some contributors, including an artist, a columnist and a few others, decided they should be paid for their services. Of course, I could not blame them, but we just couldn't do it. We thanked them for their wonderful contributions and services and bid fond farewell to them. Their material was good!

Some regular contributors suddenly stopped sending their articles and artwork. They completely chopped off all contact with *Classic Images*. I wrote asking, "What happened?" Had I done some thing to hurt them? But, to this day, no reply. It's as if they never existed. I know they did exist; I have the results of their talents in our back issues.

I am hoping none of them were like the case of Charles Crum, who began submitting artwork at the outset; his work appeared in early *8mm Collectors*, predecessor to *Classic Film Collector* and *Classic Images*. In 1965, he began a pictorial serial on a William S. Hart film, *Knight of the Trail*. The opening strips arrived on time. After three or four chapters, they ceased to arrive. The continuity was destroyed as it was to be continued in the following issue.

I wrote to Charles. The letter was returned marked "Deceased"! He had been killed in an auto accident.

Since that time, I accepted no more series for publication until the entire series was in my hands.

Then there was the columnist who reviewed films and discussed the distributors in our pages. He began submitting material calling people names and running libelous statements without back-up proof. I was forced to delete this sort of material. The publication at that time was just a hobby, and I had no time for such shenanigans. He resigned in indignation, claiming I had lost my dedication.

I patiently explained that being dedicated did not qualify me for running libelous material without proof to back up the charges.

Classic Images, *No. 30*
April 1991

I have always felt that my word was my bond. If I made a commitment, I would fulfill it ... even if it hurt. Because of that, except for a few exceptions, the contract with advertisers was always verbal. Some took advantage of it.

One well-known dealer, who is still advertising today in other publications, agreed to run a series of ads. This continuous advertising agreement earned him a discount with the stipulation that if he did *not* run the ads, we would bill him back for the difference. He stopped his advertising and refused to return the unearned discount to us. We never did collect the money, and he never advertised with us again.

His loss!

How about the guy who submitted a full-page ad with a sketch of a nude woman. I pondered over that one. Being that it was kinda artistic, I decided to run it (after he gave me an argument about it). He ran the ad twice. I received no complaints from the readers, nor did I receive payment for the ads. The guy just ignored my calls and letters.

And then there was one outfit, I'll name this one: IVY Films. Remember them? The manager verbally contracted for an ad in the first issue of our short-lived *Classic Images Review*. He did not receive the response he expected, accused us of not sending out as many as we promised (we had postal receipts) and then offered to pay for half the ad. When we turned him down, he paid for nothing. We never received the money.

Naturally, he never advertised with us again. In fact, I think they are, deservedly, no longer in business.

That was an experience!

Then we have those daring entrepreneurs who feel that everyone is getting rich running conventions. They decide to get in the act and plan their own convention, advertising it widely, expecting to pay for the expenses from the bountiful proceeds. Their convention flops, they have no money and ignore the legitimate debts they have accumulated.

Good ol' *Classic Images* is stuck again!

The best of them all was this video company, still in business on a large scale, which wanted to advertise some porno films in *Classic Images*. They were to be in a circular which contained mostly classic films. He wanted the circular inserted in one of our issues. I told him that we did not accept porno film advertising. He argued, mightily, that these were only listings. There would be only titles, no graphic descriptions. I succumbed and accepted the circular.

My hair stood on end and never returned to its soft, curly state when I saw his circular. He listed the pornos, each with a paragraph vividly describing the contents. The letters from readers began to arrive. One of them, really angry, stated that he let his entire family read the publication and that it was an insult to include such material. I agreed with him.

I couldn't retrieve the circular, but I could refuse further advertising from that honorable gentleman. He has not appeared in our pages since.

Who can forget Tom Osteen and his Fred Thomson project? Tom died several years ago. I visited Tom in his North Carolina home. His basement was full of rare films, many of them in 35mm. I noticed three 35mm cans on the floor marked with titles of rare Fred Thomson movies—*Jessie James, Kit Carson,* and *The Sunset Legion*! These films were reputed to have disappeared from the face of the earth. Tom told me he planned to issue the films to collectors in home movie size. He had the equipment to do his own processing.

He took a full-page ad in *Classic Film Collector* (forerunner to *Classic Images*). I gave him extensive editorial coverage: "Found, three lost Fred Thomson movies!"

Then gangrene set in! Tom wrote that a water main broke in his street, flooding his basement, ruining many films including the Fred Thomsons!

Letters poured in! "He's a liar ... scoundrel ... trickster.... There never were such films in his basement." Poor Tom must have received a multitude of such letters. To this day, I do not know whether it was a scam or not. I do know I saw these three 35mm cans with the Fred Thomson labels in the basement. I have a picture of those cans!

My only regret is that I didn't open them up to see what was inside!

How about my many trips to the conventions? I enjoyed them tremendously. I met so many people I had previously known only through correspondence or phone conversations. I enjoyed seeing and meeting the many celebrities. I enjoyed introducing *Classic Images* to new people, and I gratefully accepted the accolades from the readers. It was ego-nourishing!

But I did miss many of the fine films shown because I had to sit at the table and peddle my papers. That won't happen again. I will attend the conventions and enjoy all the entertainment they have to offer.

We usually sold the current issue of *Classic Images* for $1 at these events. When Lois and I left the table, we would cover everything on the table with a cloth except a pile of "our baby" and place a sign on it: "Honor System! *Classic Images* $1. Put in box."

I think there were people surreptitiously watching, waiting for us to leave. When we returned, there was usually money in the box, often not enough to cover the number of missing issues. We know that because, unbeknownst to the pilfering knaves, we had counted the issues before we left. Perhaps we should have explained what "Honor System" meant!

One of the conventioneers reported that he saw a dealer come over and help himself to a handful! We know who he is and he knows who he is. He'll probably read this item and blush. Second thought: He won't blush—he'll laugh.

I can recall another disappointment at the conventions. It was my routine to go around to the dealer tables to contact potential advertisers. Some agreed to advertise, some turned me down.

What was puzzling to me were the guys and gals who wanted to say, "No," but, instead agreed to advertise, never intending to. I would mark the individual down for an ad in the next issue and reserve the space. If the ad failed to arrive, I would contact him. He would hesitate and stall and stutter; then mutter, "I'll send it in," in a low voice.

I checked him off the advertiser's list. I knew the ad would not arrive ... and I was right. This was not an isolated case. It is difficult for me to imagine people unable to give no for an answer, but they're out there!

All was not peaches and cream in publishing *Classic Images* but I reiterate, I loved every minute of it. I miss it all except that monthly battle of the deadline when I was forced to set aside any other plans I may have had in order to get the issue out on time.

13

The Westerns

Classic Images, *No. 53*
March 1995

The Hollywood West Has Changed, But It Ain't Real!

For years I have watched and enjoyed the movies. I grew up with the likes of Tom Mix, Fred Thomson, Ken Maynard, Yakima Canutt, Wally Wales and the rest of the early cowboy heroes.

I'm not sure how many of you feel you are witnessing the real West when the actors and their horses start emoting. So, after deep and considerable thought, I decided to write this brilliant essay on Hollywood inventing its own version of the Wild West and how it, too, kept changing through the years. This will include fairly recent activities, and my opinion of them.

Of the very early Western stars, Broncho Billy Anderson and William S. Hart stand out in my mind. I was quite young when they were popular and, to me, they epitomized the Wild, Wild West as we imagined it to be. They were dressed in well-worn, disreputable clothes, sometimes looking like they had just jumped off a freight train. But we loved them for their manly, macho ways, not their taste in clothes. This, to me, was the start of the Hollywood Western. Hart, especially, was always the one who emphasized reality in his productions.

Although Tom Mix also started in those early days, he graduated to full-blown stardom in the '20s and soon became the Beau Brummell of the West, dressing for the films in sharp, snappy, always clean, tight-fitting shirts, jodhpurs and chaps. And those hats! Huge, flamboyant, ten-gallon Stetsons which I doubt the real cowboys ever saw. I think he was one of the first of the glamourous cowboys.

The likes of Fred Thomson appeared on the movie scene near the top of my favorite cowpoke list. He also was immaculately dressed with the oversized ten-gallon chapeaus and the beautifully tailored western togs.

What always amazed me was when these natty Western heroes were engaged in fistcuffs with the nasty Western villains—they never lost their hats. The antagonists are swinging at each other, they're wresting and they're pounding one another with any bulky weapon within reach. But their hats remain intact! An amazing feat! After all, those head toppers could have gotten dirty if they landed on the floor.

And how about the flawlessly dressed William Boyd as Hopalong Cassidy?

Never a wrinkle in his clothes, never a hair out of place, the Mr. Clean of the Hollywood West.

Then, melodiously bursting upon the unsuspecting public, the singing cowboys arrived! What a metamorphosis for the Hollywood Western scene. Roy Rogers, Gene Autry, Jimmy Wakely, Smith Ballew and Dick Foran were some of the yodelin' heroes in these musical oaters. They would sing to their girls, to their cows, to their horses, and to almost everything else. I never saw this, but I am sure one of them probably sang to the bad guy as he was pounding the daylights out of him, "I'll be glad when you're dead, you rustlin' rascal you."

Every big star in Hollywood wanted to do a Western. You could find all the top names in filmdom riding on the top side of Old Paint as they cantered down the trail. Clark Gable, Jimmy Stewart, Alan Ladd, James Cagney, Errol Flynn, Richard Widmark and Humphrey Bogart were a few who come to mind. They all received good direction and instruction because, I am sure, most of them couldn't tell the difference between an appaloosa, a roan, a charley-horse and a rocking horse. But big budgets and grandiose Western productions resulted from this blending of the big name stars, the big studios and herds and herds of horses and cattle.

More change! The shape of the toppers mutated from the ten-gallon Stetson high crown to flat-crowned wide brim hats. Perhaps these new hats were designed to look like mesas.

Arrivederci, pardner! Along came the spaghetti Westerns, made in Europe! Most of these were raw melodramas emphasizing start realism and highly orchestrated musical scores. The dialogue was dubbed in the few I saw. It was fun watching the lips move in one direction and the words filtering through from another, the lips sometimes going up and the sound coming down.

It was also fun watching the impassioned, incongruous faces of the cast, which somehow did not fit the accustomed Western mold to which we had become accustomed. They somehow did not fit into our mental Western facial image. One of the reasons, perhaps, was that there were few or no American Indians on the European continent. However, the films were interesting and made for good, sometimes lively entertainment.

Then we were deluged with television cowpokes: *Gunsmoke, Bonanza, Bat Masterson, Hopalong Cassidy, Maverick* and so many others, most of them in series. One thing we could count on: Whether it be an hour or a half hour time slot, when the episode was over, everything was going to be exactly as it was at the beginning of the program ... unless the powers-that-be decided to write someone out of the script. The sheriff would still be sheriff, the same hero, sidekick and heroine would still be around. If anyone had been wounded, that wound would have been healed by the next episode. Great stuff!

A bit of a side remark: Today many of our Hollywood cowboys are riding the range in Jeeps and motorcycles instead of the perennial horses.

The fast draw was the thing in the Hollywood Western. The man who could get that gun out the fastest was top dog. I enjoyed watching gun battles with both the good guys and the bad guys shooting it out with 40-shooters. They were originally called six-shooters, meaning they had the capacity to hold and fire six bullets. But in those shootouts, they kept firing the same guns over and over again, miraculously never running out of bullets—and, incidentally, seldom hitting anything.

Another side: I was always hoping that when one of the good guys remarked that he was going to clean up the town, that the next scene would show him toting a bucket and a mop in an attempt to keep this word. Really! All that dust, horse and cow droppings and, horrors, sheep droppings! And what a muddy mess when it rained.

What I really enjoyed in the Hollywood Westerns were all the great escapes. You knew that if the hero was jailed, he would refuse to remain incarcerated to await that lynch mob. He would get out! He sometimes had help. His girl or his pals would bring him tools, or a gun, or they would tie a rope from a trusted cayuse (or a wagon) to the window bars and pull the entire window out. One of the favorite escape ploys often occurred when the jailer brought him his food tray.

Sometimes he would pretend to be ill and when the jailer entered the cell to check, he would overpower him, hogtie him, grab his keys and skedaddle. And then sometimes there would be a loose board in the ceiling to which he would climb and crawl out into the roof. Also, he might engage the sheriff or the jailer in a conversation, grab him through the bars, relieve him of his keys and perhaps shout, "I'm out of here!" You could bet that none of these heroes were going to be found hanging from a tree!

So what caused me to let off steam about the changing Hollywood Western scene as compared to what the Old West was actually like? Having always been a Western fan, having seen a multitude of oaters, having read hundreds of books by the most popular Western authors, I noticed something in the last several years which seemed ludicrous and disturbed me. Down the middle of the street of a Western town come all the good guys, four or five of them. They're out in the open; they're wearing identical long coats or slickers. In many cases their guns are under those coats or slickers. And here they come, blissfully taking this midday stroll (looking grim, of course), side by side like soldiers. Any bad guy worth his salt could mow them down before they would get those outer garments unbuttoned to get at their guns.

Wonder who thought that one up. Other producers or directors must have liked it; they all used it in the few productions I had gathered up enough courage to see. This time I think Hollywood has gone too far and changed the West too much! A cowboy does not parade in the open, side by side with his pals with their shootin' irons in a position where they cannot protect themselves.

To summarize: The Hollywood Western movie today is nothing like the Old West. Nor is it like the Hollywood westerns of the '20s, '30s or '40s. Nor is it like the Hollywood Westerns of the '50s, '60s, and '70s. Now it is a new entity unto itself. I think it has gone too far, also, in vulgarity, graphic violence and excessive blood-letting. A larger percentage of our oaters than I like to say have become distasteful.

And you never know if, at the finale, the hero is going to end up in the vertical or horizontal position, dead or alive!

Classic Images, *No. 230*
August 1994

The Ghosts of Westerns Past!

Hi pardner! I'm writing this on June 6th. Audrey and I have just returned from a trip to the (almost) wilds of Montana ... Polson, to be exact.

After so many months in sunny, humid, sweltering Florida, we felt we were at the North Pole. I am not complaining. It was a glorious change. However, if we had anticipated the chilly weather, we would have brought more than one change of warmer clothes. As it was, we lived in the same cold weather outfit for the major portion of those two weeks. We felt like pioneering tramps.

We did love the area and enjoyed sanding down the goose pimples every night.

Now, about the ghost part which you may have read in the title. If you are not a new reader, you may know that I have a thing about the movies. I especially enjoy the classic Westerns. Every place we went reminded me of the moments from "oaters" I had seen.

On this trip, even the awesome, overwhelming mountains made me feel that I was in the middle of a movie scenario. Each scene produced a sense of *déjà vu* for me.

Our lodge was near an Indian reservation. Live-in teepees are probably a thing of the past, but we did see several of them—unoccupied. They were apparently used for commercial purposes by the various entrepreneurs, Indian or otherwise, who offered souvenirs, artwork, artifacts, etc., for sale. They used the wigwams in the same manner some of the fast-food chains show pictures of their hamburgers, hot dogs or whatever outside to inform people, without words, what they offer on the inside.

In the Polson area, everyone was friendly; everyone was helpful; everyone made us feel at home. We call it being "neighborly."

My first intimation that I would experience nostalgic moments and memories from past Western films and TV shows came in the restaurants. Of course, you remember Dennis Weaver and his famous character, McCloud (reruns are still appearing on the tube). Well, every smiling waitress in every eating establishment would say, upon bringing our order, "There you go!," McCloud's favorite expression.

Our forays to the various points of interest brought memory flashes from films of the past. Some of these flashes were prompted by the wildlife we saw: antelope, bison, a mountain goat, llamas (yes, llamas), several families of wild geese on Flathead Lake, right outside our window, various and sundry small animals and rodents, and a family of owls in a tree next to our cottage. (Which reminds me of one of my corny jokes which I will relate a little later in this vital, important narrative.)

We visited a Smoke Jumper's museum which contained exciting film strips, equipment displays, a replica of a fire watcher's tree top station and so many other fascinating items. Of main interest to me was an 11 × 14 lobby card displayed on the wall from the movie *Red Skies of Montana*, starring Richard Widmark, depicting a scene of a firefighter parachuting into a flaming forest, wearing the exact firefighting gear which was displayed in the museum.

I'm not letting you off the hook: here's the joke. I'll tell it as if it really happened. One of my English friends came to visit us in our cottage. One of the owls outside our window hooted.

The Englishman: "What's that noise?"

"An owl," I answered.

The Englishman: "I know it's an 'owl, but what's 'owling?"

This was an unforgettable trip. I'll always remember Montana with its forests and its thousands and thousands of pine trees, its majestic mountains (many of them snow-capped), its fresh, dry exhilarating, "chilly" atmosphere, its beautiful lakes, the absolute friendliness of everyone we met, and its various parks and museums with displays of native plants and animals (some live ... some not).

Glacier National Park was a revelation of awesome beauty! The grandeur of its snow-covered mountains, the thrill of white water rapids, the necessity to slow down while driving because of the windy, hilly roads, and the continuous vista of one of Mother Nature's finest efforts, which kept us constantly alert watching for strange, new and diverse sights, especially wildlife.

Audrey and I will not forget the huge bearskin on the wall of our cottage, just behind the potbellied stove, and we will certainly remember the huge stuffed bear in the airport at Missoula, where our plane landed, 65 miles from Polson.

We arrived home from this glorious trip to the north country. The first thing I did was to pounce on *The Motion Picture Guide* to see what movies were made with Montana in the title, in an attempt to capture and tie-in these magical moments from the films to the actual scenery.

Errol Flynn came to this area in the 1950 *Montana*; Jane Russell graced the state with her presence in the 1952 *Montana Belle*; Johnny Mack Brown visited the location twice, once in 1951 with his *Montana Desperado* and earlier with Joan Crawford in the 1930 *Montana Moon*. Bill Cody's *Montana Kid* was around in 1931 as was Lon McAllister, in 1952, with *Montana Territory*.

There may have been more; these were the only ones I could locate in my hurried, cursory inspection.

Unfortunately (or fortunately), we encountered no live bears. Had we seen one, we would have undoubtedly set a new speed record for running ... in the opposite direction.

Classic Images, *No. 11*
January 1992

Western Procrastinators

I have become a permanent fixture at the public library near us. It is nothing for me to complete a book in a day. One of the reasons is that I scan read. I find myself skipping much of the descriptive material and digesting the action. I feel that I am getting all the benefits I want from a book.

I have read many Westerns! After all, I do possess the Golden Horseshoe Award from the Buck Jones Fan Club; the Silver Boot from the Riders of the Silver Screen

Convention; an award from the Roy Rogers Fan Club; and one from the Shoot Em Ups. Therefore, I would be derelict in my loyalty if I did not read Westerns. However, that's not the reason. I have always read Westerns since I was a kid ... and thoroughly enjoy them.

So many authors exhibit symptoms of diarrhea of the pen (or typewriter, or computer) when they put their thoughts on paper. It's a toss-up whether they do it to describe the events more graphically or to demonstrate their command of the written word. Or, because they are being paid so much per word! Regardless, they interrupt the action and go on a rambling journey through word land.

Classic Images, *No. 191*
May 1991

The Two Hopalong Cassidys

I have always liked the two Hopalong Cassidys.

The Hoppy to whom I was first introduced was a rough, cussing, heart-of-gold cowboy who would just as soon fight as eat. He loved a gunfight (but would only enter one if forced) and was a likable character, always willing to help someone. He was generous to a fault, a practical joker with a great sense of humor and was willing to fight for a friend, a principle or the honor of a woman.

This was Hopalong Cassidy as originated by Clarence Mulford. He appeared in a multitude of books. I devoured them when I was much younger, and I am enjoying them once more in my retirement.

William Boyd's Hoppy was a likable character! He, too, had all the fine attributes of his counterpart, but this Hoppy was quite the dapper cowboy, natty, always dressed in spotless, black, Hollywood cowboy–style, in contrast to the literary Hoppy's well-worn chaps, dust neckerchief and disreputable hat (usually bearing bullet holes). Boyd was clean-shaven, rode a beautiful white horse (the book Hoppy's horse was a cayuse or a bronc).

I unpacked all my old books and began catching up on all the Hopalong Cassidy novels. I noticed some flagrant differences in comparing these books to the more modern Western stories; the same difference could be noted in comparing the silent older Westerns with that of the modern-day films.

The original Hoppy saga was begun in the early 1900s. Hoppy could swear a blue streak ... but you never saw the words in print. You saw, "h—l," you saw "d—n," but you never saw the worlds spelled out. God in those days was always "G-d."

What happened in film? You never saw or heard a cuss word on the screen. Remember the controversy when they permitted Clark Gable to say "damn" in *Gone with the Wind*?

Things are a bit different today.

I enjoyed those old books and films which deliberately omitted the explicit words and actions, much more than I do most of the modern movies.

I have always thought that an actor's (or should I say "writer's"?) vocabulary is mighty low, or he or she cannot be too bright, when he can't find words to express his thoughts without graphic, obscene language. There are enough words in the English language to aptly describe any given situation ... vividly.

I was in the Army four years. I know *all* the cuss words—those appearing in a book and those which are not permitted near the book. They don't shock me, they only disgust me.

And, as the TV commentator closes each of his editorials, "And, that's the way I see it today!"

King Cowboy: Tom Mix and the Movies

When I was a little lad, Tom Mix was the idol of all the kids on the block. The theaters were packed when our favorite cowpoke was on the screen. Many other cowboy stars were also popular, but Tom Mix was *The King*!

The memory of it is still with me; not the memory of what Mix films were playing or the plots, but the mental images of the thrill and excitement of seeing a Mix film.

Somehow, I missed knowledge of this book that Cinephile Bob Birchard wrote in 1993. But now I have caught up with it! This is the definitive biography of the popular Western star. Other Mix books have been written; good ones, with much Mix material. But, Bob had seen the other works and decided his would be more informative and more complete.

The amount of research spent in producing this book seems overwhelming! The result of this "digging" is many formerly obscure facts brought to the surface. Bob does not necessarily glorify his idol. He points out Mix's weaknesses and setbacks in addition to his successes. He relates previously unearthed facts about the actor's divorces and marriages and his feelings toward his bosses and competitors in his rise to the top as king of the oaters.

Listen to this: Bob has carefully researched Tom Mix's film career and has come up with 270 titles. He lists them all, most of them complete with production information, cast and a recap of the plot, when available. He haunted libraries, interviewed friends and relatives and spent countless hours divulging into magazines, studio publications, press releases and books to squeeze out every bit of information possible.

In "King Cowboy" he has divided Tom's life into sections. He begins the biography with "The Real Thing in Cowboys"; then plunges into Tom's "Selig Polyscope Films," listed by years. "Fame and Fortune" contains more geographical material and leads into "The Fox Films."

Next there is more biography with "The Drifter," and then on to his "FBO Pictures" and "Destry Rides Again." Then to "Universal Films" and then to Mascot and his only serial, *The Miracle Rider*. And then, a final biographical section, "The Last Trail."

At the end, an appendix goes into disputed credits on the star's pictures and an index of Tom's films which appear in the book ... all 270 of them.

He covers a lot of territory, this Bob Birchard! You can feel his intensity and his devotion to this Western legend. He details Tom's commitment with the various studios, his experience with the Tom Mix Circus and his untimely death.

You looking for the complete book on Tom Mix? Here it is, readable and overflowing with loads of illustrations, some of them quality frame enlargements. It has 229 pages.

King Cowboy is a paperback printed by Riverwood Press.

Classic Images, *No. 253*
July 1996

Tom Mix: Collector Supreme

Bud Norris has to be one of the foremost Tom Mix collectors in the world. You heard me: "The world." I'd bet that the famous film cowboy is constantly on his mind. I'd also bet that, next to his lovely wife, who I just met, Mix is the driving force in Bud's life. (Incidentally, Mix was born in Dubois, Pennsylvania, a short drive from Indiana, Pennsylvania.)

Bud lives in Columbus, Ohio. He attends every Cinevent in addition to the Tom Mix conventions held throughout the country. Knowing that I have always been a Mix fan, Bud has, every year, asked me to come to his home to see his Tom Mix collection.

Each year I was forced to turn him down because I was manning the *Classic Images* table, trying to sell single copies, back issues, subscriptions and advertising, and trying to explain the publication to those ignoramuses who had not heard of the classy *Classic Images*.

This year, my good friend Bob King, who usurped my job as editor of that there purty paper, decided to attend and man the *CI* table himself. This left me in left field with little to do except watch movies and sit at son Jay's table, from which he was trying to peddle some of his collection. Like most amateur collectors, he spent most of the time shopping at other people's tables. Jay, as many of you know, is president of the Jimmy Stewart Museum and every dealer in the entire universe knows of his interest in Stewart memorabilia. They converge on him and there is *always* Jimmy Stewart material available at the Cinevent, especially earmarked for Jay.

I have deviated from the main issue in this part of my monthly offering, so now I return to the Norris-Mix situation. This year I was finally able to accept Bud's invitation. I had no car, so Bud picked me up at the hotel.

We arrived at his home and went directly to the Tom Mix Wonderland in his basement, which overflows with Mix memorabilia. Bud has traveled all over the world to amass his unbelievable collection. And he has a miniature theater in which you can sit on real theaters seats and watch some of Mix's efforts.

The collection consists of posters, photos, books, artifacts and anything you can imagine (and some you cannot imagine) pertaining to the famous screen cowboy. Bud's favorite portion of the collection is a huge number of Mix postcards mounted in albums. Some are duplicated but are printed in different colors, making each card a collectible.

Another of Bud's prizes is a part from the car Mix was driving when he was killed in an accident.

He and I exchanged Mix experiences, swapping stories of having seen him in person. (When I was very young, my dad drove me into Pittsburgh for Tom's personal appearance at the Stanley Theater.)

It was a satisfying evening; one I won't forget. Right here I want to thank Bud for the opportunity of seeing these reminders of my favorite childhood movie cowboy.

It is always a pleasure to meet people like Bud who are so completely dedicated to their particular favorite. However, there aren't many of them who travel to different parts of the world to find some memento of their special people.

Bud does!

Classic Images, *No. 238*
April 1995

The Two Alamos

An eye opener for this aged classic film buff, who has always enjoyed the Western movies, occurred late last year when Audrey and I went on an Elderhostel educational expedition to the San Antonio area and discovered that there are *two* Alamos in that part of Texas.

First of all, before I explain this revelation, I don't think some of you young people know what an Elderhostel is, so I will preface this article with a short dissertation on the subject which I will entitle, "An Old Fogie's Quest for Knowledge."

Elderhostels are held in various locations throughout the world; in many instances, colleges and universities. Courses are offered on a multitude of subjects. For a set fee you receive the classes you have selected; lodging, which is sometimes provided in dormitories, sometimes in hotels and motels, or whatever other facilities are available; and, usually, meals are included.

You choose your subjects from those offered by the sponsoring organization and attend classes taught by knowledgeable people in the field; in many cases, teachers from various educational levels. You attend the sessions and absorb the knowledge you signed up to receive, and the costs are nominal.

Because of my interest in film, Audrey and I selected three courses to be taught at Fort Clark in Brackettville, Texas, which is about 120 miles from San Antonio. They were "History of Fort Clark," "The Filming of Historic Westerns in the San Antonio Area" and a course to enchant all film buffs, "Beginner's Golf!"

Our group toured Fort Clark, which is now privately owned, and found it to be fascinating. Several lectures enlightened us on the background and history of this exciting piece of Americana.

Also, our golf lessons educated us on how exasperating the game can be. It was not an easy task to hit that ulcer-generating spheroid and have it go any appreciable distance, or in the direction intended. I will never look at a golf ball again ... until the next time I decide to play.

To us, the highlight of the trip was our discovery of Alamo Village. I had never dreamed of its existence. Our lecturer was Richard L. Curilla from my old alma mater, Penn State. When he heard about *Classic Images* and our other mutual interests, he and James "Happy" Shahan, Village founder, handed me an Alamo Village press kit, which tells the story of the historic film site so much more completely and effectively than I can. That description will appear after I tell you about the Westerns which have been filmed there.

We learned that, in addition to John Wayne's *The Alamo*, over 50 big screen, TV and educational movies were shot at the village, some recently. Memorable films such as *Two Rode Together, Bandolero, Lonesome Dove, Rio Diablo, Gambler v. Good Old Boys, The Roy Rogers Show, Six Gun Heroes, The Spirit of the Alamo, Bad Girls* and so many others, had their birthplace at this location.

Now, here's the story of the "First Movie Location Built in Texas."

> Alamo Village Movie Location on the Shahan HV Ranch in Brackettville, Texas, has an exact replica of the most famous of Texas Shrines—the Alamo. Built for John Wayne's epic movie *The Alamo*, the adobe mission and fortress took almost two years to build and set a Hollywood record for the most money spent on a movie set.
>
> Construction started in September of 1957, and filming began in August of 1959, according to Village and ranch owner James T. "Happy" Shahan. One month before construction was completed, the cost had come to about $12 million. It was the largest budget spent on making a film in the United States at that time.
>
> The crew built the Alamo and building of Alamo Village with a dedication to authentically reconstruct San Antonio during the 1800s. More than a million adobe bricks were made and used in construction, as well as 12 miles of water pipe, 30,000 square feet of imported Spanish roofing tile and a million square feet of concrete flooring. Thousands of dollars in nails, wiring, lath and plaster also went into the Alamo building project. Yet one of the most difficult tasks facing Wayne and Shahan was finding and transporting the largest herd of real Texas Longhorns ever used in a motion picture.
>
> Alamo Village is a complete 1800s town with jails, saloons, general stores, hotels, stables, a church, bank, school and blacksmith shop. It has served movie production companies as a fort, a hacienda, an early frontier town and a deserted Mexican village. Alamo Village is stocked with stagecoaches, wagons, buggies, surreys, guns, props and set dressings. A herd of registered Texas Longhorn cattle roams the ranch. There are also saddle horses, goats and sheep.
>
> In addition to being the first movie set built in Texas to film major movies, TV shows, travelogues and national commercials, Alamo Village also serves as the training ground for developing and promoting young talent. Some of these have been singers Johnny Rodriguez, Dottsy and Valentino.
>
> The location of Alamo Village and the Shahan Range covers 30 square miles. Visitors are welcome at any time. The nearest town is Brackettville. It is 120 miles west of San Antonio on US Highway 90. Del Rio, on the Mexican border, is 32 miles west of Bracketville. San Antonio is served by all major airlines. There are excellent accommodations seven miles from the Village at Fort Clark Springs (210) 563-2943. Accommodations are also available at Del Rio and Uvalde which is 40 miles east.

Here's Sam again! While we toured the Village, in addition to a Western barbecue, they staged a Wild West–type shootout, much like we have seen at the various Western collectors' conventions. I think some of those in our Elderhostel group thought they were using real bullets. I, with my vast "shoot-out experience," knew better. It was easy for me to determine the fakery by deduction. I noticed when one of the villains bit the dust, he wriggled considerably until he found a spot where he could be dead comfortably. Also, nary a drop of blood was shed. What good's a shootout without plenty of gore?

After our visit to the various locations at Brackettville, Audrey and I spent the day in San Antonio to visit the real, original, honest-to-goodness Alamo. It has been kept in fine condition and has hosted thousands of visitors. The Alamo at the fort was kinda dilapidated—it looked like it had actually been in the battle. In fact, it had ... kinda!

Every time a film was shot at Alamo Village, walls were moved, roofs raised or lowered, and room interiors changed—often shrunk or enlarged to accommodate the current requirements. There was constant construction necessary for the various fisticuffs, shoot-outs and, of course, more than one simulated battle of the Alamo.

We were disappointed that, at the real Alamo, no cameras were permitted in the hoary, yet modernized, edifice. We did take a picture of the exterior in order to compare the two historic sites.

The battery in my camera had died while we were still at Alamo Village. It's a weird battery, and I was unable to purchase one in Bracketville. So, any pictures in the Village you see here are courtesy of fellow Elderhostelian traveler Mike Virgilio of Norwalk, Connecticut, or from the press kit I received.

Once we were in San Antonio, I was able to find this oddball battery, insert it and have some courageous soul take the picture of Audrey and myself with that unfaithful camera. And, for the information of those ignoramuses who question it, I have not become bald-headed. Admittedly the hairs have thinned out, but I still have one or two atop my noggin. They become strangely invisible when my picture is taken.

Classic Images, *No. 281* November 1998

Broncho Billy, the First Reel Cowboy

Ray Nielsen, whose "Ray's Way" featuring his many interviews with movie personalities graced the pages of *Classic Images* for years, has now accumulated a mass of material and coordinated it all into a video documentary: *Broncho Billy, The First Reel Cowboy*.

Footage for this feature was contributed by David Shepard, Bob Birchard and the Museum of Modern Art. Ray has knitted these filmclips into a fascinating bit of movie Americana which was televised in late July on AETN, the Arkansas Educational TV Network where Ray worked for many years.

The various scenes from the movie's infancy are in black-and-white; some scratched, some scratchless and some footage tinted; condition depending, of course, on the quality of the original material. Modern portions of this documentary have excellent color and are fascinating to watch. It's all good-quality video!

I inserted the cassette into the VCR and was immediately captivated by the familiar voice of the narrator: Hugh O'Brian.

Anderson's screen name was Gilbert M. Anderson; his real name was Max Aaronson. He was extremely popular and became known as Broncho Billy who appeared in over 130 BB silent films.

He had three roles in the pioneering first film to have a storyline, the 1903 *The Great Train Robbery*. He even fell off his horse in one scene.

In this video we also see his first appearance on the screen as a messenger boy and his last in a sound film, much older, of course, as an extra in an audience.

His first appearance as the cowboy star was in the 19XX *Broncho Billy's Redemption*. The screen character went on to extreme popularity and film immortality.

The first cowboy movie star went into partnership with George K. Spoor to form Essanay Film Manufacturing Co., which set up in Niles, California, in 1912.

Charlie Chaplin began working for Essanay in 1914. This video includes scenes of Chaplin in Essanay comedies.

On the road to making millions (which he later lost) Anderson made over 500 films; approximately 50 have survived.

In 1958, Anderson received an Academy Award as a film pioneer. The televised Oscar program ran over its allotted time, and unfortunately, this portion did not appear on the tube. Some scenes of a talking Anderson do survive and appear on this video.

There is much to hold the interest of the classic movie buff in this documentary. The Western enthusiast, especially, can experience the birth of his beloved oaters.

This video should become an integral part of every classic silent film collection.

It can be purchased from AETN, PO Box 1250, Conway, AR 72033.

14

Jungle Stuff

Love Affair with Tarzan

Like so many really literate people in the world, I am enamored with Tarzan! I have always liked Tarzan ... in print and on the screen.

My first contact with the famous ape-man was in the '20s. As a kid, I went to see *Tarzan and The Golden Lion*. I remember nothing about the picture, of its stars James Pierce and Natalie Kingston, but I do recall how much I was enthralled by this unique hero!

Later on, I was equally thrilled with Frank Merrill as *Tarzan the Mighty* and *Tarzan the Tiger*. "Look at the muscles on that guy!"

This romance with the mighty screen ape man continued until I was introduced to the original Edgar Rice Burroughs' Tarzan in print through the pages of *Argosy* magazine, to me the most wonderful publication that ever existed.

I read every word of Burroughs' Tarzan in print, haunting the library. Then I started on his Mars series and continued through the Pellucidar and Venus series. I think I have read everything of Burroughs that has appeared in print in commercial publications.

I had, through this copious reading, built a mental image of Burroughs' Tarzan, which completely overshadowed the screen ape man from my mind. Sure, I enjoyed Johnny Weissmuller ... but he wasn't Tarzan! Tarzan was articulate; he spoke well. Weissmuller's character could not! Tarzan in print was a different animal altogether from the screen image jungle men. All the other Tarzans (Buster Crabbe, Glenn Morris, Herman Brix a.k.a. Bruce Bennett, Lex Barker, Gordon Scott, Jock Mahoney and the rest) suffered by comparison.

When I began collecting films, I was able to obtain Elmo Lincoln's *Tarzan of the Apes*. "He's muscle-bound," I groaned to myself. "He can't act," I groaned again.

Lincoln was a bit on the hammy side, as were most of the silent screen actors and actresses with their histrionics, exaggerated gestures and dramatic poses. But, that very first Tarzan film, until recent years, was the closest to Burroughs' original narrative of any of its successors.

The recent Greystoke, *The Legend of Tarzan*, started out like it was to be a true Burroughs Tarzan but it, too, deviated from the original story and took off on a tangent.

Don't get me wrong! I enjoyed the Tarzan movies, but this was not the Tarzan envisioned by the famous author. Let's say I tolerated the screen Tarzans, all of whom compared unfavorably to the ape man who gave me so many hours of delightful reading.

Through the pages of *Argosy* and other magazines, I became acquainted with other jungle men of the type, whose activities eventually turned up on the movie screen and were equally disappointing to me.

From *Argosy*, I read Otis Adelbert Kline's *Jan of the Jungle*, which turned up on the screen as a serial, *Call of the Savage*, with an inept Noah Beery, Jr. It was terrible!

From *Blue Book* magazine, William Chester's "Hawk of the Wilderness" was transferred to the screen in a serial of the same name with Bruce Bennett starring as Kioga. He should have remained in the Tarzan films!

Through *Famous Fantastic Mysteries*, I was introduced to C.T. Stoneham's "The Lion's Way," which was translated to the screen by Buster Crabbe as Kaspa in *King of the Jungle*. This portrayal, to me, was closer to the Stoneham's book character than most of the Tarzans.

All three of the above had less than successful sequels written; these did not appear on the screen. Jan appeared once more in *Argosy*'s "Jan in India"; Kioga was to appear in at least three more novels in *Blue Book*; and the English author, Stoneham, wrote a sequel called "Kaspa, the Lion Man."

So, who were the best Tarzans? Personal taste would best dictate the answer to that. Everyone has his own selection. I guess Weissmuller was the most popular; others imitated him. Frank Merrill tickled my palate as a child. I have his *Tarzan The Tiger* on video. Some day I'll get around to viewing it to see if Mr. Merrill stands the test of time. I hesitate because I have had so many of my childhood screen memories shattered.

Of the more recent ape men, I personally enjoyed Ron Ely, who starred on the TV series. Jock Mahoney was good.

Christopher Lambert made for an intelligently portrayed Tarzan. If only they had stuck to the original story as promised in the pre-release publicity. Bruce Bennett was also an intelligent Tarzan, as was Gordon Scott.

In fact, let's get right down to facts: If you are a Tarzan fan ... they're all great.

Tarzan will not die! There will always be new and different ape men; the new century has already brought them. Even Disney has entered Tarzan land.

Classic Images, *No. 303*
September 2000

Tarzan and the Golden Lion

When I was a kid, 350 years ago, I became addicted to the works of Edgar Rice Burroughs. I eagerly pounced on everything he wrote. Frequently I had my nose buried in pulp magazines of the era: magazines such as *Argosy*, *Blue Book*, and *Amazing Stories*. I followed the adventures of such characters as John Carter, Caron Napier, Davie Innes and ... *Tarzan*!

I have kept tabs on the Tarzan movies, from the groundbreaking *Tarzan of the Apes* with Elmo Lincoln to Modern Jungle operas. I did miss some of the more recent Tarzans; however, I made it a point to see Disney's recent version.

I had viewed all the early Tarzan movies when they were originally released. Not long ago I was given the opportunity of once again watching the 1927 *Tarzan and the Golden Lion*, which starred James Pierce as the famous ape man. It had been considered a lost film.

Want to know what I was thinking as I watched this rare movie? My exact words, spoken aloud, were, "I wish I knew French!" That's the language in which the titles appear. It seems a print of this rare film was discovered in France. It was edited down and appeared on French TV. The title: *Tarzan et Les Mon D'or*.

Now, how does James Pierce rate as a film Tarzan, compared to the many others who portrayed the ape man? After deep considerable concentration, I have decided that he was a rather inept Tarzan, even if he did swing on the vines once! He entered the scene with a becoming haircut. I explained it to myself, "This Tarzan has been out of the jungle and has experienced civilization! He has already mated his beloved Jane and has lived in Europe. Jane probably personally trimmed his hair; she didn't want him looking like a wild man!"

Don't get me wrong; I thoroughly enjoyed this lost treasure. I got a charge out of the frequent scenes in which large groups of natives charged through the jungle, back and forth, over and over again. I figured they were practicing for some sort of athletic event, perhaps the jungle Olympics. These runners were groups of Tarzan's beloved Waziri and their antagonists (natives in support of the villains).

The biggest surprise of all was the appearance of Boris Karloff! Yes, our Boris Karloff portraying Amaza, a mean ol' ferocious savage. He was menacing! His body was stained and he wore a death's head helmet with horns. His was not a big part but, as always, he played his character convincingly.

Although I couldn't do much with the French titles, I was able to follow the action somewhat by translating some of the words which I did remember from my extensive reading, and from my high school days, years before the Civil War, when I did take a course in that language.

Because of my French illiteracy, I greeted the end with a sigh, grateful that I was finally able to see the James Pierce Tarzan, and hoping I didn't misinterpret any of the action.

My apologies to James Pierce aficionados who revere and hallow his memory, but I thought Frank Merrill, from the silent years, was a superior ape man. Even barrel-chested Elmo Lincoln rated higher. I thought all the Tarzans of the sound era, including Herman Brix (Bruce Bennett), were more acceptable.

I could never differentiate between Burroughs' great apes, of which Tarzan became king, and gorillas. They looked alike to me. In the very first *Tarzan of the Apes* novel, he locks horns (while a member of a great ape tribe) with ape-like Bolgani, the gorilla.

Through poetic license the movies have changed these jungle man-like creatures to chimpanzees. And, get this ... one of the chimpanzees is wearing a loincloth. Perhaps the film people got tired of that particular chimp relieving himself on their camera.

Burroughs' Jad Bal Ja (hope I've spelled it correctly), the original Golden Lion in the book, is now Jab in this movie version. He does figure prominently in the plot.

Tarzan's Jane is played by Doris Dunbar; Edna Murphy plays her sister. A familiar face on the silent screen, Harold Goodwin, is a friend of Tarzan. The villain of the piece, Esteben Miranda, is played by Frederick Peters who, so help me Hannah, could pass for a twin of Rodney Dangerfield. I had a difficult time accepting Rodney Dangerfield as an antagonist to Tarzan of the Apes. In the film, Miranda only got respect from Boris Karloff.

The story: An old man staggers through the jungle and brings news of a lost tribe of lion worshippers living with an unbelievable hoard of diamonds and other jewels. He draws a map and shows Tarzan the way to the lost tribe. Sneaky Rodney dons a leopard skin like Tarzan's and tricks the information from the old man, who is in such bad shape he can't tell the difference between Tarzan and Rodney Dangerfield. Incidentally, both leopard skins were designed to be the very latest in jungle attire, with a single strap going over the shoulder. How chic!

The good guys and the bad guys all wind up at a huge pagoda-like building which is the home of this violent, barbaric lost tribe which worships Numa the lion.

Edna is captured and is to be sacrificed to Numa, the sacred lion. Tarzan arrives on time and kills Numa. When the high priest of the tribe sees this, he kills himself.

The villains find the fabulous jewels, but Tarzan's lion Jab finds the villains and eliminates them. So long, Rodney!

Do I sound opinionated, narrow-minded, and having too much fun at the expense of this Tarzan? I probably am! But, don't forget, we're talking about the idol of my youth!

However, seriously, it was a pleasure and certainly worth seeing this rare film Tarzan for whom so many Burroughs fans have been pining for such a long time.

Classic Images, *No. 220*
October 1993

Lost World Reflections

THE LOST JURASSIC PARK WORLD

I saw *Jurassic Park* and have been thoughtfully meditating about it ever since.

As you long-time readers know, I'm a sucker for any prehistoric film in which the dinosaurs look like dinosaurs and move naturally, whether by animation, electronics or any other of the modern techniques developed. I am not overly thrilled at the monster films in which men walk around masquerading as the huge reptiles. Example: Godzilla. Nor am I overjoyed to see modern miniature reptiles (like the iguana) parading around with simulated horns, wings, ears or whatever, as in the Hal Roach *One Million B.C.* or the sound version of *The Lost World*.

Before I comment on *Jurassic Park*, those who have been with *Classic Images* for so many years know the publication was founded because of a dinosaur movie, the silent version of *The Lost World*. I do not intend to go into a long narrative about that because it has been told and retold.

Now, back to *Jurassic Park*. With all the bally hoo, with the countless TV teasers, with the deluge of advertising and promotion, and with the news that the film was breaking attendance records, I succumbed. I lifted my mattress and withdrew enough money to take a trip to *Jurassic Park*.

What did I think of the film? I liked it! But, I compare all prehistoric animal films to the works of Willis O'Brien, who made such masterpieces as the silent version of *The Lost World* and the original *King Kong*.

Yes, I did enjoy the film, but it was a letdown for me. The animation was superb. The animals looked like they really were alive. But, I felt the filmmakers spent too much time on the buildup in order to engender suspense. There were too many closeups of sections of dinosaur bodies, offering you only fleeting glimpses of some of the monsters, grudgingly giving you flashes and sounds of these huge behemoths. I sat there drooling, hoping to get a good view of a whole dinosaur and watch him in action so I could pass judgment on the animation.

This finally happened, but I felt too much time was spent getting there. The buildup crept along ever so slowly as the producers continued to drop "monster hints" and gradually sped up the pace of the film to finally reach the climax.

Throughout the picture I was muttering, "Let me see the monsters!" And, they finally did. It reminded me of the many TV murder mysteries where they show you only the shoes of the killer as he is performing his own particular brand of execution.

I can't help comparing *JP* with the silent *The Lost World*, which I have seen 5256 and a half times. In that film, the minute our explorers reach their destination, which is a plateau, the action explodes on the screen. You begin to see giant reptiles, many of them, in all shapes and forms. No fancy closeups of a moving tail, or a blinking eye, or a glimpse of a side of a dinosaur; you get to see the entire reptile. The only closeups I can recall are those of the dinosaur heads, mostly while they are eating. And they looked real! Even with the primitive animation of the '20s, whereby the models were moved just a fraction of an inch and photographed a frame at a time, they looked authentic! What imagination (not to mention sweat and tears) went into this pioneering film!

The only masquerading I remember is Bull Montana strutting around as an ape man.

I will never forget a scene, a long shot, in which a group of dinosaurs are feeding off a carcass. What an intricate operation that must have been for the filmmakers. What a tremendous amount of time and Herculean effort it must have taken to bring that scene to the screen. Imagine, moving all the parts of all the models a fraction of an inch at a time to coordinate the action during this prehistoric banquet.

I liked *Jurassic Park*: I enjoyed the story and the animation. It was a good film, despite those (perhaps fancied) weaknesses which appeared probably only in *my* mind. (Incidentally, I like *all* movies. I'm the guy who cries during a Western when the horse dies.)

Now, my greatest ambition, my fondest wish, my ideal dream, my utmost fantasy is: I wish I had all the money they spent on just promoting *Jurassic Park*. I'd go out and find, or *build* a dinosaur myself.

Classic Images, *No. 263*
May 1997

The Lost World (1997)

I know I have been consistent in boring you many times relative to my fascination with the 1925 *The Lost World*. Right now, it is difficult for me to believe that over three years have passed since I wrote the article "The Lost *Jurassic Park* World," comparing the recent film blockbuster with that early silent film.

I promised myself that I would not again, in these pages, talk about that early film which affected my life. (Enough was enough!) But, here I go again, February 1997, breaking my vow.

Here's why! Several months ago, I was taking a walk in one of the local malls and suddenly became mesmerized in passing Walden's bookstore when I saw a paperback entitled, "The Lost World."

I entered the store and scanned the book. It was not a rehash or review of my beloved silent film, but a brand new novel by Michael Crichton, a sequel to his previous *Jurassic Park*. "There is a man with talent," I thought. "Perhaps I'll buy the book." Then I saw the price of the paperback—$7.95. My frugal, thrifty, chintzy soul rebelled and made me renege. "Perhaps I'll buy it another time." Even though the cover stated that it had been on the *New York Times* list as the #1 bestseller, I still returned to my mall trek bookless.

Last week, I went to a used book sale and found a mint copy of that very same pocketbook for 50¢. After three seconds of deep consideration about finances, I bought it.

Tonight, February 8, 1997, Audrey and I went to a movie. The previews of coming attractions indicated that a sequel to *Jurassic Park* has been made and would appear at that theater soon. Its title: *The Lost World*. By the time this article sees print, you will probably have seen *The Lost World*, and it will surely be breaking attendance records.

Let me tell you about my experience with the book. First of all, I reached page 61, and Crichton described an RV named Challenger. My mind immediately reverted to the early *Lost World* and envisioned Wallace Beery's beaded Prof. Challenger of 1925.

Was it possible that Crichton was patterning this modern *LW* from the earlier version? Not so! The use of the name was either a coincidence or Crichton deliberately wanted to titillate me with the mention of that scientist's name created in the earlier book and film by Sherlock Holmes' author, Sir Arthur Conan Doyle.

I continued reading ... up to a point. My *Lost World* had evolved into a new world. I have frequently mentioned in the past that today's world has passed me by. I have not kept up with modern technology. Computers bewilder me, as does this word processor I am using to write this article. The millions of people on-line astonish me; the Internet itself astonishes me; and the new technology with all its unfamiliar (to me) words and phrases confounds me.

The story line of this *The Lost World* becomes technical. The computer and the sciences play major roles in the plot, and I had difficulty following it because much of the technology and many of the words and expressions were over my head … way over!

Some of the dinosaur names are completely unfamiliar to me. When I lived in my own archaic, prehistoric, pre-computer age so many years ago, science was unaware of some of the lizards' mentioned. However, to be fair, there are sketches of the various reptiles in front of the book.

Much of the scientific terminology befuddled me.

I've excerpted a couple of sentences from the narrative to give you an example of what I ran into. No doubt, a scientist would delight in them.

In describing one dinosaur, "Small Cretaceous carnivore—two meters from pes to acetabulum. In point of fact a rather ordinary theropod."

Sam: "What?"

Here's another: "Slide after slide of little pale spheres that looked like cotton balls, while she nattered on about polysaccharide bonding angles and the Campanian-Maastrichtian boundary. Jesus, it was boring."

Sam: "Right!"

Here they're talking about a slide sample: "This is a gross histologic section through the superficial epidermis. Those patchy, ragged gaps are where the postmortem necrotic change has eroded the skin surface. But what is interesting is the arrangement of the epidermal cells. You'll notice the density of chromatophores, or pigment-bearing cells. In the cut section you see the difference between the melanophores here, the allophores, here. The overall pattern is suggestive of a lacerta or amblyrhynchus."

Sam: "What? … what?" Conan Doyle, where are you? I just remembered I hated all the science classes I was forced to attend when I went to school. Now, I know why!

I know that more knowledgeable movie buffs will happily devour the book and its concept, but I could not. I put the book aside and it remains on my night table, the contents only partially assimilated by my brain.

At this point, I don't know how the book ends. Perhaps when the movie is released and comes our way, I'll go to see it and get the urge to resume reading the book. At least I'll find out what happens to the characters and their quests in *The Lost World*.

The main character in the book, Levine, is an egotist; he's pompous, arrogant and completely unlikable. I like likable people … and happy endings. I hope this one has a happy ending.

I often see the name of the versatile Michael Crichton in the credits on TV. He is listed as the author, or producer, or has some other important function on much of the entertainment that appears on the tube.

He is a fine, intelligent writer. I admire him and envy him for the knowledge he possesses on the science of today and his ability to turn it into an imaginative, almost believable fantasy. I wish I could understand it!

I also have the greatest admiration for the technicians of the film industry who are able to produce Crichton's dream images and make them appear real. I retain that same feeling about the wizards who concocted the original 1925 *The Lost World*.

I am sure when this current *The Lost World* comes to town, I'll be one of the first in line at the theater. I still have a thing about dinosaur movies.

Classic Images, *No 288*
June 1999

Piqued at *The Lost World*

Before I get started, I want to mention some trivia which will be of no interest at all to any of you. In 1960, I saw and was disappointed in the then-new version of *The Lost World*. Claude Rains starred as Prof. Challenger. Instead of animation, they used live lizards and, by camera wizardry, enlarged them to appear as giants.

Now, back to the present! I was lazily reclining in a recliner (of course), scanning the TV programs listed in the local paper, when I saw it: "Sir Arthur Conan Doyle's The Lost World." I was horrified to see that it started tonight ... right now! I leaped to the TV and turned to the station just as the opening credits ended. Thus, I was unable to see who made the film ... and when. "If this happens to be a new version of my beloved *The Lost World*, I will check the credits at the end of the program."

It was! The opening sequences take place in an auditorium where Prof. Challenger is describing the lost world which could be reached by traveling up the Amazon River. "Yippee! It's starting out just like the 1925 version. This ought to be good!"

As in the silent version, the raucous audience is heckling Challenger, laughing and jeering, until he blasts out at them. Challenger challenges anyone in the audience to accompany him up that South American river to prove the existence of this prehistoric world.

The same people who volunteered for the adventure in the 1925 version accepted the dare: Malone (played by Lloyd Hughes in the silent version), Lord Roxton (Lewis Stone), Prof. Summerlee (Arthur Hoyt) and the girl, who is a reporter in this case (Bessie Love). In the original version she is the daughter of Maple White, who had disappeared in the jungles of the lost world. Wallace Beery, of course, was Prof. Challenger, and Bull Montana was the ape-man.

We next see the explorers paddling up the Amazon, true to the 1925 film. But, here the plot deviates. I was eagerly looking forward to seeing the new version of Bull Montana's ape man. Surprise! There is an entire tribe of ape men!

We are also introduced to a tribe of natives who are eager to eradicate the explorers. The film then goes off on a tangent reverting to the style of the old B films with their oft-repeated clichés and situations. We are introduced to a female Tarzan and a group of exotic native girls.

"Where are the dinosaurs?" I asked. They *do* arrive, in much smaller quantities than Willis O'Brien's earlier effort. (I will never forget a scene in the 1925 version: a long shot of a group of dinosaurs feeding off a carcass. I was amazed because every movement of these monsters was made one frame at a time. It must have taken weeks to shoot that one scene which only lasted a few moments on the screen.)

With today's advanced technology, the animation of these monsters is superior, and they do appear to be real. An imposing tyrannosaurus is discovered along with pterodactyls and other various and sundry prehistoric giant reptiles.

I'm thinking to myself, "I can't wait to see how they handle the sequence when the huge dinosaur gets free and terrorizes the city." However, at this point, the producers decided it would be simpler and more convenient to have a pterodactyl get loose rather than the oversized reptile. "This would also be in keeping," they must have temporized, "with the original novel as dreamed up by Sir Conan Doyle."

So, the explorers play it economically smart. They will carry a pterodactyl egg with them back to civilization and let it hatch there. *Only!* ... the egg gets broken, and the city dwellers do not get to experience a live prehistoric *any*thing!

Actions of these prehistoric creatures are lifelike. However, one scene irritated my cynical senses. The huge, mountainous tyrannosaurus is chasing our featured couple through the jungle. This big creature could have overtaken them in an instant and stomped them with one giant step. However, throughout the scene and a series of heart-stopping takes, he gets no closer to these delectable morsels.

The movie ends happily, and I prepared myself with pen and paper to record the credits when the appeared. The TV station, in its infinite penny-pinching wisdom, decided to divide the picture, slicing it into two parts to allow half of it for the film's credits and the other half to promote future programming.

I was watching on a comparatively small screen TV, and when they halved the picture each half was so tiny I couldn't read the credits. What I was able to decipher, because it was in larger type, was that the film was shot in Canada. I don't know who the actors were; I don't know when the movie was made; and I don't know the studio which produced it.

Other than the action appearing on the screen, I know few details of this production. And, being of a decrepit old age, I've forgotten some of that. I know it will be televised again, and I plan to pounce on it at that time. Meanwhile, I beseech thee.... Can any of you fill in the blank spots? Frankly, I'm miffed, irked, vexed ... and piqued!

Classic Images, *No. 314*
August 2001

A More Complete *The Lost World*!

The Lost World (1925) First National. Cast: Wallace Beery (Prof. Challenger), Lewis Stone (Sir John Roxton), Bessie Love (Paula White), Lloyd Hughes (Edward Malone)

One of the big surprises of the new millennium to me is the long-hoped-for release of the 1925 *The Lost World* containing 50 percent more footage than the previous versions available to classic film collectors.

The original theater release of this film is listed at ten reels, approximately 100 minutes; this one is timed at 93 minutes. So, there are a few minutes still wandering around out there, awaiting rightful return to their heritage.

Initially, in this version, there is a short introduction to Sir Arthur Conan Doyle, the author, who also gave us Sherlock Holmes. Next, we finally get to see Gladys, the lady who inspired our hero, Malone, to join the *Lost World* expedition in order to "face death without flinching." We see her again at the end of the picture as she introduces Malone to her new husband. She didn't have the courtesy to wait for him! But, that didn't bother Malone because he didn't wait either. He had Paula White.

There are additional scenes in a hut before the explorers take off for the interior. There is interplay between the explorers with Jocko the monkey and other jungle creatures.

Summerlee's insatiable search for knowledge is shown in his interest in the flora and fauna. In one scene, his curiosity gets the better of him and he is tossed into the air when he accidentally springs a trap made with a bent tree.

There are also bits and pieces throughout the film that have been reinserted, apparently having been eliminated during the editing process of the abbreviated five-reel version. I am reviewing the VHS version of this release, but it is also available in DVD which has additional footage including a commentary with Roy Pilot, author of "The Annotated *Lost World*"; 13 minutes of unseen outtakes; and a choice of two stereo music scores, one traditional and the other with a more modern flair. A 20-page booklet, featuring a reproduction of the original film's souvenir program, is also included.

The quality of this print is good and it's well worth having! It's tinted, and the titles are sharp and clear. In addition, it has 13 minutes of animated prehistoric monster outtakes. This version was made from eight different prints to get the best quality now possible. It was produced for video by David Shepard and Serge Bromberg.

Watching the video was a revelation to me, and it was all very enjoyable, except for the musical accompaniment. I personally did not like what the Alloy Orchestra (yes, the one I complained about in the last issue) did for background music. They feel that the sound of fast percussion beat is accompanied by a weird reedy instrument (I couldn't identify it) and, in some cases, a series of musical phrases with a lack of melody. One can always turn the volume down ... I did!

We all know that the animation was supervised by Willis H. O'Brien. Harry O. Hoyt directed the dramatic portions.

Index

"Acetate Won't Wait" 156
"The Accompanists" 186
Ackerman, Forrest J 189
Aitken, Harry 153
Aitken, Roy E. 17, 25, 26, 153
Allyson, June 195
Armstrong, Bob 97
"The Awakening" 222

Baby Peggy 31
Baker, Benny 30
Barry, Don "Red" 28
Beck, Calvin T. 29
Bennet, Spencer G. 28
Binney, Constance 29
Blackhawk Films 57–63, 74–76, 160, 232
Bloom, Harry 180
Bouchard, Enrique J. 178
Bradley, Walley 15
Broncho Billy 254
The Buck Jones Rangers 95
Burr, Raymond 191–193
Burroughs Bibliophiles 107
"But!" 146

The California Cinecons 130
Canterbury Films 175
Canutt, Yakima 27
Carson, Sunset 97
CED players 83
The Chaplin Mutuals 224
Cine Service Vintage Films 174
Cinecon 12, 117
Cinecon sites 20
Cinephile guests 21, 22
Cinevent 91
Cineventing 125

Clampett, Bob 29
Clark, Jerry 182
"Classic Clips Book?" 36
Classic Film Collector 1, 11, 7, 16
"Classic Film Potpourri" 148
Classic Images 1, 7, 8, 23, 34; one hundredth issue of 79
Classic movie, definition of 67–68
Cody, Iron Eyes 96
"Collecting Autographs" 150
Columbus Cinevent 125
Commins, Frank 37
Crnkovich, Tony 34

Dean, Eddie 116
Dean, Priscilla 30
Dobbins, Cal 11, 182
Donnachie, William 170
Dwan, Allan 29

8mm Collector 1, 7, 9, 10
Entertainment Films 176
Estates, Lt. Col. Oscar 181
European Market 178

Fairbanks, Doug 15, 202
FBI investigation 52, 77
Festival Films 179
Film Classic Exchange 173
"Film Collecting Metamorphosis" 142
"Film Convention Lament—1996" 126
Film fanatics 141
Films of the Golden Age 35
Finney, Ed 170

Fiorentino, Nick 38, 173
Fox, Red 175
Francis, Cal 38
Franklin, Grady 17
Furman, Savannah 97

Gardner, Earle Stanley 191–193
"The Ghosts of Westerns Past" 247
Gish, Lillian 2
Glenn Photo Service 177
Goodrich, Jim 37
Goudal, Jetta 30
Griss, John 170

Hamilton, Neil 23
Hardy, Oliver 90
Hartney's Milestone Films 172
Havoc, June 20
Haynes, Steve 91
Hayworth, Rita 151, 231–232
Home taping 84
"Home Theaters" 139
"The 'Hoppy' Decision" 72
Horak, Jan-Christopher 156

"I Saw Sparrows or Why Not Let the Collectors Have These Movies?" 46
Illegal dupes 41, 81, 84
"The Impactors!" 188
"Is It Me?" 225

JEF Films 179
Jett, Martha 37
Jurassic Park 259, 260, 261

Katchmer, George 183
King, Bob 33
Kinkade, Harold 182
Kleiner, Arthur 27
Kolodny, Howard 89
Kornick, Mike 17, 182
Kuster, Patrick 38

Laimans, Sue 32
Landis, Cullen 24
Lang, Fritz 28
Laurel, Lois 31
Laurel, Stan 8, 15, 27, 199
LeVeque, Eddie 28
Levin, Alice 152
Lone Ranger 96
The Lost World 1, 3, 5, 9, 5, 259, 261, 262, 263, 264, 265
Love, Bessie 6
Loy, Myrna 120
Lyden, Pierce 31
Lynch, Kerry 37

Maltin, Leonard 1, 2
Marafioti, Dominick 96
"Mason ... Perry Dead or Alive?" 191
McMahon, Lou 37
McWhorter, George T. 107
Meginnis, I. K. 176
"Memory of the Stars" 193
Minot Films 174
Mirsalis, Jon 118
Mix, Tom 106, 244, 250–252
Moore, Colleen 30, 145, 197

"Movie Critics and Camera Angles" 208
"Movie Memorabilia" 58
"My FBI Scare" 138

National Cinema Service 179
Nielsen, Ray 110, 112
Niles Films 174
"Nitrate Won't Wait" 155
Norris, Bud 106, 251
Norward Enterprises 176

O'Brien, George 114

Parkchester Films 175
Petrova, Olga 27
Phelan, Martin D. 166

Qualen, John 30

"Rarity or Quality?—1997" 149
Reel Images 179
Rubin, Jay 165
Rubin, Samuel K. 6, 14, 17, 34, 35, 45, 145, 215, 216, 219, 221, 230, 234–243
"Rumblings and Grumblings" 213

Schlesinger, Mike 130
Serling, Phil 90
Shephard, David 165
Shepherd, Scott 96
"Show Biz" 214
Slide, Tony 155
Smith, Dave 19

Society for Cinephiles 87, 134
"Sons of the Desert" 97
Stewart, Jimmy 195
Stingley, John 91
Syracuse Cinephile Society 88

"The Tape Thing" 65, 68, 71, 80
Tapeworms 62
Tarzan 256, 259
"Thirty Years!" 226
Thunderbird (Morcraft) Films 177
Tom Mix Festival 106
Torme, Mel 198
"The Toy That Grew Up" 185
"TV Potpourri" 211
"The Two Alamos" 252
"The Two Dougs" 196
"The Two Hopalong Cassidys" 249

United Artists 8 175

Vaughn, Robert 118
Video discs 60, 83
Voss, Tom 166

Watsofilms 40
Weber, John 88, 90
Western Film Festival 110
"Western Procrastinators" 248

www.ingramcontent.com/pod-product-compliance
Lightning Source LLC
Chambersburg PA
CBHW081546300426
44116CB00015B/2776